SCHOLARS' GUIDE TO
WASHINGTON, D.C.
FOR
AUDIO RESOURCES

SCHOLARS' GUIDE

TO WASHINGTON, D.C.
FOR

AUDIO RESOURCES

SOUND RECORDINGS IN THE ARTS, HUMANITIES, AND SOCIAL, PHYSICAL, AND LIFE SCIENCES

JAMES R. HEINTZE

with contributions by
TRUDI W. OLIVETTI

Consultants
MICHAEL H. GRAY
LESLIE C. WAFFEN

Editor
ZDENĚK V. DAVID

WOODROW WILSON INTERNATIONAL CENTER FOR SCHOLARS

SMITHSONIAN INSTITUTION PRESS
WASHINGTON, D.C.
1985

Scholars' Guide to Washington, D.C., no. 11

This work was developed with the support of The American University Library, 4400 Massachusetts Avenue, Washington, D.C. 20016.

Library of Congress Cataloging in Publication Data

Heintze, James R.
Scholars' guide to Washington, D.C. for Audio Resources.

(Scholars' guide to Washington, D.C. ; no. 11)
Bibliography: p.
Includes indexes.

Supt. of Docs. no.: SI 1.20:Sch6/6
1. Sound recording libraries—Washington, D.C.—Directories. I. Olivetti, Trudi W. II. David, Zdenek V. III. Woodrow Wilson International Center for Scholars. IV. Title. V. Series.
ML15.W2H44 1985 026'.001554'025753 84-600234
ISBN 0-87474-516-0
ISBN 0-87474-517-9 (pbk.)

Designed by Elizabeth Dixon

CONTENTS

FOREWORD

This guide is sponsored by the Woodrow Wilson International Center for Scholars, the nation's "living memorial" to its twenty-eighth president. It is the eleventh volume in a reference series describing the scholarly resources of the Washington, D.C., area. Begun in 1977, these *Guides* were inspired, in part, by the accumulated lore about scholarly materials that was developing among fellows in the Wilson Center.

Covering sound recordings in the arts, humanities, and sciences, this guide reflects the Wilson Center's long standing interest in the history and theory of motion pictures, television, and broadcasting. From 1975 to 1984 a dozen scholars held fellowships at the Center in the audiovisual fields. In addition, since 1978 the Center has been producing radio programs, built around the fellows and guest scholars, as well as drawing upon meeting and conference participants. In 1984 the radio offerings were expanded into a weekly program entitled DIALOGUE, which is distributed by National Public Radio and the Longhorn Radio Network.

Taken as a whole, the series of *Guides* exemplifies the Wilson Center's "switchboard function" of facilitating connections between the vast resources of the nation's capital and those who have scholarly or practical needs—or simply curiosity. These *Guides*— like the Center's annual fellowship program—are designed to serve the national and international scholarly communities. Each year, at least 20,000 visiting scholars come to Washington from elsewhere in the United States and abroad to pursue serious research. The *Guides* are designed to inform scholars about the possibilities for engaging in research on particular topics in Washington. The *Guides* cover the accessible organizations of the metropolitan area of Washington, but they are not merely of local importance. In the city's libraries, archives, and data banks, in its universities and research centers, and especially in the federal agencies and international organizations concentrated here, Washington holds resources that are of national—indeed of worldwide—significance.

The series of *Guides* is under the general editorship of Zdenek V. David, the Wilson Center Librarian, who has devised the basic format. Elizabeth Dixon is largely responsible for the book design and liaison with the publisher. Consultants for the preparation of this particular *Guide* were Michael H. Gray, Tape and Music Librarian at the Voice of America, and Leslie C. Waffen, Reference and Acquisitions Archivist in the National Archives. Wilson Center staff members providing advice and assistance were Peter Braestrup, Prosser Gifford, and George Liston Seay. The author of this volume, James R. Heintze, is currently Associate Librarian at American University; Trudi W. Olivetti, a cataloger at the National Gallery of Art Library, also contributed to its preparation.

The Center thanks the American University Library, and in particular Librarian Donald D. Dennis, for support of the *Guide* and for facilitating the author's work on this project.

The Center has now prepared *Guides* for scholars in the fields of Russian/Soviet (2d rev. ed. 1983), Latin American and Caribbean (1979), East Asian (1979), African (1980), Central and East European (1980), Middle Eastern (1981), South Asian (1981), Southeast Asian (1983), and Northwest European (1984) studies, as well as a *Guide* covering film and video collections (1980). All were published by the Smithsonian Institution Press (P.O. Box 1579, Washington, D.C. 20013). A forthcoming volume will survey resources in the Washington area for scholars interested in Southwest Europe, including France, Italy, Malta, Portugal, Spain, and ancient Rome.

Washington, D.C.   James H. Billington, Director
April 15,1984   Woodrow Wilson International Center for Scholars

INTRODUCTION

Purpose. This volume is intended to serve as an introduction to audio resources in Washington, D.C., and the surrounding metropolitan area. Surveyed are collections of sound recordings and organizations that produce sound recordings or provide information, research, or teaching concerning audio resources. Although this work is directed primarily to serious researchers, many others, including the casual listener and those who have a strong interest in collecting sound recordings, will also find its contents useful.

The value of utilizing sound recordings in conducting research cannot be overemphasized. In this medium are primary source materials that often are not available in printed format. Such sources include speeches, discussions, documentaries, lectures, oral history interviews, on-the-spot and other field recordings, radio broadcasts, musical performances, poetry and dramatic readings, and other recordings of significant historical events. Today, virtually every discipline in the arts, humanities, and sciences has primary recorded source material, which can be of major importance to scholars. In effect, hearing the voice of a significant historical figure or the sound of a historical event may provide us with a deeper, more personal, insight into that person or event than can be expressed through its printed counterpart. One need only imagine, for example, what a loss to mankind it would be if the recorded speeches of Franklin D. Roosevelt or the recorded comments by Thomas Edison and other notable figures did not exist.

Aside from primary sources and musical recordings, the *Guide* surveys collections and producers of pedagogical materials. In this it calls attention to the growing availability of sound recordings, particularly on cassette tapes, for teaching purposes in the humanities, social and natural sciences, and especially in the medical and management areas.

The nation's capital is unsurpassed as a resource center for sound recordings. Together, the Library of Congress and the National Archives and Records Service hold the most comprehensive, if not the largest, collections in the country. Unlike other cities, Washington has literally dozens of federal libraries, armed services libraries, and libraries affiliated with embassies, museums, and art galleries. In addition, hundreds of national associations have Washington, D.C. offices, some of which produce or maintain collections of sound recordings.

Overall, Washington area resource collections contain some 1.5 million sound recordings. Approximately 1 million recordings are commercially produced and represent a broad spectrum of arts, humanities, and sciences. The remainder consist of primary source recordings, including not only those mentioned above but also press conferences, historic radio conversations, sound recordings produced during geographical explorations, war combat accounts and other actualities, presidential in-

augural committee activities, press briefings, monitored shortwave radio broadcasts from throughout the world, congressional hearings, and recordings by world leaders, political figures, and prominent entertainers. Many of these collections have remained, however, little known to scholars.

Researchers have access to most of the sound recording collections in Washington. As noted in the *Guide,* however, there are some collections that are classified and closed to the public. These include, for example, such National Archives holdings as the Martin Luther King Assassination Collection (RG 272) and recordings in the Nixon Presidential Materials Project.

The purpose of this *Guide* is to introduce to the scholar and other interested individuals the rich and varied audio resources of the nation's capital. It is hoped that this volume will help to stimulate the use of recorded sources by researchers.

Scope and Content. This *Guide* covers over 400 collections, organizations, and agencies, located in the Washington, D.C. area. Each entry provides basic information, such as names, addresses, telephone numbers, and descriptions, of holdings and services. Although every effort has been made to make this survey comprehensive, its contents are not exhaustive. The size of a number of collections examined precluded citing more than a sampling of representative recordings.

Although most, if not all, recording formats representing the development of wire, disc, and tape technology are included in this study, it is not intended to be a directory of formats. Generally, the use and handling procedures of recordings differ from agency to agency; rare recordings and those issued in unusual formats are available to the researcher only through copies made on preservation tape. Researchers are advised, therefore, to check with the individual(s) responsible for a given collection for specific information on the format of the collection and to determine the current policy on listening procedures.

The main body of this *Guide* is divided into two parts. Part I examines Washington-area resource collections in libraries (government, academic, public, and special); archives and manuscript repositories; museums and galleries; embassies; religious bodies; services for the handicapped; and data banks. Each entry describes the size and content of the sound recording collection, as well as access to the holdings. Readers should be aware that although the principal emphasis in this section is on an organization's sound recordings, each institution is likely to have comparable or larger collections of printed materials. For more detailed information on the printed materials in the collections cited in this volume, readers may wish to consult one or more of the regional *Scholars' Guides* listed in the bibliography. A companion volume in the audiovisual field, *Scholars' Guide to Washington, D.C. Film and Video Collections* (Washington, D.C.: Smithsonian Institution Press, 1980) by Bonnie G. Rowan, is relevant as well.

Part II focuses on Washington-area *organizations* that, primarily, serve as sources of information and assistance to researchers. A number of these institutions produce, or have collections of, sound recordings. Included are broadcasting organizations; research centers; academic departments and programs; United States government agencies; associations (academic, professional, and cultural); and publications and print media. Each entry describes the organization's objectives, services, research activities, materials, and products, especially as they relate to sound recordings.

Brief introductions provide additional information about each section, as well as listings of supplemental reference tools. For example, these introductory notes deal with sound recording preservation and oral history (section B), and provide information on collections or artifacts that represent the development of both the radio and phonograph (section C), on Freedom-of-Information Act procedures (section L),

and on procedures concerning the production and handling of sound recordings in the federal government (section L).

At the back of the book, readers will find a series of appendixes: record stores and other distributors of sound recordings; recording studios and transcription services; radio broadcasting stations; audio collections by size; housing, transportation, and other services; federal government holidays; and standard entry formats.

The *Guide's* topical coverage encompasses all of the arts, humanities, and social, physical, and life sciences. The time frame spans from the beginning of recorded sound experiments during the nineteenth century by such persons as Thomas Edison, Alexander G. Bell, Emile Berliner, and others, to the present. The geographic scope is world-wide, covering audio resources pertaining to the United States and other regions. As a special feature of this *Guide,* the author has included information on, and concise descriptions of, rare and historic examples of radios and sound recording and playback apparatus found in Washington, D.C.

Methodology. In the initial stages of this study, the author compiled a list of all Washington-area libraries, and other institutions and organizations thought to hold audio resources. The bibliography at the end of this volume contains the printed reference sources consulted in the compilation of this list. Each collection and organization was then surveyed by the author in person or by telephone. Numerous catalogs and other printed materials were examined for both additional information and descriptions of collections. Relevant printed sources describing individual holdings are cited within respective entries in the body of this *Guide.*

As the project evolved, the author met with curators, librarians, and other individuals responsible for various collections and organizations who, in turn, pointed out additional sound recording resources. Furthermore, the author and/or assistant to the project attended meetings of pertinent associations, in particular the Music Library Association (MLA), Oral History in the Mid-Atlantic Region (OHMAR), and the Association for Recorded Sound Collections (ARSC) in order to elicit suggestions and support for the project. (On June 22, 1983, at a meeting of the latter organization, the author presented a paper, "Sound Recording Collections in the Washington, D.C. Area," which focused on little-known but significant sound recording collections.) In the final stages of the project, a draft of each entry was forwarded to the respective organization for review as well as up-dated information. The survey was completed in early 1984, and data should be considered current as of that time. For possible future revisions of this work, suggestions by readers for additions, changes, and improvements are welcome and should be addressed to either the author or the Librarian, Woodrow Wilson International Center for Scholars, Smithsonian Institution Building, 1000 Jefferson Drive, S.W., Washington, D.C. 20560.

Acknowledgments. Special gratitude is extended to Trudi W. Olivetti who not only assisted the author in initiating this project but also for devoting innumerable hours to examining the vast holdings in the Smithsonian Institution and in a number of other organizations in Washington and northern Virginia. She also contributed a number of entries, helped in the compiling of information on oral history collections in the Washington area, and is author of the essay on oral history (p.96). The author wishes to express his gratitude also to Zdeněk V. David, Librarian of the Woodrow Wilson International Center for Scholars and editor of the Wilson Center's *Scholars' Guides,* whose principal guidance and untiring help made the preparation of this work possible; to Donald D. Dennis, University Librarian at American University, who has generously provided support for this study; to Michael H. Gray, Chief of the Tape and

Music Libraries at the Voice of America, and Leslie C. Waffen, Reference and Acquisitions Archivist in the Special Archives Division of the National Archives and Records Service, for their consultation services; to Samuel Brylawski, who spent many hours helping to identify significant collections in the Motion Picture, Broadcasting and Recorded Sound Division of the Library of Congress; to Walter W. Weinstein of the Bureau of Standards for providing a tour and special access to the museum holdings; to Elliot N. Sivowitch of the Division of Electricity and Modern Physics of the National Museum of American History for compiling a list of historic phonograph apparatus held in the Smithsonian Institution, Pamela M. Henson, Historian in the Smithsonian Institution Archives, for pointing out significant oral history materials there; to Donald A. Ritchie of the Senate Historical Office for offering valuable advice for identifying oral history materials and sources in the Washington area; and to the other authors of the *Guides* in this series, whose earlier work paved the way for the present study: Steven A. Grant, Michael Grow, Hong N. Kim, Purnima M. Bhatt, Kenneth J. Dillon, Bonnie G. Rowan, Steven R. Dorr, Enayetur Rahim, Patrick M. Mayerchak, and Louis A. Pitschmann. In addition, Laura Taylor and Wendy Hejnar assisted the author in typing a number of drafts, as well as providing other services. Finally, the author is indebted to the many institutions that granted access to their collections and responded cheerfully to the author's inquiries.

HOW TO USE THIS *GUIDE*

The following comments are made to facilitate the use of this reference work. For additional explanations concerning particular types of collections and organizations (libraries, museums and galleries, U.S. Government agencies), see the Introductory Note to each section.

Format. The main body of this *Guide* is divided into seven collection sections (A-G) and six organization sections (H-N). Within each section, entries are arranged alphabetically by the name of the individual collection or organization. In those sections where United States government libraries, archives, and agencies are cited, functional descriptors precede the generic name; e.g., *Labor Department* rather than *Department of Labor*. In section D, embassies are given their official titles as indicated in the *Diplomatic List* but are arranged alphabetically according to their geographic name.

Standard Entry Form. At the beginnings of the collections section and the organizations section are standard entry formats (see also Appendix VII), which outline the categories and sequence of information contained within each entry of the respective sections. The numbers of the entry form correspond to the numerical arrangement of each entry. If a particular number does not appear in an entry, that category of information was either not applicable or not available. If a single institution or organization has more than one entry in the *Guide,* references to all entries are gathered under the main entry and also in the Name Index.

Cross-References. Two principal types of cross-references are used in the main body of this *Guide:* those that refer the reader from institutions or organizations that have more than one entry and those that link special collections which are dispersed, such as National Public Radio, the current materials of which are held on-site (entry B33), while retired holdings are housed in the Library of Congress (entry A41), and National Archives and Records Service (entry B27). There are also cross-references in the individual sections to relevant collections and/or organizations entered in other sections, e.g., cross-references in section A (Libraries) to Section M (associations that have libraries).

Indexes. Three indexes provide access to information in the text from several perspectives. The *Personal Names Index* includes the names of individuals that appear on recordings described in this *Guide* and that are located in libraries and other despositories in the Washington, D.C., area. The *Subject Index* covers rather broad categories and includes geographic headings. The *Organizations and Institutions Index*

contains their names and the subdivisions of highly differentiated agencies grouped under the main entry in the index.

Names, Addresses, and Telephone Numbers. This information is subject to frequent change, particularly for government agencies and highly differentiated organizations where reorganization and personnel changes occur often. All telephone numbers include area codes (202, for the District of Columbia; 301, for the Maryland suburbs; and 703, for the Virginia suburbs) to assist researchers placing telephone calls from outside the Washington area. Where possible, the author has also cited toll-free (800) numbers. When dialing local calls from within the Washington metropolitan area, the area codes should be ignored.

Abbreviations. The following abbreviations are used herein: ips (inches per second), lp (long playing), RG (Record Group), and rpm (revolutions per minute).

COLLECTIONS

Collections Entry Format

1. General Information
   a. address; telephone numbers
   b. hours and days of service
   c. conditions of access
   d. name/title of director and key staff members
2. Size and Subjects of Collection
   a. general holdings
   b. sound recordings and related materials (transcripts, scores, manuscripts)
3. Notable Holdings
4. Facilities for Study and Use
   a. availability of audiovisual equipment
   b. reservation requirements
   c. fees charged
   d. reproduction services
5. Bibliographic Aids Facilitating Use of Collection

NOTE: The collections entry format outlines the categories and sequence of information contained within each collection entry. The numbers of the entry format correspond to the numerical arrangement of each entry. If a particular number does not appear in an entry, that category of information was either not applicable or not available.

A Libraries (Government, Academic, Public, Special)

Introductory Note

The libraries in the nation's capital available to researchers are extensive and varied, and they include public, special, academic, federal, and college and university libraries. Cross-references are provided to additional libraries not described in this section.

The Library of Congress (A41) is by far the most important source of audio materials in this section, followed in size by the Voice of America libraries (A72). The combined holdings of the National Library of Medicine (A55), libraries of special organizations, and the major college and university libraries also provide excellent support for advanced study. Among university and college libraries, the following have the largest holdings of audio resources: University of Maryland (A68 and A70), American University (A5), Catholic University of America (A15), and Montgomery College (A47). Among public libraries the same is true of those maintained by the following jurisdictions (in the order of size of holdings): Prince George's County (A61), Montgomery County (A48), Fairfax County (A21), and the District of Columbia (A42). For size estimates of audio collections in the Washington, D.C. area, see Appendix IV.

Researchers interested in the cooperative arrangements among these libraries in the audiovisual and other fields should contact the Metropolitan Washington Library Council, 1875 Eye Street, N.W., Suite 200, Washington, D.C., 20006 (telephone 202/223–6800, ext. 458). Currently some 250 libraries work together in the council to exchange information and to coordinate activities in the region. The Library Council's publications include *Axis,* a bimonthly newsletter, and *Master Calendar,* a guide to library-related events.

Other local network associations that promote library cooperation include the Consortium of Universities of the Washington Metropolitan Area (K7) and the Washington Theological Consortium (E9). In addition, the Council on Library Resources, Inc., a private operating foundation established in 1956, administers programs as well as grants to and contracts with individuals and organizations for solving problems facing libraries nation-wide, especially those of academic and research libraries. For information, contact the Council on Library Resources, Inc., 1785 Massachusetts Avenue, N.W., Washington, D.C., 20036 (telephone 202/483–7474).

Additional guides to libraries in the Washington, D.C. area include *Library and Reference Facilities in the Area of the District of Columbia,* 11th ed. (Washington, D.C.: American Society for Information Science, 1983), and the annual *American Library Directory* (New York: Bowker).

A1   Alexandria Library (City of Alexandria)

1 a. *Central Branch*
717 Queen Street
Alexandria, Virginia 22314
(703) 838–4555

b. 9:00 A.M.–9:00 P.M.   Monday–Thursday
9:00 A.M.–6:00 P.M.   Friday
9:00 A.M.–5:00 P.M.   Saturday
1:00 P.M.–5:00 P.M.   Sunday

c. Open to the public. Reciprocal borrowing privileges extended to those in metropolitan Washington area.

d. Jeanne G. Plitt, Director

2. The Alexandria Library has two other circulating branches besides the main branch with total holdings of 308,859 books, over 504 periodical titles, and other materials. Each branch tends to specialize somewhat in certain subjects, although each has a basic public library general collection.

3. Notable holdings of the Alexandria Library.

SPECIAL SERVICES DIVISION
5651 Rayburn Avenue
Alexandria, Virginia 22311

Frederic W. Boots, Chief of Special Services

Records
(703) 998–0650

Mary E. Crumplar, Library Assistant for Phonograph Records

As of June 30, 1983, total audio holdings for all three branches of the library were 5,080 titles. As with most public libraries, the record collection is of a general nature, covering music, spoken arts, children's records, and instructional materials. The music collection includes folk, classical, jazz, and musical comedy. The instructional recordings include European and Oriental languages, shorthand, typing, and physical exercise.

Alexandria Library—Special Services Division—Talking Books Department   See entry F2

**American Association of Community and Junior Colleges (AACJC)
Library   See entry M4**

**American Association of University Women (AAUW) Educational
Foundation Library   See entry M6**

A2   American College of Cardiology—Griffith Resource Library

1 a. *Heart House*
9111 Old Georgetown Road
Bethesda, Maryland 20814
(301) 897-5400, ext. 258

  b. 9:00 A.M.–5:00 P.M.   Monday–Friday

  c. The library is open to the public. Because of the advanced level of the materials in the collection, health care professionals with interests in cardiovascular medicine will find the library particularly useful. Audiovisuals are loaned for periods of three weeks. Arrangements for loans can be made by letter, telephone, or in person.

  d. Linda Blackburn, Librarian

2. The library emphasizes the acquisition of current materials that contribute to meeting its own continuing education program and the continuing educational needs of practicing cardiovascular professionals. The library's collection consists primarily of books, journals, and audiovisuals. Included in the audiovisual holdings are approximately 1,500 video and audio cassettes and slides.

  The audio cassettes consist of lectures presented in the college's continuing education program, covering virtually every area of cardiology. The tapes are directed not only to physicians but also to practicing nurses and medical technicians. There are also tapes of panel discussions and medical conventions held throughout the United States.

3. Examples of series of audio tapes that individuals may expect to find in the collection include *Journal Club: Cardiology* (CIBA Pharmaceutical Co.), *Self-Learning Series* (American College of Physicians), *AVMD Continuing Medical Education Programs* (Audiovisual Medical Marketing), and *Medical Services Digest* (Merck Sharp & Dohme International). An example of an audio-taped convention is *The American College of Cardiology & New York Medical College: Clinical Decisions in Cardiovascular Disease,* New York, 1979 (38 cassettes).

  The college also produces its own series of audio cassettes, *ACCEL* (American College of Cardiology Extended Learning), which is available for purchase or for use in the library. Each tape is based on a continuing education program conducted by the college. A single tape is issued monthly, some having slides and printed booklets. Many of the tapes focus on subjects in the field of cardiovascular disease. An audio cassette program catalog lists 45 tapes in the series. Two of the programs are truly unique and deserve mention: *An Oral History of Twenty-Five Years of American Cardiology 1949-1974* (compiled and edited by E. Grey Diamond, M.D., 5 cassettes, program 24); and *Heart Sounds and Auscultation I and II* (E. Grey Diamond, M.D., 2 cassettes, programs 11 and 34). Using a stethoscope with a cassette player, individuals may hear a variety of sounds produced by the heart.

4 a. On-site listening equipment is available in independent study rooms.

   b. No reservation requirements.

   c. There is a charge for some services provided to persons who are not members of the college.

   d. On-site audio duplication facility and photocopy service are available.

5. There is an integrated author/title/subject catalog. The library has a collection of reference books and periodical indexes for audiovisual materials in medicine. Available, also, is on-line access to all MEDLARS databases, such as, MEDLINE, AV-LINE, CATLINE.

The two principal publications of the college are its journal, *The American Journal of Cardiology* (monthly), and the *Griffith Resource Library Monthly Literature Service,* the latter consisting of abstracts of current professional articles.

A3 American Institute of Architects (AIA) — Audio-Visual Library

1 a. *1735 New York Avenue, N.W.*
Washington, D.C. 20006
(202) 626–7495
(202) 626–7493 (Reference)

   b. 8:30 A.M.–5:00 P.M.   Monday–Friday

   c. Open to the public but by appointment only. Audio tapes are not circulated.

   d. Michelle Jones, Assistant Manager of Audio-Visuals
Sheryl Romeo, Slide Librarian

2–3. The library has a collection of films, slide shows, and some 60 audio cassette tapes consisting of 1979–1980 "Convention Seminars" of the AIA. Included are presentations on various subjects including time management, marketing services, and how to start an architectural firm.

4 a. On-site listening facility is available.

   b. Prior appointment is recommended.

   c. Fees charged for purchase of tapes.

   d. Audio cassette tapes may be duplicated.

5. A list of tapes is available. The AIA publishes a number of materials including the monthly *Architecture: The AIA Journal* and the bi-weekly *AIA Memo* .

American Psychiatric Association (APA) Library   See entry M19

American Society of International Law (ASIL) Library   See entry M24

A4 American University—Department of Language and Foreign Studies —Language Laboratory

1 a. *Asbury Building, Lower Level*
Massachusetts and Nebraska Avenues, N.W.
Washington, D.C. 20016
(202) 885–2396

b. 9:00 A.M.–9:00 P.M. Monday–Thursday
9:00 A.M.–4:30 P.M. Friday
11:00 A.M.–4:00 P.M. Saturday
Hours may vary during summer session.

c. Open to members of the AU community and D.C. consortium of colleges and universities.

d. Terry Owsley, Director

2. The American University Language Laboratory is a university-wide service and resource facility, which provides mediated classroom services and learning materials for over 200 users a day during regular school sessions.

3. Laboratory holdings include an audio-tutorial collection of audio cassette and reel-to-reel tapes exceeding 7,000 entries in languages, humanities, and natural, social, economic, politicial, and behavioral sciences. A typewritten inventory of holdings lists audio tapes for such languages as Arabic, Cambodian, Shangai Chinese, Mandarin Chinese, Czech, French, German, Hebrew, Hindi, Hungarian, Indonesian, Irish, Japanese, Polish, Portuguese, Russian, Spanish, Swedish, Thai, and Vietnamese. The spectrum of audio tapes representing the humanities and sciences is broad. For example, the catalog lists audio tapes on topics such as energy, history of World War II, ecology, biology, water management, pollution, law, and economics.
Included in the laboratory's holdings is a video-tutorial library of over 400 hours of television materials in languages, humanities, biological and environmental sciences, and law.

4 a. On-site listening equipment is available.

b. Reservations are required.

c. No fees charged except those for duplication of tapes.

d. Tapes may be duplicated, but patrons must either supply their own blank tapes or purchase blank tapes in the laboratory.

5. The laboratory's holdings are listed in an "Inventory of Audio and Video Tapes (Fall, 1980)."

A5 American University Library

1 a. *Massachusetts and Nebraska Avenues, N.W.*
Washington, D.C. 20016
(202) 885–3232 (Librarian's Office)
(202) 885–3238 (Reference)

b. 8:00 A.M.–Midnight   Monday–Thursday
8:00 A.M.–10:00 P.M.   Friday
9:00 A.M.–9:00 P.M.   Saturday
11:00 A.M.–Midnight   Sunday
Hours vary during summer.

c. Open to qualified scholars for on-site use only. Circulation extended to faculty, staff, and students, and graduate students of member universities of the Washington Consortium.

d. Donald D. Dennis, University Librarian

2. The library is a major supporting facility for a variety of undergraduate and graduate liberal arts programs. As of August 1983, the collection includes some 433,972 books, 2,562 periodical subscriptions, a number of rare book collections, and an extensive variety of non-print materials, including microforms, films, filmstrips, slides, disc recordings, and video and audio cassette recordings.

3. Notable holdings of the library.

Media/Microforms Department
(202) 885–3250 (Service Desk)
(202) 885–3252 (Librarian's Office)

Diana Vogelsong, Head, Media/Microforms

This department holds some 16,400 reels of microfilm, 262,000 items of microfiche, and other non-print materials, including films, video cassettes, slides, and audio cassettes.

Audio recordings include 504 cassettes focusing on a broad spectrum of subjects, including music (mostly classical and jazz), plays, poetry, and speeches. Included among these tapes are a number of National Public Radio (NPR) productions whose subjects include politics, history, foreign policy, and war. One notable NPR series is *A Question of Place: Sound Portraits of Twentieth-Century Humanists*. The music collection also includes the series, *Great Men of Music* (produced by Time–Life), which focuses on classical music, and totals 100 cassettes.

Additional recordings are maintained in the Multi-Media Collection held in the Reserve Room, lower level. Multi-Media includes books accompanied by cassette/disc recordings. Currently the collection has 38 discs and 15 cassettes whose subjects are international folk music, electronic and computer music, radio commentators, and ethnomusicology, among others.

Record-Score Collection
Kreeger Building, Room 218
(202) 885–3264

9:00 A.M.–7:30 P.M.   Monday, Wednesday, Thursday
9:00 A.M.–9:00 P.M.   Tuesday
9:00 A.M.–5:00 P.M.   Friday
10:00 A.M.–2:00 P.M.   Saturday

James R. Heintze, Head

The collection includes some 8,350 discs, 7,500 music scores, and 800 reel-to-reel and 20 cassette recordings. The disc collection is primarily music (all styles and periods), including classical, jazz, popular, American musical theater, and international folk

music. All discs are commercially produced. Notable disc series include *Recorded Anthology of American Music* (sponsored by the Rockefeller Foundation; over 200 discs) and *Composers Recordings, Inc.* (the emphasis is on contemporary music; over 300 discs). Included in the disc collection is approximately 150 titles of spoken arts materials, including speeches, plays, and poetry.

The reel-to-reel collection includes some 250 tapes of faculty concerts and guest artist performances and lectures, from 1965 to the present. Notable guest lecturers include Andre Watts, Leon Fleisher, Dimitri Kabalevsky, Milton Babbitt, Antal Dorati, Olivier Messiaen, John Duke, and Mstislav Rostropovich. The library also has 165 reel-to-reel tapes produced by the United Nations Radio Division. These tapes consist of interviews with ambassadors and other world dignitaries and span the period 1974–1979. A set of recordings of United Nations proceedings from 1946 to 1963 are held in the Motion Picture, Broadcasting and Recorded Sound Division of the Library of Congress (A41). The 20 cassette recordings consist of music education instructional materials.

4 a.   On-site listening is available in both the Media/Microforms Department and the Record-Score Collection.

b.   No reservation requirements. However, American University faculty and students receive first consideration.

c.   There are fees charged for duplication of sound recordings.

d.   A duplication facility is available in the Media/Microforms Department. Individuals must provide blank tapes. Copyright laws apply.

5.   All materials are accessed through author/title and subject card catalogs. Both the Media/Microforms Department and the Record-Score Collection have separate catalogs as well. Typewritten guides to spoken word recordings and the series of United Nations tapes are available, as well as other in-house and standard guides.

A6   American University—Washington College of Law (WCL) Library

1 a.   *Alvina Reckman Myers Hall*
American University
Massachusetts and Nebraska Avenues, N.W.
Washington, D.C. 20016
(202) 885–2625

b.   8:00 A.M.–Midnight   Monday–Friday
9:00 A.M.–Midnight   Saturday
10:00 A.M.–Midnight   Sunday
Hours vary for exam periods, holidays, and summer session.

c.   Open to American University faculty and students and members of the Bar. Others must apply for permission to use the library. Government Documents Depository collection open to the public. Collections are only for use in the library. Individuals interested in receiving a library orientation tour are invited to contact Gary McCann in the reference office (202/885–2625).

2.   The library has an excellent collection of law materials, including books, periodicals, a microform collection, federal and state statutes, legal encyclopedias and

digests, archival materials. Other special materials include books from the personal collection of the late Richard Baxter, former judge on the International Court of Justice, the Hague.

3. The audiovisual collection of the WCL library includes more than 35 discs, 10 audio cassettes, and a small video collection. One principal collection of audio discs is a series of lectures produced by the American Bar Association, Section of Real Property, Probate and Trust Laws. Some of the subjects covered include techniques for the preservation of historic landmarks (Eugene Morris), the lawyer's role in financing real estate development (John Gose), legal assistants and word processing in probate practice (David R. Brink), income tax planning (B.T. Bowles), and the Interstate Land Sales Full Disclosure Act (John Kerr and John McDowell). Another series of four discs deals with current decisions by the United States Supreme Court. Other discs deal with various legal practices, such as, medical and dental malpractice (Robert Miller and R. Crawford Morris).

The eight audio tapes in the collection include the following: *How to Take and Pass a Law School Examination* (Irving Younger); *The Psychiatrist and the Law* (Los Angeles: Pacifica Tape Library, c. 1975); *Attica Prison: A Montage* (Los Angeles: Pacifica Tape Library, c. 1972); *We must Enlarge the Prison Gates* (Daniel Berrigan); *Our Prisons Shouldn't be Reformed, They Should be Abandoned* (Ramsey Clark); *Prisons, Prisoners, and Parole* (Clinton Duffy); *Trial Techniques* (Irving Younger); and *1981 Individual Income Tax Refresher Course* (Sidney Kess).

4 a. On-site tape listening and viewing equipment is available.

b. Students, faculty, and staff associated with WCL and The American University are granted listening privileges. Other individuals must obtain special permission.

c. No fees charged.

d. Photocopying services are available.

5. Author/title and subject card catalogs are available as is a host of legal indices. The library publishes maps, acquisitions lists, and various bibliographies, which are available in the reference office. The library's computerized research database access includes WESTLAW, LEXIS, and OCLC.

American Women Composers, Inc. (AWC)—Music Library
See entry M26

A7 Andrews Air Force Base (AAFB) Library

1 a. *Building 1642, Stop 140*
Andrews Air Force Base, Maryland 20331
(301) 981-6454

b. 10:00 A.M.–9:00 P.M.   Monday–Thursday
10:00 A.M.–6:00 P.M.   Friday
10:00 A.M.–4:00 P.M.   Saturday
1:00 P.M.–4:00 P.M.   Sunday and holidays

c. The library is not open to the general public, but it is available for use by military personnel, their dependents, and civilian employees of AAFB.

   d. Thelma Hollomon, Acting Head Librarian

2–3. The library has approximately 34,000 books, a number of periodicals, pamphlets, and newspapers. Non-print materials include microforms, art prints, war games, video tapes, disc and cassette recordings. Subject emphasis includes science and technology, philosophy, history, languages, political science, and foreign affairs. Special collections are maintained to support various base operations: The video tape collection supports academic studies on the base. One notable series is the *College Level Evaluation Program*, which consists of 30 video cassettes.

4 a. On-site listening equipment is not available. Recordings must be borrowed and listened to on an individual's personal equipment.

   b. No reservations are required.

   c. No fees are charged.

   d. A photocopy facility is available.

5. The library has a card catalog, which has author/title and subject access.

A8 Antioch School of Law Library

1 a. *1624 Crescent Place, N.W.*
   Washington, D.C. 20009
   (202) 265–9500

   b. Open 24 hours   Monday–Thursday
      8:00 A.M.–Midnight   Friday–Sunday
      Scholars who are not members of the school may not use the library after midnight.

   c. Open to scholars, law students, and attorneys. Only members of the school may borrow materials.

   d. Jose Coutin, Head Librarian
      Eddie Caparis, Associate Librarian

2. The library has a broad spectrum of materials in support of the school's law programs. Currently, holdings include 58,000 books, 424 periodical titles, a variety of microforms, and sound recordings.

3. As of May, 1982 the library held 154 audio cassettes, most of which are commercially produced by the American Law Institute, American Bar Foundation, American Bar Association, and Condyne. Subjects include litigation, liability, damages, corporations, evidence, legal research, legal writing, medical malpractice, legal ethics, and property. Approximately 10 cassettes consist of Antioch class lectures.

4 a. On-site listening equipment is available. Individuals must ask the librarian for permission for use of equipment.

   b. No reservation requirements.

   c. No fees charged.

d. Photoduplication facility is available.

5. The library maintains a variety of biliographic aids to the printed materials collection, such as the *Legal Resource Index*. The audio tapes are listed on a typewritten list, which provides subject access only.

A9 Arlington County Central Public Library

1 a. *1015 North Quincy Street*
   Arlington, Virginia 22201
   (703) 527-4777

   b. 9:00 A.M.–10:00 P.M. Monday–Thursday
      9:00 A.M.–5:00 P.M.   Friday–Saturday
      1:00 P.M.–9:00 P.M.   Sunday

   c. Open to the public. Arlington County residents may obtain a borrower's card. Metro users are eligible for borrowing privileges. Non-resident students enrolled in colleges and universities in Northern Virginia will be issued a card limited to the period of enrollment.

   d. Lelia Saunders, Library Director

2. The Central Library is the main branch of the Arlington County Public Library System, which has six additional branches. The library contains 500,000 books, over 1,000 periodical titles, foreign language books including European and Oriental languages, a strong business collection, microforms, college catalogs, and vocational information. The library also subscribes to DIALOG, a bibliographic reference database.

3. Notable holdings of the Central Public Library.

SPECIAL SERVICES
1015 North Quincy Street, Second Floor
Arlington, Virginia 22201
(703) 527-4777, ext. 43

Nancy Cavanaugh, Coordinator of Special Services

Among the audiovisual materials in Special Services is a collection of approximately 7,000 commercial long-playing disc recordings representing general subjects. These include classical, folk, and popular music, spoken arts, sound effects, and a wide variety of language instruction (including Gaelic and some Indian dialects). There is also a collection of children's records in the children's room. The records are all located at the main library. There are cassettes in the collection, especially foreign language instruction.
   The library has a reading machine for the blind and is a regional depository for materials sent by the Library of Congress. The Arlington County Library records the *Washingtonian Magazine* as a service for other local libraries, because this publication is not recorded by the Library of Congress.

Virginiana Collection
(703) 527-4777, ext. 52

Sara Collins, Virginiana Librarian

The Virginiana Collection contains material on Arlington County local history, photographs, correspondence, notebooks, and records of individuals active in civic and political affairs.

The audio holdings include some 50 one-hour oral history interviews, which were produced as part of a project begun during the Bicentennial and cover recollections of individuals spanning from 1895 to the present. Persons interviewed are long-time Arlington County residents and others prominent in county affairs. Topics discussed include rural life, urban development, business, civic activities, government, social life, historic landmarks, churches, and celebrations.

Transcripts are available by appointment. In addition, 22 interviews of the Folk Arts Oral History Program are held in the Archive of Folk Culture in the Library of Congress (B19). All of the tapes focus on community life in Arlington County. Excerpts from the project are published in *Traditions and Ideas By Those Who Remember*.

4 a. Some on-site listening available (library card required for use). Records circulate for three weeks.

b. No reservation requirements.

c. No fees charged, except for overdue items and for use of DIALOG.

d. A photoduplication facility is available.

5. The record collection is completely cataloged, the card catalog for which is on the 2nd floor. The library also has *Phono-Log* and the *Schwann Record and Tape Guide*. Each oral history tape in the Virginiana Collection has an index to its contents, but there is no general index to the collection at present.

Arlington County Public Library—Talking Book Service   **See entry F5**

A10   Arnold and Porter Law Library

1 a. *1200 New Hampshire Avenue, N.W.*
Washington, D.C. 20036
(202) 872–3994

b. 9:00 A.M.–5:00 P.M.   Monday–Friday

c. Not open to the public. Individuals may borrow recordings through interlibrary loan only.

d. James W. Shelar, Librarian

2–3.   The library contains some 20 to 25 audio cassette tapes produced by the Arnold and Porter Law Library, as well as a number of other firms. The tapes are used mostly for continuing education of lawyers belonging to Arnold and Porter and dealing with trial practice.

5.   There is a card catalog with cassettes listed under various subject headings.

Association for the Study of Afro-American Life and History, Inc. —
Library   See entry M31

A11 Atomic Industrial Forum (AIF)—Audiovisual Library

1 a. *7101 Wisconsin Avenue*
   Bethesda, Maryland 20814
   (301) 654–9260, ext. 251

 b. 9:00 A.M.–5:00 P.M.   Monday–Friday

 c. Open to serious researchers for on-site use. A number of films and video tapes are available for loan and purchase.

 d. Marge Wasson, Audiovisual Services Manager

2. The Atomic Industrial Forum, founded in 1953, is an association of industrial firms, research and educational organizations, labor groups, and governmental agencies, which work to develop and utilize nuclear energy for constructive purposes.

3. AIF maintains two libraries. The main library has a collection of some 1,500 books, 1,200 technical reports, and 250 journal and newsletter titles focusing on nuclear energy, nuclear technology, alternative technologies, electric power produced by nuclear energy, and regulatory and administrative laws that pertain to nuclear energy. There is also a vertical file of historical and current materials, including speeches, biographies, news clippings, and maps.
   A separate audiovisual library contains 16mm films, video tapes, photographs, and slide/tape presentations. One slide/tape focuses on nuclear energy and women. Although the audiovisual library has only a few slide/tape presentations, they serve as an excellent source for referring individuals to other organizations with more resources.

4 a. On-site listening facility is available.

 b. Contact the organization to schedule an appointment.

 c. Fees are not charged to listen to recordings.

5. A list of films and video tapes available for loan and purchase can be obtained by calling the audiovisual library. AFI publishes a monthly newsletter, an annual report, and a monthly periodical, *Nuclear Industry.*

A12 Bowie State College—Thurgood Marshall Library

1 a. *Bowie, Maryland 20715*
   (301) 464–3398 (Main Library)
   (301) 464–3453 (Media Services)
   (301) 464–3338 (Music Listening Laboratory)

 b. 8:00 A.M.–10:00 P.M.   Monday–Thursday
   8:00 A.M.–5:00 P.M.   Friday
   8:00 A.M.–4:00 P.M.   Saturday
   6:00 P.M.–10:00 P.M.   Sunday

 c. The library is open to scholars for on-site use only.

 d. Courtney Funn, Director of Library Services
   Vera Chesley, Director of Media Services

2. The library functions as a support system for the entire curriculum of the college. The library holdings consist of books, periodicals, microforms, and various special collections and materials, including vertical files and newsletters, a Negro collection, and a Maryland collection of materials on history, geography, government, education, and other topics pertaining to and emanating from the State of Maryland and its counties.

3. Notable holdings of the library.

Music Listening Laboratory
Martin Luther King, Jr., Communication and Fine Arts Center

9:00 A.M.–5:00 P.M.   Monday–Friday

The library's sound recordings are held in the Music Listening Laboratory. The laboratory contains some 1,180 commercial disc recordings of music of all periods, including instrumental, vocal, and choral music, operas, oratorios, and cantatas, folk and ethnic music, popular music, music designed for teaching children, music designed for filmstrip viewing, and a few rare recordings. The laboratory also contains some 3,000 music scores, which serve as a complementary collection to the recordings. The laboratory also holds all the prepared audio tapes of music-class assignments, seminars, recitals, and concerts of the college choir, concert and jazz bands, representing works of graduating seniors, and guest artists.

4 a. On-site listening facility is available in the Music Listening Laboratory.

   b. Reservations by telephone are recommended.

   c. No fees are charged.

   d. Patrons may make copies of selections from the collection. A photoduplication facility is available only in the main library.

5. The main library's card catalog is arranged by author/title and subject for books and sound recordings, which are interfiled. The Music Listening Laboratory maintains a separate card catalog. Only the prepared audio tapes have not been cataloged.

A13 Brazilian-American Cultural Institute (BACI) Music Library

1 a. *4201 Connecticut Avenue, N.W., Suite 211*
   Washington, D.C. 20008
   (202) 362–8334

   b. 10:00 A.M.–7:00 P.M.   Monday–Friday

   c. Open to the public.

   d. José Neistein, Institute Director
   Paulo Costa, Record and Tape Librarian

2–3. The library has approximately 1,000 commercial disc recordings, produced in Brazil of Brazilian music, both classical and popular. The library also has 10 audio tapes of special concerts and events of Brazilian-American culture taking place throughout the country.

4 a. On-site listening equipment is available.

b. No reservation requirement, but it is recommended that individuals telephone in advance of visiting the library.

c. No listening fees charged.

d. Some duplication of sound recordings is possible.

5. A 1980 record inventory is available.

Broadcast Pioneers Library (BPL)   **See entry B8**

A14   Business and Professional Women's Foundation—Marguerite Rawalt Resource Center

1 a. *2012 Massachusetts Avenue, N.W.*
Washington, D.C. 20036
(202) 293-1200

b. 9:00 A.M.–5:00 P.M.   Monday–Friday

c. The Resource Center is open to the public. Reference service is available by mail and telephone. Sound recordings may not be borrowed. Individuals are requested to telephone or write in advance for an appointment.

d. Cheryl A. Sloan, Head Librarian

2. The Business and Professional Women's Foundation, founded in 1956, seeks to improve women's status in the economic sector and to assist in the integration of women into all occupations. The foundation's programs are varied, including educational assistance through scholarships and loans, research activities about women, the dissemination of information, often in the form of publications, on women and work. The foundation's Resource Center serves as a special working library in support of these programs.

The Marguerite Rawalt Resource Center holds a comprehensive collection on women and employment, totaling some 5,500 books and over 15,000 research and conference reports, journal articles, papers, speeches, and at least 100 different periodicals.

3. Included in the collection are some 300 reel-to-reel tapes for and about women consisting of speeches, conventions, interviews, and panel discussions. Subjects include biography, child care, congresswomen, economics, political action, role and status of women, legislation, higher education, crime prevention, discrimination in employment, and rights of women. The majority of the tapes were produced from 1950–1975. Although many of the tapes concern the foundation's activities, there are also tapes representing the activities of other professional women's clubs.

A few of the tapes that represent the collection include: Address at the Luncheon of the National Council of Negro Women, Eleanor Roosevelt, February 26, 1955 (T01); "The Role of Women in American Leadership," Mary I. Bunting, October 5, 1962 (T50); Address before the U.S. Congress, February 18, 1943, Madame Chiang Kai-Shek (original tape at National Archives and Records Service, 1967) (T88); Address at Awards Program of American Association of University Women, Coretta Scott King, June 17, 1969 (T143); "Progress of Women," Margaret Chase Smith, July 16, 1969 (T148); *Women in Politics*, recorded in Washington, D.C., April, 1968, for

the League of Women Voters; as well as interviews with Al Mark, Ethel Payne, Billie Farnum, Spencer Oliver, Mary Brooks, Kathryn Stone, Dorothy V. Busy, and Mrs. Robert Kintner (T134–135).

4 a. On-site listening equipment is available.

b. Appointments in advance are preferred.

c. No fee for listening to sound recordings.

5. The foundation has three indexes filed in a folder labeled "Oral History Collection Catalog." A card catalog is also available to researchers. The foundation has published an array of research tools including, *Research Funding Sourcebook* (1981), *Women & Work in U.S. History: An Annotated Bibliography* (1976), and *The Woman Manager in the United States: A Research Analysis and Bibliography* (1981). A flyer describing the programs and publications of the foundation is available free upon request.

A15   Catholic University of America—John K. Mullen Memorial Library

1 a. *620 Michigan Avenue, N.E.*
Washington, D.C. 20064
(202) 635–5055 (Office of the Director)
(202) 635–5070 (Reference)
(202) 635–5077 (Schedule Information)

b. 8:00 A.M.–11:45 P.M.   Monday–Thursday
8:00 A.M.–8:00 P.M.   Friday
9:00 A.M.–8:00 P.M.   Saturday
Noon–11:45 P.M.   Sunday
Hours vary during summer.

c. Open to the public for on-site use only. Visiting scholars may be eligible for temporary courtesy borrowing by inquiring at the Office of the Director of Libraries (Room 318). Normal borrowing privileges are extended to Catholic University faculty, staff, and students, and faculty and eligible students of the Washington Consortium.

d. Eric L. Ormsby, Director of Libraries

2. Catholic University library holdings include some 1,136,953 books, 7,754 periodical titles and extensive non-print materials representing all of the humanities and most sciences.

3. Notable holdings of the library.

Humanities Library
Mullen Building, Room 312
(202) 635–5075

Blue Gutekunst, Head Librarian

The Humanities Library has over 2,000 microforms, 2 filmstrips, and 3 audio tapes, as well as one cassette (*The Difficulty of Medieval Poetry*, BFA Educational Media), and two reel-to-reel tapes (a Drama Department thesis and *Improving Voice and Articulation*, by Hilda Fisher).

Music Library
Ward Building, Room 101
(202) 635-5424

9:00 A.M.-9:00 P.M.	Monday-Thursday
9:00 A.M.-6:00 P.M.	Friday
11:00 A.M.-5:00 P.M.	Saturday
1:00 P.M.-8:00 P.M.	Sunday

Hours vary during summer.

Betty Libbey, Head Librarian

The Music Library has 15,000 music scores, 472 microfilms, 9,000 disc recordings, 430 cassette and 464 reel-to-reel tapes. The disc recordings are commercially produced and represent a broad range of music (all styles and periods) including classical, jazz, and popular. Of note are 200 recordings of Gregorian chants and a complete set of Louisville Philharmonic Society recordings representing contemporary classical music. The cassettes and reel-to-reel tapes are mostly duplicates of the disc collection made for reserve and archival purposes. One notable cassette tape is a lecture presented by Eric Routley on English hymnody.

Nursing/Biology Library
Nursing Building, Room 212
(202) 635-5411

9:00 A.M.-10:00 P.M.	Monday-Thursday
9:00 A.M.-9:00 P.M.	Wednesday-Thursday
9:00 A.M.-6:00 P.M.	Friday
1:00 P.M.-5:00 P.M.	Saturday
1:00 P.M.-9:00 P.M.	Sunday

Nellie Lee Powell, Head Librarian

The Nursing/Biology Library has 2,766 microforms, 106 video tapes, 40 films, 491 filmstrips, 5,738 slides, and 678 audio cassettes. The audio tapes focus mostly on nursing and are produced by J.B. Lippincott Company and Concept Media. A few tapes consist of lectures on nursing presented at Catholic University. One notable lecture was presented by Sister Callista Roy. A few additional tapes focus on medicine and psychology.

Reference/Social Service/Social Sciences Library
Mullen Building, Room 206
(202) 635-5070

Harriet Nelson, Coordinator

The library contains non-print materials, including over 200,000 microforms, 1,092 disc recordings, 55 cassette and 51 reel-to-reel audio tapes. The disc collection includes 546 titles and consists primarily of drama and language recordings. Included are a number of recordings of poetry. The cassette tapes consist mostly of lectures on history and psychology. Two notable series include *Middle Ages in Europe* (Sussex Tapes International, 11 cassettes) and *Walter Kerr's Guide to the Theater* (Teaching Resources Films, 6 audio cassettes). The reel-to-reel tapes include a number of travel topics on Latin America produced by the Pan American Union.

4 a. On-site listening equipment is available at all of the libraries described above, except the humanities library.

b. No reservation requirements.

c. No fees charged except for on-line searching of AVLINE.

d. Photocopy facilities are available. Generally, duplication at all libraries is conducted only for reserve and archival purposes.

5. All of the libraries retain card catalogs having access by author/title and subject. The Music Library also has musical form and artist access. Their recordings are shelved by accession number. The recordings in the Reference/Social Service/Social Sciences and the Nursing/Biology libraries are shelved in call-number order in one area of each respective library, even though the cards for recordings are interfiled with cards for books. Access to AVLINE is also available in the latter library.

A16 Catholic University of America—Robert J. White Law Library

1 a. *102C Leahy Hall*
620 Michigan Avenue, N.E.
Washington, D.C. 20064
(202) 635–5155

b. 8:00 A.M.–Midnight   Monday–Friday
9:00 A.M.–Midnight   Saturday–Sunday

c. Open to students of law for on-site use only.

d. John R. Valeri, Head Librarian
Patrick Petit, Associate Librarian

2. The library's holdings include some 96,000 books, 27,000 microforms, about 250 journals, and a number of looseleaf and treatise services in various legal areas.

3. Non-print holdings include 25 audio cassette tapes on various legal subjects, such as probate, property law, and evidence and other trial techniques.

4 a. On-site listening equipment is available.

b. Prior appointment is required.

c. No fees charged.

d. Photocopy facility is available.

5. Inquire at the Reference Desk for assistance in locating sound recordings.

A17 Children's Hospital Medical Center—Library

1 a. *111 Michigan Avenue, N.W.*
Washington, D.C. 20010
(202) 745–3195

b. 8:30 A.M.–5:00 P.M.   Monday–Friday
8:30 A.M.–5:00 P.M.   Saturday
1:00 P.M.–5:00 P.M.   Sunday

c. Open to the public. The library is for use primarily by hospital staff. Borrowing privileges are extended only to members of the hospital.

2–3. The library has approximately 120 audio cassette tapes. Children's Hospital Medical Center Library subscribes to *Audio-Digest,* a series of cassettes dealing with a variety of medical topics including pediatrics, ophthalmology, and anesthesiology. The library also has a number of separate tapes that focus on pediatrics, nursing, and pastoral care.

4 a. On-site listening equipment is available.

b. It is recommended that individuals telephone or write for more details on the collection before visiting the library.

c. No fees charged.

d. Photocopying facility is available.

5. A list of holdings with locations is available.

C.J. Jung Library and Information Center   See entry A39

Columbia Historical Society Library   See entry B10

A18 Columbia Hospital for Women—Medical Library

1 a. *2425 L Street, N.W.*
Washington, D.C. 20037
(202) 293–6560

b. 9:00 A.M.–5:00 P.M.   Monday–Friday

c. Open to qualified researchers with special permission.

d. Elizabeth M. Haggart, Librarian

2–3. The library's principal subject strengths are gynecology and obstetrics. The library subscribes to *Audio-Digest,* and has tapes from 1971 to the present.

4 a. Contact the library for information regarding listening facilities and borrowing privileges.

A19 Columbia Union College—Theofield G. Weis Library

1 a. *Flower and Carroll Avenues*
Takoma Park, Maryland 20912
(301) 891–4218

b. 8:00 A.M.–10:00 P.M.   Monday–Thursday
8:00 A.M.-1:00 P.M.   Friday
6:00 P.M.-10:00 P.M.   Sunday
Hours vary during the summer.

c. Open to the public for on-site use only.

d. Margaret von Hake, Head Librarian

2–3. The library has some 400 commercial disc recordings of mostly classical music (all styles and periods). There are some spoken-word recordings in the collection as well. The library also has a small number of audio tapes of the *H.M.S. Richards Lectureship* series produced on campus, and consisting of guest and faculty lectures. The library also has a partial run of the series, *Aspire, Tape of the Month*, produced by the Seventh-day Adventists, for 1982–1983. For more information on this series, see Seventh-day Adventists, entry E5.

4 a. On-site listening equipment is available.

b. No reservation requirements.

c. No fees charged.

5. The library has a card catalog having author/title and subject access. Cards for recordings are interfiled with cards for books.

DeSales School of Theology—Library   See entry E2

A20 District of Columbia General Hospital—Medical Library

1 a. *19th Street and Massachusetts Avenue, S.E.*
Washington, D.C. 20003
(202) 675–5348

b. Open to the staff of the District of Columbia General Hospital. Outside researchers must telephone or write requesting permission to use the library.

c. 8:30 A.M.–4:30 P.M.   Monday–Friday

d. Dale Eliasson, Librarian

2. The library has some 8,800 books and 600 periodical subscriptions on a broad range of medical topics.

3. The library subscribes to the audio cassette series, *Audio-Digest* from the 1960s to the present. Topics include pediatrics, surgery, internal medicine, obstetrics, and otolaryengology.

4 a. On-site listening equipment is available.

5. The library maintains a card catalog with author/title and subject access.

A21 Fairfax County Public Library

1 a. *Administration*
5502 Port Royal Road
Springfield, Virginia 22151
(703) 321–9810

b. Hours vary from branch to branch.

c. Most library materials circulate, and borrowing privileges are extended to residents of the county and of most neighboring counties.

d. Edwin S. Clay, III, Director of Libraries
Anne W. Paine, Coordinator, Public Information

2. Fairfax County Public Library is the largest public library system in the state of Virginia and the fourth busiest suburban public library in the United States. Including the central regional branch located in Fairfax City, the system has 20 branches, which provide over a million books, films, recordings (tapes and discs), video cassettes, and other miscellaneous materials. Special library services include talking books, outreach to the homebound, a bookmobile, meeting rooms for public use, free movie and story times for children, and book discussions for adults.

3. As of June 30, 1982 the audio collection at Fairfax County Public Library consisted of 22,391 discs and 5,812 cassettes. The collection is spread out over most branches, with the largest collection at the central branch. Subject areas include classical music, musicals, popular music and jazz, folk music, children's records, plays, poetry, speeches, and language instruction.

4 a. On-site listening equipment is available in some branches.

b. No reservation requirements.

c. No fees are charged.

d. No duplication of tapes available. Photocopy facilities are available in most branches.

5. The record collections in all branches are fully cataloged, and there is a system-wide card file for full access to audio holdings. The library system also has a microfiche and printed catalog, including author, title, and subject indexes, which include full cataloging for recordings recently acquired.

Fairfax County Public Library—Talking Book Service   **See entry F8**

A22 Fairfax Hospital—Jacob D. Zylman Memorial Library

1 a. *3300 Gallows Road*
Falls Church, Virginia 22046
(703) 698–3234

b. 4:00 P.M.–10:00 P.M.   Monday–Friday
9:00 A.M.–2:00 P.M.   Saturday
12:00 Noon–5:00 P.M.   Sunday
8:30 A.M.–4:00 P.M.   Monday-Friday (additional hours for hospital personnel only)

c. Open to the public.

d. Alice J. Sheridan, Library Director

2.   The library contains 10,000 volumes in the fields of medicine, nursing, allied health, and hospital administration and management. Some 600 books and 40 audiovisual items are added annually.

3.   The library contains approximately 300 audiovisual programs, including more than 150 audio cassettes. In addition, the holdings include *ACCEL (American College of Cardiology Extended Learning) for Nurses* and *Audio-Digest,* whose topics include pediatrics, internal medicine, and psychiatry.

4 a.   On-site listening facilities are available.

 b.   Hospital personnel receive first priority.

 c.   There are no fees charged to listen to recordings.

 d.   A photocopy facility is available.

Federal Judicial Center—Media Library   See entry L2

A23   Folger Shakespeare Library

1 a.   *201 East Capitol Street, S.E.*
Washington, D.C. 20003
(202) 544-4600

 b.   8:45 A.M.–4:30 P.M.   Monday–Saturday

 c.   The collection is open only to scholars with proper identification.

 d.   O.B. Hardison, Jr., Director

2.   Housed in an elegant building that is classical in approach and Tudor in interior decorative details, the carefully selected collection exceeds 200,000 volumes and 40,000 manuscripts on the theme of Elizabethan England and Renaissance Europe.

3.   The library has a small collection of disc recordings of Shakespeare's plays and of music performed during Shakespeare's time. In addition a number of talks and conferences presented in the library have been recorded on tape.

4 a.   Limited on-site listening equipment is available.

 b.   Reservations are required.

 c.   No fees are charged.

 d.   Photoduplication and microfilming services are available.

5.   The library follows the Library of Congress classification schedules. Finding aids include: a dictionary card catalog; *Catalog of Printed Books of the Folger Shakespeare Library,* 28 vols., 1970 and a volume Supplement, 1976; and a 3-volume *Catalog of Manuscripts of the Folger Shakespeare Library,* 1971. The author/title and subject card catalog is conveniently located between the library's two reading rooms. The recordings, however, are not cataloged.

The Folger Shakespeare Library bookstore is described in Appendix I.

A24 Food and Drug Administration (FDA)—Medical Library

1 a. *5600 Fishers Lane, Room 11B40*
Rockville, Maryland 20857
(301) 443–1538

b. 7:30 A.M.–5:00 P.M.   Monday–Friday

c. Open to the public. Audio materials are used only in the library.

d. Elizabeth C. Kelly, Director

2. The purpose of the Medical Library is to collect and disseminate information for the benefit of FDA scientists and administrators. The collection is extensive in the fields of pharmacology, medicine, and biostatistics, and includes books, journals, newspapers, indexing and abstracting services, microfilm, microfiche, a collection of FDA publications, and sound recordings.

3. The audio collection includes 500 cassettes principally on medicine. Some of the series include: *Audio-Digest* (topics include anesthesiology, family practice, internal medicine, obstetrics and gynecology, opthalmology, otolaryngology, pediatrics, and psychiatry); *Voices* (American Journal Review in Opthalmology (1876–1981); *Today's Therapeutics* (1973–1976); *Today's Surgery* (1975–1979); and *Medcom: Famous Teachings in Modern Medicine* (library has 10 titles).

4 a. On-site listening equipment is available.

b. Reservations are not required.

c. No fees are charged to listen to sound recordings.

d. Photoduplication facility is available.

5. Audio tapes are treated and cataloged as periodicals and filed in title/chronological order. Audio tapes are shelved in a listening room.

Ford's Theatre (Interior Department—National Park Service)—Petersen House Library   See entry C2

A25 Fort Myer Post Library (Army Department)

1 a. *Building 469*
Fort Myer, Virginia 22211
(703) 692–9574

b. 12:00 Noon–9:00 P.M.   Monday, Wednesday, Thursday
12:00 Noon–6:00 P.M.   Tuesday
10:00 A.M.–6:00 P.M.   Saturday

c. The library is open to active military personnel, employees of the Department of the Army, and retired military personnel.

d. Vacant, Post Librarian

2–3. Library holdings include 40,000 books, 210 periodicals, 100 microfilm titles, and 2,000 disc and 400 commercial audio cassette recordings, the latter constituting a broad spectrum of music, including popular music, jazz, folk, and classical music. The library also has a few spoken arts recordings.

4 a. On-site listening equipment is limited.

c. No fees are charged to listen to the recordings.

5. The library has a card catalog in which the disc recordings can be accessed by performer's name and title. The cassette recordings are not cataloged.

Freer Gallery of Art (Smithsonian Institution)—Library   **See entry C3**

A26 George Mason University—Fenwick Library

1 a. *4400 University Drive*
Fairfax, Virginia 22030
(703) 323–2391

b. 7:30 A.M.–Midnight   Monday–Thursday
7:30 A.M.–6:00 P.M.   Friday
9:00 A.M.–5:00 P.M.   Saturday
1:00 P.M.–9:00 P.M.   Sunday

c. Open to scholars for on-site use. George Mason University is the host institution of the Consortium for Continuing Higher Education in Northern Virginia , whose primary goal is to foster inter-institutional cooperation while broadening the base of learning opportunities for adult students. Reciprocal borrowing privileges exist among the libraries of member institutions.

d. Charlene Hurt, Director

2. Fenwick Library is the central collection on the main campus of George Mason University and contains over 236,000 book volumes, 312,000 microforms, and 3,000 periodical subscriptions. On-line computer access to bibliographic and information data bases is available. Library materials not available at the university may be borrowed through interlibrary loan.

3. Notable holdings of the library.

SPECIAL COLLECTIONS DIVISION
Fenwick Library, Second Floor
(703) 323–2251

8:30 A.M.–5:00 P.M.   Monday–Friday
Call in advance to verify hours and availability of material.

Ruth Kerns, Special Collections/Public Services Librarian

The University Library is building special collections containing primary resources materials to be used by scholars in their research. Two of these collections are of special interest to researchers in oral history:

Federal Theatre Project Collection (FTP).—This collection contains the major playscripts, radio scripts, set and costume designs, music scores, photographs, and administrative papers related to the Works Progress Administration (WPA) Federal Theatre Project of 1935–1939. With the support of the National Endowment for the Humanities, it was placed on permanent deposit at George Mason University by the Library of Congress. The audio portion of this collection includes 238 interviews, which equals some 280 hours of tape, plus 10 video tapes. Of these, 171 interviews are transcribed equaling 8,000 pages; all transcribed interviews are abstracted and indexed. The continuing oral history research program related to the FTP was organized to gather interviews with former participants. It is being expanded to include interviews with former members of other WPA arts projects, including actors, producers, directors, and designers. Oral histories currently in the Fenwick Library collection include the following: Bill Baird, Philip Barber, Anne Barlin, Howard Bay, Eubie Blake, Nadia Chilovsky, Elizabeth Cohen, Joseph Cotten, Howard Da Silva, Leonard De Paur, Mura Dehn, Lehman Engel, John Houseman, Emmet Lavery, Paula Lawrence, Albert Maltz, E.G. Marshall, John Randolph, Earl Robinson, Ben Russak, Arnold Sungaard, and Virgil Thomson. A number of recordings representing the WPA (from the 1930s) are held in the National Archives and Records Service (B27). An excellent source for the study of the Federal Theatre Project is *Pickaxe and Pencil: References for the Study of the WPA* (1982). Also a detailed description of the FTP is published in *Special Collections in the Library of Congress* (1980).

Northern Virginia Oral History Project.—This is a collection of some 75 interviews relating to the history of Northern Virginia , with the major focus on Fairfax County. The collection consists of 50 to 60 tapes, most of which have been transcribed. Local history subjects covered include schools, churches, dairy farming, transportation, and community life. For further information concerning these collections contact the Special Collections Librarian or Roy Rosenzweig, Director of Oral History Program, Department of History.

A/V Library Resource Center
Fenwick Library, Second Floor
(703) 323–2605

Helen Grissom, Non-book Librarian/Audiovisual Coordinator

The Media/Music Collection is in the Media-Music Room and comprises 1,785 disc recordings of mostly classical music with some spoken arts, and 1,231 circulating scores. The 226 audio tapes are related to curricula of the departments of English, Music, Nursing, Psychology, Biology, and Education, as is an ongoing collection of the original master reels and cassette copies of the George Mason University weekly interview programs, *Frankly Speaking,* produced by Public Relations, and aired on local and regional radio stations.

4 a. On-site listening equipment, either through a central stereo system, carrels, or portable cassette players, is available in Fenwick Library. Some equipment is also available in the Special Collections Division.

  b. No reservation required.

  c. No fees charged.

  d. Arrangements may be made for duplication of some materials in the George Mason University Library collections, consistent with copyright regulations. Contact the Special Collections Librarian or the Audiovisual Coordinator for special requests.

5.   Sound recordings in Fenwick Library Media/Music Collection are fully cataloged. A partial description of Federal Theatre Project holdings can be found in *Performing Arts Resources*, vol. 6 (1980), pp. 63–69. A directory of the Northern Virginia Oral History Project Collection is in progress.

A27   George Washington University—Jacob Burns Law Library

1 a.   *National Law Center*
716 20th Street, N.W.
Washington, D.C. 20052
(202) 676–6646 (Hours)
(202) 676–6648 (Reference)

b.   8:00 A.M.–Midnight   Monday–Friday
9:00 A.M.–Midnight   Saturday
11:00 A.M.–Midnight   Sunday

c.   Not open to the public. Sound recordings may, however, be borrowed through inter-library loan.

d.   Anita K. Head, Law Librarian
Gloria Miccioli, Media/Government Documents Librarian

2.   The law holdings include some 213,000 books, 181,000 microforms, and over 1,000 journals. Legal areas include Anglo-American law, international law, comparative law, environmental law, among others. The library holds various administrative and regulatory law publications, records and briefs of the U.S. Supreme Court, and records and briefs of the U.S. Court of Customs and Patent Appeals.

3.   The library's sound recording collection consists of 183 audio cassette tapes focusing on such topics as probate and property, bankruptcy, estate planning, tax law, international law, energy, land use litigation, civil rights, trial evidence, juvenile justice, and multinational corporations. They were produced by the American Bar Association, University of Utah Education Department, Commerce Clearing House, Center for the Study of Democratic Institutions, National District Attorneys Association, National Institute of Municipal Law Officers, National Organization for Reform of Marijuana Laws, National Paralegal Institute, Practising Law Institute, Pacifica Tape Library, and Condyne/Trans-Media. Included among the tapes are lectures, seminars, and conferences, the latter including the Seventh National Conference on Law Office Economics and Management (produced by the American Bar Association) and the Sixth National Conference on Juvenile Justice (produced by the National District Attorneys Association).

4 a.   On-site listening equipment is available.

b.   Use of materials is administered through interlibrary loan.

c.   No fees charged.

d.   A photoduplication facility is available.

5.   The library maintains a card catalog with author/title and subject access. The audio tapes are cited on a typewritten list.

A28 George Washington University (GWU) Medical Center—Paul Himmelfarb Health Sciences Library

1 a. *2300 Eye Street, N.W.*
Washington, D.C. 20037
(202) 676-2961 (Hours)
(202) 676-2850 (Reference and On-line Bibliographic Service)

b. 7:30 A.M.–Midnight   Monday–Thursday
7:30 A.M.–10:00 P.M.   Friday
10:00 A.M.–10:00 P.M.   Saturday
10:00 A.M.–Midnight   Sunday
Hours vary during summer.

c. Open only for the use of GWU Medical Center students, faculty, staff, and other GWU students enrolled in medical school courses.

d. Shelley Bader, Director of the Library

2. The Himmelfarb Library serves as a repository for materials designed to assist medical and allied health students with the general curriculum and specific courses. Such materials normally include both books and periodicals.

3. Notable holdings of the library.

Bloedorn Audio-Visual Study Center
(202) 676-2856

8:30 A.M.–10:00 P.M.   Monday–Thursday
8:30 A.M.–6:00 P.M.   Friday
10:00 A.M.–6:00 P.M.   Saturday
10:00 A.M.–10:00 P.M.   Sunday

Lynn Povanda, Manager
Susan Press, Purchaser of Software

The Audio-Visual Study Center owns more than 800 audiovisual titles in the basic sciences and clinical medicine. Materials include those purchased from commercial or other academic sources, as well as many produced by the GWU Medical Center. Representative titles include *Anatomy: Guides to Dissection; Physiology: Illustrated Lecture in Renal Physiology; Cardiac Physiology; Psychiatry: Simulated Psychiatric Patient Interviews; Pediatrics: Infant at High Risk;* and *Radiology: Basic Diagnostic Radiology.* A wide variety of audio tapes are held in the library including the series *Audio-Digest* (representing surgery, internal medicine, psychiatry, among other subjects) and *Basic Science* (lectures). There is also an oral history project underway that focuses on the medical center. Currently there are 10 interviews on the 1930s to the present.

4 a. On-site listening equipment is available.

b. No reservations required.

c. Fees are charged for duplication and on-line searches.

d. The Audio-Visual Center has a Lecture Tape Service whereby class lectures are recorded on tape and duplicated for students. A photocopy facility is available.

5.   The Resource Librarian maintains a file of media catalogs from commercial sources, health institutions, and professional health societies. Also useful is the brochure *Reference and Online Bibliographic Services*. The library also publishes *Information Interface* (10 times a year),which lists recent acquisitions as well as presenting news concerning the library.

A29   George Washington University—Melvin Gelman Library

1 a.   *2130 H Street, N.W.*
Washington, D.C. 20052
(202) 676–6047 (Reference)
(202) 676–6845 (Hours)
(202) 676–6558 (Information)

b.   8:30 A.M.–Midnight   Monday–Friday
10:00 A.M.–Midnight   Saturday and Sunday

c.   Open to scholars for on-site use. Identification is required to enter the building. Borrowing privileges are extended to George Washington University faculty and students, and Washington Consortium faculty and eligible consortium graduate students. Visitors are required to telephone or write in advance in order to make arrangements to listen to audio tape recordings.

d.   Connie K. McCarthy, Acting University Librarian

2.   The library holdings include 994,328 books and 9,805 periodical subscriptions with major subject strengths in American studies, business administration, higher education, geology, health care administration, historic preservation, international relations, Judaic studies, and urban and regional planning.

3.   Notable holdings of the library.

Reserves & Media Resources Division
(202) 676–6378

8:30 A.M.–10:00 P.M.   Monday–Friday
10:00 A.M.–6:00 P.M.   Saturday
12:00 Noon–10:00 P.M.   Sunday

Diane S. Hollyfield, Chief

This division maintains non-print materials, including some 43,000 microforms, 154 video tapes, 104 films, and 1,677 music titles and 498 commercially produced spoken-word titles of audio cassettes, and over 60 reel-to-reel recordings of lectures and other presentations.
   The collection of music cassettes is general in scope and represents all styles and periods. The spoken-word subjects include education, literature, science, American studies, and management science.
   One notable collection is a set of oral history cassette and reel-to-reel tapes with interviews by Mary Jo Deering. One notable interview is with Elmer Kayser, former George Washington University historian and resident of the District of Columbia, who recalls what Georgetown was like in the past. A by-product of this interview is available in the library as a slide/tape presentation, *Elmer Kayser's Washington*. Kayser is also interviewed concerning the history of George Washington University. This

interview is available as a slide/tape presentation, *Campus—Past and Present with Commentary by Elmer Kayser*. Transcripts for these interviews are available in the library.

A third oral history project, *Integration of the Montgomery County Schools*, also conducted by Mary Jo Deering, is available in the library. Transcripts (with some restrictions on their use) are available in the library's Special Collections Division (202/676–7497). Individuals who are working with oral history materials may want to consult: Mary Jo Deering and Barbara Pomeroy *Transcribing Without Tears: A Guide to Transcribing and Editing Oral History Interviews* (George Washington University Library, 1976).

The reel-to-reel tape recordings consist of the series *Lectures in Miniature*, presented by George Washington faculty speaking on science and humanity topics, and the series *The Voice of History* (55 tapes), which are copies of original recordings of the voices of significant twentieth-century intellectual thinkers.

4 a. On-site listening equipment is available.

b. Telephone or write in advance to make arrangements to listen to audio cassette and reel-to-reel tapes.

c. No fees charged.

d. Photocopy facility is available. Contact the library regarding current duplication policy for recordings.

5. Materials are listed in a card catalog, which provides author/title and subject access. Cards for recordings are interfiled with cards for books in the main library. The Reserves & Media Resources Division has a separate catalog. Individual finding aids are available for the oral history tape collection.

A30 Georgetown University—Fred O. Dennis Law Library

1 a. *Georgetown University Law Center*
600 New Jersey Avenue, N.W.
Washington, D.C. 20001
(202) 624–8260 (Hours)
(202) 624–8033 (General Information)
(202) 624–8375 (Reference)
(202) 624–8029 (Media Office)

b. 8:00 A.M.–Midnight   Monday–Friday
9:00 A.M.–10:00 P.M.   Saturday
10:00 A.M.–Midnight   Sunday
Hours vary for Media Office.

c. Open to scholars, attorneys, and students of law for on-site use only.

d. Robert Oakley, Law Librarian
Gary Bravy, Media/Reference Librarian

2. Library holdings include about 300,000 books and periodicals, 100,000 microforms, with special emphases placed on administrative, comparative, and international law.

3.   The library contains approximately 125 audio cassettes on a wide variety of legal topics. Many of the cassettes are produced by Condyne/Trans-Media.

4 a.   On-site listening equipment is available.

b.   Individuals must make arrangements to pick up headphones at the circulation desk; listening equipment is located in the Media Office.

c.   No fees are charged.

d.   A photoduplication facility is available.

5.   The library's materials are arranged in a card catalog. Most of the sound recordings have been cataloged and filed according to accession number and are available in the media area.

A31   Georgetown University—Joseph Mark Lauinger Library

1 a.   *37th and O Streets, N.W.*
Washington, D.C. 20057
(202) 625–4173 (Reference)
(202) 625–3300 (Library Hours)

b.   8:30 A.M.–Midnight   Monday–Thursday
8:30 A.M.–10:00 P.M.   Friday
10:00 A.M.–10:00 P.M.   Saturday
11:00 A.M.–Midnight   Sunday

c.   Open to scholars for on-site use only. Sound recordings may be borrowed only by faculty and students of Georgetown University. Sound recordings in the Woodstock Library do not circulate.

d.   Joseph E. Jeffs, University Librarian

2.   Library holdings include some 975,000 books, 12,800 periodical subscriptions, and a variety of non-print materials. The library's principal subject strengths lie in languages and linguistics, international relations, history, government, and theology.

3.   Notable holdings of the library.

Audio-Visual Learning Resource Center
(202) 625–4123

8:30 A.M.–11:00 P.M.   Monday–Thursday
8:30 A.M.–10:00 P.M.   Friday
10:00 A.M.–6:00 P.M.   Saturday
1:00 P.M.–10:00 P.M.   Sunday

Mark Cohen, Head

The collection consists of approximately 100,000 items of microforms, 350 video tapes, 450 films, 28 filmstrips, 3,500 audio cassettes, and 2,000 disc recordings. All recordings are commercially produced. The audio cassette collection is general but broad in scope and includes spoken arts, plays, poetry, and music recordings (all styles and periods). The cassette collection is also maintained on reel-to-reel format. The disc collection is an archival one from which duplicate recordings are made on cassette format.

Special Collections Division
(202) 625–3230

9:00 A.M.–4:45 P.M.   Monday–Friday

Jon Reynolds, University Archivist

The Special Collections Division has a number of significant audio tape collections on a variety of topics. The most significant collections are listed below.

Eugene McCarthy Historical Project: Oral History Series.—The series includes 714 oral history interviews on the subject of Senator Eugene McCarthy's 1968 Presidential primary campaign. The series includes interviews with political figures and celebrities, such as Ernest Gruening, Lee Metcalf, Allard Lowenstein, Henry Reuss, Ralph Yarborough, Myrna Loy, and Mary Travers; however, the strength of the collection lies in the interviews with the grass roots workers who were the real source of the distinctive nature of the campaign. A limited number are open to researchers.

Eugene McCarthy Historical Project: Audio Tape Series.—The series includes 650 audio tapes documenting the 1968 Presidential primary campaign of Senator Eugene McCarthy. Includes recordings made at speeches, rallies, and television shows, as well as supporting statement from a wide variety of celebrities.

Georgetown University Archives: Special Events Series.— Includes 613 audio recordings of speeches, symposia, and convocations at Georgetown University, 1953-1965. Speakers include Walter Reuther, Leonard Hall, Claire Booth Luce, Senator Mike Mansfield, Robert D. Murphy, Abba Eban, Edward Bennett Williams, and Paul Horgan.

Georgetown University Archives: Georgetown University Forum.—The series includes the master tapes of 1355 programs of the Georgetown University Forum, a public affairs radio show 1947–1972. Speakers include a wide variety of public figures, many at an early stage in their careers. A representative sampling would include Richard Nixon, William C. Bullitt, Henry Kissinger, John Kenneth Galbraith, Eduardo Frei, and Richard V. Allen.

Horace B. McKenna, S.J. Papers: Autobiographical Tape Series. —The series consists of 20 autobiographical and interview tapes, containing reflections on Fr. Horace B. McKenna, S.J.'s 51-year ministry among black Catholics. The tapes outline his childhood, notiviate years, and work in Southern Maryland, Philadelphia, and Washington, D.C. Fr. McKenna discusses the impact of the Depression, the Civil Rights Movement, *Humanae Vitae,* inner-city poverty, and the changing role of blacks within the Catholic Church.

Center for Applied Linguistics: Negro American Dialect Series. —The Center for Applied Linguistics developed a program between 1965–1970 to study characteristics of black language in Washington, D.C. Included in the Negro American Dialect Collection are audio tapes, entitled "Conversations in an American Negro Dialect." The series of six tapes provides a look at black dialect, culture, and family life through numerous interviews.

Lawrence Suid Collection.—More than 125 oral-history interviews with figures in the motion picture industry and the Department of Defense, concerning relations between the Department and motion picture production.

Woodstock Theological Center Library
(202) 625–3120

9:00 A.M.–5:00 P.M.   Monday–Friday

Thomas Marshall, Librarian

The Woodstock Theological Center Library, located at the rear, lower level, of the Lauinger Building, contains a small collection of audio cassette tapes, principally on Catholicism. Specific topics and titles include abortion (4–5 items) and the series *Pacem in Terris* (2 items), among others. Most notable is the set of Jesuit summer provincial conferences of New York and Maryland for the years 1977 and 1982. Represented on the tapes are well-known Jesuit speakers and lecturers, including Avery Dulles, Thomas Clarke, Joseph Fitzmyer, David Hollenbach, Donald Campion, Joseph O'Hare, Vincent O'Keefe, Joseph P. Whelan, and Howard Gray.

4 a. On-site listening equipment is available.

   b. No reservation required.

   c. No fees charged.

   d. The Audio-Visual Learning Resource Center has a duplication facility. Individuals should inquire regarding the library's duplication policy.

5. The library has a main catalog (author/title, subject) in which cards for sound recordings are interfiled with cards for books. The Audio-Visual Learning Resource Center has a separate catalog. Sound recordings in the Woodstock Library are indexed by author in a card catalog, and given an accession number.

A32 Georgetown University Medical Center—John Vinton Dahlgren Memorial Library

1 a. *3900 Reservoir Road, N.W.*
   Washington, D.C. 20007
   (202) 625–5224 (Reference)
   (202) 625–2105 (Audiovisual)

   b. 8:00 A.M.–Midnight   Monday–Friday
   9:00 A.M.–Midnight   Saturday and Sunday

   c. Open to scholars and students of medicine for on-site use.
   The audiovisual materials do not circulate.

   d. Naomi Broering, Head Librarian
   Margaret Keiser, Audiovisual Librarian

2. The library contains some 115,000 books and subscribes to approximately 1,500 journals.

3. Special collections include a rare book collection, slide/tape presentations, and a small number of video and audio cassette tapes. Specifically, the audio cassette/slide programs include the series *Famous Teachings in Modern Medicine* (Medcom) and focuses on a number of medical topics. Individual audio cassettes consist of various series including *Audio-Digest* (pediatrics, surgery, anesthesiology, obstetrics and gynecology, otorhinolaryngology, family practice, internal medicine, opthalmology, and psychiatry) from 1974 to the present. The holdings also include a number of cassette tape presentations in the series *ACCEL* (American College of Cardiology Extended Learning).

4 a. On-site listening equipment is available.

b. No reservations required.

c. No fees are charged for listening to sound recordings.

5. The library has a card catalog that provides author/title and subject access. The library is formulating plans for providing on-line access to library materials. The library publishes a monthly newsletter which notes recent acquisitions. Access to *AVLINE* is available.

Hirshhorn Museum and Sculpture Garden Library (Smithsonian Institution)   See entry C5

A33   Howard University—Allan Mercer Daniel Law Library

1 a. *2900 Van Ness Street, N.W.*
Washington, D.C. 20008
(202) 686–6684

b. 8:00 A.M.–Midnight   Monday–Friday
9:00 A.M.–9:00 P.M.   Saturday
10:00 A.M.–Midnight   Sunday

c. Open to the public for on-site use only. Audiovisual materials do not circulate.

d. Judy Dime-Smith, Law Librarian
Myung Kim, Assistant Librarian in Charge of Audiovisual Materials

2–3. In addition to books and periodicals on law, the library has a variety of non-print materials located in a separate Audio-Visual Room. These materials include audio cassette tapes.
Currently the library owns approximately 200 individual audio cassettes produced by California Continuing Education of the Bar, Institute for Continuing Legal Education, Kenneth B. Sabo Co. of California, Condyne Law Tapes, and the Practicing Law Institute. Subjects are varied including constitutional and criminal law, contracts, civil procedures, corporation law, equity, estate planning, and probate. The library also has the series *Legal Research Slide Tape Programs* (20 volumes) produced by BNA Educational Systems.

4 a. On-site listening equipment is available.

b. No reservations required.

c. No fees charged.

5. The library has a card catalog with author/title and subject access. The Audio-Visual Room holds a typewritten list of audio cassette materials.

A34   Howard University—Center for Ethnic Music Library

1 a. *Fine Arts Building, Room 3004*
Washington, D.C. 20059
(202) 636–7080

b. 9:00 A.M.–5:00 P.M.   Monday–Friday

c. Open to the public.

d. Janet Johnson, Secretary

2. The Center for Ethnic Music is a valuable resource for scholars working on African or Afro-American research. A number of the center's materials are unique.

3. Resources for African studies include an extensive collection of commercial recordings, and numerous field recordings, including the entire catalog of the African Library Association. Music from virtually all parts of the African continent are included. There are also tape recordings of original compositions by Nigerian artists, tribal, folk, and café music of West Africa, and demonstrations of Nupe and Ewe music and of African rhythms and drumming.

Resources for Afro-American music include close to 700 disc recordings of jazz, blues, and college choir music. The center has all of the disc recordings from the Fats Waller estate (close to 1,000 78-rpm discs). Other special holdings include the Earl Fatha Hines collection of recordings, tapes, and books, the Billy Taylor collection (video tapes), the Thomas Dorsey sheet music collection, and the Pearl Bailey collection of arrangements. The center also has a number of oral history tapes of jazz and gospel artists, as well as the complete disc collection of the Howard University Jazz Ensemble, 1976 to the present.

4 a. On-site listening equipment is available.

b. Prior reservation is advisable to ensure the availability of equipment.

c. No fees are charged.

d. Some duplication of sound recordings are provided; however, individuals must supply their own tapes.

5. All of the center's holdings are cataloged in three books; sound recordings have event and subject access. A description of the African holdings is printed in the center's *Final Report,* volume 4: *Activities and Acquisitions* (August 1977).

A35 Howard University—Department of Afro-American Studies Resource Center

1 a. *Founders Library, Room 300*
500 Howard Place, N.W.
Washington, D.C. 20059
(202) 636–7242

Mail:
P.O. Box 746
Howard University
Washington, D.C. 20059

b. 9:00 A.M.–5:00 P.M.   Monday–Friday

c. Open to the public for on-site use. A number of books, films, and audio tapes circulate.

d. E. Ethelbert Miller, Director

2. The purpose of the center is to acquire and disseminate information related to black studies, with emphasis placed on material that is reflective of the progressive movements in the world today. In addition, lectures, poetry readings, and meetings are held on a regular basis within its facilities. Library holdings include books, periodicals, films, slides, video tapes, and disc, reel-to-reel, and cassette recordings.

3. The sound recordings both commercial and private include approximately 250 audio cassettes consisting of lectures, panel discussions, interviews (oral history), poetry readings, performance, and speeches. Topics and significant persons represented in the collection include: Africa (Randall Robinson, Robert Mugabe, Julius Nyerere, Walter Rodney, Leopold Senghor, and Ibrahim Mohammed Babu); black social and political thought in the U.S. (Ralph Abernathy, Amiri Baraka, H. Rap Brown, Eldridge Cleaver, Angela Davis, Louis Farrakhan, Dick Gregory, Alex Haley, George Jackson, Martin Luther King, Elijah Muhammad, Betty Shabazz, William Strickland, Malcolm X, and Marcus Garvey); Caribbean and Latin America (Martha Cobb, Robert Hill, and Walter Rodney); education (Tony Brown, Richard K. Dozier, and Cliff Johnson); history; literature (James Baldwin, Amiri Baraka); music; psychology; religion (Raqib Esa and Oliver Hill); and sociology (Andrew Billingsley, Don Hopkins, and James Shephard).

The library also contains some 350 commercial disc recordings consisting of jazz performances.

4 a. On-site listening equipment is available. Sound recordings may, however, be listened to in one of the other campus libraries.

b. Reservations are required.

c. No fees are charged.

d. Duplication of sound recordings is not permitted. Access to a photocopy machine is provided.

5. The center's card catalog is arranged by author and subject. The tape collection is cataloged in a typewritten *Audio Cassette Tape Listing* with access first by subject and second by speaker/lecturer, artist. The disc collection is accessed under artist's name in a card catalog.

A36 Howard University Libraries

1 a. *Founders–The General Library*
500 Howard Place, N.W.
Washington, D.C. 20059
(202) 636–7253 (Reference)

b. 8:00 A.M.–10:00 P.M.   Monday–Thursday
8:00 A.M.–9:00 P.M.   Friday
9:00 A.M.–6:00 P.M.   Saturday
Noon–9:00 P.M.   Sunday
Hours vary during summer.

c. Open to scholars for on-site use only.

d. Kenneth Wilson, Acting Director of University Libraries

2. The Howard University Library system contains some 1,242,553 books, 21,402 periodical subscriptions, and a variety of non-print materials. Subject strengths include Africa, Afro-American life, literature and history, Afro-American religion, engineering, physical sciences, medicine, theater, business, and economics.

3. Notable holdings of the libraries.

DIVINITY LIBRARY
1240 Randolph Street, N.E.
Washington, D.C. 20017
(202) 636–7282

8:30 A.M.–10:00 P.M.   Monday–Thursday
8:30 A.M.–5:00 P.M.   Friday–Saturday

Irene Owens, Head Librarian

The Divinity Library contains a variety of non-print materials, including over 1,300 microforms, 81 video tapes, 6 films, 133 filmstrips, 168 slides, and 185 audio cassettes. The audio cassette collection consists primarily of theological lectures/sermons ranging from those presented by Martin Luther King, Jr., to Evans Crawford, a Howard University faculty member.

FINE ARTS LIBRARY
Fine Arts Building, Room 1014
Fairmont and 6th Streets, N.W.
Washington, D.C. 20059
(202) 636–7071

8:30 A.M.–8:00 P.M.   Monday–Thursday
8:30 A.M.–5:00 P.M.   Friday
1:00 P.M.–5:00 P.M.   Saturday

Carrie Hackney, Head Librarian

The collection includes 850 titles of commercial disc recordings, most of which focus on historical and classic jazz. Although the collection is basic, there are a number of hard-to-find, or out-of-print items.

HEALTH SCIENCES LIBRARY
600 W Street, N.W.
Washington, D.C. 20059
(202) 636–6433

8:30 A.M.–Midnight   Monday–Thursday
8:30 A.M.–5:00 P.M. Friday–Saturday
1:00 P.M.–Midnight   Sunday

Joseph Forrest, Associate Director
Julia C. Player, Assistant Librarian, Reference/Audio-Visuals

The Health Science Library has a variety of non-print materials including some 1,700 microforms, 300 video tapes, 150 kits, 40 sets of slides, and 250 titles of audio cassettes. Specifically, the audio cassette collection focuses on clinical microbiology, drugs, geriatrics, leadership/training, neurology, and cardiology.

MANUSCRIPT DIVISION
Moorland-Spingarn Research Center
Founders Library
500 Howard Place, N.W.
Washington, D.C. 20059
(202) 636-7479

9:00 A.M.–1:00 P.M., 2:00 P.M.–4:30 P.M.   Monday–Friday
By appointment only. Scholars are permitted only to use transcripts, some of which have restrictions placed on them.

Elinor D. Sinnette, Oral History Librarian

The Manuscript Division has a number of oral history collections. Collections currently being processed include those on black military history, Howard University history, Alpha Kappa Alpha Sorority, and the Shriners. The largest and most complete of these holdings is The Ralph J. Bunche Oral History Collection, formerly known as the Civil Rights Documentation Project. It includes some 671 reel-to-reel tapes and transcripts covering all facets of the Civil Rights Movement of the 1950s and 1960s. Represented are activities in all areas of the United States, such as desegregation in New York City schools, the Freedom Summer in Mississippi, and student participation in the movement. The interviewees of the tapes are both the leaders and those in the grass roots element. Some examples are Ella Baker, Julian Bond, Marion Barry, Burke Marshall, Gloria Richardson Dandridge, and Cardinal Patrick O'Boyle. A card catalog with subject and oral author access has been established for the collection. More work is expected to be done to improve access and verify bibliographic information. An annotated compilation entitled *Bibliography of Holdings of the Civil Rights Documentation Project* is available upon request.

The Manuscript Division also holds a collection of audio tapes, primarily of lectures and speeches given over the years at Howard University. They include: "African Influence on Chilean Music"; Bassa church music and sermons; Gabriel D'Arboussier on African economic development (1967); Shirley Graham Du Bois, "Africa, the Middle East, and the Western World" (1970); Liberian music; Miriam Makeba singing songs in English and in African languages; Josha Nkomo, "The Crisis in Central Africa" (1959); J. Osibodu, "Western African Highlife" in English and in African languages; Sidney V. Peterson, "South Africa: The Birth of the New Language" (1939); Mary H. Umolu, "My Experiences in Nigeria" (1967).

PHARMACY LIBRARY
College of Pharmacy Building
2300 4th Street, N.W.
Washington, D.C. 20059
(202) 636-6545

8:30 A.M.–8:00 P.M.   Monday–Thursday
8:30 A.M.–5:00 P.M.   Friday
1:00 P.M.–5:00 P.M.   Saturday

Jei Kim, Head Librarian

The Pharmacy Library's non-print collection includes some 3,000 slides, and approximately 300 audio cassettes. Most of the audio tapes are commercially produced and focus primarily on pharmaceutical topics, drugs, and drug abuse. The most notable series in the collection is *Voice*, produced by the American Society of Hospital Pharmacists.

4 a. On-site listening equipment is available.

   b. No reservation requirements.

   c. No fees charged.

   d. Duplication of recordings is not allowed in the Divinity and Fine Arts libraries. Inquire at the other libraries regarding their duplication policy. Photocopy facilities are available.

5. There are various cataloging procedures in use in the library system. The Divinity Library interfiles its card catalog on their audio materials and books. The Fine Arts Library has an in-house catalog in both manual and machine-readable formats, with artist/title access. Researchers should also refer to the special publication, *The Glenn Carrington Collection: A Guide to the Books, Manuscripts, Music and Recordings* (1977). The Health Sciences Library has its catalog on microfilm, and consists of three sections: author, title, and subject. They also have a shelf-list card catalog. Access to AVLINE is also provided here. The Pharmacy Library has a separate audio cassette catalog, which provides title and subject access only.

A37 Inter-American Development Bank—Felipe Herrera Library

1 a. *801 17th Street, N.W.*
   Washington, D.C. 20577
   (202) 634–8382 (Information)
   (202) 634–8388 (Library)

   b. 9:00 A.M.–5:30 P.M.   Monday–Friday

   c. Special permission must be obtained to use the library.

   d. Fernando Arbelez, Chief
   Martha Solares, Librarian

2. The Inter-American Development Bank, established in 1959, serves as an important catalyst for the economic and social development of its member countries in Latin America. It achieves this goal by providing capital for financing various economic and social projects, and by promoting and encouraging both public and private investment in the region.

The library has 60,000 volumes, periodicals, newspapers, a number of maps, and non-print materials, including microforms and sound recordings. Topics include business and finance, economics, and development, focusing primarily on Latin America and the Caribbean countries.

3. Audio materials include 50 disc and 25 cassette recordings of popular music representing most of the countries of Latin America.

4 a. On-site listening equipment is not available.

   b. Special permission is required for research.

   c. No fees are charged.

5. A booklet describing the Inter-American Development Bank is available upon request.

A38 John F. Kennedy Center for the Performing Arts Library (Library of Congress)

1 a. *Roof Terrace, North Gallery*
Washington, D.C. 20566
(202) 287-6245

b. 10:00 A.M.–6:00 P.M.   Tuesday, Thursday, Saturday
10:00 A.M.–8:30 P.M.   Wednesday, Friday

c. Open to the public.

d. Peter J. Fay, Head Librarian

2. The Performing Arts Library, established in 1979, is linked together with the Library of Congress in a common enterprise that serves the general public, the researcher, and the performers, designers, and musical artists working in the Kennedy Center. Access to materials is provided in two ways. First, the Performing Arts Library has its own collection of some 3,000 reference books, a substantial number of periodicals on the performing arts, sound recordings, videotapes, posters, programs, playbills, and heralds. Second, the Performing Arts Library has a direct link to the vast resources of the Library of Congress (A41) through a video display terminal, which provides ready access to its vast storehouse of information about recent books and about organizations and legislation concerned with the performing arts, and through an audio link that allows individuals to listen to sound recordings from the Library of Congress's large collections.

3. The library maintains a basic collection of classical, jazz, folk, and popular music on some 2,000 discs and approximately 60 cassettes. The disc collection duplicates that held in the library at the White House (A73). To some extent, recordings are acquired to match works that have been performed at the Kennedy Center.
The library is also the repository for the on-going Kennedy Center Oral History Project, funded by Warner Communications. The project consists of a series of informal interviews on videotape of Kennedy Center honorees. Currently, interviewees include Leonard Bernstein, Aaron Copland, Lillian Gish, Benny Goodman, Helen Hayes, Eugene Ormandy, and Leontyne Price. A few transcripts are available. However, tapes may not be duplicated. A correspondence file for background information on the project is located in the Motion Picture, Broadcasting and Recorded Sound Division (A41). For additional information on the project, contact Geraldine M. Otremba, Deputy Director of Operations at the Kennedy Center (202/254–3164).

4 a. On-site listening facility is available.

b. To listen to recordings held in the Library of Congress requires a 48-hour advance reservation.

c. No fees charged.

d. The library does not duplicate recordings.

5. The library has a card catalog with author/title and subject access. Most of the discs held in the library are listed in *The White House Record Library*, 2 vols. (Washington, D.C.: The White House Historical Association, 1973, 1980). A special publication that describes the library is *The Performing Arts Library of Congress and the Kennedy Center* (1979).

A39 C.J. Jung Library and Information Center

1 a. *2948 Brandywine Street, N.W.*
Washington, D.C. 20008
(202) 363–9220

b. 9:00 A.M.–4:00 P.M.   Monday, Friday
9:00 A.M.–1:00 P.M.   Wednesday

c. Library is open only to members of the C.J. Jung Association. For a small fee, however, individuals may apply for membership.

d. Virginia McCormick, Office Manager

2–3. The library has a number of private audio recordings including 50 cassette tapes consisting mainly of seminars and lectures related to Jung, dreams, and relaxation techniques. Examples of titles in the collection include *The Role of Mind in Cancer Therapy* (O. Carl and Stephanie Simonton, 1974; cassette no. T54) and *Relaxation Training Program* (Thomas Budzynski, 1974; cassette no. T1).

4 a. On-site listening equipment is not available.

b. Prior appointment is recommended.

c. There is a fee for application for membership available from the information center.

d. Requests for duplication of tapes are treated on an individual basis only.

5. The library has a handwritten list of audio materials.

A40 Labor Department Library

1 a. *Francis Perkins Building*
200 Constitution Avenue N.W.
Washington, D.C. 20210
(202) 523–6992 (Reference)

b. 8:15 A.M.–4:45 P.M.   Monday–Friday

c. Open to the public for reference use only. The audio collection is for use primarily by the staff of the Department of Labor.

d. Sabina Jacobson, Library Director

2. The library has an extensive collection of materials in the fields of labor and economics. Holdings include some 535,000 books, 3,200 periodicals, a number of foreign official documents, including foreign labor-union materials, and publications of the International Labor Organization.

3. The audio cassette collection includes 20 tapes focusing on the subject of management. The tapes are produced by the American Management Association. Recordings of the Department of Labor for 1941 and 1955–1969 are held as RG 174 in the National Archives and Records Service (B27).

4 a. On-site listening equipment is not available.

b. Prior appointment is recommended.

c. No fees charged.

d. A photoduplication facility is available.

5. The library has two dictionary card catalogs for pre- and post-1975 acquisitions. There is also the *United States Department of Labor Library Catalog,* published by G.K. Hall (1975), and a list of *Periodicals Currently Received by the U.S. Department of Labor Library* (1980).

A41 Library of Congress

1 a. *Thomas Jefferson Building*
1st Street, S.E.
(between Independence Avenue and East Capitol Street)

John Adams Building
2nd Street, S.E.
(between Independence Avenue and East Capitol Street)

James Madison Building
Independence Avenue, S.E.
(between 1st and 2nd Streets)

Mail:
10 First Street, S.E.
Washington, D.C. 20540
(202) 287–5000 (main number)

b. General Reading Rooms: Main Reading Room, Thomas Jefferson Building, second floor; and the Thomas Jefferson Reading Room, John Adams Building, fifth floor:
8:30 A.M.–9:30 P.M. (stack service to 9:00 P.M.)   Monday–Friday
8:30 A.M.–5:00 P.M. (stack service to 4:00 P.M.)   Saturday
1:00 P.M.–5:00 P.M. (stack service to 4:30 P.M.)   Sunday
Closed on all holidays except Washington's Birthday, Columbus Day, and Veterans Day. Division hours are noted below.

c. Open to researchers over high school age for on-site use. Interlibrary loan service (exclusive of periodicals, newspapers, and non-print materials) is available to other libraries.

d. Daniel J. Boorstin, The Librarian of Congress

2. The Library of Congress, founded in 1800, is the nation's library. It currently holds over 80 million items and is growing by 7,000 every working day. Researchers, especially those from outside of the Washington area, who are planning to visit the Library should plan on allowing extra time to become acquainted, not only with its services, but also with the buildings themselves. For example, the architecture and decoration of the Jefferson Building is a wonder in itself, and visitors can expect to find some 112 major paintings, 20 pieces of sculpture, as well as an array of additional

artistic decorations. In addition, at any one time, there are one or more major exhibits of either books or artifacts being presented. Exhibition halls located in the Jefferson and Madison buildings are open to the public from 8:30 A.M. to 9:30 P.M., Monday–Friday and 8:30 A.M. to 6:00 P.M., Saturday, Sunday, and holidays.

Because of the size and diversity of its collections, users may have some initial difficulty locating various collections. An orientation theater is located in the Visitor Services Center at the west entrance of the ground floor lobby of the Jefferson Building. There, an 18-minute slide-sound presentation, *America's Library*, is shown hourly from 8:45 A.M. to 8:45 P.M., weekdays, and 8:45 A.M. to 5:45 P.M., weekends and holidays. In addition, free guided tours leave periodically from the Visitor Services Center from 9:00 A.M. to 4:00 P.M. weekdays. Researchers should obtain a copy of *Guide to the Library of Congress* (1982), available in the sales shop in the Visitor Services Center. The guide describes in detail all of the Library's divisions and services. It also includes a handy street map of the immediate area, as well as library hours and pertinent telephone numbers.

In order to develop successful search strategies, researchers should be aware of the following important points. First, not every item held in the custody of the Library is cataloged. In fact, certain sizeable portions of the holdings remain uncataloged. Second, there is no comprehensive catalog or finding aid incorporating all of the collections. In conducting research, scholars may have to shuttle back and forth between the Main Reading Room catalog and varous other catalogs held in separate divisions. Third, collections received by the Library of Congress are often dispersed. For example, manuscripts and papers of a given donated collection may be sent to the Manuscript Division (B20) whereas recordings in the same collection are sent to the Motion Picture, Broadcasting and Recorded Sound Division (A41). Therefore, scholars can expect to visit two or more divisions when conducting certain research projects. Fourth, researchers can expect a delay of two or more hours for retrieving materials, particularly printed items, after requests have been submitted, and frequently they will receive a "not-on-shelf" response.

The Library of Congress facilitates research projects in a number of ways. First, professional reference staff are readily available in all areas of the Library. Second, private study desks and listening rooms, reserve-book shelves, advance print and nonprint reserve service, and limited stack passes are available to serious researchers. The Study Facilities Office (202/287–5211) of the General Reading Rooms Division (202/287–5530) receives applications and requests for private study desks and reserved book shelves. All stack services for the general collections are handled by the Collection Management Division (202/287–7400). Researchers can also confer with the divisional reference librarians for additional special requests.

AFRICAN AND MIDDLE EASTERN DIVISION
Hebraic Section
John Adams Building, Room LA 1006
(202) 287–5422

8:30 A.M.–5:00 P.M.   Monday–Friday

Myron M. Weinstein, Head

The Hebraic Section has a number of oral history transcripts of tapes produced by the Institute of Contemporary Jewry of Hebrew University. These transcripts are on microfilm in the series, *The New York Times Oral History Program*. Specifically the transcripts are divided into the following parts: I: Jewish Communities (4 reels); II: World War II: The Holocaust, Resistance and Rescue (9 reels); IIa: The Yom Kippur

War (1 reel); and III: Zionism and Israel (9 reels). Researchers should refer to the printed guide, *Oral History Guide No. 1: A Bibliographic Listing of the Memoirs in the Micropublished Collections* (1976) and *Oral History Guide No. 2* (1979), published by the Microfilming Corporation of America.

ASIAN DIVISION
Japanese Section
John Adams Building, Room LA 1014
(202) 287-5431

8:30 A.M.–5:00 P.M.   Monday–Friday
8:30 A.M.–12:30 P.M.   Saturday

Hisao Matsumoto, Head

The Japanese Section has a series of oral history interviews under the collective title *American Studies in Japan, Oral History Series*. The series is produced by the American Research Material Center of the University of Tokyo and currently consists of 14 interviews in transcript format with professors and journalists. All interviews are in Japanese. LC lacks several numbers in the series of 14 interviews, specifically nos. 7, 8, 11, and 12.

The Motion Picture, Broadcasting and Recorded Sound Division (A41) has recordings on tape of prominent Japanese authors and poets who appeared in various LC-sponsored programs beginning with Tanigawa, Shuntaro on April 15, 1970 in the International Poetry Festival, individual poetry readings recorded for the Archive of World Literature on Tape, and Japanese Traditional Songs (April 13, 1983). Total of seven recordings.

Southern Asia Section
John Adams Building, Room LA 1018
(202) 287–5600

8:30 A.M.–5:00 P.M.   Monday–Friday
8:30 A.M.–12:30 P.M.   Saturday

Louis A. Jacob, Head

The Southern Asia Section has been involved in the Library of Congress' World Literature on Tape program. Currently 12 Pakistani poets have been recorded reading selections from their own works. The recordings were produced in Pakistan. A list and biographical file and copies of the recordings are held in the Southern Asia Section. Researchers who desire to listen to the tapes should refer to the Motion Picture, Broadcasting and Recorded Sound Division (A41). Individuals who need background and other information should consult the Head of the Southern Asia Section.

COPYRIGHT OFFICE
Cataloging Division
James Madison Building, Room 513
(202) 287–8040

8:30 A.M.–5:00 P.M.   Monday–Friday

Susan Aramayo, Chief
John Raoul Lemat, Assistant Chief

Information & Reference Division
(202) 287–6800
(202) 287–9100 (24-hour service for application for a claim to copyright)

8:30 A.M.–5:00 P.M.   Monday–Friday

Joan Doherty, Assistant Chief

Records Management Division
(202) 287–8445

8:30 A.M.–5:00 P.M.   Monday–Friday

Ann Hallstein, Chief

Approximately half a million works are registered annually by the Copyright Office. However, only a portion of these materials are selected for inclusion in the Library's general holdings. The remaining materials including sound recordings are held under the custody of the Copyright Office. Scholars should be aware, therefore, that the Copyright Office is an important resource for information and materials not available elsewhere in the Library.

The Cataloging Division produces a record for each copyrightable work received. These records are published in the series, *Catalog of Copyright Entries,* which is divided into eight parts, including Nondramatic Literary Works, Serials and Periodicals, Performing Arts, Motion Pictures and Filmstrips, Visual Arts, Maps, Sound Recordings, and Renewals.

The catalog of sound recordings is an excellent and unique source of information on sound recordings, and includes recordings that are selected by the Motion Picture, Broadcasting and Recorded Sound Division for inclusion in its holdings, as well as recordings retained under custody of the Copyright Office. Therefore, researchers will find recordings cited in this catalog that are not included in the general card catalogs or the catalog, *Music: Books on Music and Sound Recordings.* In addition, the identification and access to a particular recording and its contents are provided more explicitly in this catalog than in other Library of Congress catalogs. For example, a researcher can access a sound recording through any one of all titles cited on a particular recording, as well as by name of record manufacturer and number.

Information on and access to sound recordings held under the custody of the Copyright Office is provided by the Information & Reference Division. There is no charge for a search conducted on-site by a researcher for a recording held by the office. However, for a fee, the Copyright Office will conduct a search of their holdings. Sound recordings may not be duplicated.

To register a claim to copyright, individuals should contact the Copyright Office at (202) 287–9100, or for additional information, (202) 287–8700. All forms are supplied free of charge. There is a fee charged for certification of registration. Individuals should refer to a handy booklet, *Copyright Basics,* for additional information.

HISPANIC READING ROOM
Thomas Jefferson Building, Room LJ 239
(202) 287–5397

8:30 A.M.–5:00 P.M.   Monday–Friday

John Hebert, Assistant Chief
Georgette Dorn, Head of Reference

The Hispanic Reading Room has custody of the Archive of Hispanic Literature on Tape. The archive was established in 1942 as a means of providing for posterity original voice recordings on magnetic tape of contemporary Iberian and Latin American poets and writers. To date, close to 500 authors, representing the following countries, have been recorded reading selections from their own works: Argentina (47); Barbados (1); Belize (1); Bolivia (7); Brazil (64); Chile (34); Colombia (27); Costa Rica (4); Cuba (24); Dominican Republic (5); Ecuador (15); El Salvador (1); French Guiana (1); Guatemala (15); Haiti (13); Honduras (2); Jamaica (1); Mexico (58); Nicaragua (4); Panama (14); Paraguay (6); Peru (29); Portugal (10); Puerto Rico (19); Spain (35); Surinam (1); Uruguay (21); Venezuela (33); and United States (Chicano authors; 1). At least five of these authors are Nobel prize winners: Vicente Aleixandre (Spain), Miguel Angel Asturias (Guatemala), Juan Ramón Jiménez (Spain), Gabriela Mistral (Chile), and Pablo Neruda (Chile).

Access to the archive is provided through a published catalog, The Archive of Hispanic Literature on Tape: A Descriptive Guide (1974) and a typewritten list, Archive of Hispanic Literature on Tape: 1983, updating the former, and available for reference on-site. The archive is also described in Special Collections in the Library of Congress (1980).

Four of the recordings are available in the form of long-playing discs. They can be purchased through the Motion Picture, Broadcasting and Recorded Sound Division (A41). In addition, the Recorded Sound Section will also reproduce for nonprofit institutions and for noncommercial purposes copies of the tapes in the archive. In order to request reproduction of any of the readings in the archive, contact Georgette Dorn in the Hispanic Reading Room. She will provide an exact cost estimate, which varies according to the length of the reading and the cost of postage. She will then transfer the request to the Recorded Sound Section. Up to ten copies of each tape may be reproduced without the written permission of the author. After ten copies have been made, the author's or his executor's written permission must be obtained. Researchers may listen to recordings on-site.

The Hispanic Reading Room has pamphlets that describe the various manuscript and book collections available to researchers.

MAIN READING ROOM
Thomas Jefferson Building, First Floor
(202) 287–5520

8:30 A.M.–9:30 P.M.   Monday–Friday

Gary Jensen, Head

The collection of reference books available to researchers in the Main Reading Room totals over 17,000 titles, most of which are in the humanities, social sciences, and bibliography. The Library of Congress Main Reading Room Reference Collection Subject Catalog (2nd edition; 1980) will help researchers locate desired books in the various alcoves in the Reading Room.

Scholars may wish to begin their search for various types of audiovisual reference materials and sound recordings in the card or computer catalogs in the Reading Room. For example, in searching for oral history materials focusing on bibliography, congresses, phonotape catalogs, etc., researchers would look in the catalogs under the subject heading "Oral History." Individual entries indicate in which area given items are located. These catalogs, therefore, draw together items focusing on similar topics but located in different areas of the Library of Congress. Because of the size of the Library's collections, however, not all materials are listed in the card catalogs. Researchers may need to use specialized indexes and finding aids.

The traditional access tool for the LC collection is its 20-million card catalog. However, this catalog was frozen December 31, 1980. Cataloging by computer was begun for English language titles in 1968. As of January 4, 1981, the automated record became LC's official record of holdings from that date forward.

The Library of Congress Information System (LOCIS) is accessible through SCORPIO (Subject-Content-Oriented-Retriever-for-Processing Information-On-Line) and MUMS (Multiple-Use-MARC-System) commands. Both access the MARC (Machine-Readable-Cataloging) database, a comprehensive catalog record, which is available on tape for purchase from LC's Cataloging Distribution Service and which serves now as the basis for the *National Union Catalog*.

SCORPIO can be used to access post-1968 LC holdings of printed materials about all aspects of sound recordings by subject (LC subject headings). MUMS provides author, title, and component-word access to LC records of holdings cataloged since 1963 or in process, and LC's name authority files.

LC's computer catalog center (202/287-6213), located off the Main Reading Room, contains public computer terminals. The staff will instruct researchers in the use of terminals, which then may be used free of charge. For a fee, the staff will perform bibliographic searches. Data output is available in a variety of forms.

MICROFORM READING ROOM
Thomas Jefferson Building, Room 140-B
(202) 287-5471

8:30 A.M.–9:30 P.M.	Monday–Friday
8:30 A.M.–5:00 P.M.	Saturday
1:00 P.M.–5:00 P.M.	Sunday

Alan Solomon, Head

The Microform Reading Room holds over 1½ million items. The collection includes a number of series of oral history interviews in both microfilm and microfiche formats. A number of these collections can be accessed through the reading room card catalog under the heading "Oral History." Materials acquired after mid-1982 have been entered in the on-line automated catalog.

The following list of relevant collections has been abstracted from a typewritten guide to special collections in the Microform Reading Room. The typewritten guide was prepared in February 1981 by Lois Korzendorfer.

Alice Lloyd College, Appalachian State University, Emory and Henry College and Lees Junior College: Appalachian Oral History Collection (Microfilm no. 49530), 20th century.—Over 300 memoirists recall life in the Appalachians, including a college dean, miners, farmers and housewives. Printed guide, *Oral History Guide No. 2*.

American Film Institute: Louis B. Mayer Oral History Collection (Microfilm no. 49528; Microfiche no. 5185), 20th century, Part 1.—People associated with all aspects of the motion picture industry— from technical persons to directors—recall their early days; over 150 memoirists; each interview is indexed. Printed guide, *Oral History Guide No. 2*.

British Broadcasting Service, Monitoring Service: Summary of World Broadcasts (Microfilm and Microfiche no. 5174), 1939–1972 microfilm and 1973+ microfiche.— Summaries of radio news transmissions that have been monitored by the BBC; divided into broad geographical areas.

California State University, Fullerton: Community History Project, Anaheim (Microfilm no. 49515), 20th century.—Fifteen residents of Anaheim, California recall their earlier days. Index on film and printed guide, *Oral History Guide No. 2*.

California State University, Fullerton: Community History Project, Fullerton (Mi-

crofilm no. 49516), 20th century.—Twelve people recall life in Fullerton, California, in the early part of this century. Index on film and printed guide, *Oral History Guide No. 2.*

California State University, Fullerton: Japanese-American Oral History Collection (Microfilm no. 49517), 20th century.—Interviews with 70 people involved with Japanese relocation camps during World War II, both as evacuees and workers at the camps. Index on film and printed guide, *Oral History Guide No. 2.*

California State University, Fullerton: Richard M. Nixon Oral History Collection (Microfilm no. 49527), 20th century.—In nine sections (e.g., Nixon Family History, R.M. Nixon in High School, Whittier College Years), interviewees provide background information and personal reminiscences of their contacts with Mr. Nixon. Printed guide, *Oral History Guide No. 2.*

California State University, Fullerton: San Juan Capistrano Community History Project (Microfilm no 49519), 20th century.—Twelve memoirists speak about the early history of this community. Printed guide, *Oral History Guide No. 2.*

California State University, Fullerton: Southeastern Utah Oral History Collection (Microfilm no. 49518), 20th century.—Residents of this area speak about their life and work; of the 34 interviewees, many are Indians. Index on film and printed guide, *Oral History Guide No. 2.*

CBS News Television Broadcasts (Microfiche no. 5193-5204), 1975+.—Includes transcripts of the CBS daily news broadcasts, plus public affairs broadcasts, such as "60 Minutes" and "CBS Reports." Printed index, *CBS News Index.*

China Missionaries Oral History Collection of the Claremont Graduate School, Claremont, California (Microfilm no. 49512), 20th century.—In addition to 44 memoirs, this collection contains biographical sketches of the missionaries; also includes an overview of the collection. Index on film and printed guide, *Oral History Guide No. 1.*

East Asian Institute of Columbia University: Chinese Oral History Project (Microfilm no. 49508; Microfiche no. 5123), 1911–1949, Part 1.—Recollections of prominent Chinese leaders of that time; seven memoirists. Printed guide, *Oral History Guide No. 1.*

Marshall University, Huntington, West Virginia : Oral History of Appalachia (Microfilm no. 49520), 20th century.—Interviews with approximately 125 working class people who lived most of their lives in the Appalachian Region; interviewees were at least 65 years of age in 1972. Printed guide, *Oral History Guide No. 2.*

New Orleans Jazz Oral History Collection of Tulane University (Microfilm no. 49702), 20th century.—Forty-five musicians and other people recall life in New Orleans during the early 20th century. Printed guide, *Oral History Guide No. 2.*

University of Hawaii: Pacific Regional Oral History (Microfilm no. 49509; Microfiche no. 5121), 20th century.—38 memoirists document the growth of the United Public Workers Union in Hawaii. Printed guide, *Oral History Guide No. 1.*

Tennessee Regional Oral History Collection of the Memphis Public Library (Microfilm no. 49514), 20th century, Part 1.—Nine interviewees talk about life in and around Memphis. Printed guide, *Oral History Guide No. 2.*

University of California, Berkeley: Agriculture, Water Resources and Land Use, Oral History Collection (Microfilm no. 49526), 20th century.—Twenty-four people chronicle the development of water-use institutions, agricultural development, and land use planning in the state of California. Index on film and printed guide, *Oral History Guide No. 2.*

University of California, Berkeley: Books and Printing in the San Francisco Bay Area, Oral History Collection (Microfilm no. 49529), 20th century.—Twenty-one participants and observers of the printing movement of the Bay area are interviewed. Index on film and printed guide, *Oral History Guide No. 2.*

University of California, Berkeley: Forestry, Parks and Conservation Oral History Collection (Microfilm no. 49703), 20th century.—Forty-five oral histories provide background information about the development of the conservation movement in this country. Printed guide, *Oral History Guide No. 2.*

University of California, Berkeley: Russian Emigres Oral History Collection (Microfilm no. 49701), 20th century.—Recollections of 10 Russian refugees from the San Francisco Bay area provide insights into life in Russia before, during, and immediately after the Revolution of 1917. Printed guide, *Oral History Guide No. 2.*

University of California, Santa Cruz: Regional Oral HistoryProject, Economic, Social and Cultural, Central California Coastal Area (Microfilm no. 49521), 20th century.—Approximately 12 individuals recall life in central California in the early part of this century. Index on film and printed guide, *Oral History Guide No. 2.*

Wallace, Henry Agard, Diary and Reminiscences (Microfilm no. 49522-49523), 20th century.—The diary (Microfilm no. 49522) consists of 42 volumes from 1935-1946. The reminiscences (Microfilm no. 49523) consist of transcriptions of recorded interviews, sections of his diary, selections from his correspondence and papers, and selections from transcriptions of telephone conversations. Printed guide to reminiscences, *Oral History Guide No. 2.*

Woods Highway Truck Library Oral History Collection (Microfilm no. 49511), 20th century.—Twenty memoirists provide insights into the birth and early development of the American trucking industry. Printed guide, *Oral History Guide No. 1.*

Additional oral history collectionsin the Microform Reading Room include the Sangamon State University, Springfield, Illinois, Oral History; Slave Narratives; and Southeastern Utah Regional Oral History Collection.

Copies of transcripts of additional oral history collections in printed format are held in the custody of various other divisions of the Library of Congress. The Reading Room is equipped with several microfilm and microfiche readers and printers.

MOTION PICTURE, BROADCASTING AND RECORDED SOUND DIVISION
Performing Arts Reading Room (LM 113)
James Madison Building
(202) 287-7833

8:30 A.M.–5:00 P.M.   Monday–Friday
8:30 A.M.–5:00 P.M.   Saturday, by appointment only.

Samuel Brylawski, Reference Librarian, Recorded Sound Reference Center
Edwin Matthias, Reference Librarian, Recorded Sound Reference Center

The Motion Picture, Broadcasting and Recorded Sound Division holds close to 1½ million recordings. Approximately 900,000 recordings are commercial (lp and pre-lp), and the rest consist of noncommercial recordings in a variety of formats, including cylinders, wire recordings, aluminum, zinc, acetate-covered glass and aluminum, rubber compound, and translucent plastic discs, and tape in virtually all reel and cassette formats. There are over 300,000 pre-1970 instantaneous lacquer recordings, as well as 200,000 78-rpm discs. Recordings available to researchers include vinyl discs and rare recordings that have been transferred to preservation magnetic tape. The library has received a number of compact disc recordings, which are not yet cataloged. A large majority of the commercial recordings have never been cataloged; there are no shelflists or subject and geographic indexes. Commercial recordings are shelved alphabetically by manufacturer and numerically by manufacturer's number.

To identify a given collection or locate and retrieve an individual recording, researchers should be aware of a number of search strategies. First, although the division

maintains extensive and separate card catalogs for both commercial and noncommercial recordings, most recordings have never been cataloged. Therefore, when cards are not in the catalog for a certain item, it is necessary that the researcher obtain a manufacturer's name and number for commercial items so that a search of the stacks can be undertaken. The Reference Center maintains an excellent collection of published guides and discographies for this purpose. A number of collections held in the library are cited and described in various published reference tools (see category 5, p.58, for LC publications). The most important publication of this sort is *Special Collections in the Library of Congress: A Selective Guide* (1980). Of the 269 LC special collections in this compilation, 39 contain sound recordings and are described in considerable detail below. Another important reference tool is *The Rigler and Deutsch Record Index—A National Union Catalog of Sound Recordings.* (For a full description of this book, see Association for Recorded Sound Collections, Inc. (M29).) The Reference Center collection of published discographies and rare and out-of-print serials, including information on individual recordings, subjects and formats, is extensive. Researchers outside the Washington, D.C., area are well advised to thoroughly examine readily accessible Library of Congress-related tools before coming to the library. A great deal of time and expense can be saved by doing so.

When a given collection and its contents are cited in the card catalog, researchers should be aware that, in some cases, not every item within a collection has been cataloged. Therefore, the finding aid or correspondence folder for that particular collection should be consulted. These aids may include correspondence between the donor and the Library of Congress, lists compiled by the Library or the donor, and significant background information on the collection. In addition, various subject folders are available to researchers. For example, the folder on "Oral History" contains clippings, letters of inquiry, and news items regarding various Library of Congress-related collections. The researcher should also be aware that several collections have been broken up and shelved among the general holdings by label, name, and number. A reference librarian is available to assist the researcher.

Individuals should also be aware of the procedures involved for listening to a recording. First, a researcher completes a listening request form in the Recorded Sound Reference Center. In most cases, it will be possible to listen to disc recordings the same day the request form is completed. A request must be submitted by 3:00 P.M. in order to obtain recordings the following day. Researchers outside the Washington area can send requests by phone or letter, so that recordings can be placed on reserve for the day of visit. Individuals must supply the pertinent information appropos the requested material, such as the call number, and the record manufacturer's name and number. If materials are not located, the staff will need additional time to make in-depth special searches. Next, a listening position will be assigned by the Music Division staff on the day of arrival. Listening hours are 9:00 A.M. to 5:00 P.M., Monday through Saturday. A brochure describing the procedures in detail is available from the Recorded Sound Reference Center.

Following is a complete list of collections held in the Motion Picture, Broadcasting and Recorded Sound Division and described in *Special Collections in the Library of Congress: A Selective Guide* (1980).

Amateur Hour Collection: 3,100 broadcast disc recordings, 500 audio tapes, 550 films, and 7,000 pieces of documentation. American Forces Radio and Television Service Collection, 1940s to present: 150,000 broadcast recordings. George Antheil Collection: 6 recordings of film scores by Antheil. *Arthur Godfrey Time* Collection, 1949–1957: 3,000 instantaneous disc recordings. Ernest Bloch Collection: voice recordings of Ernest Bloch. Damrosch Family Collection, 1937–1941: 254 discs of *The Music Appreciation Hour.* Jessica Dragonette Collection, 1930s: 369 disc recordings

and complete transcriptions of 37 radio broadcast programs. Geraldine Farrar Collection, 1904–1906: 50 disc recordings of radio broadcasts and other performances of G. Farrar. Irving Fine Collection: 40 audio tapes of the composer, I. Fine. John Ross Frampton Collection (dispersed), 1912–1930s: 747 discs of piano performances. General Foods Corporation Collection, 1930s and 1940s: 200 radio broadcast transcription discs. German Speech and Monitored Broadcast Collection, 1930s and 1940s: 2,500 German speeches and radio broadcast recordings. George and Ira Gershwin Collection, 1926 and 1928 (noncommercial): 250 disc recordings of both commercial and noncommercial productions. H. Vose Greenough Collection, 1930s–1940s: 1,021 acetate discs and 793 audio tapes of music performances in the Boston area. Oscar Hammerstein II Collection: dictaphone belts of recorded pre-versions of musical shows. Wally Heider Collection, 1930s–1950: 1,900 discs and 1,350 audio tapes of popular music recordings. Jack Kapp Collection, 1930s–1940s: cartoon drawings related to the recording industry. A.F.R. Lawrence Collection, 1930s: 2,320 test pressings and 745 instantaneous discs of speeches, popular music, and radio broadcasts. C.P. MacGregor Company Collection, 1930s–1977: 4,200 disc and 1,500 audio tape broadcast recordings and scripts of radio programs. NBC Radio Collection, 1933–1970: 175,000 NBC radio broadcast recordings. National Press Club Collection, 1952 to present: 830 recordings of speeches presented at the National Press Club (B32). National Public Radio Collection (B33): consists of radio broadcast recordings of cultural programs. Office of War Information Collection, 1940s: 50,000 acetate disc recordings consisting of domestic and foreign radio broadcasts of news, reports, and entertainment. J. Robert Oppenheimer Collection: 70 recordings of lectures and interviews of Oppenheimer in tape, wire, and disc formats. Wilfrid Pelletier Collection, 1938–1949: 575 discs of broadcast music programs. Rachmaninoff Archives: 700 commercial disc recordings and a few private discs. Sigmund Romberg Collection, 1934–1935: 543 commercial and noncommercial discs, some of which are transcriptions of radio shows. Arnold Schoenberg Collection: wire and disc recordings. John Secrist Collection: 1,700 discs. Benedict Stambler Archive of Recorded Jewish Music: 1,400 commercial recordings of Jewish music. Raymond Swing Collection, 1940s–1953: several hundred broadcasts of Swing. John Toland Collection, 1970s: 150 audio cassette tapes of interviews related to Nazi Germany. United Nations Recordings Collection. Voice of America Collection, 1945–1960s: 65,000 broadcast recordings of VOA music programs.

Following are collections not described in *Special Collections in the Library of Congress: A Selective Guide* (1980) but which are also located in the division.

John R. Adams Collection, 1890s–1945.—5,436 78-rpm discs; consists of a wide array of subject matter, including 57 Berliner Gramophone Company 7-inch discs issued in the mid-to-late 1890s; several rare ethnic recordings, mostly in Spanish and Polish, and one disc by George W. Johnson, one of the first Blacks to produce a commercial recording; 49 Societe Italiana di Fonotipia discs (1904–1915), 830 Columbia discs, 3,072 Victor Records, 8 Zenophone discs (1899–1901), and 7 Department of State Victory-discs.

American Legion Collection, late 1940s.—82 discs; includes radio programs of the series *This is Our Day, Decision Now!,* and *This is Our Duty.* Subjects covered include armed services recruiting, health, politics, and social problems, as well as the acceptance speech of Paul H. Griffith, National Commander in 1946.

American Medical Association Collection, 1958.—11 discs; radio spots and the radio program series, *Health Magazine of the Air,* including such notables as Henry Fonda, Douglas Fairbanks, Jr., Ralph Bellamy, Tyrone Power, Patti Page, and Mel Allen.

American Psychological Association Oral History of Psychology Collection, 1971–

1980.—64 audio tape interviews; all of the interviewees are prominent in the field and include Rudolph Arnheim, Fred Thorne, J.B. Rhine, B.F. Skinner, Heinz Ansbacher, Harry Harlow, and Harold Burtt.

American Red Cross Collection, 1947–1953.—61 discs; this set of recordings consists of radio programs and spot announcements. One program features Bob Hope and Bing Crosby. Radio series include *In Your Name, Errand of Mercy, 1949 Fund Campaign,* with Ingrid Bergman, Fred MacMurray, and Joan Leslie, and *1951 Fund Campaign.*

Audio-Scriptions, Inc. Collection, 1936–1945. Several hundred aluminum disc recordings, including the series *Library of Voices,* speeches by some 45 members of Congress, and others; radio programs, performances, addresses. A wide array of politicians, entertainers, musicians, and poets, as well as individuals such as Mary Pickford, Harry Truman, Harold Ickes, Ethel Barrymore, Eddie Cantor, Loretta Young, Tyrone Power, and Orson Welles.

Joel Berger Collection, 1901–1915.—209 disc recordings; mostly of Russian origin and feature over 40 singers of the Imperial Russian Opera. Most of the recordings were issued by the Berliner Gramophone Company and its descendent, The Gramophone Company. Included also are Russian Zonophone and Russian Pathé recordings.

Berliner Collection, 1892–1900.—Published and unpublished recordings issued by the Berliner Gramophone Company, which invented and introduced the disc recording. A number of these recordings were acquired as part of various gift collections. Among these discs are musical performances by the Sousa Band as well as various individual musicians, native American music, and several voice recordings of Emile Berliner and family members. Access to the recordings is provided, in part, through the catalog, *Berliner Records in the Library of Congress.* The collection also includes a number of significant papers, including laboratory notebooks, documents regarding litigation, photographs, correspondence, scrapbooks, and published copies of Berliner's patents. (For additional information on these Berliner items, see the John R. Adams Collection and the Isabelle Sayers Collection.)The Berliner collection also includes laboratory equipment used by Berliner in his experiments with the development of the phonograph. These include 1 graphophone type AT, without reproducer and with nonworking mechanism; 1 copper master of a recording marked E. Berliner in Washington, D.C., September 1887; 1 turntable mechanism (solid), 8 inch with spindle; 1 experimenter's box containing crane supports, arm support, experimental diaphragm, and in bamboo style; 1 experimenter's box containing 3 diaphragms, 6 diaphragm supports, 8 metal diaphragms, 9 mica and mica-laminated diaphragms, and 1 small box of nuts and bolts; 3 small packages of compounds. In addition, there is 1 Edison home phonograph, without reproducer and with nonworking mechanism, 1901, and 50 zinc recording blank plates, 1890, in the collection.

CBS Radio Collection, May 13–26, 1957 (397 tapes) and 1960–1967 (several hundred items).—Includes recordings of programs, news conferences, speeches, state-of-the union addresses, musical programs, comedy and quiz programs, soap operas, golf tournaments, special broadcasts, news coverage of the Kennedy assassination, space program coverage, the Kentucky Derby and other horse races, Republican National Convention coverage, coronation ceremonies for Pope Paul VI, U.N. Security Council coverage, and coverage of civil rights debates and marches. Individuals represented include, in part, Presidents Eisenhower, Kennedy, and Johnson, and various senior advisors and officials. Programs are indexed by title in the Special Collections catalog as well as in a chronologically arranged shelf list.

Central Intelligence Agency Collection, 1959–1962.—230 audio tapes; consists of shortwave monitorings of Fidel Castro speeches.

Douglas, Justice William O., Collection, early 1950s.—46 audio tapes; folk and

traditional music recorded on-site during several Asiatic trips; includes music recorded in the Himalayas, Afghanistan, and India of dances, songs, and chants. The collection also includes 28 reels of movies.

Film Promotion Records, 1928-1930s.—Over 80 discs; soundtrack excerpts, which were played during designated weeks by radio stations for promotion of forthcoming movies. These discs produced by Paramount and MGM studios were distributed to various radio stations throughout the country. Each disc cites the week that the recording was to be aired. A considerable number of singers and major entertainers are represented in the collection, including Joe Penner, Judy Garland, Bing Crosby, Jeanette MacDonald, Dorothy Lamour, Greta Garbo, and Nelson Eddy.

Gridiron Club Collection, 1947, 1956-1978.—119 reel-to-reel tapes and 15 non-commercial discs. The recordings document the annual Gridiron Club spring dinner and other functions of the club. Included are satiric skits, songs, dances, and speeches, which are performed by members of the journalists' club in honor or at the expense of the then-current Presidential administration. The collection is restricted from public access until 2006, unless the written permission of the president or historian of the Gridiron Club is obtained.

Hartt College Organ Festival Collection, 1972 to the present.—Audio tape of Annual International Contemporary Organ Music Festival; includes many premiers played under composers' supervision. Representative organists include Leonard Raver, David Craighead, Catharine Crozier, and Clyde Holloway. Program notes are located in the division's correspondence file.

Hempel, Frieda, Collection, 1930s.—20 sound recordings; consists of radio broadcasts and live performances by German soprano Frieda Hempel (1885-1955). Some of the recordings were produced by Carnegie Hall Company.

Historic Addresses Collection, 1935-1941.—1,500 aluminum discs, produced by Historic Records Co; consists of speeches, broadcast discussions, musical selections, World's Fair addresses, the Democratic Convention for 1936 and the National Education Association Convention for 1938. Individuals represented in the collection include Albert Einstein, President and Eleanor Roosevelt, King George VI, Pope Pius XI, Neville Chamberlain, Queen Wilhelmina, Henry A. Wallace, Cordell Hull, Winston Churchill, and Lord Halifax.

House of Representatives Sessions Collection, February 21, 1979 to the present.—The House Recording Studio records the daily sessions of the House of Representatives (B17). After 60 days, audio tapes are forwarded to the Motion Picture Broadcasting and Recorded Sound Division of the Library of Congress. There individuals may listen to the tapes or have one or more tapes duplicated after 30 days from the date of recording. These tapes can be purchased in reel or cassette format. Individuals should use the *Congressional Record* as a point of reference to the collection. The Recorded Sound Section has a useful finding aid, which lists each session, including the date and time. Refer to the booklet, *House Broadcasting System: An Introduction,* which includes additional information on the program.

Kemp, Hal, Collection, 1934-1939.—140 acetate and RCA electrical transcription discs; this collection consists of audio tape copies from the University of Wyoming collection of original discs of Hal Kemp and his orchestra as well as guest soloists, including Skinnay Ennis, Bob Allen, Kay Thompson, Judy Star, and Harry Wilbert.

Kettering, Charles F., Oral History Project, November 29, 1977-May 18, 1978.—8 oral history interviews on 12 audio cassettes; examines the life of Charles F. Kettering, founder of the Kettering Foundation, Dayton, Ohio, and is based on recollections of persons who knew and worked with him. Time period covered is from 1912-1958. Interviewees include Thomas M. Boyd, Robert G. Chollar, Samuel Gould, Dale Groom, Carroll A. Hochwalt, Frederick J. Hooven, David Rike, and William Treharne.

Library of Congress Chamber Music Concerts Collection, 1937 to the present.—Several hundred audio tape recordings of concerts presented at Coolidge Auditorium in the Library of Congress. The collection is valuable not only because it represents a wide array of visiting artists and performing groups, but also because the concerts have been recorded live. Many of the works performed have been premiers. Currently some 35 concerts a year are being recorded. A partial list of performing ensembles include Budapest String Quartet, Coolidge Quartet, Albeneri Trio, London Quartet, Paganini Quartet, Stuyvesant Quartet, Kroll Quartet, Krasner Chamber Ensemble, New Music Quartet, Curtis Quartet, Juilliard Quartet, New York Pro Musica, Beaux Arts Trio, Virtuosi di Roma, Boston Woodwind Quintet, Eastman String Quartet, New York Woodwind Quintet, Philadelphia Woodwinds, Deller Consort, Brazilian String Quartet, Zurich Chamber Orchestra, Metropolitan Opera Studio, and the Toulouse Chamber Orchestra. Some notable artists include Rudolf Serkin, Ralph Kirkpatrick, Virgil Fox, Jennie Tourel, Artur Balsam, and Alexander Schneider.

McBride, Mary Margaret, Collection, 1937–1954.—Disc recordings (1,132 hours) of radio broadcast shows of talk-show hostess, Mary M. McBride (also used the name, Martha Deane). Informal interviews and discussions with a wide array of notable persons on WOR (Mutual Broadcasting System) and later, CBS and NBC, including James Thurber, Fannie Hurst, Eleanor Roosevelt, Janet Flanner, James Melton, Basil Rathbone, Rube Goldberg, Edgar Guest, Bruce Catton, Anatole Litvak, Fred Allen, Gracie Fields, Faith Baldwin, Wanda Toscanini Horowitz, Herbert Agar, Mary Roberts Reinhart, Charles Laughton, Langston Hughes. Recordings in this collection are available only after they have been transferred to tape.

Marine Corps Combat Recordings, 1943–1945.—1,500 discs (originally Amertape filmstrip or Armour Wire formats); based on Marine Corp correspondents' accounts in the field, which focus on Pacific campaigns of World War II (the majority recorded in Saipan); include battle experiences and eyewitness accounts.

Marlboro School of Music Archives, 1966–1978.—3,000 audio tapes; The Marlboro School of Music, under the direction of Rudolf Serkin in Vermont has recorded its dress rehearsals and performances. Many of the musicians recorded at these concerts of chamber music have since attained international stature. The collection is presently restricted and will not be available to the public until 2003.

Matthews, Brander, Collection, 1929–early 1950s.—110 reel-to-reel tape transcriptions from aluminum discs. During the period, Columbia University engaged in a project of recording radio programs (both from commercial radio and, in some cases, short-wave transmissions from Europe) and actual events taking place on the campus. Represented in the collection are poets and playwrights reading their own works, presidents, senators and other politicians, librarians, and academicians. There are speeches, musical concerts, dialect recordings, ethnomusicological recordings, and various recordings representing the U.S. Navy. A partial list of individuals in the collection includes John Erskine, Edgar Lee Masters, Robert Frost, Cornelia Otis Skinner, Walter Damrosch, Franklin D. Roosevelt, Lowell Thomas, Conrad Aiken, Austin Chamberlain, John Hall Wheelock, John Gould Fletcher, Herbert Hoover, George Russell, Thomas Edison, Albert Einstein, King George V, Amelia Earhart, Aldous Huxley, Gertrude Stein, Huey P. Long, Joseph W. Byrnes, and Rudyard Kipling.

Mead, Margaret, Collection, 1930s–1970s.—1,000 recordings (500 listening hours); consists of reel-to-reel and cassette tapes of anthropology field expeditions and commercial discs (lps and 78 rpm), consisting of radio and television sound transcriptions, commercial educational discs and tapes. The papers of Margaret Mead are held in the Manuscript Division (B20) and the films in the Motion Picture and Television Reading Room, Room 336, James Madison Building (telephone 202/287–1000).

Motion Picture Film Synchronous Disc (Vitaphone) Collection, 1926–1930s.—75 discs; these discs were designed to play in synchronization with their respective films. Film studios represented include Paramount, Warner Brothers, First National Pictures, M-G-M, RKO Pathe, United Artists, Talking Pictures Epics, Inc., and Universal Studios. Included are discs for such films as *The Revelers, Gold Diggers of Broadway, Black Waters, Noah's Ark, Madame Q, The Iron Mask, Phantom of the Opera, Show Boat, The Man Higher Up, Eddie Peabody, Naughty Baby, Trader Ginsberg, Our Modern Maidens, The Divine Lady, Puttin' on the Ritz, The Pagan, Voice of the City,* and *The Desert Song*. This collection is growing and the researcher should inquire of current holdings at the time of research.

Naval Research Laboratory Collection, 1918, 1943–1948.—Audio tape recordings of 14 discs; subjects include interviews, speeches, music performance of the U.S. Navy Band, submarine testing at different speeds (1918), Naval Research Laboratory twentieth anniversary (1943) and twenty-fifth anniversary (1948), and firing of V-2 rocket at White Sands, New Mexico. Individuals represented include Admiral A.H. Van Kueren, Admiral Harold G. Bowen, and E.H. Krause.

Navy Oral History Project, 1951–1952.—121 audio tape recordings on the history of Naval radio, which focuses on the years 1898–1934. A number of individuals were interviewed by S.C. Hooper. Topics include signalling by radio during 1911–1912, history of nationalization of radio, aviation radio, radio code, wireless companies in 1915, construction of original transpacific and transcontinental Navy radio stations (1916), and introduction of radio into the armed services.

The Navy Reporter Collection, July 5–November 30, 1945.—9 audio tapes of a radio program featuring various service personnel; consists of interviews, farewell addresses, musical segments, variety programs, news of the world spots, and lectures, such as that on post-war farming presented by Clinton Anderson, Secretary of Agriculture on December 7, 1945. Significant figures in the collection include General Omar Bradley, Robert Goodwin, Ben Moreel, Rear Admiral Lawrence Dubose, and Admiral W.M. Callaghan.

Office of Education Collection, 1935–1940.—Several hundred 16 inch discs; included are the following series of radio broadcasts: "World is Yours (1936–1940)," "Democracy in Action (1939–1940)," "Gallant American Women (1939–1940)," "Let Freedom Ring (1937)," "Education in the News (1935–1938)," "Have You Heard? (1936–1937)," "Brave New World (1937–1938)," and "Answer Me This (1936–1937)," and miscellaneous recordings from 1935–1939. Subjects are varied.

Osborne, John, Collection, 1970s.—700 audio cassette tapes; these recordings were made by Osborne during the 1970s when he was senior editor and columnist for *New Republic* magazine, and wrote "The Nixon Watch" and "The White House Watch" political columns. Represented in the collection are interviews with national and international political figures, copies of broadcast speeches, press conferences, and personal recordings. The collection is restricted from public use until June 29, 1992.

Randall, Edwin T., Collection, 1930s–1970.—1,000 recordings, produced by Friendly World Broadcasting Co. (Wallingford, Pennsylvania); consists of radio conversation programs, such as "Friendly World" and "Yankee in the Heart of Dixie," both conducted by Edwin T. Randall. Appearing on the programs was a wide variety of individuals from grass-roots persons to well-known figures, including, for example, Albert Einstein, Eleanor Roosevelt, Pearl Buck, Clarence Pickett, Stewart Udall, Norman Cousins, Linus Pauling, Chester Bowles, Marjorie Swann, Kathleen Lonsdale, and Jerome Frank.

Recorded Lectures, Inc. Collection (Chicago, Illinois), early 1940s.—11 discs; lectures presented by various individuals on timely topics, including nutrition, speech, American culture, education, and Pan American trade.

Roosevelt, Theodore, Association Collection, 1965–1970.—25 items, including sound recordings and films. Includes interviews, narrations, and discussions, recollections, mostly focusing on the life of Theodore Roosevelt.

Sayers, Isabelle, Collection, 1895–1955.—Paper documents and machines; pre-1925, several thousand discs, cylinders, and other sound recordings. This collection, one of the richest in existence, documents the development of the phonograph industry. It includes several hundred early phonograph manufacturers' catalogs and 21 Berliner discs, as well as many very rare cylinder and disc machines (some dating from the 19th century), automatic music rolls, and thousands of discs and cylinders.

Smith, K.R., Collection, 1931–1948.—1,298 16-inch and 12-inch electrical transcriptions. These recordings, produced by World Broadcasting System, Associated Music Publishers, and Muzak, were leased to radio stations throughout the country and provided smaller, non-network, radio stations with recordings for broadcast of classical and popular music performed by nationally known musicians. This collection is shelved by manufacturer name and number and is partially accessible through the catalogs of the companies available in the Recorded Sound Reference Center.

Voice of America "Conversations with African Writers" Collection. —65 audio tape interviews with African literary figures originally broadcast by VOA African Service in 1975. The writers represent 20 English-speaking African countries. See *Special Collections in the Library of Congress* (1980) for a description of the broadcast recordings of VOA music programs.

Voices of the Silents Collection, 1973–75.—3 audio tapes; interviews with silent film personalities made by Jean Tucker, Assistant Information Officer, Library of Congress. Interviewed are Karl Brown, Lillian Gish, Joseph Henabery, Anita Loos, and Miriam Cooper Walsh. The collection includes edited and unedited transcripts of the recordings.

WOR Radio Archive, 1930s–1950s.—18,000 discs; comprises one of the most complete archives in existence of a radio station. Sound recordings include early radio documentaries, news broadcasts of WOR and Mutual network, music programs produced by WOR and others, and coverage of New York City and national events. The sound recordings are being transferred to tape by RKO General and will be made available to researchers in periodically released groups as they are taped. Indexes to the sound recordings will also be produced by RKO General. Documents in the collection include WOR programming, engineering, public service, and business. The collection is particularly rich in documenting works of writer-producer Phillips H. Lord, creator of such radio programs as "Counterspy" and "Gang Busters." The latter is represented by copies of the FBI files from which episodes were based, drafts for episode scripts, and final scripts. Yet other documents outline the station's public service broadcasts, news operations, music programming, and engineering experiments with facsimile broadcasting and television.

WRC Radio Collection, October 31–November 6, 1955.—71 audio tapes; a sample week of broadcasts from WRC and WRC-FM, Washington, D.C. The recordings represent all of the programs carried on these stations for one full week. Included are radio dramas, sports programming, religious and public service broadcasts, talk shows, quiz shows, news, advertisements, and disc jockey programs. A chronological log of the stations' broadcasts during the week and the respective shelf numbers for the tapes is available.

MUSIC DIVISION
Peforming Arts Reading Room (LM 113)
James Madison Building
(202) 287–5507

8:30 A.M.–5:00 P.M.   Monday–Saturday

Donald L. Leavitt, Chief
Jon Newsom, Assistant Chief
Elizabeth H. Auman, Head, Reference Section

The holdings of the Music Division are extensive and include over 4 million pieces of music and some 300,000 books and pamphlets, programs, microforms, and periodicals focusing on almost every aspect of music. The greatest strengths are in opera, music of the United States, and Western art music in general. Even though the Music Division does not have custody of musical sound recordings, researchers will most likely need the facilities of this division and the adjacent Recorded Sound Reference Center, both of which are located in the Performing Arts Reading Room. For example, if a researcher wished to examine the Rachmaninoff Archives (the most extensive collection of Sergei Rachmaninoff holographs, personal papers, and memorabilia outside the Soviet Union), he/she would have to visit both divisions: the manuscript and printed portions of the archives are under the custody of the Music Division, the set of 700 sound recordings in the archives are held in the custody of the Motion Picture, Broadcasting and Recorded Sound Division.

The Performing Arts Reading Room has 16 multipurpose listening and viewing rooms, and at least 18 additional listening stations. Listening hours are 9:00 A.M. to 12:00 noon, Monday through Friday. The Music Division holds an excellent collection of discographies and record manufacturers' catalogs. The most frequently consulted of these, however, are in the Recorded Sound Reference Center. A substantial number of sheet music items in the collection are not to be found in the card catalog or database. Researchers should, therefore, consult a reference librarian if an item is not cited in the card catalog.

The card catalog has three principal classifications: the "M Class" catalog of music is organized by medium and type, title of work and name of composer; the "ML Class" catalog focuses on the history and literature of music; the "MT Class" catalog focuses on works of music theory, teaching, appreciation, and analysis.

Many of the principal collections held in the Music Division are cited in *Special Collections in the Library of Congress: A Selective Guide* (1980). For a comprehensive bibliography of books and articles focusing on collections in the Music Division, see Carol June Bradley's *Music Collections in American Libraries: A Chronology* (Detroit: Information Coordinators, 1981). Readers should also be aware of *The Music Division: A Guide to Its Collections and Services* (1972) and the printed catalog, *Music, Books on Music and Sound Recordings*. The latter is also available in a microfiche edition. For a comprehensive description of collections in the Music Division, see D.W. Krummel's *Resources of American Music History: A Directory of Source Materials from Colonial Times to World War II* (University of Illinois, 1981).

POETRY OFFICE
John Adams Building, Room LJ 320
(202) 287–5394

Nancy Galbraith, Head

The Poetry Office is in charge of the Archive of Recorded Poetry and Literature. Recordings are held in the custody of the Recorded Sound Reference Center of the Motion Picture, Broadcasting and Recorded Sound Division.
   Begun in 1943, the archive now contains selected works of over 1,000 poets, including poetry readings and literary events held in the library's Coolidge Auditorium. There are also a number of copies of private collections, including, for example, that of the American poet Lee Anderson (1896–1972). Other literary figures in the collection include John Berryman, E.E. Cummings, Robert Frost, T.S. Eliot, and Robert Lowell. Recorded also is the National Poetry Festival of 1962, the Shakespeare Festival of 1964, a symposium on American Literature in 1965, the Dante Symposium of 1965, Lillian Gish's 1969 lecture on motion pictures, Colleen Dewhurst and George C. Scott in a recitation, Herman Wouk and James Dickey reading from their works, an unrehearsed interview with H.L. Mencken, and nine Pulitzer Prize poets reading their own poems.
   For a list of poets and literary programs, see *Literary Recordings: A Checklist of the Archive of Recorded Poetry and Literature in the Library of Congress* (1981). The checklist provides the name of the person, group, or event recorded, dates and places of recording, titles or first lines of poems, and an index to names of persons who have recorded for the archive. For recordings made after 1981, researchers can check the card catalog for noncommercial recordings in the Recorded Sound Reference Center.
   Tapes of many of these recordings may be purchased if their use will be limited to noncommercial educational and cultural purposes. Long-playing literary discs may also be purchased from the Motion Picture, Broadcasting and Recorded Sound Division.

4 a-b. Availability of listening equipment and reservation requirements are noted in the discussion of the Motion Picture, Broadcasting and Recorded Sound Division.

   c. No fees are charged.

   d. Duplication of sound recordings is available in the Motion Picture, Broadcasting and Recorded Sound Division. Researchers should also take note that self-service, coin-operated, photocopying machines are available in all buildings. In addition, the Photoduplication Service, Room G-1009, John Adams Building (202/287-5640) provides, for a fee, photostats, microfilms, and other photocopies of materials in the Library of Congress.

5. In addition to the published reference tools listed under appropriate divisions above, scholars may consult various other publications mentioned below, which are more general in nature. For example, the *Annual Report of the Librarian of Congress,* the *Quarterly Journal of the Library of Congress,* and the *Library of Congress Information Bulletin,* all include information and feature articles on significant sound recording collections, as well as current developments on sound recording preservation and major gifts to the library. Major LC catalogs include the following.
   The National Union Catalog, Pre-1956 Imprints. Currently published by the Mansell Company in England, 754 vols. This catalog supersedes the following two titles.
   A Catalog of Books Represented by Library of Congress Printed Cards Issued (from August 1898 through July 1942), 167 vols. Supplement: cards issued August 1, 1942–December 31, 1947, 42 vols.

The Library of Congress Author Catalog: A Cumulative List of Works Represented by Library of Congress Cards, 1948–1952, 24 vols.

The National Union Catalog: A Cumulative Author List Representing Library of Congress Printed Cards and Titles Reported by Other American Libraries. Cumulation for 1953–1957, 28 vols., available in reprint from Rowman and Littlefield; cumulation for 1958–1962, 54 vols., out of print; cumulation for 1963–1967, 72 vols., available from J.W. Edwards; cumulative for 1956–1967, 125 vols., available from Rowman and Littlefield; cumulative for 1968–1972, available from J.W. Edwards; cumulation for 1973–1977, available from LC Cataloging Distribution Service. Currently published by the library in nine monthly and three quarterly issues with an annual cumulation, the catalog covers some 1,100 U.S. and Canadian libraries.

Monographic Series. An aid to locating works published as a series; the series is printed in three quarterly issues and an annual cumulation.

Library of Congress-Books: Subjects, A Cumulative List of Works Represented by Library of Congress Printed Cards. For 1945 and later imprints, this catalog is arranged alphabetically by LC subject headings and by author under subject headings. Cumulation for 1950–1954, 20 vols., available in reprint from Rowman and Littlefield; cumulation for 1955–1959, 22 vols., available in reprint from Rowman and Littlefield; cumulation for 1960–1964, 25 vols., and for 1965–1969, 42 vols., available from J.W. Edwards; cumulations for 1970–1974, 100 vols., available from Rowman and Littlefield. Since 1975, this catalog is being published under the following title.

Subject Catalog. Continues the preceding work, published in three quarterly issues and an annual cumulation, available from LC Cataloging Distribution Service.

National Register of Microfilm Masters. An annual publication; the 1969 and later issues are available from LC Cataloging Distribution Service.

NOTE: The library of Congress Federal Theatre Project Collection is on permanent loan to the George Mason University Library (A26). Additional components of the Library of Congress are discussed in entries A38, B19, B20, and F9.

Library of Congress—National Library Service for the Blind and Physically Handicapped (NLS/BPH)   See entry F9

A42 Martin Luther King, Jr., Memorial Library (District of Columbia Public Library)

1 a. *901 G Street, N.W.*
Washington, D.C. 20001
(202) 727–1111 (Hours)
(202) 727–0321 (Information)

b. 9:00 A.M.–9:00 P.M.   Monday–Thursday
9:00 A.M.–5:30 P.M.   Friday–Saturday
1:00 P.M.–5:00 P.M.   Sunday
Hours vary during summer.

c. Open to the public. Residents of the District of Columbia may borrow materials. Borrowing privileges extend to persons residing in some neighboring jurisdictions.

d. Kathleen Wood, Central Librarian

2. The Martin Luther King, Jr., Memorial Library is the main collection in the District of Columbia Library system. The library contains some 429,038 books, approximately 2,768 periodicals, as well as newspapers and other printed materials.

3. Notable holdings of the library.

Audiovisual Division
Room 226
(202) 727–1265

Marcia Zalbowitz, Chief

This division has some 2,237 films on such subjects as history, literature, art, technology, business, philosophy, biography, fiction, entertainment, and sociology for all ages. There is also a circulating collection of 3/4-inch video cassettes, and a small rental collection of 1/2-inch video cassettes for home use only. In addition, the division has a small circulating collection of audio cassette tapes and recordings, with the principal focus on the spoken word.

Language and Literature Division
Room 223
(202) 727–1281

Octave S. Stevenson, Chief

This division has approximately 677 recordings of foreign language instruction.

Music Division
Room 209
(202) 727–1285

Mary Elliott, Chief

The Music Division contains the greatest number of audio recordings. Currently, there are some 20,000 recordings of classical music of all styles and periods. There is also a large reference collection that includes excellent examples of contemporary music from the 1970s to the present. American musical theater is well represented. Some 900 jazz albums, that are part of a gift, have made this genre well represented also. Overall, the division's collection has been characterized as having an excellent array of commercially released recordings.

Washingtoniana Division
Room 307
(202) 727–1213

Roxanna Deane, Chief/Oral History Project Director

An Oral History Research Center was established in the Washingtoniana Division in 1982. A principal objective of the center is to serve as a clearinghouse for information on oral history projects being conducted throughout the city and to collect materials regarding persons, neighborhoods, institutions, and events that enlarge the public understanding of the history of the District of Columbia. Both tapes and transcripts are systematically collected. Currently, the Washingtoniana Division holds the following collections.

   Celebracion de la Mujer Latina Project.—A completed project of tapes in Spanish. The director of the project is Barbara Zulli D'Emilio.
   Changing Communication in the Family.—Produced by the Capital Children's Mu-

seum, this project consists of taped interviews of adults over 60 years-of-age who reflect on childhood experiences. Project director is Tom Lane.

Jewish Historical Society Oral History Project.—Some 28 persons who have been long-time residents in the District of Columbia have been interviewed. The collection consists of both tapes and transcripts, and its project director is Ellen Robinson Epstein.

Latino Youth Community History Project.—Produced by the Latin American Youth Center, this project documents the history of the D.C. Latino community. Interviews are in Spanish and were conducted by high school students.

Washington Entreprenuers Project.—Produced by Strayer College (A65), this collection consists of copies of taped interviews with long-term metropolitan area business persons.

The center also conducts workshops and initiates and encourages projects that serve to document the history of the District of Columbia. Individuals can contact Roxanna Deane for additional information.

4 a. On-site listening equipment is available.

b. No reservations required.

c. No fees are charged.

d. Photoduplication facility is available. Audio duplication facility is not available. Patrons may bring their own portable tape recorders into the Music Division to record discs.

5. All divisions have card catalogs where individuals may search under author, title, subject, and musical form.

Martin Luther King, Jr., Memorial Library (District of Columbia Public Library)—Services for the Blind and Physically Handicapped See entry F10

A43 Mary Riley Styles Public Library (City of Falls Church, Virginia)

1 a. *120 North Virginia Avenue*
Falls Church, Virginia 22046
(703) 241-5030

b. 9:00 A.M.–9:00 P.M.   Monday–Thursday
9:00 A.M.–5:00 P.M.   Friday–Saturday
1:00 P.M.–5:00 P.M.   Sunday (October through May only)

c. Open to the public. Library cards issued to any person who lives in, works in, pays taxes to, teaches in, or attends school in Falls Church City. Reciprocal borrowing privileges also exist for residents of neighboring counties of Virginia, Maryland, and the District of Columbia.

d. Deane Dierksen, Library Director

2. The collection of the Mary Riley Styles Public Library includes over 76,000 books, current and popular magazines and newspapers, over 500 large print books, a number of art reproductions, and audiovisual materials. A variety of services are available.

3. Notable holdings of the library.

Record Collection

Chung Ahn, Audiovisual and Adult Services Librarian

The record collection consists of over 5,000 commercial disc recordings of the general nature usually found in a public library. The musical portion is about 50 percent classical, and the rest is comprised of jazz, folk, musicals, and popular music. The language-instruction recordings include both European and Oriental languages, and other instructional material includes speed handwriting and aerobics. The collection also includes children's records and the spoken arts (literature and history). There is also a small collection of some 150 state-donated cassette tapes, which does not circulate. Other cassettes are part of the library's collection of nostalgia kits, and multi-media programs on historical subjects.

Falls Church Historical Collection
Virginia Room

Anna W. Rupps, Associate Librarian in Charge of the Collection

The Falls Church Historical Collection combines materials which had belonged to the Falls Church Historical Commission with other items already in the Falls Church Public Library. The purpose of the collection is to acquire all available documentation pertaining to the City of Falls Church, its citizenry, history, culture, and government. General works dealing with other areas will be added when they are necessary to provide a context for events in Falls Church. The collection includes photographs and supporting documentation, maps, Falls Church Historical Commission's reports and publications, city records, pamphlets, slides, scrapbooks, newspapers, and family histories.

The oral history portion of this collection consists of some 180 tapes with transcriptions of interviews with older citizens of Falls Church, covering 1850 until the present. Some effort was made to gather information on genealogy, but the major emphasis is upon recollections of the changing scene of Falls Church. Other oral history materials include some 30 tapes that focus on city affairs and government.

4 a. On-site listening available. Records circulate for 14 days, with a borrowing limit of 10 items at one time.

  b. No reservations required.

  c. No fees charged, unless items are overdue.

  d. Photoduplication is available.

5. The disc collection is completely cataloged, and may be accessed through the library's main catalog. Indexing of the oral history tapes in the Virginia Room is not yet complete.

A44 Maryland College of Art and Design Library

1 a. *10500 Georgia Avenue*
 Silver Spring, Maryland 20902
 (301) 649-4454

  b. 8:30 A.M.–4:00 P.M.   Monday–Friday

c. Open to the public for on-site use only. Borrowing privileges extended only to members of the college.

d. Laura C. Pratt, Head Librarian

2. The library's collections include some 7,500 books, two-thirds of which focus on art, 23 art periodical titles, and approximately 13,000 slides.

3. The library has approximately 127 commercial disc recordings of classical, jazz, and rock music. The library collects disc recordings primarily for the jacket art and not for their musical content.

4 a. On-site listening equipment is not available.

b. No reservation requirements.

c. No fees charged.

d. Photocopy machine is available.

5. The sound recordings are not cataloged.

A45 Maryland National Capital Park and Planning Commission (M–NCPPC) Montgomery County Planning Department Library

1 a. *8787 Georgia Avenue*
Silver Spring, Maryland 20907
(301) 565–7507

b. 9:00 A.M.–5:00 P.M.   Monday–Friday

c. Open to the public for on-site use by appointment only.

d. Jan Holt, Librarian
Mary Goodman, Librarian

2. The Maryland National Capital Park and Planning Commission is a bi-county agency in Maryland whose jurisdiction includes Montgomery and Prince George's counties. Some of its functions include the determination of land use and park development and management in these areas. The library serves as a resource center for the commission.

3. The library has 33 audio cassette tapes of the American Society of Planning Officials Planning Conference "Planning for Varied Lifestyles," held in 1973 in Los Angeles and the same organization's 1975 conference held in Vancouver, Canada. Subjects for both conferences include land use, housing, urban transit, agricultural land preservation, zoning, environmental psychology and design, and water quality management.

4 a. On-site listening equipment is not available.

b. Prior appointment is recommended.

c. No fees charged.

d. Photocopy facility is available.

5. An in-house list of tapes organized according to conference is available.

A46 Marymount College of Virginia —Ireton Library

1 a. *2807 North Glebe Road*
Arlington, Virginia 22207
(703) 522–5600, ext. 284

b. 8:30 A.M.–11:00 P.M.   Monday–Thursday
8:30 A.M.–5:00 P.M.   Friday
9:00 A.M.–5:00 P.M.   Saturday
2:00 P.M.–11:00 P.M.   Sunday
Hours vary during holidays.

c. The collection is available to scholars for on-site use only. Marymount is a member of the Northern Virginia Consortium.

d. Deborah Leather, Director, Learning Resources and Services

2. Marymount College is a liberal arts institution with masters level programs in business, education, human resources development, liberal studies, and nursing. The Ireton Library collection includes some 65,000 volumes, 435 periodical subscriptions, 685 audiovisual titles, and partial holdings in ERIC from 1975 to the present.

3. The audio collection at Marymount consists of some 250 commercial disc recordings focusing on classical music, language instruction (predominantly Spanish), and spoken arts. This colleciton also includes a collection of no more than 100 audio cassette tapes, which are mostly spoken arts.

4 a. On-site listening facilities are available.

b. No reservations are required.

c. No fees are charged.

d. Duplication of sound recordings is not permitted.

5. The disc collection is not cataloged. The audio cassettes, however, are given full cataloging and are accessible through the main card catalog, which has author/title and subject access.

A47 Montgomery College Libraries

1 a. *51 Mannakee Street*
Rockville, Maryland 20850
(301) 279–5066 (Reference, Rockville Campus)

b. 8:00 A.M.–10:00 P.M.   Monday–Thursday
8:00 A.M.–4:30 P.M.   Friday
9:00 A.M.–5:00 P.M.   Saturday

c. The library is open primarily to faculty, staff, and students of the college, and residents of the community. Books and recordings circulate. Residents of Montgomery County, Maryland, may apply for borrowing privileges. Recordings circulate from individual libraries. Interlibrary loan is not available for recordings.

d. Donald J. Fork, Director, Educational Support Services
   Joan Elbers, Coordinator of Reader Services

2. Montgomery College maintains libraries on each of its three campuses: Rockville, Takoma Park, and Germantown. Library materials include books, periodicals, and non-print items used in support of the college's curricula.

3. Notable holdings of the libraries.

Rockville Campus Library
51 Mannakee Street
Rockville, Maryland 20850
(301) 279–5066

8:00 A.M.–10:00 P.M.   Monday–Thursday
8:00 A.M.–4:30 P.M.   Friday
9:00 A.M.–5:00 P.M.   Saturday

Rawland G. Cresser, Campus Director, Educational Support Services
Joan S. Elbers, Coordinator of Library Readers' Services

The Rockville Campus Library houses approximately 5,000 commercial lp discs and some 600 audio cassettes, representing a basic collection of classical music, jazz, country, rock, musical comedy, and spoken arts.

Takoma Park Campus Library
Takoma Park, Maryland 20912
(301) 587–4090, ext. 242

8:00 A.M.–9:00 P.M.   Monday–Thursday
8:00 A.M.–4:30 P.M.   Friday

LaVerne Miller, Campus Director, Educational Support Services

The Takoma Park Campus Library holds some 1,400 commercial audio cassettes representing the fields of education, literature, English, general science, nursing and allied health programs, office studies, and approximately 997 reel-to-reel audio tapes on education, music, English language, and office studies. These are primarily instructional materials, which do not circulate but are available for use in the Learning Laboratory. The library also has some 1,300 commercial lp discs focusing mostly on classical music, jazz, country, and rock.

Germantown Campus Library
20200 Observation Drive
Germantown, Maryland 20874
(301) 972–2000, ext. 312

Polly Proett, Campus Director, Educational Support Services

The Germantown Campus Library holds some 1,850 commercial lp discs focusing primarily on music, poetry, drama, and literature. An additional 250 commercial audio cassettes are part of some 216 instructional kits.

4 a. On-site listening equipment is available.

b. Reservations are not required.

c. No fees are charged.

d. Photoduplication facilities are available. Duplication of sound recordings is not permitted.

5. Each campus library has a catalog in book format with author, title, and subject access. Most disc recordings are listed in these catalogs. Audio tapes are accessed through a number of typed lists.

A48 Montgomery County Department of Public Libraries—Rockville Library

1 a. *99 Maryland Avenue*
Rockville, Maryland 20850
(301) 279–1637 (referrals to special collections and specialists)
(301) 279–1953 (Rockville Library)
(301) 279–1944 (Films Office)

b. 9:00 A.M.–9:00 P.M.   Monday–Thursday
9:00 A.M.–5:00 P.M.   Friday–Saturday
Hours vary during the summer.

c. Open to the public. Borrowing privileges are extended to individuals living in some surrounding jurisdictions. You may locate an available item by calling the libraries. Arrangements can be made to send it to the branch library of your choice.

d. Agnes M. Griffen, Director of the Department of Public Libraries
Patricia A. Tarin, Chief of Public Services
Jane Tucker, Chief of Technical Services

2. The Department of Public Libraries consists of four regional libraries and fifteen community and branch libraries. As of July 1983 the system contained 64,500 disc and cassette recordings, representing such subjects as classical, jazz, folk, and popular music, spoken arts, sound effects, and instructional materials. Most of the libraries contain small circulating collections of recordings. Not all libraries, however, have on-site listening equipment.

3. Notable holdings of the library.

Maryland Municipal Collection
Rockville Library
(301) 279–1953

Anne Bledsoe, Reference Librarian
Patricia Burt, Reference Librarian/Oral History Specialist

The Maryland Municipal Collection is maintained in a separate room and includes materials that focus on Maryland history, with an emphasis on Montgomery County. Such materials include books, periodicals, maps, Maryland state documents, books by Maryland authors, and audio recordings, some of which are oral history tapes with transcripts.

Specifically the audio collection includes a series of approximately 500 reel-to-reel tapes called *Montgomery County Comments*, which is a public service radio program produced by the Office of Information of the Montgomery county government. The tapes span the period 1970–1980, and focus on Montgomery County government

programs, bank surveys, consumer affairs, crime, noise control, drug and alcohol abuse, education, and energy.

Another series, *Montgomery County Historical Society Oral History Tapes & Transcripts,* include over 35 audio cassettes and 11 reel-to-reel tapes of interviews with at least 27 individuals residing in the county. The original set of these recordings and transcripts are deposited in the Montgomery County Historical Society, Inc. Library (B23).

Another series, *Marie Bennett Oral History Tapes and Transcripts,* produced by the Montgomery County League of Women Voters, Inc. (B24), consists of 57 cassettes of interviews with 27 individuals on various subjects, reflecting the social history of Montgomery County, Maryland.

The Municipal Collection also has a set of *Vinton Lecture Series Tapes* (1971–1973, 1975), consisting of 9 audio cassettes focusing on planning issues of Montgomery County and an additional 12 cassettes dealing with mental health.

4 a. On-site listening equipment is available in five branch libraries only; Bethesda, Long Branch, Gaithersburg, Twinbrook, and Olney.

   b. No reservation requirements.

   c. No fees charged.

   d. Photoduplication available at most libraries.

5.   The library system has a number of book catalogs, which identify which libraries own the book or record you want. See especially the *Phonograph Record Catalog* where you may search under composer, author/title, subject, and musical forms. The Maryland Municipal Collection of audio materials has a separate index card shelf list. Some, but not all, oral history tapes are cataloged in the adult book catalogs. Cassettes with transcripts are filed in acquisition order.

Montgomery County Department of Public Libraries—Services for the Physically Handicapped   See entry F11

Montgomery County Historical Society, Inc., Library   See entry B23

A49 Mount Vernon College Library

1 a. *2100 Foxhall Road, N.W.*
    Washington, D.C. 20007
    (202) 331–3475

   b. 8:00 A.M.–Midnight   Monday–Thursday
      8:00 A.M.–8:00 P.M.   Friday
      9:00 A.M.–5:00 P.M.   Saturday
      2:00 P.M.–10:00 P.M.   Sunday

   c. Open to the public. Borrowing privileges extend to the college community and to graduate students and faculty in the Washington Consortium of Universities.

   d. Lucy Cocke, Director

2. The audio collection of this small college library is surprisingly comprehensive. The library currently holds more than 1,500 commercial lp disc recordings, 800 reel-to-reel tapes, and 400 cassettes on a variety of topics. The bulk of the collection is in music, mostly classical, covering a wide historical range from the medieval period to the present. Spoken arts recordings include American and European literature, speeches, historical topics, current social issues, and old radio programs. One group of tapes consists of interviews with artists and other well-known Americans, such as Margaret Mead, Frank Lloyd Wright, Robert Penn Warren, and Aaron Copland. Instructional material includes a series on ear training and a variety of European language instruction recordings.

3. Special series in the library's audio collections include the *Recorded Anthology of American Music,* produced by New World Records, and a series of tapes produced by Pacifica Radio in California. This series concentrates on current (usually controversial) political issues, women's studies, and communication topics. The library also holds archival recordings pertaining to the history of the college and recordings made by the college's singing group.

4 a. On-site listening facilities are available.

   b. No reservation requirements.

   c. No fees charged.

   d. Photoduplication available. An audio laboratory with extensive tape duplication equipment is available.

5. The audio collection has been cataloged and is accessible through the main card catalog.

A50 National Aeronautics and Space Administration (NASA) — Headquarters Library

1 a. *600 Independence Avenue, S.W.*
    Washington, D.C. 20546
    (202) 453–8545

   b. 8:00 A.M.–4:30 P.M.   Monday–Friday

   c. Open to the public.

   d. Mary Anderson, Chief

2. The library holdings include most NASA publications and publications of its predecessor, the National Advisory Committee on Aeronautics (NACA).

3. Audio materials include some 35 tapes of luncheon colloquia speakers, some of whom are well-known in the field. Meetings were held three to four times a year. Additional information on this collection is sketchy at this time. Individuals should contact the library regarding the current status of the holdings.

4 a. On-site listening equipment is not available.

   b. Prior appointment is recommended.

   c. No fees charged.

d. Photoduplication facility is available. Audio duplication is not available.

5. The library has a microfilm copy of a card file spanning 1915 to 1962 on aeronautics and astronautics, which is available to outside researchers. NASA publications are regularly cited in *NASA Publications* and in its bi-weekly *Scientific and Technical Aerospace Reports* (STAR). A number of materials are available free from the Public Information Services (202/755–8341).

National Air and Space Museum (NASM) (Smithsonian Institution)—Library   See entry C6

National Association of Secondary School Principals (NASSP)—Library See entry M39

A51 National Bureau of Standards (NBS) (Commerce Department)— Library and Information Services Division

1 a. *Route 270 and Quince Orchard Road*
  Gaithersburg, Maryland 20760
  (301) 921–3451 (Reference)

  Mail:
  Library and Information Services Division
  National Bureau of Standards
  Administration Building, Room E06
  Gaithersburg, Maryland 20899

b. 8:30 A.M.–5:00 P.M.   Monday–Friday

c. Open to the public. Use of audiovisual materials requires special permission.

d. Patricia W. Berger, Chief, Information Resources and Services Division
  Marvin A. Bond, Chief, Resources Development

2. The library holds about 200,000 volumes and currently receives over 2,500 journals. Subject strengths include physics, chemistry, engineering, mathematics, and statistics.

3. The library has in storage approximately 125 audio reel-to-reel tapes consisting of narrations on various topics, interviews, and press briefings, and a number of films.

  Of more significance, however, is the NBS Oral History Program held in custody by the library. The program was initiated to capture the recollections of former distinguished scientists and program managers. Some twenty persons have been interviewed during the period 1976–1983, including: A.V. Astin, director; R.D. Huntoon, deputy director; W.R. Tilley, chief, technical information and publications; W.F. Snyder, radio science and engineering; J. Rabinow, engineering and inventions, ordnance research and development; J. Hilsenrath, computer science and mathematics; F.J. Rossini, thermodynamics and thermochemistry; G.C. Paffenberger, former chief, dental research; and C.M. Sitterly, authority on atomic spectra. Most of the tapes have been transcribed. A useful source to be used in conjunction with the interviews is *Measures for Progress: A History of the National Bureau of Standards* (1966). Contact

Karma Beal, Acting Historical Information Specialist (301/921–3401), for current information on access to the collection as well as for interviews not cited above.

___

National Center for Devices and Radiological Health (Health and Human Services Department—Public Health Service—Food and Drug Administration)—Library   See entry L8

___

National Clearinghouse for Alcohol Information (NCALI) (Health and Human Services Department—Public Health Service—Alcohol, Drug Abuse, and Mental Health Administration—National Institute on Alcohol Abuse and Alcoholism)—Library   See entry L9

___

A52 National Clearinghouse for Bilingual Education Library

1 a. *1555 Wilson Boulevard, Suite 605*
Arlington, Virginia 22209
(703) 522–0710, ext. 216
(800) 336–4560 (toll-free)

   b. 8:30 A.M.–5:30 P.M.   Monday–Friday

   c. Open to the public.

   d. Christiane Paulos, Coordinator of Resource Collection

2. The National Clearinghouse for Bilingual Education Library was established in 1977, and specializes in the fields of bilingual education, English as a second language, second language learning, and language acquisition. Holdings include over 1,200 books, 250 newsletters and journals, a vertical file collection, and various curriculum materials. In addition, the library receives all materials produced under Title VII of the Department of Education.

The Clearinghouse has its own in-house database, BEBA (Bilingual Education Bibliographic Abstracts). The database is available through BRS (Bibliographic Retrieval Service) and currently contains some 12,000 items.

3. The library's audiovisual materials include some 40 cassettes and filmstrips consisting of curriculum materials and focusing on bilingual education.

4 a. Contact the library regarding available listening facilities.

   b. An appointment is recommended.

   c. Fees are charged for computer searches.

   d. A photocopy facility is available.

5. All of the library's materials are indexed in BEBA (Bilingual Education Bibliographic Abstracts).

A53 National Defense University (NDU) (Defense Department)—Library

1 a. *Fort Lesley J. McNair*
4th and P Streets, S.W.
Washington, D.C. 20319
(202) 693–8437

b. 8:00 A.M.–4:30 P.M.   Monday–Friday (closed every alternate Friday)

c. Audio materials are reported to be in storage and not available.

d. J.T. Russell, Library Director
Julia Mayo, Chief of Reader Services

2. The National Defense University Library is a support facility for the two main colleges of NDU: the National War College and the Industrial College of the Armed Forces. The library holds some 255,000 monographs and 1,100 journal subscriptions with the principal focus on history, economics, government, international relations, and security studies.

3. The library holds only a nominal amount of sound recordings, including several hundred cassette tapes for language instruction. Most foreign languages are represented in this collection, which is housed in the Industrial College of the Armed Forces Building.
The Division of Special Collections (202/693–5066) has a number of audio tape recordings of lectures presented at NDU, as well as two video tape cassettes, including *Dedication of the National Defense University by President G.R. Ford on January 18, 1977* and *J. Carlton Ward, Distinguished Professor: January 17, 1983*.
There are a number of oral history materials focusing on the National War College and the Industrial College of the Armed Forces located in the Office of Air Force History (B37).

4 a. On-site listening equipment is available.

b. Prior appointment is required.

c. No fees are charged.

d. Duplication of Defense Language Institute tapes is permitted.

5. Individuals can consult the *NDU Handbook for Foreign Language Resources* (1981) for identifying languages represented in the audio tape collection.

National Education Association (NEA)—Library   **See entry M40**

National Epilepsy Library and Resource Center (NELRC) (Epilepsy Foundation of America)   **See entry F13**

National Genealogical Society Library   **See entry B30**

A54 National Institute of Education (NIE) (Education Department)— Educational Research Library

1 a. *1200 19th Street, N.W.*
Washington, D.C. 20208
(202) 254–5060

 b. 10:00 A.M.–4:00 P.M.   Monday–Friday

 c. Open to the public. Only employees of the Department of Education may borrow materials. Researchers may use audio tapes in library with special permission.

 d. Charles Missar, Supervisory Librarian

2. The library provides research and retrieval services in the area of education-related literature and resources. The library also furnishes audiovisual and television support to the institute, including the production of software. Holdings include over 130,000 books, 1,200 subscriptions to current periodicals, and files of all NIE-produced documents and final reports. Special materials include a rare book collection of 395 items, a microform collection, and a collection of audio tapes.

3. The audio cassette tape collection consists of 300 tapes of the series *Options in Education* produced with a grant from NIE by the National Public Radio and the Institute for Educational Leadership of George Washington University, and an additional 58 cassette tapes on education, philosophy, psychology, science, social sciences, and other miscellaneous topics. Significant individuals featured on the tapes include Marshall McCluhan, John Holt, John Joodlad, Bruno Battleheim, and Buckminster Fuller. The library also maintains a collection of 125 books on various audiovisual topics.

 NIE also has an Information and Reference Branch located at Room A-038, 400 Maryland Avenue, N.W., Washington, D.C. 20202; telephone: (202) 245–8853. The librarian is Susan Harlem.

4 a. On-site listening equipment is not available.

 b. Prior appointment is recommended.

 c. No fees charged.

 d. Photocopy facility is available.

5. The library has author/title and subject catalogs. The library has numerous reference indexes including their own published *Periodical Holdings List* (1978). Database access is through DIALOGUE, BRS, and ORBIT.

A55 National Library of Medicine (NLM) (Health and Human Services Department—Public Health Service—National Institutes of Health)

1 a. *8600 Rockville Pike*
Bethesda, Maryland 20209
(301) 496–6095 (Reference)
(201) 496–5511 (Interlibrary Loan)

b. 8:30 A.M.–9:00 P.M.   Monday–Thursday
    8:30 A.M.–6:00 P.M.   Friday
    8:30 A.M.–5:00 P.M.   Saturday
    Hours vary during summer.

c. The library is open to the public. All first-time users must obtain a registration number at the Reader Service Desk and sign the daily log each time upon entering the Reading Room.

d. Donald A.B. Lindberg, Director

2. The National Library of Medicine is the world's largest research library in a single scientific and professional field. As a national repository for biomedical literature, the library has holdings of over 3 million books, journals, technical reports, theses, microfilms, and pictorial and audiovisual materials. The library also provides extensive bibliographic, reference, and interlibrary loan services.

3. Notable holdings of the library.

LEARNING RESOURCES CENTER (LRC)
Audiovisual Resources Section
(301) 496–4244

Linda Watson, Head

The Audiovisual Resources Section (AVRS) provides for the sharing and management of audiovisual and other non-print information on medicine and the health sciences, as well as audiovisual reference service. Specifically, the section manages the Learning Resource Center and provides audiovisual reference service. The LRC houses 1,200 of the 11,600 titles in the AVLINE audiovisual collection, as well as recent issues of audiovisual journals on open shelves available for browsing. Remaining titles are housed in the stacks. The LRC also provides viewing and listening facilities. AVRS also identifies audiovisual instructional materials and manages a distribution system for their loan or sale to health professionals, supports a program for the review and preservation of historical audiovisual materials of significant value in the health sciences, maintains external relationships with health professionals and their organizations regarding the availaibility and use of audiovisual materials, and participates in collaborative studies to improve procedures for handling non-print instructional materials in health science libraries. In short, AVRS holds one of the most extensive collections of medical audiovisual materials in the country.

HISTORY OF MEDICINE DIVISION
(301) 496–5405

John Parascandola, Chief

The division's resources for the study of medical and related science history are among the most extensive of any institution in the world. There are almost 500,000 printed materials. Included in the holdings are numerous manuscripts, prints, photographs, and oral history materials.

The oral history collection consists of 84 titles of reel-to-reel tapes and transcripts. Most, but not all, tapes have been transcribed. The subject matter dates from 1926 to the present. Subjects represented include disease, medical organizations, committees, and other formal bodies, physicians, psychology (child and adult), medical legislation, medical education, research, after-dinner presentations, chemistry and bio-

chemistry, food, drugs and chemicals, public health, quackery, medical ethics, child development, nursing, medical conferences, and studies in medicine, including immunology, pathology, homeopathy, surgery, gastroenbrology, cardiology, bacteriology, cardiology, and pediatrics.

Some representative titles include: *Interview with Theodore Wiprud (and William P. Herbst)* (June 19, 1962; OH 1: discussions of Washington physicians in the 1930s); *Interview with R. Palmer Howard (and Daniel W. Humphreys)* (December 10, 1966; OH 9: general practice in the town of Oilton, Oklahoma in the 1920s and 1930s); *Transcripts and Tapes of Interviews on the Child Development Movement* (98 interviews conducted from 1967–1975; OH 20: interviews with Leona Baumgartner, Urie Bronfenbrenner, Martha Eliot, Lawrence K. Frank, Jerome Kagan, Arthur Lesser, Margaret Mead, Walter Mondale, Lois B. Murphy, Lee Salk, Lester Sontag, Benjamin Spock, Helen Thompson, and Alfred H. Washburn, etc.); *Interview with Peter D. Olch, Washington, D.C., (and Daniel L. Borden)* (OH 25: pertains chiefly to the court case of the American Medical Association, the Medical Society of the District of Columbia, the Washington Academy of Surgery, and the Harris County Medical Society, initiated by the U.S. Government in 1941); Re-recording of an Edison cylinder recording of Florence Nightingale (July 7, 1890) with an introduction by M. Adelaide Nutting (September 26, 1939; OH 30); *Transcripts and Tapes on the American Child Guidance Clinic and Child Psychiatry Movement* (79 interviews conducted from 1975–1978; OH 76); *Women in Medicine* (OH 77; interviews with 37 women and 2 men physicians, 1976–1978); *Interviews with Physicians Stationed on Ellis Island in the 1910s and 1920s, by Elizabeth Yew, 1977–1978* (OH 79); and miscellaneous tape recordings pertaining to the history of the National Library of Medicine (1959 onward; OH 70).

The easiest way to access these and oral history tapes is to consult the Shelflist Catalog, where they are listed by accession number. Cards for audio tapes are also interfiled among cards for manuscripts in the Manuscripts-Name Catalog, as well as in the Manuscript-Subject Catalog.

STAFF LIBRARY
Building 38A, Room B1N-14K
(301) 496–5780
(301) 496–6097

8:30 A.M.–5:00 P.M.   Monday–Friday

Alvin J. Barnes, Librarian

The library focuses primarily on library science materials and has a basic collection of books, periodicals, and vertical file materials. Although the library has no audiovisual materials, it does contain a small collection of audiovisual resource books. These materials are accessed most readily through the subject catalog under the topics, Audio-Visual Education, Audio-Visual Equipment, Audio-Visual Library Service, and Audio-Visual Materials.

The library has a small collection of periodicals relating to audio matters. Such serials include *Stereo Review* and *Library Technology Reports*.

The library is primarily for use by NLM staff. However, other individuals may use the library but with no borrowing privileges.

4 a.   On-site listening equipment is available in the Learning Resources Center.

   b.   Prior reservations are not required in the Learning Resources Center. Researchers desiring to listen to oral history recordings in the History of Medicine

Division are requested to write or telephone in advance, so that listening equipment can be procured and any restrictions on materials can be verified.

   c. Fees are not charged to listen to recordings.

   d. A photocopy facility is available.

5. NLM publishes a variety of catalogs and materials that researchers will find useful for identifying sound recordings as well as print materials. Catalogs include *Index Medicus* (monthly); *Cumulated Index Medicus* (annual); *Abridged Index Medicus* (monthly, with annual cumulation); *National Library of Medicine Current Catalog* (quarterly, annual cumulation); *Medical Subject Headings*; and *National Library of Medicine Audiovisuals Catalog* (quarterly, annual cumulation; see also, entry G2, for additional information on this latter catalog).

Other publications include an occasional *Fact Sheet,* which describes specific divisions and services of the library, and a list of *Publications* (1983) and a *NLM News* bulletin. NLM also publishes a series of guides to sources of information for various subjects. Each guide includes a section on audiovisual materials. Recently published guides include *Nutrition* (1982), *Nursing* (1981), and *Psychiatry and Psychology* (1981). Another bibliographic tool that researchers will find useful is *Audiovisual Aids: Programmed Instruction, and Computer Assisted Instruction in Allied Education, May, 1974 through July, 1978.* NLM also publishes a number of flyers describing MEDLARS and its various component databases. The two principal databases in the system regularly citing recent audiovisual software are AVLINE (see entry G2) and BIOETHICSLINE.

The History of Medicine Division maintains its own card catalog. The division has a number of published guides to the collection. Citations to materials published since 1964 are included in the division's HISTLINE (History of Medicine Online) database, also available to researchers, includes citations to monographs, journal articles, symposia, congresses, and other publications.

A number of oral history materials and other records are cited in the Library of Congress *National Union Catalog of Manuscript Collections.* In addition, the development of the oral history program is described and documented in the publication, *A History of the National Library of Medicine: The Nation's Treasury of Medical Knowledge* (1982).

National Public Radio (NPR)—Library   **See entry B33**

National Theatre Library Archives   **See entry B35**

A56 National Wildlife Federation—Frazier Memorial Library

1 a. *1412 16th Street, N.W.*
Washington, D.C. 20036
8925 Leesburg Pike
Vienna, Virginia 22180
(202) 797–6800, ext. 6829

b. 8:00 A.M.–4:30 P.M.   Monday–Friday

c. The libraries are open to the public but individuals may not borrow books. Interlibrary loan through colleges and universities is available.

d. Sharon Levy, Librarian

2–3. The Frazier Memorial Library has some 36 commercial disc recordings of bird songs. At least one of the recordings was produced by Roger Tory Peterson, and can be used with his various guides to birds.

4 a. On-site listening facilities are not available.

b. Individuals must write or telephone requesting permission to bring listening equipment into the library.

c. No fees are charged to use the library.

d. Recordings may not be duplicated.

5. There is no index to the sound recording collection.

NOTE: The Recorded Sound Section of the Library of Congress (A41) has one National Wildlife Federation disc recording from the radio program series, *Save America*. Topics include "Wildlife and the Farm" and "Hot Fish."

A57 Naval Air Systems Command—Technical Library (Navy Department)

1 a. *Jefferson Plaza No. 2, Room 278*
Washington, D.C. 20361
(202) 692–9006

b. 9:00 A.M.–5:00 P.M.   Monday–Friday

c. Open to military personnel, government agencies, and contractors only. Researchers require special permission to use library.

d. Pat Stone, Librarian

2. The library's holdings include 14,000 books, 300 periodical subscriptions, some 400,000 documents, and a number of audio and video tapes. Subjects include aeronautics, chemistry, electronics, math, physics, propulsion, and weapons systems.

3. The library has some 100 audio cassette tapes representing various topics in management, public speaking, and languages. A number of the tapes are produced by the American Management Associations (M15) and Peter Drucker.

4 a. On-site listening facility is not available.

5. The library has a card catalog with author/title and subject access.

A58 Northern Virginia Community College (NVCC)—Learning Resources Centers

1 a. *Annandale Campus*
8333 Little River Turnpike
Annandale, Virginia 22003
(703) 323–3128
(703) 323–3221

Alexandria Campus
3001 North Beauregard Street
Alexandria, Virginia 22311
(703) 845–6276

b. Annandale Campus:
8:00 A.M.–9:00 P.M.   Monday–Tuesday
8:00 A.M.–5:00 P.M.   Wednesday–Friday
Alexandria Campus:
8:00 A.M.–10:30 P.M.   Monday–Thursday
8:00 A.M.–6:00 P.M.   Saturday
Hours may vary from quarter to quarter.

c. The Annandale Campus is open to the public. Recordings do not circulate, except for classroom use or by special arrangement. The Alexandria Campus allows recordings to circulate to students, faculty, and residents of the surrounding community.

d. Lois Smith, Acting Director, Learning Resources, Annandale Campus
Gloria Terwilliger Brown, Director, Learning Resources, Alexandria Campus

2. The Annandale Campus has a large collection of audiovisual materials of all types, which have been acquired to support the curriculum. Audio holdings are primarily in cassette format, both independent tapes and those to be used with filmstrips or slides. Topics are varied, including art, science, business administration, computer technology, economics, education, history, literature, music history and appreciation, personal guidance, philosophy, psychology, vocational guidance, and women's issues.

The Alexandria Campus collection of over 600 cassette titles is intershelved with other library materials. It is quite similar to that at the Annandale Campus with differences reflecting the individual curricula. The bulk of the collection is in English grammar and literature and in business administration. The remainder covers the physical sciences and the social sciences, exercise and dance, police administration, and foreign language, including English as a second language. The disc collection of some 530 titles is entirely classical music, in support of the music program. These are stored in separate record bins.

3. Notable holdings of the Annandale campus.

Music Lab

8:00 A.M.–4:30 P.M.   Monday–Friday

The Music Lab is located in the Music Department and houses a separate collection of tapes and discs of primarily classical music for use by persons taking music courses.

4 a. On-site listening equipment is available in all facilities.

   b. No reservations are required.

   c. No fees are charged.

   d. Photocopy facilities are available. Duplication of audio materials is provided. Contact the Learning Resources Centers for additional information.

5. Items that have been acquired since 1979 are fully cataloged and are listed in the COMCAT for the college (including five campuses). The Learning/Multimedia lab materials are also listed by subject and by title in the *Multi-Media Catalog,* updated annually. Music Lab materials acquired before 1979 are listed on a card file in the Audio Visual Services Office of the Learning Resources Center.

Oblate College Library   **See entry E4**

A59 Office of Personnel Management Library

1 a. *1900 E Street, N.W., Room 5H27 (Reference)*
    Washington, D.C. 20415
    (202) 632–4432

   b. 8:30 A.M.–4:30 P.M.   Monday–Friday

   c. Open to the public. Materials may not be borrowed.

   d. Betty B. Guerin, Chief, Library Branch

2. This library contains mostly materials related to personnel administration with emphasis on the Federal Civil Service. Holdings include more than 70,000 books, government documents, approximately 600 periodicals, and numerous research dissertations on microform. The library also has a number of personnel documents issued by Congress, and archival material related to the Office of Personnel Management and the U.S. Civil Service Commission.

3. The library has a small collection of audiovisual materials including audio reel-to-reel tapes, video cassettes, and films. The audio tapes are few in number and include the following: *Remarks of Vice President Humphrey and John Williams Macy, Jr. on the Occasion of the U.S. Civil Service Commission's 82nd Anniversary Ceremony, January 15, 1965* (1 reel-to-reel tape); *The Minority Member as a Career Trainee* (Samuel D. Proctor, 1968; 1 reel-to-reel tape); *Equal Employment Rights in the Federal Government* (presentation to agency heads, March 17, 1966, Lyndon B. Johnson; 1 reel-to-reel tape); *Focus on Careers: Civil Service* (Roger W. Jones; 1 reel-to-reel tape); *1969 Annual Awards Ceremony* (U.S. Civil Service Commission; 2 reel-to-reel tapes); *An Overview of Federal Personnel Policy* (Seymour Berlin; 1 reel-to-reel tape); *Current Implementation of Executive Order 11222, Prescribing Standards of Ethical Conduct for Government Officers and Employees* (Karl Ruediger; 1 reel-to-reel tape); *Past, Current and Future Problems Under Executive Order 10988* (David S. Barr; 1 reel-to-reel tape); *The Practical Side of Negotiating Under Executive Order 10988* (Roy F. Renoud; 1 reel-to-reel tape).

4 a. On-site listening equipment is not available. Individuals have to make arrangements to bring in personal equipment.

b. No reservation requirements.

c-d.Photocopy facility is available.

5. The staff will make literature searches and referrals to other sources where necessary. Although on-line searching is not available to the public, the reference staff does offer some research consultation. The library publishes the monthly journal *Personnel Literature.*

A60 Prince George's Community College—Learning Resources Center

1 a. *301 Largo Road*
  Largo, Maryland 20772
  (301) 322–0462
  (301) 322–0476 (Reference)

b. Fall and spring semesters:
  8:00 A.M.–10:00 P.M.   Monday–Thursday
  8:00 A.M.–6:00 P.M.   Friday
  9:00 A.M.–5:00 P.M.   Saturday
  1:00 P.M.–5:00 P.M.   Sunday
  Semester break hours:
  9:00 A.M.–2:30 P.M.   Monday–Friday
  Closed weekends in the summer.

c. Books and audio materials circulate to college faculty, staff, and students only. The public may listen to recordings on site.

d. Leah K. Nekritz, Associate Dean for Learning Resources
  Charmaine Yochim, Coordinator of User Services

2–3. The library's collection of books, periodicals, and non-print materials support a two year college curriculum consisting of general and technical programs, as well as a large number of adult education courses. The audio collection consists of some 2,500 tapes and approximately 5,500 discs. Most of the discs are musical recordings representing all styles and periods of music. The spoken discs contain many recorded literary works from sources such as Caedmon and Spoken Arts.
  The cassette collection covers a wide range of subjects with lectures in psychology, sociology, history, and literature, foreign language instruction, and many programs on current affairs from sources such as National Public Radio (B33) and the Pacifica Tape Library, produced in California.

4 a. On-site audio listening equipment is available.

b. No reservations required but first consideration is given to members of the college.

c. No fees charged for listening.

d. A self-service, no fee, audio duplication facility is available. Individuals must provide their own blank cassette tapes.

5. The library maintains an integrated author, title, and subject card catalog. There is a separate music recordings card catalog where individuals can search under composer, title, subject, performing group, and musical form.

A61 Prince George's County Memorial Library System

1 a. *Hyattsville Library*
   6530 Adelphi Road
   Hyattsville, Maryland 20782
   (301) 779-9330
   (301) 699-3500 (Administrative Office)

   b. 9:00 A.M.–9:00 P.M.   Monday–Thursday
      1:00 P.M.–6:00 P.M.   Friday
      9:00 A.M.–5:00 P.M.   Saturday
      1:00 P.M.–5:00 P.M.   Sunday
      Hours vary during summer.

   c. Open to the public.

   d. Ron Kaye, Audio Visual Officer
      Norman Jacob, Information Officer

2. The Prince George's County Memorial Library System consists of the Hyattsville Library, Administrative Offices, and 20 additional branch libraries. As of June 1982 the system contained 21,000 titles on 89,421 commercial disc recordings and 12,480 cassette recordings of mostly classical and popular music. Other subjects represented include jazz, spoken arts, and language instruction. All of the branch libraries circulate recordings, but only some branch libraries have on-site listening facilities.

3. Notable holdings of the library system.

Hyattsville Library, Maryland Room
(301) 779-9330

John Krivak, Librarian

The Maryland Room, located in the reference area, includes materials that focus on the history of Maryland with an emphasis on Prince George's County. The collection contains some 8,000 books, 40 pamphlet drawers, maps, clippings, microfilm, newspapers and magazines, and a few oral history tapes.

   The oral history collection consists of only 12 audio cassette tapes, a few of which deal with the history of Beltsville, Maryland. The tapes are not cataloged, and transcripts have not been made. Individuals should ask for the tapes in the Librarian's Office.

Greenbelt Branch Library, Tugwell Room
11 Crescent Road
Greenbelt, Maryland 20770
(301) 345-5800

10:00 A.M.–9:00 P.M.   Monday–Wednesday
10:00 A.M.–6:00 P.M.   Thursday
1:00 P.M.–6:00 P.M.   Friday
9:00 A.M.–5:00 P.M.   Saturday

Harriet Ying, Branch Librarian

The Tugwell room, located on the lower level of the building, is named in honor of Rexford Guy Tugwell (1891–1977), former Resettlement Administration Chief, who

played a significant part in the establishment of Greenbelt, Maryland . The Tugwell Room contains materials on the history of Greenbelt, which include books, newspapers, pictures, maps, programs, letters, materials on other planned communities, and oral history tapes.

The oral history collection includes only 6 audio cassette tapes concerning the history of Greenbelt. Transcripts for these tapes have not been made.

Available also at the Greenbelt Library is the Tel-Med Tape Library consisting of over 200 recordings of health messages covering a wide spectrum of health concerns. Subjects include family planning, human sexuality, diseases, dental care, nutrition, first aid and safety, and mental health. Access to this collection is available by telephone (301/345–4080). The operator plays the recording over the phone for you. A pamphlet that lists the tapes is available from the library.

4 a. The Hyattsville Library and some of the branch libraries have on-site listening equipment.

b. No reservation requirements.

c. No fees charged.

d. Photoduplication facilities are available at most libraries.

5. All disc and cassette recordings are cataloged on microfiche. Access is by performer, composer, and subject. In addition, the cassette collection may be accessed through nine individual binders, for subjects such as jazz, rock, classical music, and spoken arts. The cassette labels are taken off the individual cassettes and placed in the binders for patrons to browse through.

Prince George's County Memorial Library System—Visually & Physically Handicapped Division   See entry F17

A62 Prince George's General Hospital and Medical Center—Saul Schwartzbach Memorial Library

1 a. *Cheverly, Maryland 20785*
(301) 341–2440

b. 8:00 A.M.–8:00 P.M.   Monday–Friday
9:00 A.M.–2:30 P.M.   Saturday

c. Open to scholars, physicians, and students of medicine.

d. Eleanor Kleman, Head Librarian

2–3. The library's collection includes books, periodicals, and various non-print materials including video and audio cassette tapes. The latter consists of two principal series: *Audio-Digest* (anesthesiology, internal medicine, obstetrics and gynocology, pediatrics, and surgery) and *ACCEL* (American College of Cardiology Extended Learning; 85 tapes). The collection includes a number of old 78 rpm disc recordings on psychiatry.

4 a. On-site listening equipment is not available. Patron must supply personal listening equipment.

b. Reservations are not required.

c. Fees are not charged for listening to audio materials.

d. The library does not have the equipment to duplicate tapes.

5. The library has a card catalog. Cards for sound recordings are interfiled with cards for books. Sound recordings are accessed by title and subject only.

A63 Smithsonian Institution Libraries

1 a. *Central Reference and Loan Services Collection*
National Museum of Natural History, Room 25
10th Street and Constitution Avenue, N.W.
Washington, D.C. 20560
(202) 357–2139

b. 8:45 A.M.–5:15 P.M.   Monday–Friday

c. Open to the public for on-site use. Visitors should call in advance for an appointment. Interlibrary loan and photoduplication services are available.

d. Robert M. Maloy, Director
Mary Clare Gray, Chief Librarian, Central Reference Services

2. The Central Reference and Loan Services Collection contains more than 60,000 books and some 600 serial titles in the reference and general holdings. Major subject areas include bibliography, biology, natural history, geology, paleontology, travel and exploration, business administration, and computer and library science. There are no audio holdings in the Central Reference Library but this library serves as the principal referral office to collections located in branch libraries throughout the Smithsonian Institution Libraries system.

3. Notable holdings of the libraries.

Museum Reference Center Library
Office of Museum Programs
Arts and Industries Building, Room 2235
9000 Jefferson Drive, S.W.
Washington, D.C. 20560
(202) 357–3101

Catherine D. Scott, Chief Librarian

This branch is the only library of materials in musiology in the country. The bulk of the collection includes books, periodicals, and an extensive vertical file collection. Audio holdings include a collection of educational slide-tape programs produced by the American Association for State and Local History and over 100 cassette recordings of the annual meeting of the American Association of Museums from 1976 to 1983.

Museum Support Center (formerly Conservation Analytical Laboratory) Library
4210 Silver Hill Road
Silver Hill, Maryland 20560
(202) 287–3666

Karen Preslock, Chief Librarian

This branch houses a collection of some 1,500 books and 60 periodical titles in the areas of conservation of museum materials and related disciplines. The library is also a referral center for audiovisual materials maintained in the Conservation Analytical Laboratory. Audio holdings include some 180 tapes of annual meetings of the American Institute for Conservation from 1980 to the present. Topics covered include the conservation of paper, paintings, furniture, and other objects; the handling and storage of museum objects; and the regulation of museum environments. Another audio collection is a series of some 100 cassette instructional tapes on various scientific analysis techniques, such as appropriate examination of materials and how to use a spectrometer.

4 a.   Listening facilities are available at some branches.

   b.   Reservations are usually required for use of any of the research facilities in the Smithsonian Libraries system.

   c.   Fees are not charged.

   d.   Photoduplication services are available at some branches.

5.   A series of small brochures for Smithsonian Institution Libraries, one for each branch, describes regulations and collection information. The *Smithsonian Institution Libraries Catalogue,* a computer microfiche guide by author, title, and subject includes all materials cataloged by the libraries since 1965. For records not yet converted to machine-readable form, researchers should consult card catalogs and other access tools located in individual branches and the Libraries' Union Catalog located at the Central Reference and Loan Services.

NOTE: Other Smithsonian Institution libraries are treated separately in this study. See Freer Gallery of Art Library (C3), Hirshhorn Museum and Sculpture Garden Library (C5), National Air and Space Museum Library (C6), and National Museum of African Art Archives (C10). Researchers should also take note of the sound recordings in the records of the Smithsonian Institution (RG 106) in the Special Archives Division of the National Archives and Records Service (B27).

Senate Library   **See entry B40**

Society of Woman Geographers—Library   **See entry M53**

A64   Southeastern University Library

1 a.   *501 Eye Street, S.W.*
   Washington, D.C. 20024
   (202) 488–8162

   b.   9:00 A.M.–9:00 P.M.   Monday–Thursday
       9:00 A.M.–8:00 P.M.   Friday
       8:30 A.M.–4:30 P.M.   Saturday–Sunday

   c.   The library is open to the public but only faculty and students of the university may borrow materials.

    d. Laurence Himelfarb, Library Director
       Bruce Snyder, Associate Director for Audio-Visual Services

2. Southeastern University, founded in 1879, hosts a number of undergraduate and graduate programs in business. The library, serving as a major support facility for these programs, has an excellent collection of business materials in finance, accounting, marketing, economics. Currently, the library has some 20,000 books and 250 periodical titles, and a variety of non-print materials including transparencies, filmstrips, and audio cassette and disc recordings.

3. The collection of commercial recordings includes some 100 audio cassettes representing such topics as auditing, introductory and intermediate accounting instructional programs, English pronunciation, and the relevance of patterns and sound in language. There are also 6 titles of tapes produced by National Public Radio on economics, international relations, and sociology. Other examples of series of cassette productions include *Drucker on Management* and *Sound of the Economy* (monthly, produced by Citicorp).
    The disc collection includes 150 titles representing a broad range of musical subjects. Cassette-disc/filmstrip kits include such subjects as music, art, earth science, microeconomics, and labor.

4 a. On-site listening equipment is available.

    b. No reservation requirements.

    c. No fees charged.

    d. A photoduplication facility is available. Audio duplication is available to faculty of the university.

5. The Associate Director for Audio-Visual Services is currently working on a book catalog for the audiovisual materials. When completed, the catalog will provide name/ title, format, subject, and performance medium access.

A65 Strayer College Library

1 a. *1100 Vermont Avenue, N.W.*
    Washington, D.C. 20005
    (202) 467–6966

    b. 8:30 A.M.–8:30 P.M.   Monday–Thursday
       9:00 A.M.–4:30 P.M.   Friday
       9:00 A.M.–12:30 P.M.   Saturday
       Hours may vary when the college is not in session.

    c. Open to the public for on-site use. Non-print media owned by the college supports the instructional programs, and cannot usually be borrowed. The material, however, is generally available for use within the college.

    d. Barbara Krell, Librarian
       David Moulton, Assistant Librarian

2. Library materials are purchased to support the college curriculum. The library has approximately 18,000 books, 130 periodicals, and non- print materials representing

a variety of business areas, including accounting, business management, data processing, office administration, and word processing.

3. The library owns 180 dictation audio cassette tapes and disc recordings for shorthand (40–260 words per minute). Other non-print materials include 120 items of software in various formats: video (1/2 inch, VHS), film-strips, slides, and audio cassette tapes. The three prominent subject areas are word processing, data processing, and management.

Washington Entrepreneurs Project
(202) 467–6966, ext. 241

Richard Voelkel, Director

This oral history archive consists of 22 interview recordings with Washington small business entrepreneurs, each having at least 30 years experience in the Washington metropolitan area. Specific interviewees include Milton Kronheim, Walter Bell, Frank Rich, W. Weschler, A. Bovello, and M. Peake. Transcripts are in the process of being approved by interviewees.

   In addition, the college has a Virginia campus where plans are underway to establish a learning resources center, which will contain non-print materials including audio cassettes. Contact: David Moulton, Librarian, Strayer College, 3045 Columbia Pike, Arlington, Virginia 22204; (703/892–5100).

4 a. On-site listening equipment is available.

 b. Reservations are required.

 c. No fees charged to listen to sound recordings.

 d. A photoduplication facility is available.

5. The library uses the Dewey decimal system for cataloging books. Sound recordings are not cataloged.

Textile Museum—Arthur D. Jenkins Library   **See entry C15**

Traditional Music Documentation Project (TMDP)—Library
See entry B50

A66 Trinity College—Sister Helen Sheehan Library

1 a. *Michigan Avenue and Franklin Street, N.E.*
Washington, D.C. 20017
(202) 269–2255 (Librarian's Office)
(202) 269–2254 (Audio-Visual/Reference)

 b. 9:00 A.M.–11:00 P.M.   Monday–Thursday
9:00 A.M.–8:00 P.M.   Friday
10:00 A.M.–5:00 P.M.   Saturday
12:00 Noon–11:00 P.M.   Sunday

c. Open to faculty and students of the college. Other individuals may use the materials on-site with permission only.

d. Sister Dorothy Beach, Head Librarian

2. The library has over 157,000 books and 605 periodical subscriptions. The holdings are broad in support of a liberal arts college program. History, literature, and political science are emphasized. Non-print materials include microforms, video tapes, films, filmstrips, slides, and audio discs and tapes.

3. The library has 22 audio cassettes consisting of classical music, 140 discs and 38 reel-to-reel tapes of spoken word titles with an emphasis in American and English literature, history, and philosophy, and some 28 individual lectures by Trinity college faculty, such as in English and history. One notable item in the collection is an audio tape recording of a speech by Pope John Paul II presented at Trinity College on October 7, 1979, during a papal visit to the United States.

4 a. On-site listening equipment is available.

b. No reservation requirements.

c. No fees are charged.

d. A photocopy facility is available. Duplication is available to Trinity college faculty and is conducted in the Language Laboratory.

5. The library's holdings are indexed in a card catalog, which provides author/title, subject, and musical form access.

A67 Uniformed Services University of the Health Sciences—Learning Resource Center (LRC)

1 a. *4801 Jones Bridge Road*
Bethesda, Maryland 20814
(202) 295–3356 (Administration)
(202) 295–3350 (Circulation/Class Reserve Desk)

b. 7:00 A.M.–11:00 P.M.   Monday–Thursday
7:00 A.M.–5:00 P.M.   Friday
12:00 Noon–11:00 P.M.   Sunday
Holiday and summer hours vary.

c. Open to public for on-site use only.

d. Chester J. Pletzke, Director, Learning Resource Center

2. The Learning Resource Center contains over 60,000 books, journals, audiovisuals and subscribes to more than 1,000 journal titles.

3. The LRC has a special collection in the discipline of military medicine. Audiovisual materials accessible to the general public include slides, slide/cassettes, video tapes, video discs, American College of Radiology Learning Resource File.

4 a. On-site equipment is available.

b. No reservation requirements.

c. No fees charged for listening to audiovisuals.

d. A photoduplication facility is available.

5. The LRC on-line catalog is accessible for searching by author, title, and subject. All available audiovisual materials are listed in the public access catalog.

A68 University of Maryland—College of Library and Information Services (CLIS) Library

1 a. *R. Lee Hornbake Library Building*
Second Floor, South Wing, Room 2115
College Park, Maryland 20742
(301) 454–6003

b. 8:00 A.M.–10:00 P.M.   Monday–Thursday
8:00 A.M.–5:00 P.M.   Friday
9:00 A.M.–5:00 P.M.   Saturday
1:00 P.M.–6:00 P.M.   Sunday

c. The library is available for use by serious scholars.

d. William G. Wilson, Librarian

2. The College of Library and Information Services Library is a support facility for CLIS programs and courses. As of February, 1982, the library held some 42,000 volumes, including 20,265 books, 4,235 volumes of periodicals, and numerous pamphlets and technical reports. Non-print materials include microforms, 149 audio cassettes, 46 disc recordings, and 52 filmstrips.

3. Sound recordings held by the library focus primarily on library science and information communications. Two examples include *Utilizing the Best of Communication Devices* (1973; cassette) by Ruth Warncke and *Can We Afford to Communicate* (1973; cassette) by Carolyn Whitenack. The library has an extensive collection of audiovisual printed materials.

4 a. On-site listening equipment is available through the Instructional Design and Support Center, Room 3114 (301/454–2558).

b. A 24-hour advance notice to reserve listening equipment is recommended.

c. No fees are charged.

d. A photoduplication facility is available.

5. CLIS librarians are available to assist researchers in locating materials of all types. The library's card catalog includes author/title and subject access. A number of cassettes can be readily identified under various "audiovisual" subject headings.

A69 University of Maryland Language Media Center

1 a. *1204 Foreign Language Building*
   University of Maryland
   College Park, Maryland 20742
   (301) 454-5728

  b. 8:00 A.M.–10:00 P.M.   Monday–Thursday
     8:00 A.M.–4:00 P.M.   Friday

  c. Open only to faculty and students of the University of Maryland .

  d. James E. Royalty, Director

2. The collection includes instructional tape recordings of the following languages: Ancient Greek, Arabic, Chinese, Danish, French, German, Hebrew, Italian, Japanese, Norwegian, Portuguese, Russian, Spanish, Swahili, Swedish, and Yiddish.

3. In addition, the collection includes some 500 reel-to-reel supplementary tapes consisting of lectures, music, poetry readings, plays. For example, there are 60 tapes of speeches by prominent Chinese leaders and lectures by specialists on Chinese and Japanese, culture, art, history, religion, literature, and foreign relations. Notable items include speeches by Chiao Kuan-hua and Huang Hua at the United Nations, an interview with Yukio Mishima, Sayo Yotsukura's lectures on the "Japanese Way of Thinking," and lectures on Japanese Noh drama, Kabuki, and Zen Buddhism.

4 a. On-site listening equipment is available to University of Maryland students only.

  b. Researchers should telephone in advance to reserve the necessary equipment.

  c. No fees are charged for listening.

5. The center has a card catalog with author and subject access. A typewritten list is available for instructional materials.

A70 University of Maryland Libraries (College Park Campus)

1 a. *College Park, Maryland 20742*
   (301) 454-4737 (Reference, R. Lee Hornbake Library)
   (301) 454-5704 (Reference, McKeldin Library)
   (301) 454-3036 (Reference, Music Library)

  b. 8:00 A.M.–11:00 P.M.   Monday–Thursday
     8:00 A.M.–6:00 P.M.   Friday
     10:00 A.M.–5:00 P.M.   Saturday
     12:00 Noon–11:00 P.M.   Sunday
     Hours vary on holidays and during summer.

  c. Open to the public, but borrowing privileges are extended only to students, faculty, and staff of the university. Visiting scholars may apply at the Circulation Department, McKeldin Library (301/454–4974) for special borrowing privileges.

  d. H. Joanne Harrar, Director of Libraries

2. The University of Maryland library system includes the following libraries: Architecture, Art, Engineering & Physical Sciences, R. Lee Hornbake, McKeldin, Music, and Nonprint Media Services, and White Memorial (Chemistry). The College of Library and Information Services (CLIS) Library (A68) is administered as a separate facility. Total holdings include over 1,500,000 books and 19,000 periodical titles, which support educational and research programs at the university.

MC KELDIN LIBRARY
Historical Manuscripts and Archives Department, Fourth Floor
(301) 454-2318

Charlotte B. Brown, Acting Head

The McKeldin Library is the main library on campus, and its collection of books, periodicals, newspapers, and microforms, and various special collections are particularly useful to graduate students, faculty, and scholars, especially for disciplines within the humanities and social sciences.

The Historical Manuscripts and Archives Department contains organizational and family papers, personal papers, manuscripts, letters, photographs, and oral history collections, many of which relate to Maryland, and official records of the University of Maryland. The audio tape collection includes several hundred items consisting of oral history interviews, speeches, news reports, panel discussions, lectures, and readings by poets. Much of the oral history and other recorded materials focuses on the history of the University of Maryland. However, some of the materials will be of interest to researchers working in other areas. For example, a number of nationally known figures have spoken at University of Maryland commencements, including Luther H. Hodges, Edmund Muskie, and Sir Peter Ramsbotham. Other recordings include such materials as lectures by Katherine Anne Porter, an interview about the shooting of George Wallace in Laurel, Maryland, and black student rights (WMAL news report, May 1972), an interview with J.R. Salamanca (author), and recordings in the Bakery and Confectionary Workers Union Collection, Cigar Makers International Union Collection, and the College of Journalism Collection, comprising the Baltimore Sun Distinguished Lecture Series. A typed list of aural materials is available. Transcripts of some of the oral history interviews are available.

R. LEE HORNBAKE LIBRARY
Nonprint Media Services (NPMS)
R. Lee Hornbake Library Building, Fourth Floor
(301) 454-4723

8:00 A.M.-11:00 P.M.   Monday-Thursday
8:00 A.M.-5:00 P.M.   Friday
10:00 A.M.-5:00 P.M.   Saturday
12:00 Noon-11:00 P.M.   Sunday

Allan C. Rough, Head

The Nonprint Media Services collection contains commercially produced audio and video cassettes and 16 mm films, which support the educational, research, and recreational needs of the university. Areas of concentration include American history, women's studies, life sciences, and drama. Currently NPMS holds approximately 6,000 titles (8,000 individual items) of audio cassette tapes. All but 12 percent are commercially produced. Locally produced recordings include instructional materials, lectures and other campus events, and oral history interviews.

MUSIC LIBRARY
R. Lee Hornbake Library Building, Third Floor
(301) 454–3036

Neil Ratliff, Fine Arts Librarian/Head of Music Library
H. Fred Heutte, Head of Reference and Circulation

The Music Library contains materials pertaining to music and dance, and includes books, periodicals, music scores and parts, and sound recordings, as well as a number of significant special collections. The library's general collections of sound recordings include some 20,000 discs, consisting of classical music (all styles and periods), folk music, and jazz. Complete sets of manufacturers' recordings include New World Records, Composers Recordings, Inc., Louisville Philharmonic Orchestra recordings, Folkways Records, and all Donemus Recordings of Dutch music. The library has only a few audio tape recordings in its core collection. One notable set comprises 35 reels of recitals by Stanley Drucker, clarinetist.

Special Collections in Music (SCIM)
(301) 454–5611

Bruce Wilson, Curator of Special Collections

Special collections that contain sound recordings include the American Bandmasters Association Research Center Collection, the Music Educators National Conference Historical Center Collection, the International Clarinet Society Collection, and the National Association of College Wind and Percussion Instructors Research Center.

International Piano Archives at Maryland
(301) 454–6479

Morgan Cundiff, Head

The International Piano Archives at Maryland, administered as a unit of the Music Library, is one of the largest collections of piano recordings in the world. The collection, including many early recordings as well as many rare discs, contains 7,650 78-rpm discs, 6,300 33⅓-rpm discs, 1,100 audio tapes, 2,300 reproducing piano rolls, and a number of microfilms. Printed materials in the collection include 3,500 music scores, a number of periodicals, and commercial record manufacturer catalogs.

In 1979, supported by a grant from the Ford Foundation, the library embarked on a major project of microfilming and indexing the collection, using a system of high-resolution microphotography. The label information and matrix numbers etched into the recordings were photographed and the basic data entered into a computer. The result was an index providing access points by composer, performer, title, and label/issue and matrix numbers. Access to the Piano Archives is by appointment only.

In addition, some 20 lp recordings based on performances in the Piano Archives are available for purchase. Contact Morgan Cundiff for a flyer.

4 a. On-site listening equipment is available.

b. Appointments to examine special collections are required.

c. No fees are charged.

d. Photocopy facilities are available.

5. Each library maintains a card catalog with author/title and subject access.

NOTE: The University of Maryland American Folklife Center, which consists of oral history interviews, recollections regarding folklore, and folksongs, is located in the Archive of Folk Culture in the Library of Congress (B19). In addition, a University of Maryland collection of radio broadcasts of station WJSV/ WTOP for 1937–1957 (RG 200: National Archives Gift Collection) have been donated to the Special Archives Division of the National Archives and Records Service (B27).

A71 University of the District of Columbia (UDC)—Division of Learning Resources—Media Services Division—Library

1 a. *Building 41, Level 1*
4200 Connecticut Avenue, N.W.
Washington, D.C. 20008
(202) 282–7999

b. 8:00 A.M.–9:00 P.M.   Monday–Thursday
8:00 A.M.–6:00 P.M.   Friday
9:00 A.M.–1:00 P.M.   Saturday

c. Open to the public for use within the library. Only UDC faculty may borrow audio materials.

d. Audrey Jones, Supervisor of Utilization and Distribution
Elizabeth Thompson, Media Specialist

2–3. A general collection used primarily to support the university's curriculum. There are 3,269 commercial disc recordings of mostly music consisting of classical music of all periods, blues, and jazz. Among these discs is the *Recorded Anthology of American Music* series funded by the Rockefeller Foundation and respresenting the heritage of American music, and a small collection of spoken arts discs, consisting mostly of plays.

The collection also includes 360 reel-to-reel and an unspecified number of cassette tapes consisting mostly of audio dictorial instructional materials for such disciplines as English, mathematics, chemistry, communications skill, and computers and data processing. Also worth noting are a number of tape recordings of various meetings and events at UDC.

4 a. An extensive listening facility is available for use by library patrons.

b. No reservation requirements.

c. No fees charged.

d. Photoduplication facility is available. A recording duplication facility is available for students and faculty of UDC. Other persons need to obtain special permission for this service.

5. The library has card catalogs arranged by author/title and subject. There is a separate card catalog for audio materials. Not all audio materials have, however, been cataloged. Disc recordings are shelved according to composers represented. The library also has a small collection of printed reference works for audiovisual materials. A descriptive brochure of the library's services is available free upon request.

Virginia Theological Seminary—Bishop Payne Library   **See entry E7**

A72 Voice of America (VOA) (U.S. Information Agency)—Music and Tape Libraries

1 a. *Music Library*
HHS-North Building, Room G-510A
330 Independence Avenue, S.W.
Washington, D.C. 20547
(202) 755-4799

Tape Library
HHS-North Building, Room 2231
(202) 755-4228

b. Music Library:
7:30 A.M.–5:30 P.M.   Monday–Friday
9:00 A.M.–3:00 P.M.   Saturday, Sunday, holidays
Tape Library:
7:00 A.M.–9:00 P.M.   Monday–Friday
9:00 A.M.–3:00 P.M.   Saturday, Sunday, holidays

c. Individuals must contact the Public Information Office of VOA stating specific requests. A 1948 law prohibits domestic dissemination, but materials are available for listening and research.

d. Michael Gray, Chief, Tape and Music Libraries
Gene Miller, Collection Manager

2. The Voice of America is the official international radio broadcasting service of the United States government, operating as part of the United States Information Agency. The VOA first went on the air in February 1942 as the radio component of the United States Office of War Information. After 1945 it became part of the Department of State, and in 1953 it was one of the elements making up the newly created United States Information Agency. The Music and Tape Libraries are resources for VOA programmers in 42 different language services broadcasting 970 hours per week. About twelve percent of that time is music, and 50 percent news or news-related.

3. The Music Library has about 50,000 commercial records, half of which are 45-rpm discs and half are lps divided into accession series for classical music, pop and rock music, jazz, ethnic and folk music, and recorded Americana. In addition to conventional musical records, the library has a collection of theme and background production music, several sets of sound effects recordings, and tapes of live jazz festivals.

The Tape Library, consisting, in part, of approximately 75,000 audio reel-to-reel and cassette tapes, is basically a working collection for the use of the broadcasters and programmers in the English and foreign language departments at VOA. Each day the library receives a large number of off-the-air tapes of noncommercial and network news and public information programs, such as, "All Things Considered," "The Today Show," "MacNeil/Lehrer Report," "WGMS at Noon." These tapes are recorded by accession numbers in the daily log book and are generally held for a period of one to three months. Important segments are taken from these recordings and maintained in a permanent archive collection, which was established in 1942.

The collection includes presidential speeches and news conferences, news items concerning senators, major diplomats, and other prominent persons, highlights of all space program events since the early 1960s, and many other important current events. Tapes that are made on-site by the staff of VOA and maintained in the library include a number of 10-minute special reports with "actualities" collected for potential use in broadcasts for programs, such as "Classical Calendar," "People in the News," "Working America," "Crime and Law Enforcement," "New Horizons in Science," "Your Health," and special features on American holidays when they occur. These programs are intended to reflect the life style of American society. There are also longer programs, which follow a prescribed format. Examples are "Studio One" which consist of half-hour reviews and excerpts of currently playing American theatrical productions, "Supreme Court," "American Writing Today," and a series of programs on American literature and history for non-native English speakers.

A number of recordings of music broadcasts and series have been donated to the Library of Congress (A41) and the National Archives and Records Service (B27).

4 a. On-site listening equipment is available.

b. Reservations are required.

c. Fees are not charged to listen to recordings.

d. Duplicate copies of tapes can be made if arranged in advance and if permitted by law or contractual agreement.

5. In the Music Library recordings are indexed through lists for each accession series and indexes of performers and performing groups. Older recordings are indexed by composer, title, and performer. Additional ready reference folders are maintained for Christmas music, broadway show recordings, film soundtracks, and other special-interest categories. Descriptive control of the tape library is accomplished through a system of log books and catalog cards, including daily sheets of Recordings Received in Program Documentation Unit (January 1962 to December 1977), recording log books (arranged alphabetically by name of speaker and chronologically thereunder for each letter of the alphabet), personality log books (arranged alphabetically by name of person), and index cards (arranged alphabetically by recurring programs not indexed in the log books).

NOTE: The U.S. Advisory Commission on Public Diplomacy, whose mission is to conduct a continuing overview of the activities of the USIA and in particular the VOA, has issued its *1983 Report*. The commission has examined VOA media and programs, such as Radio Marti, a broadcasting service to Cuba. For additional information, contact G. Richard Monsen, Staff Director at the commission (202/485–2457). The mailing address is United States Advisory Commission on Public Diplomacy, Room 600, 301 4th Street, S.W., Washington, D.C. 20547.

Washington Bible College—Oyer Memorial Library   See entry E8

Wesley Theological Seminary Library   See entry E10

A73 The White House—Record Library

1 a. *1600 Pennsylvania Avenue, N.W.*
Washington, D.C.
(202) 456–2550

c. The library is not open to the public.

2. The White House Record Library was inaugurated in 1973 during the Nixon administration. At that time, a commission was appointed to establish the collection. Its members included Willis Conover (Chairman); Paul Ackerman (country, folk, and gospel music); Johnny Mercer (popular music); Irving Kolodin (classical music); and Helen Roach (spoken word). The Record Industry Association of America presented the original collection, which consisted of 2,000 commercial lp discs to the White House.

In 1979 a new commission was appointed by the Carter administration. Its members included John Hammond (Chairman); David Hall (classical music); Bob Blumenthal (contemporary popular and Latin music); Ed Bland (rhythm-and-blues, blues, and Black gospel music); Frances Preston (country, folk, and White gospel music); John Lewis (jazz); and Paul Kresh (spoken word). At that time, 893 additional discs were added to the collection.

3. The collection represents a basic but well-defined cross-section of both music and spoken word recordings. Included are masterpieces of classical music, with an emphasis on well known performers. The collection also includes contemporary popular music, such as musicals, Latin music, rhythm and blues, Black gospel, country and folk, the latter including Anglo-American, Black, American Indian, and White gospel music. Spoken word recordings include documentaries, speeches, lectures, interviews, poetry, prose, plays, and humor.

A duplicate set of these recordings is located in the John F. Kennedy Center for the Performing Arts Library (A38) where the public has access to them.

5. The recordings are listed in *The White House Record Library,* 2 vols. (White House Historical Association, 1973, 1980).

A74 Wilkes & Artists, Chartered—Law Library

1 a. *1666 K Street, N.W.*
Washington, D.C. 20006
(202) 457–7872

b. 9:00 A.M.–5:30 P.M.   Monday–Friday

c. The library is open to qualified researchers and students of law. Sound recordings may be borrowed, but with special permission only. Interlibrary loan is available to other law libraries.

d. David W. Lang, Head Librarian

2. Wilkes & Artists is a collective organization for attorneys practicing in the District of Columbia and is organized to provide service to on-going litigation of Wilkes & Artists.

3–4. Library holdings include print materials and 33 audio cassette recordings focusing on: real estate financing, zoning law, commercial law, corporate law, and bankruptcy. Each tape features a well-known attorney or teacher. The majority of the tapes are produced by Condyne Law Tapes and span the period from 1972 to the present. Wilkes & Artists receive the recordings on a subscription basis as part of the firm's continual education program for its lawyers. The tapes include Daniel R. Mandelker lecturing on zoning laws, and Don Agustine and Peter M. Fass lecturing on partnership agreements, real estate taxes, and limited partnerships in real estate (operations and ventures).

4 a. On-site listening equipment is available.

   b. Prior appointment is required.

   c. No fees are charged to listen to sound recordings.

   d. A photoduplication facility is available.

5.   An in-house list citing the cassette recordings alphabetically by title is available.

B Archives and Manuscript Repositories

Introductory Note

The depositories discussed in this section include those formally designated as *Archives,* and those whose audio holdings focus on archival materials and/or oral histories. The largest such holdings in the Washington, D.C., area are in the National Archives and Records Service (B27) and in the Library of Congress (B19), followed in order of size by the National Public Radio Library (B33) and the Folklife Program Archive of the Smithsonian Institution (B43).

The leading source for identifying archival and manuscript collections is the *Directory of Archives and Manuscript Repositories in the United States* (National Archives and Records Service, 1978), which includes descriptions of holdings and is organized geographically. The primary reference work for the description of oral history collections (as well as manuscripts and papers) is the annual *National Union Catalog of Manuscript Collections* (Library of Congress, 1959-). Readers interested in the use of archival records in audio form will find further information in the following discussion of oral history and preservation of sound recordings.

ORAL HISTORY*.—An understanding of history has always required the piecing together of different kinds of evidence and filling in gaps. Traditionally, this evidence has been in the forms of written documentation and artifacts. In the last thirty-five years there has been a gradual increase in the recognition of oral history as an additional tool for historical understanding. As in preliterate societies of both ancient and contemporary times, the storyteller of a community can relate important information, which is completely unlike written records and which, but for the oral historian and his tape recorder, would otherwise be lost.

Since the end of the nineteenth century, the focus of historical research has gradually included the social as well as the political, the local as well as the international, and the common person as well as the elite. In this context, oral history has become "the bread and butter of the twentieth century historian" (according to Donald Ritchie of the Senate Historical Office) and has also become a valuable resource for anthropologists, historical preservationists, librarians, archivists, folklorists, and journalists.

---

*This section on oral history was prepared by Trudi W. Olivetti.

England was the first country to conduct first-hand interviews in a systematic way; the government's work for the 1801 census resulted in the compilation of the so-called Blue Books, a source for the writings of Marx and Engels, among others. In the United States, one of the first to use oral history methodology to gather information was Hubert H. Bancroft, who collected interviews from early Californians in the 1860s. There were other projects in the late nineteenth and early twentieth centuries, including the collection of "life-story interviews" for the Federal Writers Project of the 1930s, under the auspices of the Works Progress Administration.

The first formal American oral history project, which is still on-going, is that begun by the distinguished historian, Allan Nevins in 1948 at Columbia University in New York City. Other major centers exist at the University of California in Berkeley and Los Angeles, and in Texas and Kentucky. The original approach of the Columbia project was to interview the nation's most powerful and influential figures. During the 1960s the scope was expanded to cover the ordinary citizen and to record native American history, black American history, women's issues, and other such topics. Also during the 1960s, the Oral History Association was founded, with a membership that has grown to more than 1,500 institutions and individuals.

Among the growing list of reference materials on oral history are national and regional directories, conference proceedings, general histories and "how to" manuals, and catalogs or guides to specific collections and programs. *Oral History Collections*, edited by Alan Meckler and Ruth McMullin and published by Bowker in 1975, was the first national directory on the subject and, although some information was incorrect or soon outdated, its uniqueness made it an important tool. The more recent *Directory of Oral History Programs in the United States*, published in 1982 by Microfilming Corp. of America, was prepared with the collaboration of the Oral History Association. As valuable as these directories are, the rapid growth of oral history projects throughout the country has increased the need for more local guides to specific programs and regional collections.

In recognition of that need, this *Guide* includes the most comprehensive list to date of oral history programs and collections in the Washington area. Researchers will find relevant material in every section of the *Guide*, but primarily in section B. For a complete listing of entries that describe oral history materials, refer to "Oral History" in the Subject Index. Under Libraries (section A) are public library projects covering local history for each community or for the state. Libraries at universities and at professional associations have more specialized programs, covering such topics as black Americans, the history of broadcasting, and the history of women's suffrage. Universities and colleges in the area (section K) offer programs on oral history methodology and also support several on-going projects. Important collections include the Federal Theatre Project held at George Mason University (A26) and the Washingtoniana project begun in 1982 at the Martin Luther King, Jr., Memorial Library (A42).

In addition to the clearly designated oral history collections found under sections A (Libraries) and B (Archives), this *Guide* includes archival and other unique material that can be regarded as historical documents in an oral form. For example, the researcher will find speeches by a variety of people gathered from National Press Club (B32) functions over the years, or the address given by Pope John Paul II at Trinity College (A66) during his 1979 visit to the United States.

What makes the Washington area particularly rich in oral history resources is the presence of the Library of Congress, the National Archives and Records Service, the Smithsonian Institution, and the other offices and agencies of the federal government. All branches of the military have their own historical offices, which conduct various types of oral history projects (B5, B21, B36, and B37). Some government agencies have hired historians as consultants to conduct oral history, among them the National Park Service (B31), and the Army Corps of Engineers (B6). The Smithsonian Insti-

tution alone has on-going projects covering American artists, black American culture, the history of computers, District of Columbia history, the history of the Smithsonian itself, and many other topics. The National Archives and Records Service (B27) has enormous quantities of oral material representing other federal agencies. The Library of Congress (A41) has microform holdings of transcripts of oral history tapes from all over the country, as well as its own oral history collections in several of its divisions.

Coordinating this effort in the Washington area are such organizations as the Society for History in the Federal Government (B44) and OHMAR (Oral History Mid-Atlantic Region) (M50), the local branch of the Oral History Association. It was founded in 1976 and is now the largest and most active of regional groups.

It is not surprising that Washington is fast becoming another major center for oral history, because of the number and variety of its programs and collections. An example of almost any type of project being conducted elsewhere in the country can be found here. Washington, D.C. is truly a microcosm of the nation's oral history activity.

PRESERVATION OF SOUND RECORDINGS.—The preservation of sound recordings is of vital concern to institutions that hold old and rare recordings. In 1959, the Library of Congress published one of the first substantial studies, *Preservation and Storage of Sound Recordings: A Study Supported by a Grant from the Rockefeller Foundation.* The Library of Congress continues to base its handling procedures on the guidelines of this study. The Library of Congress is also experimenting with new procedures based on recent developments in technology. For example, SONY Video Communications Products Company in Lanham, Maryland, has been contracted to produce some 50 digital compact audio discs of 2 chamber music concerts scheduled for presentation in the Coolidge Auditorium at the Library of Congress. Concerning this program, see "The Library of Congress Optical Disc Pilot Program," in *Library of Congress Information Bulletin,* vol. 42, no. 37 (September 12, 1983), pp. 312–316. In addition, the National Preservation Program Office of the Library of Congress has available for viewing a 51-minute video tape presentation on preservation. Contact the Public Services Coordinator of the Motion Picture, Broadcasting and Recorded Sound Division, Library of Congress, Washington, D.C. 20540.

A research project concerning the care and handling of magnetic audio tape was completed in 1982 by the Tape Head Interface Committee of the National Aeronautics and Space Administration (L6). The committee explored the effects of tape handling and storage and recommended procedures to avoid contamination and accidental erasure of tape, as well as advice on protection, transport, and cleaning techniques. This study is available as NASA Reference Publication 1075, *Magnetic Tape Recording for the Eighties* (April 1982).

Another study underway since 1981 is under the auspices of the Polymer Science and Standards Division of the National Bureau of Standards through a five-year contract from the National Archives and Records Service. The project is titled "Prediction of the Long Term Stability of Poly-Based Recording Media (NBSIR 82-2530)" and is being carried on by Daniel W. Brown, Robert E. Lowry, and Leslie E. Smith. It focuses on the aging characteristics of audio-polyester magnetic tape. For more information, contact Alan Calmes at the National Archives (202/523–3159).

Finally, the Motion Picture, Broadcasting and Recorded Sound Division of the Library of Congress is preparing a bibliography of some 7,000–8,000 books and articles that focus on non-print preservation.

**B1   Alexandria Archaeological Research Center (City of Alexandria—
Department of Historic Resources)**

1 a. *New Torpedo Factory Arts Center*
   105 North Union Street
   Alexandria, Virginia 22314
   (703) 838–4399

   Mail:
   Box 178
   Alexandria, Virginia 22314

   b. 9:00 A.M.–5:00 P.M.   Tuesday–Saturday

   c. Prior appointment is required.

   d. Pamela J. Cressey, Director

2–3. The Alexandria Archaeological Research Center is engaged in a number of
programs relating to historic Alexandria, including historic preservation, archives,
tours, and education programs. The center also has an on-going oral history program.
A number of recorded interviews have been conducted and are available at the center
for on-site use.

4 a. On-site listening facilities are not available.

5. A number of publications are available from the center.

**B2   American Federation of Labor and Congress of Industrial
Organizations (AFL-CIO)—George Meany Center for Labor Studies**

1 a. *10,000 New Hampshire Avenue*
   Silver Spring, Maryland 20903
   (301) 431–6400

   b. 9:00 A.M.–4:30 P.M.   Monday–Friday

   c. Open to researchers by prior appointment.

   d. Fred K. Hoehler, Director
   Christine Lawson, Secretary/Oral History Project Coordinator

2–3. The AFL-CIO is a federation of national unions, state federations, and affiliated
local unions. The George Meany Center for Labor Studies serves as an educational
center where seminars, lectures, and workshops are provided for union officers and
staff throughout the country. In 1978–1980, through a grant from the AFL-CIO and
the National Endowment for the Humanities (L11), the center conducted an oral
history project whereby interviews with significant labor leaders were undertaken to
preserve the history and merger of the AFL-CIO in 1955. Some 54 interviews, each
averaging two hours in length, were completed and recorded on audio cassettes. Most
of the recordings have been transcribed. Some of the individuals interviewed include
Jack Barbash, Andrew Biemiller, Irving Brown, Jack Conway, Evelyn Dubrow, Douglas Fraser, Arthur Goldberg, Tom Harris, John Hurling, Hilda Julbe, David Mc-

Donald, Lee Minton, Abe Raskin, Stanley Ruttenberg, William Schnitzler, George Weaver, Albert Woll, and Albert Zack. The oral history project is not on-going. Contact the center during the hours of 9:00 A.M. and 4:30 P.M. for additional information.

4 a-b. Contact the center for information regarding listening facilities.

    c. Fees are not charged.

    d. A photocopy facility is available.

5. The oral history collection is not cataloged. Audio cassettes are shelved alphabetically by interviewee. AFL-CIO publications include *American Federalist* (monthly) and *Free Trade Union News* (monthly).

B3   Archives of American Art (Smithsonian Institution)

1 a. *National Museum of American Art*
     National Portrait Gallery Building
     8th and F Streets, N.W.
     Washington, D.C. 20560
     (202) 357–2781

    b. 10:00 A.M.–5:00 P.M.   Monday–Friday

    c. The archives are open to researchers but access to some materials is restricted.

    d. Garnett McCoy, Senior Curator
       Catherine M. Keen, Archives Technician, Oral History Collection

2. The Archives of American Art, founded in 1954, holds the world's largest collection of documentary material on the history of the visual arts in the United States from the eighteenth century to the present. Present archival holdings exceed 8 million items and include letters, sketchbooks, diaries, clippings, catalogs, and other original records of artists, art historians, dealers, collectors, and American art institutions. A bureau of the Smithsonian since 1970, the archives maintains a number of regional research and collecting centers throughout the country.

3. The oral history program of the Archives of American Art was begun in 1958 when interviews with Charles Burchfield, Edward Hopper, Paul Manship, and Charles Sheeler were taped. Since then, this on-going project has produced well over 2,000 interviews with artists and others associated with the field. Other individuals represented in the collection include Harry N. Abrams, Leonard Baskin, John Canaday, Roy Lichtenstein, Robert Rauschenberg, and Ben Shahn.

    Persons involved in the oral history program have also initiated special projects that focus on specific movements and artists in a specific geographic area. In the 1960s over 400 interviews were conducted with artists participating in the Works Progress Administration, one of the largest collections of primary documentation of this period. Other special projects include holdings on San Francisco Bay Area Art, artists in San Francisco, and a collection of interviews with people associated with Mark Rothko.

    Of 1,500 tapes (both cassette and reel-to-reel), some 1,300 have been transcribed and are available to researchers. A number of interviews have access restrictions, requiring written permission from interviewee or from his/her estate. Information on restrictions can be obtained from the Archives of American Art. Although transcripts

are not available in the Washington, D.C., area, researchers who have made appointments may consult transcripts in the archives' regional offices at 41 East 65th Street, New York, New York 10021; 87 Mount Vernon Street, Boston, Massachusetts 02108; 5200 Woodward Avenue, Detroit, Michigan 48202; and M.H. de Young Memorial Museum, San Francisco, California 94118.

4 a. There are listening facilities but normally only transcripts can be made available to researchers.

b. Appointments must be made to use the collection.

c. Fees are not charged.

d. Photoreproduction of transcripts is not permitted.

5. There is a card catalog for the oral history tapes arranged by person interviewed, with some subject access.

The Archives of American Art publishes a quarterly *Journal,* which contains articles based on its collections and a descriptive listing of recent acquisitions. Articles written on the oral history program have included abstracts of selected interviews.

B4 Armenian Assembly of America

1 a. *1420 N Street, N.W., Suite 101*
Washington, D.C. 20005
(202) 332–3434

b. 9:00 A.M.–5:00 P.M.   Monday–Friday

c. Open to qualified researchers by appointment.

d. Ross Vartian, Executive Director

2–3. The Armenian Assembly has custody of the Armenian Assembly Oral History Project, which consists of 600 interviews with Elder Armenian-Americans who fled Turkey during the Armenian genocide of 1915–1923. There are approximately 1,300 listening hours of tapes. Some 200 interviews have been translated and transcribed.

5. A computer index of the collection is being assembled.

B5 Army Center of Military History (CMH) (Army Department)

1 a. *200 Massachusetts Avenue, N.W., Room 4124C*
Washington, D.C. 20314
(202) 272–0291

b. 8:00 A.M.–4:30 P.M.   Monday–Friday

c. U.S. citizens may examine unclassified documents without prior permission. Unofficial researchers must have security clearance to examine classified documents.

d. Brig. Gen. Douglas Kinnard, Chief of Military History
David F. Trask, Chief Historian (202/272–0293)
Brooks Kleber, Assistant Chief (202/272–0293)

2. The Army Center of Military History advises and coordinates services on historical matters through its Army Historical Program. Programs include the preparation and publication of histories for and about the Department of the Army. All of the center's research is produced in-house. The center does not maintain any archival collection of military records; these are held at the National Archives and Records Service (B27).

3. Although the center does not have an oral history program, oral history recordings are occasionally produced in the course of research conducted on distinguished military personnel. Contact Brooks Kleber for information on such research. The center maintains an oral history program at its U.S. Army Military History Institute, Carlisle Barracks, Pennsylvania 17013. Additional oral history material relating to the Army Department is included in the Oral History Program of the Office of Air Force History (B37), and RG 335 in the Special Archives Division of the National Archives and Records Service (B27).

4 a. On-site listening equipment is not available.

5. A catalog, *Publications of the U.S. Army Center of Military History,* can be obtained free upon request.

B6   Army Corps of Engineers (Army Department)—Historical Division

1 a. *Historical Division, DAEN–ASH*
Office of the Chief of Engineers
Kingman Building
Fort Belvoir, Virginia 22060
(703) 355–2543

b. 8:00 A.M.–4:30 P.M.   Monday–Friday

c. The Historical Division collections are available for use by scholars. Individuals should telephone or write in advance to schedule a visit.

d. John T. Greeenwood, Chief
Paul J. Walker, Historian

2–3. The U.S. Army Corps of Engineers Oral History Collection contains more than 90 life-history and special subject interviews exceeding 11,000 pages in length. Most of the interviews have been recorded on cassette tape. The interviewees are retired Corps officers and civilian employees and officers' wives, as well as a limited number of active duty officers and civilians. They include former Chiefs of Engineer, officers who served as Corps District and Division commanders and as managers of major Corps construction projects, and civilian heads of major headquarters elements. Examples of distinguished interviewees include Gen. Bruce C. Clarke, Lt. Gen. Emerson C. Itschner, Lt. Gen. Arthur G. Trudeau, Lt. Gen. Walter K. Wilson, Jr., Maj. Gen. Hugh J. Casey, Maj. Gen. Claude H. Chorpening, Maj. Gen. Roscoe C. Crawford, Maj. Gen. Kenner F. Hertford, Maj. Gen. Charles G. Holle, Maj. Gen. Charles I. McGinnis, Maj. Gen. William E. Potter, Brig. Gen. Miles M. Dawson, Brig. Gen. Roy T. Dodge, Brig. Gen. William M. Glasgow, Jr., Brig. Gen. William C. Hall, Brig. Gen. Herbert D. Vogel, Brig. Gen. Orville T. Walsh, Brig. Gen. William W. Wanamaker, and Brig. Gen. Theron D. Weaver.

Topics covered include combat engineering and military construction for all twentieth century wars; peacetime overseas military construction; civil works construction, including rivers and harbors, flood control, and disaster relief; atomic bomb, missile,

and space construction programs; the role of the Corps of Engineers in New Deal relief; the Panama Canal; D.C. government; and West Point education.

4 a. Contact the Historical Division for information on the availability of sound recording equipment. In most cases, researchers will be provided with transcripts.

b. Prior appointment is recommended.

c. No fees are charged.

d. Photoduplication facility is available.

5. A catalog of oral history materials is being compiled. In addition to the already published *Engineer Memoirs: Lieutenant General Frederick J. Clarke; Engineer Memoirs: Major General William E. Potter*; and *Engineer Profiles: The District Engineer: Colonel William W. Badger,* several interviews will be published as part of these series.

B7 Association of Former Members of Congress (FMC)

1 a. *1733 Connecticut Avenue, N.W.*
Washington, D.C. 20009
(202) 332–3532

b. 9:00 A.M.–5:00 P.M.   Monday–Friday

c. Open to the public.

d. Senator Frank E. Moss
John S. Managan, President

2. The Association of Former Members of Congress has nearly 600 members and is involved in a number of educational, research, and social programs, and various grant and legislative projects. Former members of Congress lecture at various colleges and universities.

3. One of the most interesting and valuable projects undertaken by the association has been the oral history program of former congressmen. In 1982, approximately 100 oral history cassette and reel-to-reel tapes prepared by the FMC were presented to the Motion Picture, Broadcasting and Recorded Sound Division of the Library of Congress (A41). (See the *Congressional Record—House* (May 17, 1982) for the official announcement of this gift and the *Library of Congress Information Bulletin* 41 (March 19, 1982) for additional information and background on the gift.)

Individuals may access the tapes by using a finding aid filed under the title, "Former Members of Congress," in the subject vertical file in the division. Transcripts of the tapes have been deposited in the Manuscript Division of the Library of Congress (B20) and are also available on microfiche by the New York Times Microfilming Corporation.

5. The FMC publishes *Congressional Alumni News* (quarterly).

B8 Broadcast Pioneers Library (BPL)

1 a. *1771 N Street, N.W.*
Washington, D.C. 20036
(202) 223–0088

b. 9:00 A.M.–5:00 P.M. Monday–Friday

c. The library is open to the public by appointment. Researchers may spend as much time as necessary to complete projects. Telephone queries and reference questions received by mail can be handled on a limited basis, but there is a charge for research. Because the collection is unique, materials can only be used in-house.

d. Catharine Heinz, Director

2. The Broadcast Pioneers Library, established in 1971, is an archive of sources on the history of broadcasting as well as a reference facility that serves the broadcasting industry and the public. The library is dedicated to preserving and maintaining materials not available elsewhere.

BPL holdings include 11,450 books and pamphlets, 1,830 radio and TV scripts, some 277 periodical titles on broadcasting and related fields, and a number of private radio and television program collectors' catalogs and newsletters. There are 20,000 photographs covering every aspect of broadcasting and a large collection of Broadcast Pioneers' papers and scrapbooks. Audio holdings number 3,145 and include 670 oral history interviews.

3. Included among the papers that researchers should be aware of are: the Lionel F. Baxter papers, including an audio tape of a testimonial dinner (1941) honoring George Washington Carver; and various recordings included in the papers of Don Hopkins, Peter H. Bontsema, and Irene Beasley, among others. The library also has the papers of Joseph E. Baudino, Carl J. Burkland, Phillips Carlin, Robert Lewis Coe, Donald Dwight Davis, James M. Gaines, Mrs. Clyde M. Hunt, Edward M. Kirby, Robert E. Lee, John H. Norton, Jr., Charles H. Pearson, Rod Phillips, Elmo Neale Pickerill, John T. Schilling, and Gilson VanderVeer Willets. Of special interest are the Alfred N. Goldsmith papers, which contain experimental disc recordings of the first international broadcasts of March 14, 1925, and January 1926.

The library holds a collection of CBS materials dating from about 1937 to 1943. Included in it are the *Weekly Digest of Radio Opinion* (1942) with commentators Frank Blair, Quincy Howe, and Eric Sevareid, and *Overnight Service* (1942–1943), which provide digests of broadcasts by Hilmar Robert Baukhage, Morgan Beatty, Earl Browder, Frazier Hunt, Fulton Lewis, Jr., and Lisa Sergio.

The oral history collection includes interviews with prominent women broadcasters. Among them are Kathryn F. Broman, Margaret Mary Kearney, Agnes Law, Edythe Meserand, Mary Tyler Moore, Minnie Pearl, Ruth Crane Schaefer, and Betty White. Examples of other individuals represented in the collection include Robert F. Bartley, Federal Communications Commissioner (1966); Thomas H. Belviso, copyright expert and pioneer member of the NBC music department; Edgar Bergen; Ray Perkins, old time entertainer; Alfred W. Saunders, designer engineer for NBC; and Lowell Thomas.

4 a. Some on-site listening equipment is available.

b. Appointment is required.

c. Duplication of audio tapes is not allowed.

5. Of great value to scholars is the BPL referral service to other public and private collections of broadcast materials. The library's access to its own collections varies. The Oral History Project has its own card file arranged by interviewee and interviewer for accessions after 1973. The library's *Audiotapes and Cassettes in the Broadcast Pioneers Library: A Preliminary Catalog* (1973) indexes additional oral histories, speeches, and a small number of radio programs. BPL staff is currently compiling a selective guide to radio and television programming collections across the country. A number

of papers, oral history materials, and other projects are cited in the Library of Congress *National Union Catalog of Manuscript Collections* (see especially the 1978 issue in which 24 collections are described).

B9 Census Bureau (Commerce Department)—Census History Staff

1 a. *Building 3, Room 1676*
Bureau of the Census
Suitland and Silverhill Roads
Suitland, Maryland 20746
(301) 763-7936

Mail:
DUSU–Bureau of the Census
Washington, D.C. 20233

b. 7:30 A.M.–4:00 P.M.   Monday–Friday

c. Open to the public for reference inquiries. Contact the office by mail or telephone for further information.

d. Frederick G. Bohme, Chief, Census History Staff

2. The Census History Staff is establishing an oral history program. Its pilot project includes eight interviews with retired and active officials of the Census Bureau. Contact Dr. Bohme for information on the current status of the program.

NOTE: Recordings in the records of the Bureau of the Census for 1940 (RG 29) are held in the Special Archives Division of the National Archives and Records Service (B27).

4 a. On-site listening equipment is not available.

B10 Columbia Historical Society Library

1 a. *1307 New Hampshire Avenue, N.W.*
Washington, D.C. 20036
(202) 785-2068

b. 10:00 A.M.–4:00 P.M.   Wednesday, Friday, Saturday

c. Open to scholars for on-site use. Individuals are asked to telephone or write in advance for an appointment to visit the library.

d. Perry Gerard Fisher, Executive Director
Elizabeth J. Miller, Curator

2. The Columbia Historical Society is dedicated to collecting information on the history of the District of Columbia. The library contains over 15,000 books and some 60,000 prints, negatives, and other materials including sound recordings. The subjects emphasized in the library's holdings include biography, geography, and topography.

3. Currently, the library has 20 reel-to-reel tape recordings, which focus on local history. Most of the tapes are lectures and programs of nnual conventions, which are held during February. The tapes span the period 1967–1975. Representative examples of what individuals will find in the audio collection includes *Problems in Writing the History of D.C.* (Constance Green, speaker, historian) and *Outdoor Sculpture in Washington* (James Goode).

4 a. On-site listening equipment is available.

b. Telephone or write for an appointment.

c. Contact library regarding any fees charged.

5. Audio tapes are indexed in a card catalog having subject and speaker access. The society publishes a number of materials including the *Reports of the Chronicler of the Columbia Historical Society of Washington, D.C., 1951–1961* (1976).

B11 Democratic National Committee (DNC)—Press Office

1 a. *1625 Massachusetts Avenue, N.W.*
Washington, D.C. 20036
(202) 797–6575, ext. 261
(202) 797–5900

b. 9:00 A.M.–5:00 P.M.   Monday–Friday

c. Open to researchers by appointment.

d. Terry Michael, Deputy Director of Communications

2. The Democratic National Committee maintains a press office, which is responsible, in part, for recording a number of conventions and other activities relating to the Democratic Party. The creation of the sound recording collection consists of a two-fold process. First, the DNC produces the tapes and enters information on them in the DNC's book list, *Audio and Video Material Stored at the National Archives,* which is held in the Press Office. Much of the information in this catalog is organized according to tape number, the date tape was produced, and subject and event. Second, the tapes are then forwarded to the National Archives and Records Service (B27), where they are maintained as a permanent collection. To obtain special permission to listen to the tapes in the collection, or to obtain more specific information concerning the collection, individuals must first telephone or write to the Press Office. Once permission to use the collection has been obtained, individuals can then visit the Office of Presidential Libraries of the National Archives and Records Service (B27) where access to the collection can be granted in accordance with its regulations.

3. The collection consists of 1,200 reel-to-reel and cassette tapes dating to 1956 and includes DNC convention activities and speeches, radio spots and programs, fund raising dinner speeches, news conferences, addresses to the nation, state chairmans' meetings, regional conferences, TV programs including "Face The Nation (CBS)" and "Issues and Answers (ABC)," oral history interviews, Young Democrats Conferences, and national committee meetings. In short, the collection is quite extensive and varied. The tapes focus on such topics as foreign policy, domestic policy on crime, economics, health, safety, agriculture, youth, education, campaigns, Peace Corps, civil rights, business, religion, and science. Examples of recordings include: "Sen.

Humphrey Speaks at National Press Club about the Soviet Invasion of Hungary" (December 20, 1956; box 5, no. 1); "Vice-Pres. Humphrey Speaks at Goddard Memorial Awards Dinner at Sheraton Park Hotel, Washington, D.C." (March 16, 1966; box 5, no. 12); "Lyndon Baines Johnson Speaks to the Nation after Meeting with Negro Leaders at White House following Dr. Martin Luther King's Death" (April 5, 1968; LBJ 115); "Lyndon Baines Johnson Signing Auto Insurance Study Bill" (May 22, 1968; LBJ 122); "General William Westmoreland's Remarks following Swearing-in as Army Chief of Staff" (July 3, 1968; no. 227); "Governor Ronald Reagan: News Conference" (February 27, 1968; REP 30); "Harold Stassen: News Conference" (July 15, 1968; REP 38); "Address by Sen. Edmund S. Muskie to the Consumer Federation on Air Pollution, Sheraton Park Hotel" (June 30, 1969; Misc. no. 98); "Interview with Senator Alan Cranston, California, Interviewed by Joe Brady" (August 12, 1969; Misc. no. 103); "Senator Walter F. Mondale, Minnesota: A Guest on CBS Capitol Cloakroom" (August 13, 1969; Misc. no. 108); and "Interview with Senator Thomas McIntyre, New Hampshire, Recorded in the Senator's Office" (August 8, 1969; Misc. no. 109).

4 a.   Sound recording facilities are located in the National Archives and Records Service (B27) where the tapes are housed.

5.   Bibliographic aids are described in category 2 above.

B12   Dominican House of Studies—Archives

1 a.   *487 Michigan Avenue, N.E.*
Washington, D.C. 20017
(202) 529–5300

b.   10:00 A.M.–4:00 P.M.   Monday–Friday

c.   Open by appointment.

d.   Father Adrian Wade, Archivist

2–3.   General holdings in the archives consist of records of the Dominican Order in the United States, including letters, diaries, unpublished manuscripts, memoirs, maps, charts, and photographs. The archives also has a small number of oral history interviews.

4 a.   On-site listening equipment is not available.

B13   Education Department—Office of Educational Research and Improvement

1 a.   *Office of the Assistant Secretary*
Department of Education
Brown Building, Room 717
19th and M Streets, N.W.
Washington, D.C. 20208
(202) 254–6458

b.   8:30 A.M.–4:15 P.M.   Monday–Friday

c. Open to researchers.

d. Donald J. Senese, Assistant Secretary
Stephen J. Sniegoski, Historian

2. The Department of Education conducted an oral history project during 1971–1975 and 1980–1981. Interviews were conducted with various past officials of the agency. Interviews are in cassette format and most of them have been transcribed.

3. Interviewees include John Ward Studebaker, Commissioner of Education from 1934–1948; Gertrude Broderick; John Gordon Studebaker, son of the elder Studebaker and Far West Regional Director of an educational magazine; Francis Keppel, Commissioner of Education from 1962–1966; Peter P. Muirhead, Executive Deputy Commissioner of Education during the 1950s; Sidney Percy Marland, Jr., Commissioner of Education at the time of interview in 1971; Joseph H. Douglass, Executive Director of President's Committee on Mental Retardation and various posts with Department of Education; Joe Keene, official in Office of Education in 1965; John Singerhoff, official in Office of Public Information in the Office of Education during the 1960s; Arthur Harris, official in the Department of Education; and Earl James McGrath, Commissioner of Education from 1949 to 1953 (includes cassette tapes but no transcripts).

5. Oral history materials are not cataloged.

B14 Energy Department (DOE)—History Division

1 a. *Assistant Secretary for Management and Administration*
Forrestal Building
1000 Independence Avenue, S.W.
Washington, D.C. 20585
(202) 252–5235

b. 9:00 A.M.–4:30 P.M.   Monday–Friday

c. Currently, all oral history materials are closed to the public.

d. Jack M. Holl, Chief Historian
Travis Hulsey, Administrative Assistant

2–3. The History Division conducts an oral history program. The collection includes research and exit interviews conducted by DOE historians with past officials of the Atomic Energy Commission, Energy Research and Development Administration, Federal Energy Administration, and the Department of Energy. Transcripts have not been made.

5. A list of the interviews is not available.

B15 Folklore Society of Greater Washington (FSGW)—Archive

1 a. *Box 19114, 20th Street Station*
Washington, D.C. 20036
(703) 281–2228

b. 9:00 A.M.–5:00 P.M. Monday–Friday

c. Open by appointment only.

d. Kathy Westra Hickerson, President
Bill Day, Archivist

2. The Folklore Society of Greater Washington is a nonprofit, educational organization dedicated to preserving and promoting traditional folk arts in the Washington, D.C., metropolitan area. The society achieves this, in part, by sponsoring more ,than 100 concerts, dances, and workshops, as well as an annual Washington Folk Festival, throughout the year.

3. The archive includes official FSGW records, old newsletters, publicity clippings, photographs, and more than 500 audio tapes of sponsored events held between 1963 and 1984.

5. The society publishes a monthly *Newsletter*.

B16 Forest Service (Agriculture Department)—History Section

1 a. *P.O. Box 2417*
South Agricultural Building, Room 0325
Washington, D.C. 20013
(202) 447–2418

b. 8:00 A.M.–4:00 P.M. Monday–Friday

c. Open to researchers.

d. Dennis Roth, Chief Historian

2. The Forest Service maintains an oral history program. Interviewees consist primarily of both active and retired officials of the agency. The History Section not only acquires copies of interviews conducted elsewhere, but also occasionally contracts for interviews.

3. The collection currently consists of some 30 interviews, including those with Edward Cliff, Christopher Granger, and Richard McArdle. A number of interviews were conducted by the Forest History Society and the University of California at Berkeley. All of the interviews are in transcript format.

4 d. A photocopy facility is available.

B17 House of Representatives—House Recording Studio

1 a. *Rayburn House Office Building, Room B310*
Washington, D.C. 20515
(202) 225–3941

b. 9:00 A.M.–5:00 P.M. Monday–Friday

d. William C. Moody, Director

2.   The House Recording Studio records the proceedings of the House of Representatives. After 60 days, the audio tapes are forwarded to the Motion Picture, Broadcasting and Recorded Sound Division of the Library of Congress (A41).

3.   Audio tapes are available for purchase for 30 calendar days, from the date the proceeding took place on the House Floor. Video tapes are available for 60 calendar days; following the 60-day period, the original is erased and the blank tape reused. For additional information contact: Office of the Clerk, House of Representatives, Longworth House Office Building, Room 1036, Washington, D.C. 50515 (202/255–1300).

   Individuals may contact the House of Representatives to hear recorded telephone running accounts of proceedings on the Floor: (202) 225–7400 (Democratic); (202) 225–7430 (Republican).

5.   Printed information and tape duplication request forms are available from the Office of Records and Registration (Office of the Clerk).

B18   Jewish Historical Society

1 a.   *701 3rd Street, N.W.*
Washington, D.C. 20001
(202) 789–0900

   b.   Hours vary depending upon availability of personnel.

   c.   An appointment is required for use of recordings.

   d.   Haddassah Phursz, Director

2–3.   The Jewish Historical Society is devoted to preserving the history of the Jewish experience and contribution to the development of the Washington area. Their oral history project has resulted in over 30 recorded interviews with Jewish residents of Washington. Cassettes of these interviews have been placed in the Washingtoniana Division of the Martin Luther King, Jr., Memorial Library (A42). In addition, a separate project consists of 6 interviews with residents of the Hebrew Home of Greater Washington (6121 Montrose Road, Rockville, Maryland 20852), who have exemplified the Jewish contribution to the economic and social life on the East Coast of the United States. These interviews are published under the title, *To Make A Dream Come True: Stories of the Residents of the Hebrew Home of Greater Washington* (no date).

4 a.   On-site listening equipment is available.

   b.   Reservations are required.

   c.   No fees are charged.

   d.   Photoduplication facilities are not available.

B19 Library of Congress—American Folklife Center—Archive of Folk Culture

1 a. *Thomas Jefferson Building, Ground Floor, Room G152*
1st Street, S.E.
(between Independence Avenue and East Capitol Street)
Washington, D.C. 20540
(202) 287–5510

b. 8:30 A.M.–5:00 P.M.   Monday–Friday
Closed on all holidays except Washington's Birthday, Columbus Day, and Veterans Day.

c. Open to researchers over high school age for on-site use.

d. Joseph C. Hickerson, Head

2. The Archive of Folk Culture controls over 300,000 items of folklore representing every state of the country, as well as all parts of the world. It is, in effect, the largest repository of traditional documentation in the United States. Subjects include folksong, folkmusic, folktale, and oral history. Although reference service for all relevant materials under control of the archive is provided on-site, field recordings, including cylinders, discs, wires, and tapes are held in the Motion Picture, Broadcasting and Recorded Sound Division (A41). In addition, thousands of commercial recordings pertaining to folklore and ethnomusicology are also held there. The archive does have a substantial number of audio tape preservation copies available for use on-site. The archive maintains a reading room containing some 3,500 reference books and periodicals, as well as a considerable amount of manuscript material. Many of the recordings and accompanying documents are organized in special collections, a few of which are described in category 3 below.

3. Blue Ridge Parkway Folklife Project Collection, 1978. —Photographs, films, 39 cassettes and 428 reel-to-reel tapes. American Folklife Center in cooperation with the National Park Service. This field research project documents folklife along the parkway in Virginia and North Carolina. Subjects include crafts, music, church services, radio broadcasts, and interviews. Two disc recordings representing the project are available for purchase through the Recorded Sound Section, or in person at the Sales Shop (see Appendix I).
    Rosemary Killam Texas Folk Music Collection, 1971.—33 audio cassette recordings. Subjects include annual sacred singing in Round Grove, Texas; instrumental and bluegrass playing in Granbury, Texas; Fiddlers' contests in DeLeon, Lampasas, Garland, and Gatesville, Texas; "Monthly Singin'" in Fall Creek, Texas; "Musical" in Santo, Texas; and fiddle contests in Richland Hills, Texas.
    Keith Ludden Kansas Folk Music and Oral History Collection, 1980.—16 reel-to-reel tapes of interviews with individual musicians, not only about music, but also about social life. Musical groups include The Holy Ghost Band (Kansas City), Los Mariachis Tropicales (Kansas City), Ed Grisnik and his Orchestra (Kansas City), and the Kansas City Jazz.
    The University of Maryland Folklore Archives.—Includes various subjects such as Adams-Morgan school topic (1969); Henry Fuller of Sandy Spring, Maryland, talking about folktales; legends and belief tales from Silver Spring, and Thurmont, Maryland, North Carolina and West Virginia; Polish folktales; urban black lore in D.C.; Bill Clipper talking about barge work on the C&O Canal; local history of Oldtown,

Maryland; Western Pennsylvania mining folklore; folksongs from Green Gables, Maryland; Russian-Jewish folklore; and Hasidic and family lore from Baltimore, Maryland, and Washington, D.C.

Montana Folklife Survey, 1979.—144 reel-to-reel and 2 cassette tapes. A varied survey of ethnic life, including musical performances and events, singing and vocal impressions of the Turner Colony of Hutterites, wedding ceremonies, oral history interviews, Irish and German community and occupational life.

Federal Cylinder Project
(202) 287–6590

Dorothy Sara Lee, Director

The American Folklife Center established the Federal Cylinder Project in 1979 to coordinate the preservation and duplication of wax cylinder recordings (especially those located in various federal agencies and other organizations throughout the country) of the former Bureau of American Ethnology, the National Archives and Records Service (B27), Harvard's Peabody Museum, the American Philosophical Society, and the American Museum of Natural History. Included in the program are some 100 cylinder collections totaling 9 to 10 thousand cylinders. The use of wax cylinders in recording was from its inception primarily for fieldwork by anthropologists, folklorists, and musicologists. Some of the earliest cylinders include American Indian music and folktales recorded by Jesse Walter Fewkes in 1890, music of the Kwakiutl Indians from the 1893 Chicago World's Fair, and Plains Indian music recorded by Alice Cunningham Fletcher and Walter McClintock in the mid to late 1890s. Other cylinders represent African, Afro-American, Anglo-American, Missouri-French, Hispanic, and Chinese cultures. Many recordings are accompanied by field notes, published and unpublished manuscripts, and photographs. Currently, work is underway for producing finding aids for each collection.

4 a-b. Sound recording facilities for materials controlled by the archive are available for use by researchers in the Motion Picture, Broadcasting and Recorded Sound Division (A41). Reservations for use of facilities is required.

   c. No fees are charged.

   d. Photoduplication facilities are available. Depending on restrictions, duplication of some sound recordings is permitted, and is handled through the Motion Picture, Broadcasting and Recorded Sound Division (A41).

5. Access to the collection is provided through various card catalogs as well as by both published and unpublished finding aids. Card catalogs include Field Recordings (pre-1940), an item catalog arranged by AFS (Archive of Folk Song) number, title, geographical location, and performer. This catalog should be used with the published catalog *The Check-List of Recorded Songs in the English Language in the Archive of American Folk Song to July, 1940* (supplement through October 1940), which does not, however, include all of the entries in the card catalog. The companion card catalog, Field Recordings (post-1940) is arranged in the same way. Researchers should also refer to the Field Recording Collections catalog where each card cites the name of the collection, number of recordings, and description of contents. An AFS number refers researchers to the vertical files where a corresponding folder includes printed and manuscript background information on the respective collection. Individuals should consult *A Guide to the Collections of Recorded Folk Music and Folklore in the Library of Congress* (1983) where these indexes and procedures are described in detail.

The Archive of Folk Culture produces two series of publications, including *Reference Aids,* which includes general bibliographies, discographies, and directories, and *Finding Aids,* which describes aspects of the library's unique collections of folklife and ethnomusicology, including *Street Cries, Auction Chants, and Carnival Pitches and Routines* (1983) and *Virginia Field Recordings in the Archive of Folk Culture* (1983). Researchers should refer also to *An Inventory of the Bibliographies and Other Reference and Finding Aids Prepared by the Archive of Folk Culture.* Thirty-three individual collections are described in the Library of Congress *Special Collections in the Library of Congress* (1980).

The American Folklife Center has available for purchase a varied selection of disc recordings, including the series, *Folk Music in America.* Recordings may be purchased at the Sales Shop (Appendix I) or by mail from Public Services Coordinator, Library of Congress, Motion Picture, Broadcasting and Recorded Sound Division, Washington, D.C. 20540. A number of brochures describing the recordings are available free upon request from the Sales Shop and the American Folklife Center.

B20 Library of Congress—Manuscript Division

1 a. *James Madison Building, First Floor, Room 101*
Independence Avenue, S.E.
(between 1st and 2nd Streets)
Washington, D.C. 20540
(202) 287–5383

Mail:
10 First Street, S.E.
Washington, D.C. 20540

b. 8:30 A.M.–5:00 P.M.   Monday–Saturday
(Stack service ends at 4:15 P.M.)
Closed on national holidays.

c. The Manuscript Division is open to serious researchers, who must first present proper identification and complete a registration form. Because of the nature of rare materials, the division has its own requirements for obtaining access to its holdings. A brochure describing the conditions as well as services and photocopy facilities is available. Researchers from out of town are advised to obtain a copy of this brochure.

d. James H. Hutson, Chief

2. The Manuscript Division holds approximately 10,000 collections, total holdings exceeding 40 million items. Included are presidential papers, the papers of various government officials and notable Americans families, and papers of various nongovernmental organizations.

3. The Manuscript Division has a number of sound recording-related material. The recorded counterparts to the written materials held in the division are located in the Motion Picture, Broadcasting and Recorded Sound Division (A41). The first procedure for identifying materials is to consult the Master Record, which is an up-to-date computer-generated descriptive list of collections held in the division. It is available for on-site use only. In addition, descriptive typewritten aids are provided for selected collections. In any event, it is best to consult with a reference librarian during the course of research. The division has the following collections.

U.S. Capitol Historical Society Oral History Collection, 1978–1982.—2 containers; interviewees include Robert Byrd, Allyn Cox, Edward Lee Roy Elson, Jennings Randolph, Hugh Scott, and Thomas G. Steed.

Former Members of Congress, Inc. (Oral History Collection).—100 items, transcripts only. Examples of individuals interviewed include Thomas G. Abernethy, William H. Ayres, Marguerite Stitt Church, James William Fulbright, Wilbur D. Mills, John S. Monagan, Hugh D. Scott, Jr. The recordings are held in the Motion Picture, Broadcasting and Recorded Sound Division.

Suffragists Oral History Project (Regional Oral History Office of the University of California at Berkeley), 1974.—3 boxes, transcripts only. Interviewees include Helen Valeska Bary, Jessie Haver Butler, Miriam Allen de Ford, Ernestine Hara Kettler, Burnita Shelton Matthews, Alice Paul, Laura Ellsworth Seiler, Sylvie Grace Thompson Thygeson, and Mabel Vernon.

"Meet the Press" Collection, 1956 to present.—63,800 items as of 1979; include papers of Lawrence E. Spivak, transcripts of radio and television broadcasts, news clippings, scrapbooks, and lists of participants. All of the recordings are held in the Motion Picture, Broadcasting and Recorded Sound Division and some 700 photographs and drawings are held in the Prints and Photographs Division (202/287–5836). A description of the collection is printed in *Special Collections in the Library of Congress* (1980).

In addition, printed and manuscript portions of the Margaret Mead Papers, Columbia Broadcasting System Collection, and John Toland Collection, and transcripts from the Senate Historical Office Oral History Collection (B39) are held in the division.

The Manuscript Division's typewritten guide, "Collections —Performing Arts," includes the following references to radio scripts: Fred Allen, 404 radio scripts; Columbia Broadcasting System, 5,700 radio scripts; Amos and Andy, 419 selected radio scripts; Goodman Ace, 2,200 radio scripts; Albert P. Terhune, selected radio scripts; Vic and Sade, 978 radio scripts. Researchers should be aware that radio scripts were frequently not read over the air exactly as written. Therefore, in certain cases, one might need to consult both the written and recorded versions.

In addition, the division's Sigmund Freud Collection includes transcripts of numerous taped interviews of Freud's colleagues and friends.

4 d. Except for materials under restriction, most manuscripts may be copied on-site for research. The reading room is equipped with photocopy machines and microfilm reader-printers. In addition, the Photoduplication Service, Room G-1009, John Adams Building (202/287–5640) provides, for a fee, photostats, microfilms, and other photocopies of materials. Permission is required to use cameras in the reading room. Microfilm reproductions of many manuscripts are available through interlibrary loan.

5. The division has a number of catalogs, indexes, and finding aids. These include catalog cards, which briefly describe the collections available for reader use and various indexes to special collections. A separate brochure concerning finding aids is available upon request. The Library of Congress annual publication, *National Union Catalog of Manuscript Collections* (1959—) includes oral history collections held by contributing libraries and other institutions throughout the country.

B21 Marine Corps (Navy Department)—History and Museums Division

1 a. *Washington Navy Yard, Building 58*
9th and M Streets, S.E.
Washington, D.C. 20380
(202) 433–3840 (General Information)
(202) 433–3840 (Museum Information)

b. 8:30 A.M.–4:30 P.M.   Monday–Friday

c. The collection is open to researchers. Some holdings have access restrictions.

d. Henry I. Shaw, Jr., Chief Historian
Benis M. Frank, Head, Oral History Section

2.   The oral history collection in the History and Museums Division contains over 1,260 hours of tapes transcribed onto over 32,000 edited pages, and more than 6,000 individual interviews relating to Vietnam, which have not been transcribed. The oral history program was established to obtain personal narratives of the experiences and observations of active duty, reserve, and retired Marines. The period covered is 1893 to the present, and is primarily concerned with military service, Marine Corp history, Spanish American War, World Wars I and II, Korean War, Vietnam War, Blacks in the Marine Corps, and the development of Marine Corps amphibious warfare. The form of the recordings include taped presentations, briefings, debriefings, and speeches and interviews.

3.   Individuals interviewed include Lt. Gen. Joseph Charles Burger, Lt. Gen. William Henry Buse, Jr., Lt. Gen. Francis Patrick Mulcahy, Maj. Gen. Walter Greatsinger Farrell, Maj. Gen. Wood Barbee Kyle, and Brig. Gen. John Carroll Miller. In addition, 8 of the last 11 commandants of the Marine Corps have been interviewed for the program.

One notable group of recordings includes the Navajo Code Talkers Oral History Collection (1971), consisting of some 27 items. There are interviews with Philip Johnston, who originated the idea of using an Indian language in coded form for transmitting voice messages in combat situations, and with former Navajo language code talkers during World War II. Another issue-oriented set of interviews has been with enlisted Marine Security Guards who are assigned to the State Department and provide security to American consulates and embassies. Also in this group are interviews with the Marines who were part of the Iranian hostage group.

4 a.   Contact the Oral History Section regarding available sound recording equipment.

5.   In addition to a card catalog and indexes to individual transcripts, and an index to Vietnam-related tapes as a whole, there are published reference sources that provide information about the collection: *Marine Corps Oral History Collection Catalog* (1979) and *Guide to the Marine Corps Historical Center*. Individuals may also want to consult *An Annotated Reading List of United States Marine Corps History* (1971) and *Marine Corps Personal Papers Catalog* (1974).

Additional oral history materials related to the Marine Corps are included in the Oral History Program of the Office of Air Force History (B37). Recordings of Marine Corps recruiting broadcasts for 1942–1943 (RG 127) are held in the Special Archives Division of the National Archives and Records Service (B27).

B22 Maryland–National Capital Park and Planning Commission (M-NCPPC) —History Division

1 a. *4811 Riverdale Road*
Riverdale, Maryland 20737
(301) 779-2011

 b. 9:00 A.M.–5:00 P.M. Monday–Friday

 c. Contact the History Division for information on access to the collection.

 d. Bianca Floyd and Susan Pearl, Co-directors of the oral history project.

2. Bianca Floyd and Susan Pearl are directors for an oral history project, "Prince George's County Black History Study," which documents the histories of families who have lived in Prince George's County, Maryland, for several generations. To date, 15 interviews have been completed; transcripts are not yet available. The project is scheduled to be completed in 1985.

4 a. On-site listening equipment is not available.

B23 Montgomery Country Historical Society, Inc., Library

1 a. *Beall-Dawson House*
103 West Montgomery Avenue
Rockville, Maryland 20850
(301) 762-1492

 b. 12:00 Noon–4:00 P.M. Tuesday–Saturday

 c. Open to the public. There is a research fee.

 d. Mead Karras, Executive Administrator
Jane Sween, Librarian

2. The library has a wide array of materials devoted to Montgomery County, Maryland. Included are books, journals, government records, club scrapbooks, an extensive photographic collection, and oral history tapes and transcripts.

3. In 1976 the society's Oral History Committee initiated a Bicentennial Year Oral History Project on the recollections of residents of Montgomery County. The project, which lasted for several years, produced interviews with 27 individuals. Perhaps the most important person interviewed was E. Brook Lee, who is one of the most significant figures in Montgomery County history. The total number of items includes approximately 35 cassette and 11 reel-to-reel tapes with transcripts. The Maryland Municipal Collection in the Rockville Library of the Montgomery County Department of Public Libraries (A48) also has a set of these tapes and transcripts.

4 a. Individuals are asked to inquire regarding audio facilities.

 b. No reservations required.

 c. A nominal fee is charged to use the library.

d. Photocopy facility is available.

5. The library has a number of basic printed reference works, which facilitate the use of the collection.

B24 Montgomery County League of Women Voters, Inc.

1 a. *12216 Parklawn, Suite 101*
   Rockville, Maryland 20852
   (301) 984-9585

  b. 9:00 A.M.–5:00 P.M.   Monday–Friday

  c. Open to researchers by appointment.

  d. Carla Satinsky, President

2–3. The Montgomery County League of Women Voters began an oral history program through its Marie Bennett Memorial Library Fund in 1973. Their purpose was to record the reminiscences of individuals in governmental, political and community life in Montgomery County, Maryland. To date at least 27 individuals have been interviewed on such topics as politics, the origins of Chevy Chase, Maryland, the school and library systems, real estate development, and newspaper publishing. All of the 57 or so audio cassettes produced by the league are held as a permanent collection in the Maryland Municipal Collection in the Rockville Library of the Montgomery County Department of Public Libraries (A48).

4 a. On-site listening equipment is available in the Rockville Library of the Montgomery County Department of Public Libraries.

National Aeronautics and Space Administration (NASA)—History Office Archives   See entry L6

B25 National Agricultural Library (NAL) (Agriculture Department)

1 a. *10301 Baltimore Boulevard*
   Beltsville, Maryland 20705
   (301) 344-3755

  b. 8:00 A.M.–4:30 P.M.   Monday–Friday

  c. Open to the public. Reference and research services may be requested in person, by mail, telephone or telecopier. A reference librarian is on duty on the main floor of the NAL building, Monday through Friday. Self-guided audio tapes of the public services areas of the library are available and are particularly useful for researchers who need to utilize NAL resources. Inquire at the reception desk in the lobby.

  d. Joseph Howard, Director

2. The NAL collection contains the single most important body of knowledge on agricultural and related sciences in the free world. Holdings include some 1.7 million

volumes, over 23,000 journals, and more than 80 major indexing and abstracting publications in science and technolology. Many of the foreign books and periodicals are unique in the United States. The library also has a large number of non-print materials, including microfilms, microfiche, microprint, and aerial photographs.

3. Notable holdings of the library.

Information Access Division
Room 301
(301) 344–3876

Head (vacant)
Alan E. Fusonie, Historical and Preservation Program Specialist

The National Agricultural Library maintains an oral history program, which was established in 1972. The library does not conduct interviews but rather acquires transcripts from organizations involved in various agricultural and related studies. Researchers visiting NAL who would like to know how the program was begun may examine the transcript of the first "Symposium on Oral History" held at NAL, August 10, 1972. Access to the collection is handled by Dr. Fusonie in Room 301. The oral history collection is stored on the 8th floor.

To date over 400 transcripts have been acquired. Some examples of collections and interviewees are listed below.

The Appalachian Oral History Project.—5 boxes, consisting of the history and folklore of the Central Appalachian region. Access is provided through a catalog, *The Appalachian Oral History Project: Union Catalog* (1977).

University of California at Berkeley (Regional Oral History Office) Oral History Program.—Interviewees and topics include Newton Bishop Drury (parks and redwoods); John W. Gregg (landscape architecture); Horace M. Albright and N. B. Drury (conservation); Richard M. Leonard (lawyer, environmentalist, and mountaineer); Sidney T. Harding (Western water development); Edward DeWitt Taylor (San Francisco printer); Ansel F. Hall (Yosemite National Park ranger); George B. Hartzog (national parks); Loye Holmes Miller (naturalist); and Ralph W. Chaney (paleobotanist and conservationist). Included in the materials is the *California Wine Industry Oral History Project* which includes 17 transcripts focusing on history of the development of the wine industry. Interviewees include Leon Adams; Maynard A. Amerine; Philo Biane; Sydney J. Block; Burke H. Critchfield; William V. Cruess; Maynard A. Joslyn; Louis M. Martini; Otto E. Meyer; Antonio Perelli-Minetti; Louis A. Petri; Lucius Powers; Victor Repetto; Edmund A. Rossi; A. Setrakian; Brother Timothy; Ernest A. Wente; and A.J. Winkler.

Texas Agricultural Experiment Station (Texas A & M University). —Interviews with William T. Hardy, James G. Teer, and others, on such topics as veterinary medicine, range science, and more.

Forest History Society.—Interviews with Clarence F. Korstian, and others, and employees of the St. Regis Paper Company.

University of California at Davis,Oral History Program. —Interviews with Reuben Albaugh, J. Earl Coke, Harold Cole, Knowles A. Ryerson, Henry Schacht, Ruth R. Storer, and others, on such topics as animal science and poultry industry.

Soil Conservation Service, Oral History Program.—Interview with William J. Ralston.

Sierra Club Oral History Project.—Interviews with Thomas Amneus, Irene M. Charnock, J. Gordon Chelew, Nathan C. Clark, Olivia R. Johnson, E. Stanley Jones, Marion Jones, Robert R. Marshall, Dorothy L. Pepper, and Richard Searle.

The library also has a few transcripts representing the John F. Kennedy Library Oral History Program.

NOTE: Records of the Department of Agriculture for 1940–1950 (RG 16) are held
in the National Archives and Records Service (B27).

4 a.   On-site listening equipment is not available.

   d.   Photocopy facilities are available.

5.   Although there is no separate printed list of the oral history collection, most items
can be accessed through AGRICOLA (Agricultural Online Access) (G1). Information
describing NAL holdings is printed in a number of flyers and leaflets. See especially,
Information Alert, Quick Bibliography Series, and *Bibliographies and Literature of
Agriculture,* available in the Reference Room, first floor (202/344–3755). For researchers, information specialists, scientists, and librarians who need to stay abreast
of new programs, acquisitions, and current news at NAL, see *Agricultural Libraries
Information Notes* (bi-monthly).

B26   National Anthropological Archives (Smithsonian Institution)

1 a.   *National Museum of Natural History Building, Room 60-A*
10th Street and Constitution Avenue, N.W.
Washington, D.C. 20560
(202) 357–1986

   b.   9:00 A.M.–5:00 P.M.   Monday–Friday

   c.   Open to the public. Appointments in advance are recommended.

   d.   Herman Viola, Director

2–3.   The National Anthropological Archives is a depository of manuscript collections and photographs comprised primarily of material on native Americans. Audio
holdings include field recordings in the papers and documents of John P. Harrington
(1884–1961), ethnologist and student of West-Coast Amerindian languages. This collection consists of 400 wax cylinders and 1,600 aluminum discs, including music and
narration from Harrington's fieldwork with American Indians. Some of these recordings have been transcribed and some have been copied onto cassettes for use by
researchers.
   Two additional manuscript collections held by the archives had similar recordings,
which were sent to the Library of Congress (B19). These are the Frances Densmore
and Alice Cunningham Fletcher papers.

4 a.   Limited listening facilities are available.

   b.   Reservations are recommended.

   c.   No fees are charged to use the archives.

   d.   Reproduction of materials can be arranged.

5.   The archives maintains a computer-produced list of holdings arranged by tribe,
with language, informant, and limited subject indexes.

B27 National Archives and Records Service (NARS) (General Services Administration)

1 a. *8th Street and Pennsylvania Avenue, N.W.*
   Washington, D.C. 20408
   (202) 523–3218 (General Information)
   (202) 523–3232 (Central Research Room)

   b. Branch Research Room:
      8:45 A.M.–5:15 P.M.   Monday–Friday
      Central Research Room:
      8:45 A.M.–10:00 P.M.   Monday–Friday
      8:45 A.M.–5:00 P.M.   Saturday

   c. Open to researchers with a National Archives research pass, obtainable from the Central Information Division, in the lobby of the Pennsylvania Avenue entrance. Individuals must present identification, such as a driver's license. Upon signing in for the first time, researchers may wish to obtain a free copy of *A Researcher's Guide to the National Archives* (1977), which describes the principal research rooms and procedures for using the collections. This and a number of published finding aids are available free upon request in Room G-6. Researchers may want to proceed to the Central Research Room, Room 200-B, where additional aids not available in Room G-6 may be consulted.

   d. Robert M. Warner, Archivist of the United States

2. The National Archives and Records Service was created by the National Archives Act of 1934, in which provision was made for the Audio-Visual Archives Division to accession, preserve, arrange, describe, and provide reference service for still pictures, motion picture films, video and sound recordings that have been created by or for federal agencies, acquired by federal agencies in the course of their official functions, and obtained from non-federal sources, but which contain pertinent information about federal programs and activities not available in the official records.

   Throughout the years, sound recordings have become a very significant form of archival material documenting the U.S. government, not only in terms of the vast quantity of items produced, but also in the number of federal agencies represented. Today, over 70 federal agencies are represented in the accessions program. In addition to these materials, numerous gifts of sound recordings from private individuals and organizations have been accessioned.

   The National Archives houses one of the largest sound recordings collections of its kind in the world. There are over 115,000 recordings or nearly 80,000 hours of listening, reflecting the technological advancement of sound dating from 1896 to the present. The number and principal types of recordings include 75,000 discs consisting of 57,000 listening hours, 30,000 reel-to-reel tapes in a variety of reel sizes, consisting of some 12,000 listening hours. Other types of sound recordings include 15,000 dictaphone, memobelts, and memovox discs, and wire and cylinder recordings.

   The recordings consist of press conferences, panel discussions, oral history interviews, speeches, court and conference proceedings, entertainment and public affairs programs, and news broadcasts. Scripts, transcripts, and production case files relating to individual items are also accessioned. Spoken materials represent statistically 95 percent of the holdings, and music represents only 5 percent. Regarding subject

content, history represents 92 percent of the collections, language 1 percent, folklore 1 percent, popular music 5 percent, and tribal music 1 percent.

Sound recordings are organized similarly to printed materials and are assigned record group (RG) numbers with each group containing the records of a single government agency or subdivision. The Gift Collection of nongovernment donations is designated RG 200.

3. Notable holdings of the archives.

CIVIL ARCHIVES DIVISION
(202) 523-3108
Daniel T. Goggin, Director

Judicial, Fiscal and Social Branch
Room 5W
(202) 523-3089

Clarence Lyons, Chief

RG 65: Records of the Federal Bureau of Investigation.—Includes audio tapes focusing on the Martin Luther King, Jr. assassination. Closed to public access for fifty years (from 1977).

RG 272: Records of the President's Commission on the Assassination of President Kennedy.—Includes radio tape recordings (1963) of Dallas stations and the Voice of America. Tape recordings are also in the Numbered Commission Document File (1963–1964) and Office Files of Staff Members (1964), the latter including 27 dictaphone belts, and 3 NBC audio tapes. See the published finding aid, *Inventory of the Records of the President's Commission on the Assassination of President Kennedy* (1973) for a full description of RG 272.

RG 274: National Archives Collection of Records of Inaugural Committees.— NARS retains only the latest two inaugurations, which are retired eventually to the respective presidential libraries. As of this writing, NARS has sound recordings relating to the Carter and Reagan inaugural committee activities. (See RG 274 cited under the Motion Picture, Sound & Video Branch (p.136) for copies of past inaugural committee activities).

Legislative and Diplomatic Branch
Room 5E
(202) 523-3174

Milton Gustafson, Chief
Charles South, Acting Assistant Chief

RG 148: Expositions, Anniversary and Memorial Commissions.—Includes 25 sound tape recordings of the President's Commission for the Observance of Human Rights, which took place in 1968. Refer to file folder ACC No. NN 369–109 for additional information on this collection.

The Legislative and Diplomatic Branch also has in its custody a set of transcripts of oral history interviews acquired from the Senate Historical Office (B39). All interviews have been conducted with staff members of the U.S. Senate, including Ruth Y. Watt, Chief Clerk, Permanent Subcommittee on Investigation; Darrell St. Claire, Assistant Secretary of the Senate; Frank Attig, Reporter of Debates; Pat Holt, Chief of Staff; W. Featherstone Reid, Assistant to Senator Warren Magnuson; and Floyd Riddick, Parliamentarian.

Scientific, Economic and Natural Resources Branch
Room 11E
(202) 523–3059

Franklin W. Burch, Chief

RG 401: Polar Archives.—247 sound recordings. This record group contains a number of sets of collected papers and other materials, many of which contain sound recordings:

Carl Robert Eklund (1909–1962) Family Papers, 1920–1974.—27 items. This collection contains correspondence, diaries, logs, research notes, still and motion pictures, and sound recordings relating to Eklund's participation in the U.S. Antartic Service (1939–1941) as station scientific leader, U.S.-IGY Wilkes Station (1956–1957), in the Arctic, Desert and Tropic Information Center, and field trips for the Department of the Interior.

Captain Dayton Brown Papers, 1940–1971.—Includes 2 tape recordings or reports related to Navy camouflage design.

Historical materials of William J. Cromie.—Includes sound recordings made at Little America, Antarctica, in 1957; 6 items. Also includes magnetic tape recordings of theatrical performances by station personnel during the 1957 winter-over. Some of these tapes also contain segments of recorded music not related to the performances. See also, South Pole station sound recordings for 1958. 6 items. These consist of recorded interviews with station personnel, and the subjects focus on conditions there.

Espaminodas J. Demas Papers, 1926–1972.—Includes tape recordings of his explorations in the Arctic and Antarctic, 1926–1935.

John Dyer Papers.—Includes tape recordings, and aluminum disc recordings of the Byrd Antarctic Expedition no. 2, 1933–1935. Subjects include sounds of penguins and seals, Easter Island natives singing, radio conversations, and other broadcasts, and group discussions.

Lincoln Ellsworth Papers.—Includes sound recordings relating to the Antarctic Expedition, 1935–1936; 2 items.

Sound recordings relating to Eskimo studies, ca. 1946–1965.—143 items, focusing on Eskimo language and culture in Greenland, Canada, and Alaska. One special aspect of this collection are the Greenlandic songs and music.

Harrison J. Hunt Papers.—Includes sound recordings relating to Crocker Land Expedition, 1913–1917, and other events, 1964–1965; 8 items.

Oral History Interviews with Commander Schlossbach.

Overall, RG 401 represents a truly unique collection. In addition to the above papers, researchers will discover an array of recordings or radio transmissions, some of which are in wire reel format, lectures, and even comments on an Antarctic movie and book in process from 1943–1948.

NIXON PRESIDENTIAL MATERIALS PROJECT
Pickett Street Annex
845 South Pickett Street
Alexandria, Virginia 22304
(202) 756–6716

Mail:
NARS Building
8th Street and Pennsylvania Avenue, N.W.
Washington, D.C. 20408

James J. Hastings, Deputy Director
Richard McNeil, Archivist (202/756–6725)

The Nixon Presidential Materials Project contains a number of audio recordings, some of which are accessible to serious researchers. The major collection is the White House Communication Agency recordings consisting of some 7,046 audio tapes in reel format produced from January 20, 1969 to August 9, 1974. These recordings consist of public remarks, public meeting remarks, press briefings, press conferences of departmental chiefs, and transition period recordings. Transcripts are not available.

Another set of recordings was donated by Nixon and consists of some 120 reel-to-reel tapes spanning the pre-Presidential period, 1952–1968. Yet another set of 99 recordings consists of dictation discs of verbal drafts of Vice-President Nixon and outgoing White House remarks.

Sound recordings that as of this writing are closed to the public include all of the Watergate hearings, the House Judiciary Committee hearings on impeachment, the China Advance Telephone Communications for the two advance teams that preceded Nixon's trip to China, and the 950 (6,000 listening hours) White House tapes produced by Nixon during the period from February 1971 to July 1973. Eventually all of this material will be retired to a presidential library to be located in San Clemente, California.

The staff in the annex has prepared a number of useful finding aids in the form of card catalogs.

OFFICE OF PRESIDENTIAL LIBRARIES
Room 104
(202) 523–3051

Douglas Thurmond, Archivist

The Office of Presidential Libraries has custody of sound recordings accessioned from the Democratic National Committee and Republican National Committee. The office holds these materials for ten years in stack areas 2W2 as a courtesy to those organizations. The recordings are then deposited in various appropriate presidential libraries. Although there are a number of finding aids accessing the material of both committees, most of the recordings are not inventoried. The office does not assign RG numbers to those recordings, as is the normal practice in other divisions of NARS. Researchers therefore, should contact both the Democratic National Committee (B11) and Republican National Committee for various finding lists that they maintain, as well as for obtaining permission for using the recordings.

SPECIAL ARCHIVES DIVISION
(202) 523–3062
Charles Dollar, Director of the Division

Motion Picture, Sound & Video Branch
Room 2W (Administration)
Room G-13 (Reading and Research Room)

William T. Murphy, Chief of the Branch (202/523–3063)
Leslie Waffen, Reference and Acquisitions (202/786–0041)

The Motion Picture, Sound & Video Branch has custody of the majority of sound recordings in the National Archives. A number of recordings are described in various printed publications (see category 5, p.138). Other collections of recordings have never been described in any printed publication. The following list of record groups is based

on an examination of appraisal reports and inventory and accessions lists, as well as those Record Groups cited in the typewritten list, *Sound Recordings in the Audiovisual Archives* (1972), prepared by Mayfield S. Bray and Leslie C. Waffen. The following compilation is current as of June, 1983.

RG 7: Records of the Bureau of Entomology and Plant Quarantine, 1939.—1 item; a recording of greetings telephoned by Dr. Leland O. Howard from Washington, D.C., to the 50th anniversary meeting of the American Association of Economic Entomologists at Columbus, Ohio, December 27, 1939.

RG 12: Records of the Office of Education, 1912–1965.—172 items. Selected radio broadcasts produced by the Office of Education from 1934 to 1953 including programs from the series "Brave New World," "Americans All—Immigrants All," and "Democracy in Action." Programs of educational significance, 1937–1949, focusing on the role of education in wartime and including broadcasts concerning the Voice of Democracy contests, the High School Victory Corps, and the Norman Corwin production, "We Hold These Truths" aired December 15, 1941. Recordings of the proceedings of the "Midcentury White House Conference on Children and Youth," and the "White House Conference on Education," 1955 and 1965. Broadcasts of speeches and discussions by Commissioners of Education, 1938–1964, on such programs as "America's Town Meeting of the Air." Recordings of events of historical significance, 1912–1951, including several speeches by Theodore Roosevelt and a special tabloid broadcast of the coronation of King George VI.

RG 16: Department of Agriculture: Records of the Radio-Television Unit, 1940–1950.—210 items. Includes sound recordings (12-inch and 16-inch acetate and glass-base discs) of radio programs and broadcasts produced or acquired by the Radio-Television Unit on farm and agriculture topics during the period cited above. Included are programs in the public affairs series "American Farmer," "Consumer Time," "National Farm and Home Hour," "Timely Farm Topics," and "Western Agriculture," as well as additional recordings relating to the participation of the American farmer in the World War II defense effort. Examples include "Food Fight for Freedom (1943)," "The Farm Labor Challenge for 1944," "Victory Garden Tips (1944)," and "Nuts to Adolph (1943)."

Sound Recordings of Press Conferences, Speeches, Interviews, and Public Information Programs, 1971–1981.—240 items. Includes audio tapes (open reel and cassette) of recordings produced and acquired by the Radio-Television Unit covering essentially the administrations of Secretaries of Agriculture Earl Butz and Robert Bergland. Included are news conferences, press briefings, interviews, radio broadcasts, speeches, remarks, and media appearances by Butz, Bergland, and other USDA officials relating to agriculture topics such as farm price supports, food productivity, grain sale to USSR, World Food Conferences, the American Agriculture Movement, and the farmers' strike on the Mall in Washington, D.C.

RG 18: Records of the Army Air Forces, 1945.—91 items. Consists of recordings of radio programs in "The Fighting AAF" and "Your AAF" series which include actual air combat accounts obtained by radio reporters in all theaters of action and eyewitness accounts of combat. A recording of Gen. Dwight D. Eisenhower's speech at Orly Field, Paris, France, on June 18, 1945.

RG 24: Records of the Bureau of Naval Personnel, 1945.—1 item. A dramatization of the role of sailors in World War II.

RG 26: Records of the United States Coast Guard, 1937–1939.—10 items. Recordings of radio broadcasts concerning the administration of the Coast Guard and its role in the training of merchant seamen; about the history, traditions, and activities of the Coast Guard; of graduation exercises at the Academy in New London, Connecticut; and of ceremonies presenting the William S. Paley amateur radio award to

ham radio operators for keeping communications open in disaster areas. A description of the national doubles tennis matches, 1938.

RG 29: Records of the Bureau of the Census, 1940.—5 items. Recordings of a radio series entitled "Uncle Sam Calling—Story of the 1940 Census."

RG 31: Records of the Federal Housing Administration, ca. 1934. —18 items. Recordings of radio programs aimed at financial institutions, community betterment groups, property owners, contractors and building material dealers, and other businesses explaining the benefits of Government-insured loans under title 1 of the National Housing Act of 1934.

RG 38: Records of the Office of the Chief of Naval Operations, 1942–1945.—47 items. A miscellaneous collection of recordings of radio broadcasts from "The Army Hour" and the "Meet Your Navy" series concerning all aspects of the war, mainly in the Pacific theater, including eyewitness accounts by Armed Forces Radio Service war correspondents and members of the fighting forces of battles, bombing raids, air operations from aboard a carrier, Marine operations in jungles, the bombardment of Japan from aboard a battleship, and the funeral of Ernie Pyle on Ie Shima. Recordings of radio-telephone conversations between personnel in tanks as they advance in battle; of interviews with crewmen aboard a submarine; and of greetings from servicemen to their families back home. The collection also includes recordings concerning production for the war effort, the role of women in the shipbuilding industry, bond promotion, and recordings of a report to Congress on the progress of the war in Europe by Gen. Dwight D. Eisenhower. A recording of a V-E Day broadcast.

Psychological Warfare Recordings, 1943–1945.—148 items. This series consists of 16-inch glass disc audio recordings produced during World War II by the Special Warfare Branch, Office of Naval Intelligence, Office of the Chief of Naval Operations, and used as a psychological warfare tool for directing propaganda broadcasts in German, Japanese, and English to the Axis countries. Included are recordings of talks given by U.S. military personnel; news spots; anti-Fascist messages; and messages from German prisoners relayed by an announcer to the prisoners' relatives.

RG 44: Records of the Office of Government Reports, 1939–1940. —48 items. Recordings of weekly broadcasts sponsored by the Office of Government Reports known as the "Cabinet Series," the "Agency Series," and the "National Defense Series," in which President Franklin D. Roosevelt, Cabinet members, and officials of departments and agencies of the government explain federal programs and ask for public support and cooperation.

RG 46: Records of the United States Senate, 1946.—5 items. Includes Recordings of hearings on the investigation of the national defense program at the Philadelphia Signal Depot by the Senator James M. Mead Investigating Committee.

Sound Recordings of Commission Meetings, December 1975–December 1976.— 39 items. Cassette recordings of nine meetings of the Commission (restricted).

Sound Recordings of Congressional Research Seminars, August 1976–October 1976.— 18 items. Cassette recordings of five seminars focusing on welfare policy, environment, energy and the economy, oversight of the Executive Branch, support agencies of the Senate, and leadership in the Senate. Transcripts and discussion outlines are available.

Sound Recordings of Interview and Discussions with Senators and Staff on Operations and Policy-Making, June 1976–August 1976.—8 items. Cassette recordings of interviews with legislative aides and administrative assistants for Senators Ernest Hollings and Mark Hatfield describing specific functions and duties and of roundtable discussions with Republican and Democratic senators on the operation of their respective offices (restricted).

Transcripts of Commission Meetings from 1975–1976.—Includes nine meetings. The transcripts serve as a finding aid to the sound recordings of the meetings (restricted).

RG 47: Records of the Social Security Administration, 1936–1940. —6 items. Recordings of lectures accompanying filmstrips explaining social security benefits and procedures for obtaining coverage. There are also recordings of radio programs explaining unemployment benefits, and of programs recruiting warworkers.

RG 48: Records of the Office of the Secretary of the Interior, 1936–1952.—800 items. A miscellaneous collection of recordings of speeches, discussions, interviews, news, ceremonies, and musical programs, many of them of broadcasts, made by the Department of the Interior or collected by it from other government agencies and commercial sources relating to the overall functions of the department; the activities of the Bureau of Biological Survey and the Fish and Wildlife Service concerning wildlife treaties and fish and wildlife conservation; the Bureau of Mines and its work in connection with rare minerals needed for the war effort and mining hazards and safety; the functions of the Bureau of Reclamation in flood control, the development of power, the reclamation of land through irrigation, and the land settlement programs; dedication ceremonies at several Bureau of Reclamation projects; dust bowl migration and reclamation of dust bowl land; the Division of Territories and Island Possessions and its work in Alaska, Hawaii, and Puerto Rico; the work of the General Land Office; the Geological Survey; an interview in 1941 with William Henry Jackson, pioneer photographer with the Geological Survey; the national park system throughout the United States and in the territories and island possessions; the Office of Indian Affairs concerning Indian arts and crafts, improvement of sheep, grazing problems, self government, and Indians in the armed services; the Petroleum Administration Board on conservation of petroleum products, new processes for extracting oil from shale, and the transportation of oil; and the Solid Fuels Administration for War concerning the coal strike and the government takeover, on conservation of coal, and on development of synthetics from coal.

Recordings relating to Work Projects Administration disease control programs; Public Works Administration projects to combat the depression; the public housing program and prospects for postwar housing; the work of the Civilian Conservation Corps, child labor and wages and hours legislation; the role of women workers in the war effort and the contributions of civilians, including Jews and immigrants; the Social Security system and its functions; the Department of Agriculture concerning food conservation and nutrition, farm credit cooperatives, soil conservation, grazing on public lands, conservation of forests and lumber and the development of the Rural Electrification Administration and what it means to the farmer; the Office of Price Administration; the War Resources Planning Board; the National Defense Advisory Commission; the Civil Service Commission; the Office of Civilian Defense; the Bureau of the Budget; the Treasury Department concerning narcotics; the Public Health Service; the Federal Communications Commission; the State Department concerning the Pan American Union; the Veterans' Administration concerning land grants to veterans and education under the GI Bill; the Office of Alien Property; the Selective Service System; and wartime development of industry, aeronautics, scientific research, and atomic energy.

Miscellaneous recordings of the National Education Association; of the Franklin D. Roosevelt birthday celebration of 1945 and the dedication of Hyde Park, 1946; of a dramatization of the history of the United States from the Revolution to World War II; political campaign speeches of both sides in the 1940 presidential campaign; newscasts about all aspects and the progress of the war; the Allies and their contribution to the war; Adolf Hitler's Sudeten, 1938, and Danzig, 1939, speeches; President Roosevelt's "Day of Infamy" speech, December 8, 1941; discussions of the United Nations, United Nations Relief and Rehabilitation Administration, and United Nations Educational, Scientific and Cultural Organization. Marion Anderson's and other musical programs including folk and religious music.

RG 51: Records of the Office of Management and Budget: Sound Recording of President Johnson's Press Conference, May 3, 1968.—1 item. Johnson announces the beginning of the Paris Peace Conference and answers questions on prospects for peace, the 1968 presidential campaign, a tax increase, and the balance of payments problem.

Sound Recordings of Speeches, Press Conferences, and Briefings by the Director, 1970–1973.—3 items. Audio tape recordings of a speech by Director George Schultz to a dinner meeting of the Business Council, October 16, 1970; a press briefing by director Schultz on Phase II of President Richard Nixon's economic policy, October 7, 1971; and a press conference by the director on the budget from January 27, 1973.

Audio Recordings of Press Conferences, Speeches, and Briefings, 1973–1980.—10 items. Audio recordings of speeches, press conferences, and briefings by OMB directors Roy Ash, Bert Lance, James Lynn, and other persons. Included are Ash's comments on the energy crisis, and Lance's remarks before the National League of Cities on various issues. Also included is a speech on Vietnam by Dolf Droge, an assistant to Henry Kissinger, before the Leadership Training Institute.

RG 56: General Records of the Department of the Treasury, 1941–1961.—1,214 items. Recordings of radio broadcasts promoting the purchase of defense and Victory bonds and consisting of dramatic and musical programs featuring many prominent entertainers from the "Treasury Star Parade," "Treasury Salute," "Bondwagon," and "Guest Star" series. Recordings of "Minute Man" speeches consisting of short appeals promoting war bonds by important government leaders. News and discussion programs from the "American Forum of the Air," "News of the World," and several broadcasts from the "Army Hour" series, including a program on which the last Morse code message from Corregidor as received in Hawaii on May 5, 1942, is re-enacted with a voice overlay reading a coded message. There are also miscellaneous recordings and programs of historical interest including Prime Minister Churchill's address to Congress of May 19, 1943, and President Harry S Truman's radio report on the Potsdam Conference, August 9, 1945; and many other recordings by world leaders, political figures, and prominent entertainers.

RG 59: General Records of the Department of State, 1938–1961.—14 items. Recordings of addresses by Secretaries of State Cordell Hull (chiefly on the subject of reciprocal trade), John Foster Dulles, and Christian Herter. Recordings of the "Good Neighbor" series about Brazilian economic, cultural, and political history. A recording of a dramatization of the history of the world between 1918–1939, entitled "And Then Came War," narrated by Elmer Davis.

RG 60: General Records of the Department of Justice, 1941–1944. —584 items. Sound recordings of broadcasts made over facilities of the German Radio Broadcasting Corporation during World War II by Herbert J. Burgman, Douglas Chandler, Frederick W. Kaltenbach, and Robert Best. They were confiscated from the broadcasting studio in Berlin at the end of the war and introduced as evidence in treason trials of some of these individuals.

RG 64: Records of the National Archives and Records Service, 1937–1981.—248 items. Recordings of speeches, interviews, and ceremonies relating to activities of the National Archives, including the opening of the Freedom Train Exhibit, 1949; the enshrinement of the Declaration of Independence and the Constitution in the Exhibit Hall, 1952; Archivists of the United States, including Wayne C. Grover on the program "Report to the People," 1966, and James B. Rhoads on "Capital Assignment," 1968; at the 193rd anniversary of the Declaration of Independence ceremonies at the National Archives, 1969; and on WETA, Atlanta, Georgia, 1970. There are additional materials representing Frank Burke, Albert Meisel, Mabel Deutrich, Frank Evans, and Walter Robertson. There are also recordings of the proceedings of the National Historical Publications Commission luncheon meeting, June 17, 1958, and of meetings

of the National Archives Advisory Council, December 1968–May1972 (May 1969 missing).

Recordings of the proceedings of National Archives Conferences on U.S. Polar Explorations, September 8, 1967; the National Archives and Statistical Research, May 27–28, 1968; Captured German and Related Records, November 12–13, 1968; United States Foreign Relations, June 16–17, 1969; the History of Territories, November 3–4, 1969; the National Archives and Urban Research, June 18–19, 1970; Research in the Administration of Public Policy, November 19–20, 1970; Research in the Second World War, June 14–15, 1971; and the National Archives and Research in Historical Geography, November 8–9, 1971.

Recordings of opening remarks of the Archivist of the United States, the Administrator of General Services, and guest speakers at premiere showings of "Films at the Archives" festivals, 1970. (For a description of a series sponsored by the Woodrow Wilson International Center for Scholars, see entry J15.)

Audio reel tapes of formal lectures presented to the public by guest speakers on various historical topics related to the use of archival records and sources. Included are presentations by Sir David Evans of England on the history of archival practice; Alex Haley on the use of genealogical records for *Roots*; Anthony Cave-Brown on war-time code solving and deception; Herbert Gutman on slave family research; and others on various subjects dealing with the historical study of immigration into the United States.

Miscellaneous recordings of Charles A. Lindbergh's reception in Washington, D.C., and of his address to the Press Club, 1927; of Adlai E. Stevenson's acceptance of the Democratic nomination for the presidential candidacy, 1952; of state of the union messages by Presidents Dwight D. Eisenhower, 1960, and John F. Kennedy, 1961; concerning the flight into outer space of Comdr. Alan Shepard, 1961; of President Kennedy's address to the United Nations, 1961; and of sound effects of an atomic bomb explosion.

RG 69: Records of the Work Projects Administration, 1936–1942.—418 items. Recordings of performances of folk singers, madrigal singers, a cappella choirs, Negro choruses, light and grand opera companies, symphony orchestras, concert bands, dance bands, and other groups of the Federal Music Project, many with intermission talks by prominent persons about the work of the WPA. Recordings of radio programs broadcast by the Federal Theatre Project, including productions of *R.U.R., Bolero, Hamlet,* and *Murder in the Cathedral.* Speeches, interviews, and special programs on the subject of the WPA and its organization or functions, or as part of productions by or for the WPA. Recordings of programs in the radio series "Their Greatest Stories," "History in Action," "Epic of America," "Pioneers of Science," and "Portraits in Oil." Recordings of several programs in the series "Friends and Neighbors" sponsored by the Democratic National Committee in support of New Deal programs; and special programs on national defense during 1941.

RG 79: Records of the National Park Service, 1932–1976.—225 items. Recordings of the memorial service in honor of Stephen T. Mather, July 10, 1932, first Director of the National Park Service at the Bohemian Club, San Francisco; the dedication of Mammoth Cave National Park, 1947; and the dedication of the equestrian statues at the north end of Arlington Memorial Bridge, Washington, D.C., 1951. A recording of a speech by Newton B. Drury explaining the functions of the Park Service to the Commonwealth Club of California, 1946.

Ninety-nine audio tape recordings of interviews of employees of the National Park Service (NPS) and related agencies, federal, state, or private, conducted Mr. S. Herbert Evison as part of the Harpers Ferry Center Oral History Project. The purpose of the interviews was to provide aural documentation to supplement textual records relating to the history of the NPS, its practices, functions, and organization. The Oral

History Project is a continuing one and these recordings constitute the initial interviews conducted during 1962–1963. Transcripts of the interviews are available as a separate series.

Audio tape recordings (109 items) of the NPS public service radio series, "Secrets of the National Parks," documenting the historical and natural heritage of the National Park System. The series was produced in cooperation with The American University and features interviews with NPS personnel, historians, environmentalists, scientists, biologists, and other individuals who discuss, lecture, or reminisce on various aspects of the National Parks covering topics such as the history of Biscayne Bay, the Appalachian Trail, fire control, the living geyser basins, underwater archeology, and the Yellowstone wilderness. Included as guests are individuals such as Justice William O. Douglas speaking on the history of the C & O Canal, and Ansel Adams on the program "Photographer of the Parks." Several tapes include actuality recordings made on location to highlight programs, such as "Music from Wild Sounds," "Folk-Songs-Latin Style," and "Folk Tales of El Morro."

RG 82: Records of the Federal Reserve System, 1937.—1 item. A recording of the address made by President Franklin D. Roosevelt at the dedication of the Federal Reserve Building.

RG 83: Records of the Bureau of Agricultural Economics, 1939–1944.—11 items. Lectures on general agricultural subjects, the history of agriculture in the United States, and special war-related phases of agriculture, recorded in English and Spanish for use with filmstrips.

RG 85: Records of the Immigration and Naturalization Service. 1940–1945.—61 items. Recordings of radio broadcasts concerning the obligations of aliens under the Alien Registration Act of 1940, of the "You and Your Citizenship" series designed to improve understanding of the alien and his problems, and of the "Heirs of Liberty" series intended to instruct aliens in U.S. citizenship laws and the benefits of citizenship. Recordings of dramas about the Immigration Border Patrol.

RG 90: Records of the Public Health Service, 1942 and 1967.—77 items. Recordings of the proceedings of the White House Conference on Health, November 3 and 4, 1965, and of a radio broadcast about National Health Week, 1942.

RG 94. See RG 407.

RG 96: Records of the Farmers Home Administration, 1934 and 1936.—32 items. Recordings of dramatic radio programs emphasizing the role of the Resettlement Administration in the introduction of scientific farming methods, financial assistance to farmers, adjustment of farm debts, and accounts of historical incidents that influenced the life of the farmer in the 1930s. A dramatization of the sinking of the *Lusitania* and commentary on attempts to salvage her treasures. A discussion of the extortion racket in the United States.

RG 103: Records of the Farm Credit Administration, ca. 1936.—2 items. Recordings of 15-minute radio programs entitled "Homes of the Land."

RG 106: Records of the Smithsonian Institution, 1912–1941.—422 items. Bureau of American Ethnology recordings of songs and linguistic material in Indian languages, including Aleut, Mission, Chumash, Creek, and Navajo, with some translations, 1912, 1914, and 1930–1941. The Mary C. Wheelwright Collection of field cylinder recordings dating from the 1920s. Additional information on RG 106 is published in *Guide to Records in the National Archives of the U.S. Relating to American Indians* (1982). There are also recordings of the radio series "The World Is Yours," "Education in the News," "Let Freedom Ring," "Wings for the Martins," and "Women in the Making of America," broadcast by the U.S. Office of Education, 1936–1941.

RG 107: Records of the Office of the Secretary of War, 1942–1943. —37 items. Recordings from the "Orientation Service" and "What Are We Fighting For?" series of speeches to the officers and men of the armed services by war correspondents

concerning backgrounds of the war and German and U.S. war aims. Recordings of broadcasts of "The Hour of the Victory Corps" and "The Victory Hour" series, which were designed to enlist youth of high school age into the war effort.

RG 112: Records of the Office of the Surgeon General (Army), 1956.—2 items. "Brainwashing—Its Implications for Americans," an address by Major William E. Mayer, U.S. Army Medical Corps, San Francisco Naval Shipyard.

RG 117: Records of the American Battle Monuments Commission, 1937.—21 items. Recordings of the dedication ceremonies of the Meuse-Argonne war memorial at Montfaucon, France, August 1, 1937.

RG 118: Records of United States Attorneys and Marshals, 1944–1945.—23 items. Disc recordings of broadcasts by Radio Tokyo and other Japanese stations during World War II that relate to "Tokyo Rose" and her treason trial. Recordings were originally shortwave broadcasts monitored by the Foreign Broadcast Intelligence Service (see RG 262).

RG 119: Records of the National Youth Administration, 1938–1939.—19 items. Recordings of a discussion of NYA personnel on the Passamaquoddy Tidal Power Development. A radio drama about young persons who were helped by the NYA after they had been unable to find employment. A recording of the dedication of the NYA exhibit at the New York World's Fair on June 3, 1939.

RG 122: Records of the Federal Trade Commission, 1937.—2 items. Dedication of the Federal Trade Commission Building by President Franklin D. Roosevelt on July 12, 1937.

RG 127: Records of the United States Marine Corps, 1942–1943. —6 items. Recordings of Marine Corps recruiting broadcasts.

RG 129: Records of the Bureau of Prisons, 1939.—2 items. Recordings of programs released to radio by the National Parole Conference, April 17–18, 1939.

RG 130: Records of the White House Office. 1950–1953, 1959.—165 items. Recordings of radio speeches by President Harry S Truman concerning domestic and foreign affairs, remarks at ceremonies and dedications, greetings to foreign dignitaries visiting America, and many campaign speeches, 1950–1952. Greetings exchanged by President Dwight D. Eisenhower and Prime Minister John G. Diefenbaker of Canada on the occasion of the opening of the Prince Albert Radar Laboratory, June 5, 1959.

RG 131: Records of the Office of Alien Property, ca. 1930–1941. —105 items. Recordings from the records of the German-American Bund of German nationalist songs, symphonies, operatic selections, speeches by Nazi leaders, including Adolph Hitler, and similar material used at entertainments and rallies. Recordings of Bund rallies in Madison Square Garden and the Hippodrome, New York City.

RG 146: Records of the Civil Service Commission, 1965–1967.—11 items. Speeches presented by Vice-President Hubert H. Humphrey, Vice-President Lyndon Johnson, John W. Macy, Jr., and the Georgetown University Forum series (2 items), and WWDC radio station interviews with John W. Macy, Jr. Topics include employment for youth, postal revenue and Federal Salary Act, equal rights, and the Civil Service Commission. There is also a sound track for the film, *Friargraphics.*

RG 147: Records of the Selective Service System, 1969.—4 items. Audio tape recordings of random selections of the Selective Service Lottery Selection of December 1, 1969, at the National Headquarters, Washington, D.C.

RG 160: Records of Headquarters Army Service Forces, 1943–1944.—147 items. Recordings in foreign languages made for training purposes by the Army Special Training Division under the Director of Military Training.

RG 162: General Records of the Federal Works Agency, 1941.—2 items. Recordings of two radio broadcasts of speeches by John M. Carmody relating to defense housing, 1941.

RG 165: Records of the War Department General and Special Staff, 1942–1951.—

1,293 items. Miscellaneous recordings collected by the Radio Branch of the Bureau of Public Relations of the War Department, 1942–1949, relating to combat at Salerno, Anzio, and several other European sites; concerning the war in the Pacific including Gen. Jonathan M. Wainwright's surrender of Manila to the Japanese, Gen. Douglas MacArthur's arrival in Melbourne from the Philippine Islands, campaigns, air-sea rescue activities, the death of Ernie Pyle, and the Japanese surrender in the Philippines. Recordings of press conferences of Gen. Robert L. Eichelberger concerning the occupation of Japan and of Gen. Lucius D. Clay relating to the Allied occupation of Germany.

Recordings of addresses, press conferences, and interviews of Secretary of Defense Louis A. Johnson about the Armed Forces Unification Act, defense policy, and economy in defense. Recordings of addresses of the heads of the various women's services to Girls' Nation about careers for women in defense. Recordings from the Office of the Chief of Staff of testimony by Secretary of War Henry L. Stimson and others before the Select Committee on Post War Military Policy, 1945. A recording of the farewell ceremonies of General MacArthur at Haneda Airport, 1951, made by the Radio-TV Branch, GHQ, Tokyo. Many recordings in German, Japanese, and Chinese that were used by the Axis in their psychological warfare efforts during World War II.

RG 171: Records of the Office of Civilian Defense, 1939–1945. —200 items. Recordings of radio broadcasts of speeches, discussions, and dramas promoting participation in and explaining all phases of the operation of the Civilian Defense program, including broadcasts by the Office of Civilian Defense, the Office of War Information, the National Safety Council, the Commerce and Industry Association of New York, the Young Men's Christian Association, the U.S. Army, "The Burns and Allen Show," and "The Vic and Sade Show." A series of recordings about many aspects of civil defense in England.

RG 173: Records of the Federal Communications Commission, 1934–1945.—305 items. Recordings of cases heard and decided by the commission upon petitions and complaints of interested persons or upon the motion of the commission itself, involving chiefly telephone, telegraph, cable, and radio broadcasting companies and dealing with such matters as rates, facilities, quality of service, corporate organizations, assignment of radio frequencies, and transfers of ownership.

RG 174: General Records of the Department of Labor, 1941, 1955–1969.—133 items. A recording of President Harry S Truman's address to the President's Conference on Industrial Safety, 1941. Recordings made by or about the Labor Department, 1955–1969, and including press conferences, ceremonies, addresses, and interviews, mostly of Secretaries of Labor James P. Mitchell, Arthur Goldberg, and Willard Wirtz, relating to policies, programs, and functions of the Department of Labor in particular, and government-labor relationships in general.

RG 178: Records of the United States Maritime Commission, 1941–1945.—127 items. Recordings of radio broadcasts concerning the work of the commission and the importance of the merchant marine in the war effort and consisting of dramatizations, speeches, interviews, panel discussions, news commentaries, and award presentations featuring commission members, President Franklin D. Roosevelt, Carl Sandburg, Edward R. Murrow, and many other important persons. Included are broadcasts of "Information Please," "It's Maritime," "For This We Fight," "Heroes of the Merchant Marine," "Men at Sea," "Fibber McGee and Molly," "Sing Along," and "Deeds without Words."

Dramatizations of the history of the Merchant Marine, including the arrival of the *Franklin* at Nagasaki, 1799, the voyage of the *Margaret* from Salem to Nagasaki in 1801, the beginning of U.S. and Canadian shipping on the Great Lakes, and the life of whaler and writer Herman Melville.

RG 179: Records of the War Production Board, 1942–1945.—120 items. Recordings of radio broadcasts concerning the importance of increased war production, the conservation of essential materials, and the betterment of labor-management relations; also consisting of dramatizations, speeches, interviews, and entertainment, including Eleanor Roosevelt, Donald M. Nelson, Joseph C. Grew, Frank Knox, Leon Henderson, and a number of actors and actresses. Included are broadcasts of "Men, Machines and Victory," "You Can't Do Business with Hitler," and "Fibber McGee and Molly." Recordings used in training mail and messenger service personnel, secretaries, and switchboard operators.

RG 188: Records of the Office of Price Administration, 1941–1946.—202 items. Recordings of radio broadcasts concerning the importance and necessity of price controls, rationing, and enforcement of the regulations; news commentaries, dramatizations, panel discussions, speeches, and interviews featuring prominent persons, such as Chester S. Bowles, Robert S. Kerr, Donald M. Nelson, Leon Henderson, Harold L. Ickes, Harry S Truman, Robert A. Taft, Paul Porter, and Fiorello La Guardia. Included are broadcasts of "Neighborhood Call," "Hasten the Day," "OPA Weekly Report," "A Hundred Million Questions," and "You Can't Do Business with Hitler." A recording of a congressional debate concerning the extension of price controls beyond the end of the war.

RG 195: Records of the Federal Home Loan Bank System, 1945.—1 item. A sound recording created to accompany and explain a Federal Home Loan Bank Board exhibit at the Texas centennial.

RG 196: Records of the Public Housing Administration, 1938–1946.—75 items. Recordings of radio broadcasts from the "Slums Cost You Money" series concerning the need for low cost housing and explaining the federal housing programs and the role of local governmental units in its implementation, and relating to national defense housing. Recordings from the "Famous Homes of Famous Americans" series. Recordings from the "Agency Series" consisting of reports to the people by several executive agencies.

RG 200: National Archives Gift Collection, 1892–1983.—36,042 items.

ABC Collection: Radio Network News Programs, 1943–1967.—25,000 sound recordings. Includes discs of radio broadcasts from the ABC network as recorded or aired by the ABC Radio News Department. Consists of speeches, scheduled news programs, news commentaries, special events, and public affairs programming. There is coverage of presidential activities, including the events surrounding the assassination of John F. Kennedy; political conventions; congressional hearings, such as Army-McCarthy and Kefauver Crime Hearings; U.S. participation in the Korean and Vietnam wars; and a sampling of network news commentaries on these events by Walter Winchell, Drew Pearson, Elmer Davis, Martin Agronsky, and Taylor Grant.

CBS Collection: CBS Bicentennial Radio Programs, July 2–4, 1976.—4 sound recordings. Audio tapes of two bicentennial radio specials, "Festival for the Fourth" providing an audio summary of the highlights of bicentennial coverage around the world, and "America—This I Believe," a series of 35, five-minute CBS radio reports featuring interviews with a variety of Americans offering their reactions and observations on America's 200th birthday celebration. "CBS Radio at Fifty: An Autobiography in Sound," consists of 3 audio tape recordings commemorating the 50th anniversary of CBS radio on September 18, 1977.

University of Maryland Collection: Radio Broadcasts of Station WJSV/WTOP, 1937–1957.—2,600 sound recordings. Consists of disc recordings of radio broadcasts of speeches and interviews with presidents, congressmen, world leaders, and statesmen, as well as descriptions of historical events and political campaigns, news, documentaries, and public affairs programs.

National Public Radio Collection: News and Public Affairs Programs, 1971–1975.—

3,558 audio tape recordings. Includes news programs and commentaries, specifically the 90-minute daily news program "All Things Considered," congressional hearings, presidential speeches and press conferences; special events including political campaigns, space flights, and professional conferences; and public affairs broadcasts, such as "Firing Line," "National Press Club," "Ford Hall Forum," "Contemporary World Problems," and "Advances in Science." An index is available.

Town Hall Collection, 1935–1952.—Audio recordings of the public affairs program, "America's Town Meeting of the Air," a discussion forum for issues of national concern.

Radio Station WWDC Collection: WWDC Radio Documentaries, 1973–1975.—6 sound recordings. Consists of documentaries entitled "The Most Pampered Plane in the World," "Air Force One," and "UFOs—Fact or Fiction."

Emerson L. Fraser Collection: Public Service Radio Programs, 1950–1955.—49 disc recordings produced by federal agencies and non-profit public service organizations, of broadcasts, such as "Your Navy Show," "Stars for Defense," "Stars on Parade," as well as recordings produced by the U.S. Marine Corps, National Guard, Coast Guard Reserve, U.S. Air Force, American Red Cross, U.S. Army, and the March of Dimes.

David Goldin Collection: Aired by Armed Forces Radio and Commercial Radio Networks, 1932–1952.—3,200 disc recordings. Consists of radio broadcasts produced, acquired, or aired by the CBS, NBC, Mutual, and Armed Forces radio networks. Included are political speeches, interviews, combat actualities, special events, documentaries, political conventions, congressional hearings, entertainment to U.S. troops overseas, and foreign radio stations and public affairs programming.

John Hickman Collection: Historical Recordings and Radio Broadcasts, 1931–1977.—960 disc recordings of broadcasts produced, acquired or aired by CBS, NBC, Mutual and Armed Forces radio networks, as well as various educational radio stations. Included are broadcasts of addresses by Presidents Herbert Hoover, Harry S Truman, Dwight D. Eisenhower, Richard Nixon, Gerald Ford, and Jimmy Carter; speeches by Will Rogers, Senator Huey Long, Father Charles E. Coughlin, Ambassador Joseph Kennedy, Senator Gerald P. Nye, Senator Joseph McCarthy, Henry Cabot Lodge, and Supreme Court Justice Abe Fortas. In addition, there are recordings of interviews of congressional leaders relating to Watergate, Vietnam, and the Nixon impeachment hearings, press conferences with Henry Kissinger and President Carter, World War II combat conferences, recordings of special events such as civil rights demonstrations and Vietnam War protests, and congressional hearings.

Milo Ryan Phonoarchive Collections, 1939–1945.—2,500 disc recordings. A collection of original sound recordings of radio broadcasts made by CBS radio affiliate KIRO, from 1939–1941. Includes transcribed speeches, special events, and public affairs programs of World War II subjects. A separate catalog is available.

"Ladies of the Press" Collection, 1962–1967.—94 sound recordings. Broadcast interviews with notable personalities, such as Martin Luther King, Jr., Robert F. Kennedy, Pearl Buck, Dick Gregory, James A. Farley, as questioned by three women journalists.

There are other recordings of speeches of most U.S. presidents of the twentieth century, and speeches, interviews, and panel discussions by many prominent persons, including Thomas A. Edison, Admiral Robert E. Peary, Amelia Earhart, Will Rogers, Norman Thomas, Henry A. Wallace, Cordell Hull, Summer Wells, Alben W. Barkley, Adlai E. Stevenson, Gen. Douglas MacArthur, Eleanor Roosevelt, Sara Delano Roosevelt, Wendell Willkie, Winston Churchill, King George VI of Great Britain, Mme. Chiang Kai-shek, Mahatma Gandhi, and a number of Senators and Representatives, well-known singers, actors, writers, religious leaders, World War I heroes, and combat airmen of World War II.

There is also a collection of sound recordings of a television series, "Longines Chronoscope," 1951–1955, consisting of interviews and panel discussions with U.S. and world leaders in many fields, including politics, education, science, and economics.

There are also recordings of all broadcasts over at least one of the networks for the day of September 21, 1939, including the President's neutrality message delivered before Congress, of the 24 hours after the attack on Pearl Harbor, of the first 36 hours of the allied invasion of Europe, June 6, 1944, of the 3 days following the death of President Roosevelt, April 12, 1945, and of V-J Day. There are recordings of the signing of the German and Japanese surrender documents. Included also are recordings of the 1960 Democratic and Republican national conventions, of National Defense Day in 1924, the Sesquicentennial celebration of the Constitution in 1936, the centennial celebration of the American patent system in 1936, the laying of the cornerstone of the Roosevelt Library in 1939, and the Inter-Asia Relations Conference at New Delhi, India in 1947. Other recordings include hearings of the Special Senate Committee on the Communication Satellite Bill, 1962, dramas, musical events, and a series of talking books prepared by the American Foundation for the Blind. The materials described above represent only a sampling of what researchers can expect to discover in RG 200.

RG 207: General Records of the Department of Housing and Urban Development, 1966–1968.—245 items. Includes radio spot announcements pertaining to departmental programs and speeches by the Secretary, Robert C. Weaver.

RG 208: Records of the Office of War Information, 1941–1946.—1,115 items. Includes recordings of informational, news, and propaganda broadcasts released at home and beamed abroad, covering all aspects of the war effort on the home front; campaign news on the Allies and the Axis powers; domestic news; and news of the progress of the war and the defeat of Italy, Germany, and Japan.

Recordings of speeches of Presidents Franklin D. Roosevelt and Harry S Truman, and of Winston Churchill and many others; visits of world leaders to the United States; and international conferences including Casablanca (1942), Dumbarton Oaks (1944), Yalta (1945), the U.N. Conference on International Organization and the Charter signing ceremonies (1945), and the opening session of the U.N. General Assembly and the Security Council (1946). Recordings pertaining to the functions of the International Bank for Reconstruction and Development; the Internal Monetary Fund; the World Health Organization; and the U.N. Relief and Rehabilitation Administration. Miscellaneous recordings relating to the lend-lease program, U.S. aid to small nations, reciprocal trade agreements, International Red Cross activities, the death of Franklin D. Roosevelt, of atom bomb tests, and of the music of many lands. Included in the overseas broadcasts are series entitled "Uncle Sam Speaks," "Voice of Freedom," "You Can't Do Business with Hitler," and "We Fight Back"; and a series broadcast to the Japanese by Captain Ellis M. Zacharias. Domestic broadcasts include series known as "This Is Our Enemy," "Soldiers of Production," "Three-Thirds of a Nation," "Neighborhood Call," "Hasten the Day," and "Victory Front"; and a number from commercial daytime serials.

RG 210: Records of the War Relocation Authority, 1944–1945.—28 items. Recordings of radio broadcasts concerning the activities of the WRA, the record of Nisei soldiers, and speeches by Dillon S. Meyer, director of the Authority.

RG 215: Records of the Office of Community War Services, 1943–1944.—4 items. A recording made to accompany the film, "Prostitution and the War."Three disc recordings of "Tribute to the U.S. Cadet Nurse Corps," broadcast on November 13, 1944, by the National Broadcasting Company from Constitution Hall, Washington, D.C.

RG 216: Records of the Office of Censorship, ca. 1942.—2 items. Recordings of

training lectures relating to censorship of international telecommunications, telephone, registered mail, POW mail, travelers mail, and press and radio.

RG 220: Records of Temporary Committees, Commissions, and Boards, 1968–1980.—1,184 items. This RG includes extensive sound recordings focusing on the following: National Commission on the Causes and Prevention of Violence, 1968–1969 (18 sound recordings); National Commission on Marijuana and Drug Abuse, 1970–1973 (4 sound recordings); National Study Commission on Records and Documents of Federal Officials, 1975–1977 (23 volumes of transcripts of audio tape recordings); National Commission on the Observance of International Women's Year, 1977 (ca. 200 sound recordings, many of which are interviews, lectures, and oral history materials); Presidential Commission on World Hunger, 1978–1980 (2 sound recordings); Records of the President's Commission on Coal, 1979 (305 sound recordings); Commission on the Accident at Three Mile Island, 1979 (517 sound recordings); White House Conference on Library and Information Services, 1979 (38 sound recordings); Records of the White House Conference on Families (63 sound recordings); Recordings of meetings, briefings, and discussion of the National Advisory Committee (14 sound recordings).

RG 228: Records of the Committee on Fair Employment Practice, 1946.—4 items. A dramatization of the work of the committee, 1941–1946.

RG 229: Records of the Office of Inter-American Affairs, 1941–1945.—24 items. Recordings in Spanish and French of informational and propaganda broadcasts to Latin America about life in the United States, American ideology, American institutions, and the American war effort and peace aims. Included are recordings in the series, "United Nations Speak" and "Americanos Todos."

RG 235: General Records of the Department of Health, Education, and Welfare, 1942, 1947.—8 items. Recordings of broadcasts of speeches by Paul V. McNutt, ca. 1942; and of a series concerning the training and rehabilitation of the handicapped, 1947.

RG 238: National Archives Collection of World War II War Crimes Records, 1945–1946.—2,056 items. Recordings of the proceedings of the sessions of the International Military Tribunal held in Nuremberg, Germany, from November 20, 1945, to October 1, 1946, including the testimony of the Nazi defendants, and the testimony of witnesses on German aggression, concentration camps, forced labor, the Gestapo, pillage of art treasures, and other injustices and atrocities committed by the Germans.

RG 242: National Archives Collection of Foreign Records Seized, 1925–1944.—1,551 items. Recordings collected by the war crimes investigators but not used in evidence at the trials and those captured by allied forces during and after the war of speeches by Nazi officials, including Adolph Hitler, Joseph Goebbels, Hermann Goering, and Albert Speer, 1939–1944; propaganda material recorded by the Fascists in Italy; speeches of Benito Mussolini, Count Galeazzo Ciano, and other Fascist leaders; and speeches by Italian dignitaries including Pope Pius XI.

RG 243: Records of the United States Strategic Bombing Survey, 1945.—366 items. Recordings of interviews with Japanese civilians concerning the effects of American bombing on several Japanese cities, and an eyewitness account of the bombing of Hiroshima.

RG 252: Records of the Office of the Housing Expediter, 1950–1952.—73 items. Recordings of broadcasts of speeches, interviews, and panel discussions by Housing Expediter Tighe Woods and other housing officials, Congressmen, and others concerning rent control. Recordings of public hearings on rent control.

RG 255: Records of the National Advisory Committee for Aeronautics. 1942, 1947, and 1967. Includes interviews and broadcasts with Congressman Anderson, Maj. H.W. Squires, Smith De France, and others. The collection also includes a number of NASA

materials including: daily summaries of Apollo 204 review board sessions; eyewitness statements concerning the command module; voice communications with the astronauts; inspection of the burned command module; talk to the Apollo staff by Dr. Joseph Shea.

RG 262: Records of the Foreign Broadcast Intelligence Service, 1940–1947.—608 sound recordings. Includes recordings of foreign broadcasts, many in English and others in German, Japanese, and other languages, that were monitored by the service. There are broadcasts by Ezra Pound from Italy, October 2, 1941 through July 24, 1943, speeches by Adolph Hitler, Paul Joseph Goebbels, Joachim von Ribbentrop, Benito Mussolini, Marshall Henri Petrain, Pierre Laval, Hideki Tojo, and others. Other recordings include broadcasts over German radio by U.S. citizens including Frederick W. Kaltenbach, Douglas Chandler, Edward Delaney, Mildred E. Gillars ("Axis Sally"), and broadcasts originating from Japan or Japanese-held territory of news reports and commentary, including that of "Tokyo Rose." There are speeches by Presidents Franklin D. Roosevelt and Harry S Truman, King George VI of Great Britain, and other allied leaders, 1940–1947.

RG 264: Records of the Commissions on Organization of the Executive Branch of the Government, 1949.—3 items. Recordings of interviews with Herbert Hoover by Lyman Bryson, Columbia Broadcasting System's Counsellor on Public Affairs, concerning the plans for reorganization of the Executive Branch of the government.

RG 267: Records of the Supreme Court of the United States, 1955—1970.–1,138 items. Includes, in part, tape recordings of oral arguments before the Supreme Court during the 1955–1970 terms. The tapes are transferred to the archives annually, but reproductions may not be furnished until three years after the date of argument.

RG 274: National Archives Collection of Records of Inaugural Committees, 1949, 1961.—8 items. Recordings of committee meetings and press conferences and of interviews with committee members relating to plans for the inaugurals of Presidents Harry S Truman and John F. Kennedy. (See RG 274 cited under the Judicial, Fiscal and Social Branch for recent inaugural committee recordings).

RG 280: Records of the Federal Mediation and Conciliation Service, 1959.—1 item. A recording of several talks to be used with slides in connection with the mediation work of the service.

RG 286: Records of the Agency for International Development: Records of the Office of Public Affairs.—375 sound recordings of "Overseas Mission" radio series, 1952–1970 and 1971–1976.

RG 288: Records of the National Foundation on the Arts and Humanities, 1965–1979.—43 items. Recordings of speeches, meetings, panels, special programs, and media appearances featuring various officials: Senators Hubert Humphrey, Jacob Javitz, Claiborne Pell, Edward Brooke, William Proxmire, and others.

RG 295: Records of the Office of Price Stabilization, 1950–1953.—47 items. Recordings of radio broadcasts containing consumer information, consisting of talks, interviews, dramas, spot announcements, and music featuring Tighe Woods, Eric Johnston, Michael V. DiSalle, Roger Putnam, and several prominent entertainers, including, Kate Smith, Frank Sinatra, and Bob Crosby.

RG 296: General Records of the Economic Stabilization Agency, 1951–1953.—39 items. Recordings of a speech by Michael V. DiSalle, 1951, of a Reconstruction Finance Corporation conference, 1952, and of administrative hearings concerning personnel matters of the agency, 1953.

RG 306: Records of the United States Information Agency, 1950–1965.—387 items. Recordings made by or for the Voice of America for overseas release and consisting of dramatizations, reports, speeches, and interviews designed to promote better understanding of the United States. They are concerned with rural America, labor, farming, education, scientific developments, economics, the role of women in the United States,

travel, immigrants in America, conservation, politics, food inspection, public health, charitable and service organizations, literature, foreign students in the United States, the communications media, world food production, world health, the establishment of the Constitution and the concept of individual freedom, the sesquicentennial of the birth of President Abraham Lincoln, and the Korean action. Included are programs from these series: "Washington Interview," "The Puerto Rican Story," "The Jeffersonian Heritage," "Document: Deep South," "Atoms for Power," "New World of Atomic Energy," "Indian Country," "The Great Lakes," and "New Horizons in Science."

RG 326: Records of the Atomic Energy Commission, 1967.—3 items. A recording entitled "Atomic Year 25," produced to commemorate the 25th anniversary of the achievement of a controlled nuclear chain reaction at the University of Chicago on December 2, 1942.

RG 328: Records of the National Capital Planning Commission, 1953.—12 items. Recordings of the proceedings of the commission, January–April and May 22, 1953.

RG 330: Records of the Office of the Secretary of Defense, 1949–1973.—1,172 items. Recordings of press conferences, briefings, speeches, and statements of Department of Defense and other government officials, political and military leaders, and others relating to defense policy, foreign affairs, military aid, the Korean action, and other matters; and of radio and television programs, 1942–1960. Stenographic recordings of activities of the Secretaries of Defense in conference, Marine Corps Schools, Quantico, Virginia , July 23–26, 1953. There are also a number of recordings representing the Defense Advisory Committee on Women in the Service.

RG 335: Records of the Office of the Secretary of the Army, 1951–1974.—613 sound recordings. Includes recordings made for use at Army camps during Armed Forces Day. Most of the recordings, however, consist of the "Army Hour" radio program, 1942–1974. Program scripts for the program are included in the collection.

RG 341: Records of Headquarters United States Air Force, 1953.—33 items. Includes recordings from the G-2 intelligence file relating to the 1953 May Day celebration in Moscow and to unspecified "Security Information."

RG 342: Records of the United States Air Force Commands, Activities, and Organizations, 1961–1975.—256 items. Recordings of three radio broadcast series, "Great Moments to Music," "Our Date with History," and "Country Music Time." The first two series focus on various aspects of aerospace technology. The third series features live performances by country music artists and performers, such as Patsy Cline, Dave Dudley, Merle Travis, the Floriday Boys, Faron Young, and Archie Campbell.

RG 370: Records of the National Oceanic and Atmospheric Administration, 1977–1979.—32 items. Consists of a radio series of interviews with NOAA scientists, technicians, specialists, and programming officials who discuss agency programs and functions and how these activities affect the public. Some topics are historical, such as a discussion of weather patterns for presidential inaugurations and a history of oil spills. Topics of a more general nature relate to aspects of oceanography and meteorology, such as ocean engineering, solar forecasting, aquaculture, and the ozone layer.

RG 381: Records of Agencies for Economic Opportunity and Legal Services, 1964–1973.—835 sound recordings. Includes audio tapes of addresses, interviews, press conferences, and training seminars. One major emphasis is on the subject of poverty. There are also recordings of the radio series, "Voices of Vista" and "Vista Viewpoint." The series includes interviews, peformances by musicians and other entertainers. The interviews focus on hunger, migrants, the aged, and community action.

RG 398: Records of the Department of Transportation, 1970–1977.—257 items. Includes audio tapes of press conferences, briefings, speeches, interviews, and hearings and testimony. The topics covered are extensive.

RG 407 (formerly RG 94): Records of the Adjutant General's Office, 1917–1945.—

26 items. Recordings of opening exercises at Army administration officer training at North Dakota Agricultural College and at Grinnell College in Iowa, 1942. Oral history materials include accounts by Army and Air Force personnel, including James H. Doolittle, and others, of their combat experiences, 1941–1945.

RG 423: Records of the National Advisory Commission on Criminal Justice Standards and Goals, 1971–1973.—1 item. An audio recording of a radio interview aired on WISN AM/FM in Milwaukee, Wisconsin. Rev. Prenzlow discusses the background of the commission, the recently released commission report, the penal system, and court reform.

RG 429: Records of Organizations in the Executive Office of the President, 1971–1976.—271 sound recordings. Includes recordings on the Domestic Council Committee on the Right to Privacy, the Presidential Clemancy Board, meetings of the American Revolution Bicentennial Commission. There are also radio interviews, press conferences, and public service announcements.

RG 453: Records of the Commission on Civil Rights, 1961–1967.—6 sound recordings. Includes press conference and radio broadcast recordings.

4 a. Tape recorders and headphones are available for on-site use.

b. Researchers are encouraged to make arrangements in advance of their visit so that the use of audio equipment can be scheduled. Researchers may bring their personal listening equipment into the various reading rooms.

c. No fees are charged except those for duplicating recordings.

d. Duplication of recordings is provided by the staff for a fee. A price list and order forms are available. Researchers may use their own equipment to duplicate recordings without charge. Only recordings in the public domain (comprising about 60 percent of the holdings) may be duplicated. Other holdings are subject to restrictions on use as designated by the donor or agency. A leaflet that describes the procedures for ordering copies of sound recordings is available free upon request.

5. The identification of many sound recordings is provided through various bibliographic aids. The best means of identifying which record groups have sound recordings is the online printout, *List of Record Groups of the National Archives and Records Service* (January 1981). This handy tool includes a list of RGs arranged alphabetically with each RG broken down by format. Included, also, are lists of RGs arranged by operating units, as well as RGs arranged by RG number. RGs cited in the present study were identified, in part, with the use of this aid.

Researchers having RG numbers in hand can then consult various finding aid vertical files in the appropriate divisions/branches where contents of each RG are described. The Motion Picture, Sound & Video Branch, for example, also maintains various card files, including a RG control card catalog and name, subject, and series card catalogs. A typical card entry includes RG number, name or title of the record group, donor or agency, date of material and accession number, format, physical restrictions statement, and a description of the materials.

Other aids include the *Guide to the National Archives of the United States* (1974), *Sound Recordings in the Audiovisual Archives Division of the National Archives* (1972), the contents of which are cited above, *Audiovisual Records in the National Archives Relating to World War II, Audiovisual Records Relating to Naval History* (1975), *Voices of World War II, 1937–1945* (1971), *The Crucial Decade: Voices of the Postwar Era, 1945–1954* (1977), *Captured German Sound Recordings* (1978), and *Audiovisual Records in the National Archives Relating to Black History* (July 1972). Another aid, *Guide to Records in the National Archives of the United States Relating to American Indians* (1981) includes some information on record groups containing sound record-

ings. Researchers must scan each RG because the sound recordings are not separately indexed.

Most research rooms also maintain various typescript finding aids. Perhaps 15 percent of the recorded collections have such aids in the form of written transcripts, radio scripts, and general background information. For example, all remarks and speeches of U.S. Presidents are transcribed and published in the series, *Public Papers of the President.*

The National Archives publishes a journal, *Prologue* (quarterly), which frequently lists and describes recent sound recording accessions. An additional useful publication that cites printed materials is *Select List of Publications of the National Archives and Records Service* (1982). Many of the above publications are available free upon request.

B28 National Archives for Black Women's History

1 a. *1318 Vermont Avenue, N.W.*
Washington, D.C. 20005
(202) 332–1233
(202) 332–9201

b. 9:00 A.M.–5:00 P.M.   Monday–Friday, by appointment only

c. Open to researchers by appointment.

d. Guy McElroy, Museum Curator

2. The National Archives for Black Women's History evolved in 1977 from the Archives Committee of the National Council of Negro Women, established by Mary McLeod Bethune in 1939. It is the only archival repository that focuses solely on black women and includes papers, photographs, letters, and other documents relating to the history of black women and their participation in such issues as civil rights, education, health, housing, employment, and international relations.

3. There are a number of oral history tapes in this collection. Researchers wishing to use these materials should write or call the archives to make specific requests and to arrange for an appointment.

4 a. On-site listening equipment is not available.

B29 National Council for the Traditional Arts (NCTA)

1 a. *1346 Connecticut Avenue, N.W.*
Washington, D.C. 20036

b. 10:00 A.M.–6:00 P.M.   Monday–Friday

c. Only serious researchers may gain access to the collection of audio recordings. Individuals must write and describe their purpose and request an appointment at least a month in advance.

d. Joseph T. Wilson, Executive Director

2. The National Council for the Traditional Arts, founded in 1934, is a private organization that organizes and directs public presentations of the traditional folk arts. Among the council's significant annual productions is the National Folk Festival.

3.   The council maintains an archive of audio recordings of the National Folk Festival. Although an exact count of individual recordings is not available, there are approximately 800 hours of audio recordings on reel-to-reel half track stereo format. There are 60 hours of ¾-inch video recordings. Performers on the recordings are folk artists who are selected for the festival on the basis of their authenticity and excellence. It is for this reason and the professional quality of the recording that this collection is considered valuable.

4 a.   On-site listening equipment is available for some material.

b.   Prior appointment is required and may be refused.

5.   Most of the audio tapes are cataloged by means of a log-in system done at the time of performance.

B30   National Genealogical Society Library

1 a.   *1921 Sunderland Place, N.W.*
Washington, D.C. 20036
(202) 785–2123

b.   11:00 A.M.–4:00 P.M.   Monday, Wednesday, Friday, Saturday
7:00 P.M.–10:00 P.M.   Wednesday

c.   Open to the public for a fee. Materials are loaned to society members only.

d.   Lt. Col. Varney Nell, President
Lillie May Park, Librarian

2.   The National Genealogical Society Library holdings focus on American local history and genealogy. Included are 14,000 volumes and some 50 journals, as well as extensive vertical file material. Source materials include Bible records, cemetery inscriptions, and probate and vital records.

3.   Notable holdings of the library.

Glebe House
4527 North 17th Street
Arlington, Virginia 22207
(703) 525–0050

10:00 A.M.–4:00 P.M.   Monday–Friday

The Glebe House is a historic home acquired in 1983 by the society and is scheduled to become its headquarters during late 1984. A few materials are already on deposit there, including a small collection of approximately 60 audio tapes consisting of lectures on genealogy presented by society speakers at the 5th floor theatre of the National Archives and Records Service (B27). These programs are normally presented twice a month from September to May. Audio tapes are available to society members only.

4 a.   On-site listening equipment is available at the Glebe House.

c.   A fee is charged to members to borrow audio tapes; however, members may utilize available equipment at Glebe House without charge.

d.   Duplication of the audio tapes is not permitted.

National Museum of African Art (Smithsonian Institution)—Eliot Elisofon Archives—Music Collection   See entry C10

National Museum of American History (Smithsonian Institution)—Archives Center   See entry C11

B31 National Park Service (Interior Department)—Clara Barton National Historic Site

1 a. *5801 Oxford Road*
Glen Echo, Maryland 20812
(301) 492–6245

b. 10:00 A.M.–5:00 P.M.   Monday–Sunday

c. Open to the public.

d. John Byrne, Superintendent

2.   The Clara Barton National Historic Site served as National Red Cross Head-quarters, Red Cross warehouse, and Clara Barton's home from 1897 to 1904. On-site is a library containing some 300 books on Clara Barton, turn-of-the-century America, and the Red Cross, as well as transcriptions of the diaries that Barton kept while living in the house. The library also maintains a photograph reference collection containing several hundred photographs concerning Barton and her work, and several thousand photographs of the house restoration project.

3.   The Library has 3 oral history interviews in cassette format of information about Clara Barton, her home, and Red Cross endeavors. Interviewees include Barton's private secretary, Joyce Butler Hughes, who is Barton's great grand niece, and a neighbor who knew Barton. Average length of each tape is 3 hours. The tapes have not been transcribed.

NOTE: Additional materials (RG 69) representing the National Park Service are located in the National Archives and Records Service (B27).

4 a. On-site listening equipment is available.

b. Reservations to use the oral history materials are recommended.

c. No fees are charged.

B32 National Press Club (NPC)—Archives

1 a. *National Press Building*
529 14th Street, N.W.
Washington, D.C. 20045
(202) 737–2500 (General)
(202) 662–7005 (Archives and Library)

   b. 9:00 A.M.–5:00 P.M.   Monday–Friday

   c. Open to serious researchers.

   d. Barbara Vandegrift, Archivist

2. The National Press Club is an association of writers, reporters, and newsmen representing newspapers, television and radio, wire services and other media.

3. Since 1952, the NPC has recorded on audio tape luncheon speeches and other internal events. Only the current year of recordings is retained by NPC in their archives (only a few of these speeches have been transcribed). At the end of the current year, the recordings are presented to the Library of Congress, where they are added to the "National Press Club Collection," held in the custody of the Motion Picture, Broadcasting and Recorded Sound Division (A41). Currently that collection contains over 850 recordings from 1952 to 1982. Examples of speakers represented in the collection include Presidents Hoover, Truman, Eisenhower, Kennedy, Johnson, Nixon, and Carter, and an array of congressmen, cabinet members, cultural figures, and foreign leaders, such as Adenauer, de Gaulle, Sukarno, Khrushchev, and Castro. Sir Patrick Dean, Senator Charles Goodell, John Freeman, Pierre Trudeau, Carlos Restrepo, Bowie Kuhn, Melvin R. Laird, Hugh Scott, Abe Fortas, John Volpe, Nuyegen Cao Ky, Earl Butz, Golda Meir, Henry Jackson, Harold Wilson, Willy Brandt, Abba Eban, and Helmut Schmidt. Persons in the arts include, for example, Artur Rubinstein and Alex Haley.

   The NPC also regularly presents a number of tapes to National Public Radio (B33). In turn, NPR has donated their copies of the recorded speeches for the years 1971–1976 to the National Archives and Records Service (B27) and the musical events associated with certain events to the Motion Picture, Broadcasting and Recorded Sound Division of the Library of Congress (A41).

4 a. On-site listening equipment is available.

   b. An appointment is recommended.

   c. No fees are charged for listening to recordings.

   d. Researchers may purchase copies of recorded speeches.

5. NPC archives maintains a card catalog of all speeches where they are listed by name of speaker. A chronological list is also available.

B33 National Public Radio (NPR)—Library

1 a. *2025 M Street, N.W.*
      Washington, D.C. 20036
      (202) 822–2000

   b. 9:00 A.M.–5:00 P.M.   Monday–Friday

   c. Although the library is open to the public, it is regarded primarily as a working collection for NPR staff.

   d. Ricki Kushner and Margot McGann, Co-Directors

2. National Public Radio is a network of radio stations, which began broadcasting in 1971. All programs produced by National Public Radio are duplicated on reel-to-

reel tape and stored by the broadcast library. The tape collection reflects the variety of programming produced by NPR, including its news shows, "All Things Considered" and "Morning Edition," and National Press Club addresses (1976 to the present), congressional hearings, "Jazz Alive," and numerous drama programs. The last five years of programming are housed at NPR. After five years, news and information programs are sent to the National Archives and Records Service (B27), and performance programs are sent to the Library of Congress (A41).

3. The music, sound effects, and spoken word collection comprises some 4,000 commercial discs, for use by NPR staff in producing programs.

4 a. On-site listening equipment is available.

b. Prior appointment is required.

c. There are no fees charged to listen to the recordings. A fee is charged to record news programs.

d. Some of the recordings may be duplicated as long as no copyright restrictions exist. Cassette or reel-to-reel copies are available at cost.

5. The tape collection is assigned an accession number and then arranged by distribution date. The disc collection is arranged by subject. Both are cataloged and retrieved through a microfiche catalog with access by title, series title, keyword, classification number, geographic heading, and personal names. The collection spans from 1971 to mid-1982.

The NPR Publications Department offers for purchase many of its educational, cultural, and informational programs. The NPR *1983 Cassette Catalogue* lists over 200 programs for such topics as education, humanities (including the arts, language and literature, and media), science (including medical ethics and technology and the natural sciences), and the social sciences (focusing on aging, American culture, American foreign affairs, business and economics, health, history, international affairs and issues, marriage and family, psychology, social problems, special interest groups, including ethnic groups, the handicapped, and women, war and peace, and world cultures). Included among these recordings are a number of oral history interviews. The catalog also includes a list of NPR member radio stations. Contact the Publications Department at (800) 253–0808 (toll-free) for a copy of this catalog. In addition, individuals may contact the Public Information Department (202/822–2300) for information on obtaining taped copies of news programs. There is a fee for this service. Due to copyright regulations, music programs may not be taped.

A number of audio cassettes produced by NPR on accounting, economy, and capitalism are cited in *Management Media Directory* (Detroit: Gale Research Co., 1982).

B34 National Republican Congressional Committee (NRCC)— Communications Division

1 a. *320 First Street, S.E.*
Washington, D.C. 20003
(202) 479–7080

b. 9:00 A.M.–5:00 P.M.   Monday–Friday

c. Open to researchers by appointment.

d. Ed Blakely, Deputy Director, Communications Division

2. The National Republican Congressional Committee was founded in 1866 as a political organization dedicated to electing Republicans to Congress. Currently, it is the only party organization whose sole responsibility is to work for the election of Republicans to the House of Representatives. The NRCC is an autonomous unit but does work in cooperation with other party campaign organizations, such as the Republican National Committee. To promote Republican campaigns for the House, the NRCC employs a full-time professional staff to provide a wide range of support services. The Communications Division is responsible for developing campaign advertising of all types and for the transmission of congressional news statements to local radio stations. The division's GOP Radio Network is a source of information on congressional actions in a number of communities around the country.

3. NRCC has a small number of audio tapes dating from 1978 to the present, which contain spot commercials for various Republican candidates, mostly for the House. There is no index to this collection, but each reel has a listing of its contents.

In addition to its commercial production for individual GOP candidates, the Communications Division also plays a major role in the creation and production of the Republican Party's National Media Program.

4 a. On-site listening equipment is not available.

5. A brochure describing the NRCC is available to interested individuals.

B35 National Theatre Library Archives

1 a. *1321 E Street, N.W.*
Washington, D.C. 20004
(202) 628–6161

c. Not open to the general public. Scholars may, however, telephone or write requesting an appointment to visit the archives.

d. Rick Schneider, Head Librarian

2–3. The National Theatre Library Archives contain some 100 disc, cassette, and reel-to-reel recordings of productions performed there, as well as other productions, from the 1950s to the present. The discs are commercially produced. The audio tapes were produced on-site and consist of actual performances.

4 a. On-site listening facility is available.

b. Prior appointment is required.

c. There is no charge to listen to recordings.

5. There is no catalog. Materials are shelved alphabetically by title.

B36 Naval Historical Center (Navy Department)—Operational Archives Branch

1 a. *Washington Navy Yard, Building 57 (third floor)*
9th and M Streets, S.E.
Washington, D.C. 20374
(202) 433–3170

b. 7:30 A.M.–4:30 P.M.   Monday–Friday

c. Open to the public. Researchers should notify the staff before arrival. Some materials are classified and restricted.

d. Dean C. Allard, Head, Operational Archives Branch

2. The Operational Archives Branch holds archival collections relating to naval policy and strategy during the last forty years, papers of various senior naval officers, and bibliographic reference files on many naval officers dating back to the early nineteenth century. The records contain some 200,000 items.

3. The archives also has a number of oral history materials, including oral history transcripts (145 volumes) prepared by the U.S. Naval Institute and consisting of interviews with retired naval officers and officials. There are also some 30 transcripts of oral history biographies from the Office of Oral History at Columbia University of retired naval officers. In addition, the archives holds 125 taped briefings and oral history interviews with American and South Vietnamese naval personnel relating to the war in Southeast Asia.
  Researchers should also take note of the Navy Oral History Project focusing on the years 1898–1934 in the Motion Picture Broadcasting and Recorded Sound Division of the Library of Congress (A41).

5. The Operational Archives Branch has detailed finding aids for most of the individual collections. Researchers will find the following publications useful: *U.S. Naval History Sources in the United States* (1979); *Partial Checklist: World War II Histories and Historical Reports in the U.S. Naval History Division* (1973); *Declassified Records in the Operational Archives;* and *Information for Visitors to the Operational Archives.*

B37 Office of Air Force History (Air Force Department)

1 a. *Bolling Air Force Base*
Building 5681
Washington, D.C. 20332
(202) 767–5764

b. 7:45 A.M.–4:15 P.M.   Monday–Friday

c. Open to qualified researchers. An appointment arranged in advance is recommended.

d. Richard H. Kohn, Chief, Office of Air Force History
  William C. Heimdahl, Chief, Reference Services Branch (202/767–5088)

2. The Office of Air Force History maintains an extensive Oral History Program

begun during the 1950s with recordings and transcripts housed in the Albert F. Simpson Historical Research Center, Maxwell Air Force Base, Alabama. The collection includes some 1,300 interviews. Copies of a number of transcripts are held in Washington, D.C. Although many of the interviews have been conducted by the Office of Air Force History, a large number of interviews have been acquired from numerous other sources.

3. The range of topics represented is broad and encompasses Air Force activity dating to the early 1920s. All of the campaigns are well represented as are interviews with individuals responsible for the development of Air Force weapons systems. The collection includes interviews with former Secretaries of the Air Force, Chiefs of Staff, Major Command Commanders and Commanders-in-Chief, and Chief Master Sergeants. Examples of interviewees include Gen. Creighton Abrams, Brig. Gen. Cleo M. Bishop, Maj. Gen. Alden R. Crawford, Gen. Dwight D. Eisenhower, Gen. William J. Evans, Gen. Bruce Holloway, Gen. Daniel "Chappie" James, Gen. George C. Kenney, Gen. Curtis LeMay, Gen. Earle E. Partridge, Gen. Horace M. Wade, and Maj. Roland F. Fluck.

The collection is also valuable to researchers who seek information not necessarily related to the Air Force. For example, there are interviews with individuals associated with Presidential administrations, from those of Franklin D. Roosevelt to the present. There are a number of oral history materials representing the other branches of the armed forces, as well as materials dealing with civilians, such as Dean Rusk and Stuart Symington, and congressional matters.

NOTE: Recordings in the records of the United States Air Force commands, activities, and organizations for 1961–1975 (RG 342) are held in the National Archives and Records Service (B27).

4 a.   On-site listening equipment is not available.

5.   All of the materials described above are listed in the *U.S. Air Force Oral History Catalog* (1982). The catalog is quite extensive, including some 1,300 items and is current as of January 1982. There is also a microfilm index to the microfilmed collection of classified and unclassified materials. Other printed lists and guides include *Air Force Historical Archives Document Classification Guide* (1971); *Personal Papers in the Albert F. Simpson Historical Research Center* (1980); *An Aerospace Bibliography* (1978); *United States Air Force History: A Guide to Monographic Literature, 1943–1974* (1977); and *A Guide to Documentary Sources* (1973).

B38   Organization of American States (OAS) Voice Archives (Records Management Center)

1 a.   *Administration Building, Rooms B1 and B2*
17th and Constitution Avenue, N.W.
Washington, D.C. 20006
(202) 789–3849

  b.   9:00 A.M.–5:00 P.M.   Monday–Friday

  c.   Open to researchers by appointment.

  d.   Maria-Antonia Roldan, Records Specialist

2–3. The OAS Voice Archives, administered by the OAS Records Management Center, contains approximately 151 disc and 48 tape recordings spanning the period 1938–1972 and consisting of speeches, statements, and press conferences regarding inter-American issues by prominent political figures. Some of these figures include Guerrero Gutierrez, Trejos Fernandez, Galo Plaza, D. Alberto Hurtado, Lleras Camargo, Antonio Rocha, Castor Jaramillo Arrubla, Bertha Lutz, and Carlos Dávila.

Included are radio transcription recordings of the "America's Town Meeting of the Air" in 1938 and the Eighth International Conference of American States in 1938, both recorded by the National Broadcasting Company; recordings of the ceremony commemorating the 40th anniversary of the Inter-American Commission of Women in 1968, meeting of American Chiefs of State in Punta del Este, Uruguay, in 1967, the Tenth Pan-American Highway Congress in Montevideo, Uruguay, in 1967; and the meeting of ministers of labor on the Alliance for Progress in 1963.

4 a. The Voice Archives does not have listening equipment.

b. An appointment is recommended.

c. No fees are charged.

d. Researchers may tape some Voice Archives recordings on their own recording equipment.

5. A typewritten inventory of sound recordings is available for perusal in the Voice Archives. Individuals may also want to visit the OAS Columbus Memorial Library. The library contains some 3 million print and non-print items, including a small number of disc recordings on the history, culture, and development of Latin America, as well as publications of the OAS and its agencies and international organizations. The director of the library is Thomas L. Welch. Hours are 9:30 A.M.–4:30 P.M., Monday–Friday; telephone: (202) 789–6037 (Reference Desk). For additional information, see *Guide to the Columbus Memorial Library* (1982).

B39 Senate Historical Office

1 a. *United States Senate*
Washington, D.C. 20510
(202) 224–6900

b. 9:00 A.M.–5:00 P.M.   Monday–Friday

c. Open to researchers.

d. Richard A. Baker, Senate Historian

2. The Senate Historical Office collects and provides information on important events, dates, statistics, precedents, and historical comparisons of current and past activities of the Senate, for use by members' offices, the press, scholars, and the general public. A staff of five advises senators and committees on the disposition of their non-current office files, assists researchers seeking access to Senate records, and maintains a register of locations of former senators' papers. The office edits for publication the committees' older executive session transcripts and conducts oral history interviews with senior Senate staff. The photohistorian provides coverage of current Senate activities of potential historical significance and collects, for Senate and public use, older photographs illustrative of the Senate and its 1,600 former members.

3.   The office maintains a valuable array of non-print materials, including some 20,000 photographs of the activities of the Senate. Included also are a number of oral history tape recordings of senior staff members who have served in Senate-related activities for more than twenty years. The staff members who have been interviewed on tape include: Floyd Riddick, parliamentarian; Darrell St. Clair, assistant secretary of the Senate; Ruth Watt, chief clerk of the Permanent Sub-Committee on Investigations; Pat Holt, chief of staff, Senate Foreign Relations Committee; Frank Attig, reporter of debates on Senate floor; and W. Featherstone Reid, assistant to Senator Warren Magnuson. All of these staff members are currently retired. Individuals may listen to the tapes or read the transcripts in the Senate Historical Office. Most of the transcripts are available in the New York Times Microfiche collection. The Senate Historical Office has also deposited sets of transcripts in the Senate Library (B40), the Manuscript Division of the Library of Congress (B20), and the Legislative and Diplomatic Branch of the National Archives and Records Service (B27).

4 a.   On-site listening equipment is available.

   c.   No fees are charged.

5.   The Senate Historical Office publishes a number of research tools, including its *Guide to Research Collections of Former United States Senators, 1789–1928* (1983) and *The United States Senate Historical Bibliography* (1977). Additional information regarding this organization is available on request.

B40   Senate Library

1 a.   *Capitol Building, S-332*
       Washington, D.C. 20510
       (202) 224–7106 (Reference)

   b.   9:00 A.M.–5:00 P.M.   Monday–Friday and whenever the Senate is in session.

   c.   Access by a private individual requires a letter from a senator.

   d.   Roger K. Haley, Senate Librarian

2–3.   The Senate Library has approximately 250,000 volumes, including Senate and House documents, such as bills and resolutions, reports, hearings and prints, and the record of floor proceedings and debates. It does not have any audiovisual cassettes or discs. It does have, however, a set of transcripts of oral history tapes produced by the Senate Historical Office (B39). Recordings of a number of Senate hearings for 1946 and the 1970s (RG 46) are in the National Archives and Records Service (B27).

4 d.   Interlibrary loan service is not available. Photoduplication facilities are available.

5.   The library has a card catalog, and a guide *General Information and Services of the Senate Library*.

B41   Senate Recording Studio (U.S. Senate)

1 a.   *United States Capitol, Room ST71*
       Washington, D.C. 20510
       (202) 224–4977

b. 9:00 A.M.–5:00 P.M.   Monday–Friday

c. Open to researchers for telephone reference.

d. Ralph Griffith, Director

2. The Senate Recording Studio produces video and audio tapes upon requests from senators for their use only. Such programs consist of news reports, commentaries and reactions to various issues, and hearings. The Senate Recording Studio does not retain any of these tapes. Currently, there are proposals, which are being introduced in the Senate, for the videotaping of Senate sessions.

Individuals may contact the Senate to hear recorded telephone running accounts of proceedings on the floor: (202) 224–8541 (Democratic); (202) 224–8601 (Republican).

B42 Smithsonian Institution Archives

1 a. *Arts and Industries Building*
900 Jefferson Drive, S.W.
Washington, D.C. 20560
(202) 357–1420

b. 9:00 A.M.–5:00 P.M.   Monday–Friday
Scholars wishing to use the archives before 10:00 A.M. will have to make special arrangements to enter the building.

c. Open to the public. Appointments are required. There are restrictions on some materials. Permission is required to quote from archive material.

d. William A. Deiss, Deputy Archivist

2. The Smithsonian Institution Archives is the official repository of the administrative and historical records of the Smithsonian Institution, as well as of the papers of its staff. The archives' collections reflect the growth and changes of the Smithsonian itself and the development of science and art in the United States. Other than official Smithsonian documents, the archives include papers of individual scholars affiliated with the institution, papers of professional societies, such as the American Society of Ichthyologists and Herpetologists, and various special collections. The strongest subject area is natural history, but many other disciplines are well represented. Researchers should also consult entries for the other three manuscript repositories within the Smithsonian: National Anthropological Archives (B26), Archives of American Art (B3), and the Archives Center of the National Museum of American History (C11).

The principal bibliographic tool for the archives is *Guide to the Smithsonian Archives* (1983), the fourth in a series of comprehensive general guides to the holdings. The guide includes all records and manuscript collections prepared for use before July 1982. Entries for record units added since then are available in the archives. Entries for some material located in other Smithsonian archives or curatorial offices are also included.

The guide has both a general and very detailed table of contents and introductory material explaining its scope and use. Each entry has detailed information about the record unit, including type of material and a listing of finding aids. The guide has an index by form and by discipline, as well as a general personal and corporate name index. Researchers looking for audio tapes should search under "Tape Recordings"

in the form index and also at sections headed "Audio-Visual and Information Files" and "Oral History Project," both listed in the table of contents.

3.   Audio holdings at the Smithsonian Archives can be divided into four general groups. Record Unit 106 includes miscellaneous recordings from the Smithsonian Offic of Public Affairs from 1958 to the present. These are interviews and lectures given by staff or guest speakers, as well as tapes of exhibitions, openings, and other Smithsonian events. Some of the individuals represented on the recordings include Jacob Kainen, Lyndon Baines Johnson, Hubert Humphrey, Jacob Bronowski, Isaac Asimov, Sir Edmund Hillary, John Updike, Norman Cousins, Anais Nin, Ronald Reagan, Mrs. Anwar Sadat, and King Hussein of Jordan. Also included in RU 106 are tapes made of animal sounds for the National Museum of Natural History audio guide.

A second important group is Record Unit 296, including tapes from "Radio Smithsonian," 1969 to the present (H22). Individuals represented on tape include Marvin Sadik, Sir Kenneth Clark, Carl Sagan, Saul Bellow, Henry Moore, Armand Hammer, Gene Raddenberry, Rube Goldberg, Alex Haley, Nelson Rockefeller, Ted Mack, Melville Bell Grosvenor, and Jimmy Carter.

The third group includes recordings found in miscellaneous collections of personal and organizational papers. For example, RU 216 includes eleven taped lectures and a panel discussion regarding ecology recorded in 1968 for the Office of International and Environmental Programs. Other record units that have audio recordings are RU 255 Moonwatch Division, Smithsonian Astrophysical Observatory, 1956–1975; RU 7231 Waldo LaSalle Schmitt Papers, 1907–1978; RU 7279 Helmut Karl Buechner Papers, 1939–1975; and RU 7294 Audubon Naturalist Society of the Central Atlantic States, Inc., 1893–1980, and undated. Additional information about these materials can be found in the *Guide to the Smithsonian Archives* (1983).

Oral History Project
(202) 357–1420

Pamela M. Henson, Historian

This is the fourth group of sound recordings in the archives. This project was begun in 1973 in order to supplement written documentation of the archives' records and manuscript collections, focusing on persons involved with the history of the Smithsonian or persons who made significant administrative or scholarly contributions. The above-mentioned *Guide* describes 21 sets of interviews. One person interviewed is Lucile Mann, wife of William Mann, a former zoo director. Mrs. Mann described expeditions she often made with her husband throughout the world. Mrs. Mann also provided the Smithsonian with recorded narration for the film made of the Smithsonian-Firestone expedition to Liberia in 1940. Other interviewees include Charles G. Abbot, John Warren Aldrich, Richard Eliot Blackwelder, James C. Bradley, Fenner A. Chace, Jr., Richard Sumner Cowan, John C. Ewers, Jennie V. Emlong, Herbert Friedmann, Horton H. Hobbs, Jr., Robert P. Multhauf, Paul H. Oehser, Watson M. Perrygo, Harald A. Rehder, Nathan Reingold, Leonard Peter Schultz, Senate of Scientists, Frank A. Taylor, Alexander Wetmore, and Fred Lawrence Whipple. Information about other oral history projects being conducted at the Smithsonian can be obtained through this office.

4 a.   Limited listening facilities are available.

b.   Reservations are required.

c.   Fees are not charged.

d.   Some duplication is permitted. Scholars should inquire.

5.   In addition to the *Guide* mentioned above, most record units in the archives have their own finding aid and index, computerized and on paper. All interviews in the Oral History Project are fully transcribed as well.

B43   Smithsonian Institution—Office of Folklife Programs—Folklife Program Archive

1 a.   *955 L'Enfant Plaza, Suite 2600*
Washington, D.C. 20560
(202) 287-3424

  b.   9:00 A.M.–5:00 P.M.   Monday–Friday

  c.   Open to the public. Appointments are required.

  d.   Peter Seitel, Director
Richard Derbyshire, Archivist

2–3.   The Folklife Program Archive includes some 12,000 hours of audio tapes representing complete coverage of live events at the American Folklife Festival, produced since 1967, plus field work documentation in support of the festivals and other special events.

The tapes are arranged by year collected and have not been organized by subjects represented. The programs offered during each festival have varied, although certain series have appeared in succession for more than one year at a time and can be considered to some extent as entities in themselves. Every festival includes music and the folklife archive is a rich depository of these performances, including an enormous range of international folk traditions in instrumental and vocal music. Interviews have also been conducted with many of the performers.

Another subject grouping can be described as regional affiliation; several festivals have represented certain states or larger areas in the United States (New England, the Pacific Northwest, the Upland South) and also countries in other parts of the world. Another series presented from time to time is Native Americans. Tribes from throughout the country have come to the festival to demonstrate their dances and customs.

A series that has been presented often since 1972 centers on occupational folk cultures. For example, in 1976, participants included radio employees, actors, police, brick layers, carpenters, steel workers, and fire fighters.

Another interesting series is "Old Ways in the New World" for which various ethnic groups were identified who have immigrated to the United States. This program centered on the ways in which these groups changed or did not change as compared to their counterparts in the "old country."

In addition to these series, the festival has offered special features, such as a children's program, a program honoring the International Year of the Handicapped, and programs on folk housing.

During the course of some of the festivals, two oral history projects were conducted with participants on-site. These were the Family Folklore Program, conducted between 1974 and 1977 and in 1981, and the Ethnic Activities Project, conducted in 1976, which dealt with the experiences of immigrants to the United States. In addition to these two projects, oral history materials can be found throughout the archive.

4 a.   Audio equipment is available for use at the archive.

   b. Reservations are required.

   c. Fees are not charged.

   d. Standard Smithsonian reproduction procedures and fees apply. Researchers should request information at the archive.

5. Although indexes to all collections are not yet available, it is possible to locate items through existing inventories and program descriptions. The holdings of the archive are listed in a chronological inventory, which includes a description and names of persons represented on each tape. The archive also maintains administrative and background information for each festival program, which can be useful to researchers in locating data.

B44 Society for History in the Federal Government

1 a. *Benjamin Franklin Station, Box 14139*
       Washington, D.C. 20044

   b. There is no formal office. Researchers must contact the society by mail.

   d. David Allison, Executive Secretary

2. The Society for History in the Federal Government is concerned, among other endeavors, with oral history programs within the federal government. Its members are working to implement ways in which little-known oral history collections can be identified and accessed. In addition, the society has studied the matter of oral history donor restrictions versus challenges under the Freedom-of-Information Act. Contact the society for additional information.

5. The society's Committee on Federal Historical Programs has issued a *Report* (June 30, 1982) regarding the current status of various aspects of Federal oral history programs.

B45 Society of the Cincinnati

1 a. *Headquarters and Anderson House Museum*
       2118 Massachusetts Avenue, N.W.
       Washington, D.C. 20008
       (202) 785–2040

   b. 1:00 P.M.–4:00 P.M.   Tuesday–Saturday
       The museum is closed on Mondays, Sundays, and national holidays.

   c. Individuals must telephone or write for an appointment to listen to the recordings.

   d. John D. Kilbourne, Director

2. The Society of the Cincinnati, founded in 1783, is a patriotic organization devoted to perpetuating the history and ideals of the founding fathers of this country. One of its recent endeavors was the celebration of the 250th anniversary of the birth of George Washington, first president general of the society. An exhibition of manuscripts, prints,

and other materials related to him was presented. The society also conducts a series of concerts presented by local and nationally known artists in the Anderson House Museum. Many of these concerts have been recorded and are included in the special collections holdings in the society's library.

3. The society's library holds a variety of materials including the archives of the society, private papers, muster rolls, orderly books and other manuscripts pertaining to the Revolutionary War, as well as other aspects of U.S. history, and some 75 reel-to-reel tape recordings of the concert series for the years 1976–1981. Two such concerts included the American Chamber Orchestra, with William Yarborough, conductor on March 13, 1982, and the United States Air Force Chamber Orchestra, with guest pianist Barbara Ryland on February 13, 1982.

4 a. On-site listening equipment is not available.

b. An appointment is required.

c. No fees are charged.

B46 Soil Conservation Service (SCS) (Agriculture Department)—History Office

1 a. *South Agricultural Building, Room 6121-S*
Washington, D.C. 20013
(202) 447–4543

Mail:
P.O. Box 2890
Washington, D.C. 20013

b. 8:00 A.M.–4:30 P.M.   Monday–Friday

c. Open to the public. Researchers must telephone or write in advance in order to obtain a visitor's pass.

d. Douglas Helms, Historian

2. The Soil Conservation Service maintains an oral history program consisting of interviews related to the history of the agency. Efforts are also made to acquire interviews on the history of conservation and the environment.

3. Currently there are some 25 interviews in process, which are not yet available to researchers. Eleven other interviews are open and include Donald A. Williams, administrator, SCS; Gordon Zimmerman, head of information, SCS; Ervin L. Peterson, assistant secretary of Agriculture (responsible for SCS, 1954–1960); William Van Dersal, biologist and deputy administrator for watersheds, SCS; William M. Johnson, deputy administrator for natural resource assessments; William B. Davey, deputy administrator for water resources, SCS; Theodore B. Plair, head, Woodland Conservationists; William J. Ralston, assistant to the administrator for legislative affairs; Verle G. Kaiser, agronomist and expert on conservation in the Palouse region; and Lee T. Morgan, worked with early wind erosion conservation districts. Cassette and reel-to-reel tapes are housed in the History Office. Scholars, however, will be asked to use the transcripts. A few copies of SCS transcripts have been deposited in the National Agricultural Library (B25).

4 a. On-site listening equipment is not available.

5. Contact Douglas Helms (202/382–0042) for the most recent typed list of interviews.

B47 State Department—Bureau of Public Affairs—Office of the Historian

1 a. *2401 E Street, N.W., State Annex 1, Room 3100*
Washington, D.C. 20520
(202) 632–8888

b. 9:00 A.M.–5:00 P.M.   Monday–Friday

c. Access to the building is restricted. Appointments with department personnel should be made in advance.

d. William Z. Slany, Historian

2–3. The State Department conducts an on-going oral history program of interviews with former department officials. To date, no more than 20 interviews have been conducted. A number of tapes have been transcribed. The interviews are restricted. Contact the Office of the Historian for additional information.

Recordings representing the State Department for 1938–1961 (RG 59) are held in the Special Archives Division of the National Archives and Records Service (B27).

B48 Supreme Court Historical Society

1 a. *111 2nd Street, N.W.*
Washington, D.C. 20002

b. 9:00 A.M.–5:00 P.M.   Monday–Friday

c. Open to the public for reference inquiries.

d. Gary Aichele, Executive Director

2. The Supreme Court Historical Society, founded in 1974, conducts historical research on the history of the Supreme Court and the entire judicial branch of the federal government. Recently, the society has established an oral history program, but as of yet, no interviews have been conducted. Contact the society on the current status of the program. Recordings in the records of the Supreme Court for 1955–1970 (RG 267) are held in the Special Archives Division of the National Archives and Records Service (B27).

5. The society publishes the *Yearbook* and a quarterly newsletter.

B49 Takoma Park Historical Society

1 a. *Municipal Building*
7500 Maple Avenue
Takoma Park, Maryland 20912
(301) 585–3542

b. 9:00 A.M.–5:00 P.M.   Monday–Friday. Hours may vary.

c. Materials may be examined with special permission only.

d. Roderick Davis, President

2–3. The Takoma Park Historical Society is engaged in a number of projects relating to historic Takoma Park, including historic preservation of buildings, markers, and archives. The society has also conducted a number of oral history interviews, some of which are stored in the Takoma Park Library, 101 Philadelphia Avenue, Takoma Park, Maryland 20912. Contact the society, not the library, for permission to examine the tapes.

4 a. Researchers must supply listening equipment.

B50 Traditional Music Documentation Project (TMDP)—Library

1 a. *3740 Kanawha Street, N.W.*
Washington, D.C. 20015
(202) 363–7571

b. Hours by appointment.

c. Library open to serious researchers who should telephone or write for an appointment to visit.

d. Curt Wittig, Director

2. The Traditional Music Documentation Project is an independent non-profit organization whose purpose is to identify and document examples of traditional African music. The results of the project's work are a research library containing an extensive collection of discs and reel-to-reel tapes of music and oral data, and books and periodicals on African music totaling approximately 3,000 items. The collection is a valuable resource for Africana. Materials in the collection represent primarily Nigeria; Zimbabwe; Southern, Central, and Eastern Africa; Mozambique; and Zaire.

3. The disc collection includes a complete set of Hugh Tracey's *The Music of Africa Series* (210 discs), which represent the pioneering work of Tracey in recording the music of Central and Southern Africa. In addition, the disc collection includes other traditional African music on such labels as Folkways, Caprice, Ocora, Bärenreiter, Vogue, Disque, and Teuveren. The tape collection includes numerous hours of music of Nigeria recorded by Wittig during his visit there. TMDP has also produced 13 albums on its own Kaleidophone label. These are excellent examples of traditional music from Kenya, Tanzania, Uganda, Mozambique, Malawi, Zaire, Rhodesia, South Africa, Zambia, and Rwanda including chants, praise songs, ballads, instrumental

music, and a well-known Yoruba folk opera. A set of these recordings is also located in the Record-Score Collection of the American University Library (A5).

In support of the audio collection, TMDP maintains a collection of reference books and periodicals.

4 a. Listening equipment is available.

b. Researchers should call ahead to make arrangements.

c. No fee is charged for visiting the library.

d. The director will tape examples of music for classroom-use based on the TMDP collection. A fee is charged for this service.

5. TMDP does not have a card catalog. The Tracy series is, however, indexed in the *Catalogue [of] The Sound of Africa Series* (Roodepoort, South Africa: International Library of African Music, 1973). All of the Kaleidophone discs are indexed in Ruth Stone's *African Music and Oral Data: A Catalog of Field Recordings, 1902–1975* (Bloomington: Indiana University, 1976). TMDP's *Kaleidophone Record Catalog 1976* is available free on request.

B51 Treasury Historical Association (THA)

1 a. *Main Treasury Building*
15th Street and Pennsylvania Avenue, N.W., Room 2434
Washington, D.C. 20220
(202) 566–8087

b. 9:00 A.M.–5:00 P.M.   Monday–Friday
Hours may vary

c. Materials held by the Treasury Historical Association are available to researchers.

d. Abby Gilbert, Chairperson, Oral History Committee

2. The Treasury Historical Association, a non-profit organization founded in 1973, is dedicated to preserving the history of the Treasury building, as well as other buildings in Washington which are related historically to events or persons associated with the Department of the Treasury. The association also conducts research projects focusing on the history of the department.

3. The THA Oral History Program has resulted in two sets of interviews: John Snyder, secretary of the Treasury under Truman interviewed by Richard P. Schick (includes transcripts, but not tapes), and William Heffelfinger who served from 1917–1962 in various fiscal posts in the department, interviewed by John Harter (includes 17 audio tapes with transcripts).

The oral history materials are on deposit in the Treasury Department Library (Elizabeth Knauff, Chief, 202/566–2777). Library hours are 9:00 A.M.–5:00 P.M., Monday–Friday. Photoduplication services are available.

Recordings representing the Department of the Treasury for 1941–1961 (RG 56) are held in the National Archives and Records Service (B27).

5. THA can provide copies of a history of the Treasury building to interested individuals.

University of Maryland —Libraries—International Piano Archives at Maryland   See entry A70

B52 Virginia History and Genealogy Collection

1 a. *Alexandria-Lloyd House*
220 N. Washington Street
Alexandria, Virginia 22314
(703) 838–4577

b. 9:00 A.M.–5:00 P.M.   Monday–Saturday
9:00 A.M.–1:00 P.M.   Saturday (summer hours)

c. Material must be used in the library.

d. Allan Robbins, Librarian in Charge of Lloyd House

2–3. The Virginiana collection contains material on the history of Virginia with special emphasis on Alexandria from 1749 to the present, some 8,000 volumes. The oral history collection includes 15–20 cassettes of older Alexandrians; some of these are transcribed. Other audio holdings are 4-years worth of meetings of the Alexandria Historical Society and an important collection of the lectures of the Alexandria Library Company, founded in 1794. This literary society was disbanded in the nineteenth century and begun again in the 1950s, at which time recordings were made. The Virginiana collection has the complete audio holdings of the Alexandria Library Company lectures, which are primarily on literary and historical subjects.

4 a. On-site listening equipment is available.

b. No reservations are required.

c. No fees are charged.

d. Duplication facilities are available.

5. Recordings are fully cataloged with a central locator file and union list in each branch.

B53 Washington Metropolitan Area Transit Authority—Planning and Development Division

1 a. *600 5th Street, N.W.*
Washington, D.C. 20001
(202) 637–1206

c. Access to the collection is provided by appointment.

d. Albert Rhoor, Project Officer, Metro History Project

2. The Washington Metropolitan Area Transit Authority has conducted a Metro History Project, which includes 40 oral history interviews. The project was initiated by Darwin Stolzenbach. Most of the tapes have been transcribed. Plans are underway

to deposit the entire collection in the Melvin Gelman Library of George Washington University (A29).

4 a. On-site listening equipment is not available.

B54 The White House–Office of the Press Secretary—News Summary and Audio Services

1 a. *White House, Room 165*
Washington, D.C. 20500
(202) 456–2950 (News Summary and Audio Services)
(202) 456–2320 (Information)

d. William Hart, Director

2. White House Audio Services provides by telephone one or two recorded daily news actualities of the President. These pieces are intended for broadcast and are suitable for scholars desiring the most current news on various issues concerning the Executive Branch. This service is provided 24 hours a day via the following telephone numbers: (800) 424–9090 (toll-free) and (202) 456–7198 (for the D.C. area).

Recordings representing the White House Office for 1950–1953 and 1959 (RG 130) are held in the Special Archives Division of the National Archives and Records Service (B27).

3. Copies of broadcasts are maintained on-site.

B55 William Alanson White Psychiatric Foundation—Archives

1 a. *1610 New Hampshire Avenue, N.W.*
Washington, D.C. 20009
(202) 667–3007

b. 10:00 A.M.–4:00 P.M.   Monday–Friday

c. Open by appointment only.

2–3. The foundation has some 2,000 disc recordings of lectures of psychiatrist Harry Stack Sullivan.

4 a. On-site listening equipment is not available.

C Museums and Galleries

Introductory Note

Museums and galleries in the Washington, D.C., area have some of the best audio resources in the region. Besides sound recordings, they hold artifacts and items in public exhibit. They maintain libraries, and special archives, and sponsor research activities, concerts, lectures, and other presentations.

The Smithsonian Institution's National Museum of American History (C11) houses the most extensive collection of artifacts representing the development of radio and phonograph technology. There are both early experimental devices used by Alexander G. Bell, Thomas Edison, Emile Berliner, and others, and examples of later technological developments. However, not all items in the museum are on display.

Scholars interested in artifacts should consider other repositories as well. The National Bureau of Standards Museum (C7) has a collection of early radios and phonographs. The Navy Memorial Museum (C13) has a Naval Electronics Exhibit exemplifying the development of radio communications, componentry, and navigational aids. The Motion Picture, Broadcasting and Recorded Sound Division of the Library of Congress (A41) has a substantial collection of Emile Berliner's experimental apparatus and laboratory equipment used in his work with the phonograph. The National Archives and Records Service (B27) has a few items, mainly General Electric and Webcor wire recorders, and an Edison cylinder player. For information, contact Charles Mayn, Director of the Recording Laboratory, Preservation Policy and Services Division (202/523-3263). The Naval Research Laboratory (4555 Overlook Avenue, S.W., Washington, D.C. 20375) occasionally borrows artifacts from the Smithsonian Institution for its displays. Contact Linda Greenway, Exhibit Manager, Information Services Office, Naval Research Laboratory, for information (202/767-2541). Also of interest is an early phonograph used by President Wilson in the Woodrow Wilson House (C16).

The annual *Official Museum Directory* (Washington, D.C.: American Association of Museums, 1971-), and the triennial *American Art Directory* (New York: Bowker, 1899-) are the standard reference works for museums and art galleries, respectively.

C1   Anacostia Neighborhood Museum (Smithsonian Institution)

1 a. *2405 Martin Luther King, Jr. Avenue, S.E.*
Washington, D.C. 20020
(202) 287–3380

b. 10:00 A.M.–6:00 P.M.   Monday–Friday

c. The museum is open to the public. Researchers desiring to use the media collection must telephone or write to the Research Department requesting an appointment. Recordings and other materials may not be borrowed.

d. John R. Kinard, Director

2. The Anacostia Neighborhood Museum's collections and activities reflect American history with an emphasis on Afro-American life and culture, especially community life in the Anacostia area of metropolitan Washington, D.C.

3. Notable holdings of the museum.

Research Department
190 Fort Place
Fort Stanton Park
Washington, D.C. 20020
(202) 287–3380

9:00 A.M.–5:15 P.M.   Monday–Friday

Louise Hutchinson, Historian and Director of Research

The Research Department maintains an oral history collection of some 96 audio cassettes produced in support of a special exhibition entitled "Anacostia Story." The oral history project, begun in 1972, is based on interviews with Anacostia neighborhood senior citizens' recollections, experiences, and comments as residents of the area. An organization associated with this project is the Anacostia Historical Society, which consists of residents of Anacostia and whose purpose is to examine their local history and have their research available to others through a series of lectures.

4 a. On-site listening facility is not available. With special permission, researchers may bring their own listening equipment into the museum.

b. An appointment is required.

c. No fees are charged.

c. Should researchers wish to obtain copies of the oral history recordings, permission must first be obtained from the informants.

5. An inventory catalog of the cassette collection is available. Recordings are arranged chronologically. For further historical background on the Anacostia area, see *The Anacostia Story: 1608–1930* (Smithsonian Institution Press, 1977).

C2 Ford's Theatre (Interior Department—National Park Service)— Petersen House Library

1 a. *511 10th Street, N.W.*
   Washington, D.C. 20004
   (202) 426–6830

   Museum:
   516 10th Street, N.W.
   Washington, D.C. 20004
   (202) 426–6924

   b. 9:00 A.M.–5:00 P.M.   Daily except Christmas

   c. Contact Frank Hebblethwaite to arrange for an appointment to visit the library.

   d. Frank Hebblethwaite, Acting Curator

2. The Petersen House Library has a collection of printed materials that focus on the history of Ford's Theatre, the Civil War period, and the life and assassination of Abraham Lincoln.

3. The library also maintains a collection of approximately 30 audio tapes spanning 1975–1983 consisting of lectures and music focusing on the events surrounding the assassination of Lincoln. Lecturers include John Brennan, Clinton Case, William C. Davis, David Gaddy, Joseph George, Harold Holzer, John Kelly, John Lattimer, Robert Marcotte, Maude Motley, Mark Neeley, Betty Ownsbey, Julian Raymond, Bert Sheldon, Richard Sloan, Elmer Stein, Beth Waldow, and W.N. Walton.

4 a. On-site listening facilities are available.

   b. There are no fees charged to listen to recordings.

   c. Photocopy facility is not available. Individuals may duplicate recordings but must supply the equipment to do so.

C3 Freer Gallery of Art Library (Smithsonian Institution)

1 a. *12th Street and Jefferson Drive, S.W.*
   Washington, D.C. 20560
   (202) 357–2091

   b. 10:00 A.M.–5:00 P.M.   Monday–Friday

   c. Researchers must contact the library for an appointment to use the sound recordings.

   d. Ellen Nollman, Librarian

2. The Freer Gallery of Art Library is a reference unit designed to supplement the art objects in the gallery and the research conducted by staff members, visiting scholars, students, and the general public. The library currently contains approximately 30,000 volumes, half of which are in Asian languages related to the gallery's collections, and some 100 periodicals.

3. The library contains over 65 lectures on reel-to-reel and cassette format of lectures presented at the gallery by well-known art historians and other scholars. Topics include architecture, Islamic art, Chinese, Japanese and Israeli art, ceramics, furniture, and archeology variously presented by John Carswell, Stuart Fleming, Ernest Grobe, Henry Hodges, Marilyn Jenkins, Thomas Lawton, Sherman Lee, Margaret Medley, John A. Pope, John Rosenfield, Laurence Sickman, and others. One notable recording is a lecture presented by Senator Hugh Scott in September 1973.

4 a. On-site listening facilities are limited.

  b. An appointment is required.

  c. Fees are not charged.

  d. Photoduplication facilities are not available. Recordings may be duplicated with prior permission.

5. An index to the lectures is not available.

C4 Gadsby's Tavern Museum (City of Alexandria—Department of Historic Resources)

1 a. *134 North Royal Street*
  Alexandria, Virginia 22314
  (703) 838–4242

  b. 10:00 A.M.–5:00 P.M.   Tuesday–Saturday
    1:00 P.M.–5:00 P.M.   Sunday

  c. Open to scholars by appointment.

2. Gadsby's Tavern Museum is dedicated to the historic preservation of its three buildings constructed in 1770, 1792, and 1878. The museum maintains a library and research room. Holdings consist of 400 books, focusing on eighteenth-century life.

3. The museum has scheduled an oral history program to begin in 1984 and will emphasize the restoration of the buildings and recent history from the 1920s to the present.

4 c. Fees are charged to see the museum.

5. Publications include a selection of pamphlets and interpretive bulletins.

C5 Hirshhorn Museum and Sculpture Garden Library (Smithsonian Institution)

1 a. *8th Street and Independence Avenue, S.W.*
  Washington, D.C. 20560
  (202) 357–3223

  b. 10:00 A.M.–5:00 P.M.   Monday–Friday

  c. Open to qualified researchers. Recordings may be listened to but researchers may not quote from them.

  d. Anna Brooke, Librarian

2.   The Hirshhorn Museum's subject emphasis is modern painting and sculpture. The library houses research materials that support primarily the needs of the curatorial staff. Currently the library has some 12,000 books and 50 periodicals.

3.   Audio holdings in the library include the archival record of public programs held at the museum since it opened. These are lectures and symposia conducted by staff, art historians, and artists. Titles include "John Canaday, American Realism," "Dialogue: Work by David Hockney," and a Red Grooms interview for "Radio Smithsonian" (H22), Mr. Lerner on "Gregory Gillespie," and Robert Rosenblum on "The Art of Andy Warhol" and "Twentieth-Century Canadian Culture: A Symposium."

4 a.   Listening equipment is limited.

   b.   Reservations are required.

   c.   Fees are not charged.

   d.   A photoduplication facility is available.

5.   There is a card catalog with author/title and subject access.

Marine Corps (Navy Department)—History and Museums Division
See entry B21

C6   National Air and Space Museum (NASM) (Smithsonian Institution)—
Library

1 a.   *6th Street and Independence Avenue, S.W., Room 3100*
Washington, D.C. 20560
(202) 357–3133
(202) 357–1300 (Reference)

   b.   10:00 A.M.–4:00 P.M.   Monday–Friday (Library)
10:00 A.M.–5:30 P.M.   Daily except Christmas (Museum).
Additional hours are added in the summer.

   c.   Open to the public by appointment. The library also serves professionals from government and private industry. Researchers must sign in and receive a visitor's pass at the guard's desk on the first floor of the museum. Materials do not circulate. The audio tape collection may be used by the public by special arrangement. Recorded tours of the museum are available for a fee. The tours cover the museum's most historic exhibits. On the tours, individuals will hear recordings of Neil Armstrong, first man on the moon; Yuri Gagarin, first man in space; Chuck Yeager, first man to break the sound barrier. Tours are available in English, French, German, Spanish, and Japanese. For more information call (202) 371–1310.

   d.   Frank A. Pietropaoli, Head Librarian

2.   The library at the National Air and Space Museum is part of the system of Smithsonian Institution libraries that supports the research and exhibit programs of the institution and the specialized interests of the staff and the public it serves. Library holdings include over 30,000 books, close to 500 periodicals, and 500,000 technical reports. Non-print materials include microfilm, some 900,000 photographs, 2,000 films,

and over 800 cassette and reel-to-reel tapes and approximately 100 disc recordings. Subject strengths include history of aviation and space, flight technology, aerospace industry, aerospace biography, lighter-than-air technology, rocketry, earth and planetary sciences, and astronomy.

3.   Sound recordings consist of lectures, ceremonies, meetings, presidential addresses, speeches, presentations, original radio broadcasts, and oral history interviews with Hershel Abbott, Edwin "Buzz" Aldrin, Douglas A. Campbell, Benjamin D. Foulois, Charles Lindbergh, and others, on aeronautical topics pertaining to World War I and II, the Korean War, and NASA programs. There are also a number of commemorative recordings of various space flight missions, and several presidential addresses by Truman and Eisenhower.

4 a.   Individuals must supply personal tape recorders to listen to sound recordings.

b.   Individuals must make arrangements in advance for using audiovisual materials.

c.   There are no fees charged for using the library. Fees are charged, however, for the reproduction of photographs, as well as for recorded tours.

d.   Audio recordings may be reproduced by special permission in limited cases. Photograph and microfiche reproduction is available. A photoduplication facility is also available.

5.   Reference aids include biographical indexes, dictionaries, atlases, and periodical indexes. Card catalogs include author/title and subject access. A useful aid to some of the sound recordings is a computer generated NASM Oral History Master List. Access to both general and specialized databases is provided.

The NASM library publishes a semi-annual *Library Bulletin,* which announces new acquisitions, a guide to the library, and a number of education leaflets on various topics. In addition, a list of various taped interviews is included in *Prelude to the Space Age: the Rocket Societies, 1924–1940* (1983).

C7   National Bureau of Standards (NBS) Museum (Commerce Department)

1 a.   *Route 270 and Quince Orchard Road*
Gaithersburg, Maryland 20760
(301) 921–3403

Mail:
National Bureau of Standards Museum
Washington, D.C. 20234

b.   8:30 A.M.–5:00 P.M.   Monday–Friday

c.   Open to the public.

d.   Karma Beal, Acting Historical Information Specialist

2.   This museum is designed to preserve and display apparatus and other memorabilia illustrative of the past scientific work of NBS for the information of visitors, for the inspiration of present and future staff members, and as a part of the historic record of the evolution of the science of physical measurements.

Currently the museum has 625 items, of which some 100 items, representing major achievements since NBS was established in 1901, are on display. The remainder of the artifacts are in storage on-site.

3.   Although few in number, the audio-related apparatus held in the museum are significant. On display is the first AC radio receiver (museum number M-166), which was developed in 1922 by P.D. Lowell and F.W. Dunmore and which established home-use of radio and made the radio broadcasting industry possible. This particular radio, manufactured in 1923 by Radio Instrument Co., used three stages of vacuum-tube radio-frequency amplification, a crystal detector, two audio frequency stages, and a telephone-receiver loudspeaker. Also on display is a Decremeter, 1912, type D, developed by F.A. Kolster and manufactured by John Firth, New York. Its tuning range is 75–3,000 meters. This instrument measures the wavelength and decrement of the damped wave trains used in spark radio-telegraphy at that time. Another significant item is the NBS secondary standard magnetic tape cassette (serial no. B-25-00), which is the standard by which all other commercially manufactured cassettes are measured.

Items held in storage include the following: a Bauer Tinkertoy radio set, circa 1954, an example of printed circuits and automatic production of electronics (refer to the article, "Project Tinkertoy: Modular Design of Electronics and Mechanized Production of Electronics," in *NBS Technical News Bulletin,* vol. 37 (November 1953), pp. 161–170, for information on this historic development); and a 45-rpm record player representing an early design utilizing a wafer tube amplifier. This unit was built to show the feasibility of the tube and has three tubes, one of which is a "glass-front" tube so that the inside construction can be seen as well as the hot cathode. A turntable, mounted on a lucite box, and 5 additional early examples of radios, 1940s–1950s, are also in storage.

4 c.   No fees are charged.

d.   The taking of photographs is permitted. A photoduplication facility is available.

5.   The museum's two principal publications listing items on display include *Museum: National Bureau of Standards* and *Catalog of Artifacts on Display in the NBS Museum* (November 1977). For artifacts in storage, researchers should consult a document vertical file. Contact Karma Beal (301/921–3403) for information on this file.

Scholars pursuing the NBS role in the development of radio communications should refer to NBS publications *Measures for Progress: A History of the National Bureau of Standards* (1974) and *Fifty Years of Radio in the National Bureau of Standards,* an address presented by J. Howard Dellinger. Relevant technical publications are cited in the series *Publications of the National Bureau of Standards,* 1901 to the present.

C8   National Gallery of Art—Education Department Film Office

1 a.   *6th Street and Constitution Avenue, N.W.*
Washington, D.C. 20565
(202) 842–6272

b.   10:00 A.M.–5:00 P.M.   Monday–Friday

c.   Open to the public by appointment only.

d.   Margaret Parsons, Program Production Coordinator

2–3. The Education Department at the National Gallery has holdings of some 400 audio tape recordings of art historical lectures presented at the gallery from 1974 to the present. Some representative titles include "Restoration of Venetian Art and Architecture," "The Art of Paul Klee," "Manet and Modern Paris," and "The Small Crucifixion by Grünewald." These lectures were delivered by visiting scholars and by National Gallery staff.

Other audio holdings consist of proceedings, symposia, and conferences held at the gallery from 1980 to the present. These symposia are frequently related to exhibitions held at the time and include the following: "David Smith," "Claude Lorrain," "Raphael before Rome," and the "Middle Atlantic Symposia in the History of Art."

A third category of audio holdings are edited radio talks by gallery personnel, including, for example, "El Greco and Late 16th and Early 17th Centuries in Toledo," "Napoleon and the Louvre," "Rembrandt's Self Portraits," and "Charles I as Collector and Patron." Many of these presentations are broadcast locally over radio station WGMS (Appendix III). Finally, the gallery has a few recorded interviews with art historians and artists, such as Anthony Caro, Henry Moore, Robert Motherwell, and James Rosati.

4 a. Limited listening facilities are available.

  b. An appointment is required.

  c. No fees are charged.

  d. Duplication of sound recordings is not permitted.

5. The collection is arranged chronologically and can be accessed by staff only. A subject and speaker card file is in progress. Many of the lectures and symposia presented at the National Gallery of Art are described in its *Annual Report.*

In addition, the National Gallery of Art maintains an audio studio where recording and editing sessions for the gallery's radio talks, slide programs, television presentations, and recorded tours are conducted and produced. Information on audiovisual services is included in the *Annual Report.*

NOTE: The library at the National Gallery of Art, which contains mostly printed materials, has 4 disc recordings of lectures presented by architect Walter Gropius, an interview with Louise Nevelson, an exhibition recording on popular culture, and a recording by Joseph Beuys. Contact a reference librarian (202/842–6511) for further information and access to the collection.

C9 National Gallery of Art—National Gallery Orchestra

1 a. *6th Street and Constitution Avenue, N.W., Room West 110*
  Washington, D.C. 20565
  (202) 842–6075

  b. 9:00 A.M.–5:30 P.M.   Monday–Friday

  c. Access to the collection is provided by special permission only.

  d. Richard Bales, Conductor

2–3. The National Gallery Orchestra maintains an archive of recorded concerts presented at the National Gallery of Art from 1943 to the present. These concerts

have included not only the National Gallery Orchestra but also soloists and other ensembles from throughout the world. Of note to music scholars are the numerous world premiers and first Washington performances presented there. One significant event is the American Music Festival recorded by National Public Radio (B33) for broadcast throughout the United States. The Sunday evening concerts are broadcast live from radio station WGMS (Appendix III).

4 a. On-site listening equipment is not available.

   b. Appointments are required.

   c. Fees are not charged.

5. All of the musical programs presented each year at the gallery are listed and described in the Gallery's *Annual Report*.

C10 National Museum of African Art (Smithsonian Institution)—Eliot Elisofon Archives—Music Collection

1 a. *318 A Street, N.W.*
   Washington, D.C. 20002
   (202) 287–3490, ext. 72

   b. 9:00 A.M.–5:30 P.M.   Monday–Friday

   c. Researchers must call in advance for an appointment.

   d. Edward Lifschitz, Curator of Education

2–3. The Eliot Elisofon Archives Collection contains approximately 50 music and other sound recordings. In addition to recorded tapes made by Elisofon during his many visits to Africa, there are the following items in the collection: "Fourth Triennial Symposium of Traditional African Art" (April 1–4, 1977); "Francis Bebey Recital" (June 23, 1974); and "Frere Cornet and William Fagg Lecture" (March 1976).

4 a. On-site listening equipment is available.

5. Individuals should ask for assistance from the staff for identifying materials in the collection.

NOTE: The National Museum of African Art library houses a collection of more than 5,000 books and 40 periodical titles in the traditional and contemporary arts of Africa, including sculptural and decorative arts, ethnography, anthropology, crafts, architecture, archeology, ancient history, oral tradition and folklore, Afro-American arts, and African retentions in the New World. Contact the library for additional information (202/287–3490, ext. 67).

C11 National Museum of American History (Smithsonian Institution) (formerly National Museum of History and Technology)

1 a. *12th Street and Constitution Avenue, N.W.*
   Washington, D.C. 20560
   (202) 357–2510

b. Department offices and research facilities:
8:45 A.M.–5:15 P.M.   Monday–Friday
Public Exhibits:
10:00 A.M.–5:30 P.M.   Daily except Christmas and New Year's days.
Additional hours are added in the summer.

c. Appointments are required for using research facilities and other non-public areas. Exhibit areas are open to the public. Exhibits may be photographed, but permission is required for publication of photographs.

d. Roger G. Kennedy, Director

2. The collections in this museum are enormously varied, reflecting the changes in emphasis of American history topics the museum has undergone. Subjects covered by research and exhibition activities include cultural history, the history of mathematics and physical sciences, the history of technology, and political history.

3. The National Museum of American History has an excellent collection of artifacts on exhibit representing the historic development of recorded sound technology as well as radio communications. Current exhibits are drawn from a number of divisions and are described below.

Sound Recording Exhibit: Phonautograph, 1857, manufactured by Leon Scott, Paris, France; Thomas Edison's first phonograph, 1877, manufactured by S. Bergmann & Co.; experimental machine, 1881, Volta Laboratory (the cylinder carries the recording, "G-r-r-G-r-r, There are more things in heaven and earth, Horatio, than are dreamed of in your philosophy; G-r-r,I am a graphophone and my mother was a phonograph."); experimental apparatus, 1880–1886, Volta Laboratory (includes an experimental recorder with large wooden diaphragm, an experimental recorder with metal diaphragm, and a tool for turning a record blank before recording); A.W. Hall's phonograph, 1879, New York (this was the third U.S. phonograph patent); experimental disc type machine, no date, Volta Laboratory; Edison phonograph, 1888 (the first Edison phonograph out of the toy class); cutting machine, 1881, Volta Laboratory; Bell and Tainter's graphophone, 1887, manufactured by American Graphophone Company (the first commercially acceptable machine in the phonograph class); A.G. Bell phonograph, no date (model utilizes an extremely small diameter record); Berliner gramophone, 1888 (this machine was reconstructed by the inventor from some original parts of the machine used in the first public demonstration of Berliner's gramophone at the Franklin Institute in Philadelphia, May 16, 1888); graphophone, 1898, type AG, American Graphophone Company; Berliner hand-operated gramophone, circa 1897; graphophone, 1897 (coin-operated machine); Victor Talking Machine, 1903, Victor Talking Machine Company; Thomas Edison home phonograph, circa 1898 (plays 2-minute records and features an inconvenient gate to support the outer edge of the mandrel, which must be opened and closed with each record change); Victor phonograph, 1911–1925, model XI, Victor Talking Machine Co., Camden, New Jersey; Victor orthophonic, 1925, Victor Talking Machine Co.; Volta Laboratory tape recorder, 1886; The Telegraphone, 1899, style D.C. 110 (this was Poulson's wire recorder manufactured by American Telegraph Company); Berliner's tape recorder, 1882 (includes the electromagnetic coil, which was part of the original apparatus).

Men and Machines of American Journalism Exhibit: Carbon microphone transmitter, 1926 (used on NBC network broadcasts); KDKA broadcast microphone, 1920 (used for first radio broadcast); Emerson radio, 1938; Crosley "Pup" radio, 1924; RCA portable radio, 1940; General Motors "Midget" radio, 1936; Zenith Transistor radio, 1955. A catalog of this exhibit is available.

Amateur Radio Station NN3S1 Exhibit: Includes two independent operating con-

soles, equipment for high-frequency operations, and capability for electronic keying, slow-scan TV, radioteletype, and satellite communication.

Other artifacts representing the development of radio communications from the Smithsonian collections are exhibited on a loan basis in the Navy Memorial Museum (C13).

ARCHIVES CENTER
John Fleckner, Archivist
(202) 357-3270

10:00 A.M.-4:30 P.M.   Monday–Friday

The Archives Center of the National Museum of American History was established in 1982 as a clearinghouse for information regarding historical documents and manuscript materials located at the center and in various curatorial offices of the museum. The center advises and collaborates with museum curators and other staff to acquire new collections, prepare collections for research use, assist and supervise research use, and create and maintain research tools, such as guides, indexes, and inventories. The Archives Center operates three major program areas: Manuscript Collections, Collection of Business Americana, and the Historical Photograph Collection.

The Manuscript Collections are described in detail in *Guide to Manuscript Collections in the National Museum of History and Technology* (1978). Information about collections acquired since then is maintained by the Archives Center. The *Guide* includes a general and detailed table of contents, introductory material describing the use of the guide and regulations regarding the collections. The entries are arranged by curatorial department and have detailed descriptions of collections, including arrangement, types of materials, and finding aids. The index includes personal and corporate names and subjects. Researchers are advised to consult this guide and Archives Center staff in locating audio tapes held as part of manuscript collections at the museum. Noteworthy audio collections and related material can be found in the curatorial departments mentioned below.

DEPARTMENT OF SOCIAL AND CULTURAL HISTORY
Division of Community Life, Room 4100
Carl H. Scheele, Curator
(202) 357-2385

The Division of Community Life has approximately 4,000 lp and 78 rpm (10 in, 12 in, and 16 in transcription) disc recordings, including jazz, big band, blues, country, and rock and roll, dating from 1903 to the present. The collection represents more than 1,000 entertainers. Many recordings are vintage discs issued by RCA Victor. Notable in the collection are 300 recordings of the Beatles over a 20 year period, and Armed Forces Radio and Television Service (300 transcription discs) recordings of the 1940s and 1950s. Yet another collection includes the series Hit of the Week Records consisting of some 40 fibrous base discs of the 1930s. The collection also includes 10 Edison cylinders dating from 1903–1912. The recordings are indexed by record manufacturer and title of recording in a card catalog. Listening facilities are not available.

Allan Herschel Company Collection, circa 1906–1956.—The Allan Herschel Company of North Tonawanda, New York, and its predecessors manufactured carousels and other amusement park rides. Documents include catalogs, price lists, advertisements, articles, photographs, sales records, correspondence, and phonograph records. The recordings include four 78-rpm discs specially produced by the Howell Custom Co., Buffalo, N.Y., for Allan Herschel. Manufacture numbers are 1438, 130, 136, and 148. These were designed for amusement devices and consist of both band and

organ performances. Works include "Zacatecas-March," "1001 Nights Waltz," "I'm Thinking of You," "Italian Nights," "Heavens Artillery-March," "King of the Air-March," "Too Young" (Jefferson Music Co.), and "The Thing."The Smithsonian catalog number for these recordings is 312369.11. There is no finding aid for the collection.

Division of Musical Instruments, Room 4124
Cynthia A. Hoover, Curator
(202) 357–1707

This division has a sound recording collection consisting of some 100 tapes of musical performances presented during the 1960s at the National Museum of American History. Many concerts feature restored instruments from the division. There is also an oral history interview, with transcript, with organist E. Power Biggs, as well as commercial recordings maintained for reference purposes by the division's staff. Other notable recordings include audio tapes gathered in connection with field trips, dealing with traditional music of various parts of the United States.

DEPARTMENT OF HISTORY OF SCIENCE
Division of Electricity and Modern Physics, Room 5025
Arthur P. Molella and Paul Forman, Curators
(202) 357–1840

This division has custody of both sound recordings and artifacts. Sound recordings include experimental Columbia microgroove recordings (12 inch), 1943–1946; tape recordings (12 reel-to-reel 3 inch, 7 inch) representing geophysical phenomena, including whistlers (lightning discharges) IGY-year 1957–1958, dawn chorus (Aurora Borealis) 1GY-year 1957–1958, Luxembourg Effect (ionospheric cross-modulation), and Jupiter noise (radio noise from planet Jupiter atmosphere); tape recordings representing programming, including first radio transatlantics representing shortwave pickup from 2LO England and rebroadcast in the United States (two 7-inch reels), and a collection of 320 reel-to-reel tapes of the Dial-A-Joke program of New York Telephone Company, 1965–1982. Over 200 comedians are represented; tape recordings representing engineering standards, including National Stereophonic Radio Committee test tape, 1960 (one 7-inch reel); recordings representing science entertainment, including songs by Arthur Roberts on topics in physics (1 reel); and 16-mm film audio-related items, including sound-on-film experiments of Joseph Tykociner. The division has some 75 reels of 16-mm footage pertaining to the historical and experimental work of Bell Telephone Laboratories and Western Telegraph Company. These latter items include some audio-related material.

Audio artifacts include phonographs, headphones, tone arms, loudspeakers and additional headsets, and radio communication items consisting of receivers, recording equipment, and microphones. Other items include electronic and computer music equipment and apparatus representing engineering standards in audio. This material is described in detail below.

Phonographs include Avery Fisher hi-fidelity system, 1937–1938; Lincoln Engineering pneumatic turntable, ca. 1950; RCA Orthofonic console, 1927; RCA acoustical/electrical transducer system, 1927; Philco Photoelectric system, 1940; Vadasz Mikiphone portable phonograph, 1917; NBC studio turntable, ca. 1939; Columbia 1p attachment, 1948; RCA 45 rpm attachment, 1948; Rabco Servo-controlled turntable (ST-4), 1971; Decca type WRP-2 portable 78-rpm player, ca. 1940; and RCA demonstration Golden Throat system, 1952.

Headphones include a collection of Koss experimental devices from the 1950s–1960s: Koss Stereophones, 1958; model K/2 plus 2; model ESP-6; model KO-747;

model Pro 4AA; model KO-727B; model K6; model ESP-9. The Koss collection also includes prototype earplate, model 4AA; experimental earplate casting; Koss mold for early diaphragm, ca. 1960; unmounted mylar diaphragm; molded top plate for driver; mylar diaphragm for driver; and first cambric diaphragm, 1958 stereophones.

Tone arms include Dubilier electrostatic/electromagnetic pickup, 1925; Dubilier electrostatic pickup, 1925; Fortin experimental electrical pickup, 1912; Western Electric Rubberline recorder, 1926; Western Electric pickup, model 2A; and Magnavox tone arm, circa 1925.

Loudspeakers and additional headsets include a collection of some 75 loudspeakers from 1919–1972. Included are a variety of balanced-armature, moving coil, electrodynamic, and permanent magnetic types representing Music Master, Crosley, Magnavox, Federal Telephone, General Electric, Jensen, Western Electric, RCA, Dictograph Products, UTAH, Alden Manufacturing Co., Jewett Radio, Freed-Eisemann, Stromberg-Carlson, Silvertone, Capehart, and Fisher. There is also a collection of communications headphones (mostly 1000/2000 ohm) representing technology of 1915–1930 of such manufacturers as Western Electric, Lambert Schmidt, Murdock, Stromberg-Carlson, Federal Telephone, Nathaniel Baldwin, Kellogg, Tower, C. Brandes, Leich Electric, Twin-tone, Trimm Radio, and Brush.

High fidelity receivers include E.H. Scott philharmonic AM-FM receiver, 1939; E.H. Scott high fidelity receiver, 1936; Philharmonic Radio Company (Avery Fisher) receiver, 1937–1938; McMurdo-Silver receiver, 1936; and Scott Casseiver, 1971.

Magnetic recording equipment includes Webcor wire recorders, 1947–1951; applied Magnetic Corporation cartridge wire recorder, 1953; Magneto phone, 1945; Air-King wire recorder, 1949; Brush "Soundmirror" tape recorder, 1952, model MK-401; Magnecorder, 1952; Scott casseiver, 1971; Pentron tape recorder, 1959; Mohawk "Midgetape" recorder, 1962; Sony portable recorder, 1961, model EM-1; and Wilcox-Gay tape recorder, 1962.

Microphones include WFLA Florida-Western electric transmitter, 1925; Stromberg-Carlson transmitter, 1920; KDKA broadcast microphone, 1920; NBC/RCA "bullet" condenser microphone, 1925; NBC/RCA suspension carbon transmitter, 1925; NBC/RCA "camera box" condenser microphone, 1927; NBC/Western Electric inductor dynamic microphone, 1931; NBC/RCA inductor microphone, 1935, type 50-A; NBC/RCA ribbon microphone, 1931, type 44-A; Western Electric inductor, 1929, type 618-A; Westinghouse condenser microphone, 1932; Ballantine condenser microphone, 1930; BBC type AXB ribbon microphone, 1936; Phillips-Thomas glow discharge microphone, 1926; Sony condenser microphone, 1965, model C-38; Neumann microphone, 1976, model U-47 FET; Electrovoice microphone, circa 1956, type 726; and RCA studio microphone, 1950, type 77-A.

Electronic and computer music equipment includes RCA Mark 1 music synthesizer, ca. 1954; Music Composing Computer, 1971, built by the TRIADEX Corporation and designed by Joseph Fredkin and Marvin Minsky; Theremin, 1930, manufactured by RCA, applies the heterodyne principle to electronic music, designed by Leo S. Theremin, Soviet Union acoustical engineer; Rhthmicon, 1931, built by Leo S. Theremin.

Apparatus representing engineering standards in audio includes General Electric apparatus used in the Uniontown, Pennsylvania receiving tests in 1960 for stereo FM; stereo decoder manufactured by Antal Csisattka of General Electric Receiver Division. The complete apparatus includes decoder, audio amplifier, two loudspeakers, FM stereo exciter for transmitter. This GE-Zenith stereo FM system adopted by the Federal Communications Commission in 1961 as the United States standard.

Division of Mathematics, Room 5128
Uta C. Merzbach, Curator
(202) 357–2392

This division has an oral history collection, begun in 1967, consisting of 270 tapes with transcripts of interviews documenting the history of computers and other mathematical devices. An alphabetical listing of transcripts by interviewee is available.

Division of Mechanisms, Room 5014
Otto Mayr, Curator
(202) 357–3188

This division has custody of both sound recordings and artifacts, including phonographs, wire and tape recorders, and experimental apparatus.

Experimental A.G. Bell Collection.—About 200 items, including photophonic recordings representing variable density/variable area on glass plates recorded at the Volta Laboratory in the 1880s. Attempts were made in 1966 to recover the audio modulation (Bell Laboratories, in conjunction with a committee at the Smithsonian Institution and the Library of Congress). One word, "barometer" was recovered; speaker unknown (one reel-to-reel tape).

Berliner Collection, 1880s–1890s.—Includes recordings and experimental devices: first Berliner gramophone recording, 1887, zinc plate, 6 inches square; Berliner record pressed into white glass, 1888; 3 zinc plates, 7 inches in diameter; Berliner commercial records, includes 3 hard rubber discs, 7 inches in diameter. These are among the earliest American commercial recordings; Berliner matrix, heavy metal plate, 10¼ inches in diameter; Berliner disc recording, made in 1888; Berliner phonautogram, wooden frame, 11 inches in diameter; Berliner gramophone recordings, 1887, 1890, and 1895; zinc disc, 8 inches in diameter.

Additional recordings include examples of Edison and Columbia experimental recordings dated 1878–1920s and 1945, respectively. Among these is an Edison tin foil recorded at the Smithsonian Institution on April 18, 1878. There is also a collection of wire recordings made on a Telegraphone, ca. 1920, including several political speeches. In addition there are 4 dictaphone cylinders on which broadcasts from the Little America Expedition, 1935–1936, are recorded.

Phonographs in the division's collections include some 20 items from the Volta Laboratory: Tainter phonograph, 1886; Bell experimental disc graphophone; Chichester Bell and Sumner Tainter graphophone; and Bell-Tainter experimental recorder-reproducer. Berliner items include Berliner gramophone exhibited at Franklin Institute, 1888; gramophone with Clarks improvement, 1898; gramophones, 1887; and experimental apparatus, 1882. Edison phonographs include phonograph, tin foil; phonograph with stethoscope, 1887; "Amberola 50" phonograph with 11 Amberol records; tin foil phonograph made by Bergmann; cylinder phonograph, 1911; Edison talking doll, ca. 1890, includes Jack and Jill and Mother Hubbard recordings; Edison opera phonograph; GEM phonograph, 1911; and some 100 accessories, mostly phonograph horns. Columbia graphophones include type B, 1889; type C made by J.H. White, 1890; type K, made by American Graphophone Co., 1893; type N; and 2 graphophones type A, one of which was made by T.H. MacDonald in 1898.

Oliver Read Collection.—About 75 items, including Multiphone, Regina Hexaphone, Ritz Portable, Princeton Talking Machine Talk-o-Phone, Busy Bee, and Pathe. Additional items include 30 dictaphones representing technology from 1890 to the 1930s.

DEPARTMENT OF HISTORY OF TECHNOLOGY
Division of Mechanical and Civil Engineering, Room 5014
David Noble and Carlene Stephens, Curators
(202) 357-3188

This division has custody of the Julian Hinds Collection, which includes a transcription of an oral history interview with Hinds conducted at the University of California at Los Angeles. Hinds served as an engineer, 1930-1941, and as general manager and chief engineer for the Metropolitan Water District of Los Angeles, 1951-1956.

DEPARTMENT OF NATIONAL HISTORY
Division of Political History, Room 4109
Edith P. Mayo, Curator
(202) 375-2008

This division has a collection of 100 16-inch radio transcription discs from the World War II period and produced by radio station WCAU in Philadelphia, Pennsylvania. Researchers can expect to find presidential and campaign speeches of Franklin D. Roosevelt, Wendell Wilkie, Harry Truman, Winston Churchill, Dwight D. Eisenhower, and Herbert Hoover. There is also a collection of 30 reel-to-reel television and radio presidential advertisements (broken down by market area) dating from 1976 to the present. These feature radio campaign spots for the 1980 presidential primary of Jimmy Carter, Barry Commoner, and George Bush, among others. Other notable items include cylinder recordings of speeches by Calvin Coolidge, Theodore Roosevelt, William Jennings Bryan, and William Harding and spanning the period 1896-1920.

DEPARTMENT OF PUBLIC PROGRAMS
Josiah O. Hatch, Assistant Director
Room 5103
(202) 357-2124

The purpose of this office is to present public programs in the museum, such as concerts. It also provides other programs, such as educational outreach into the Washington community, especially for schools and for senior citizens, and for publications in the museum. Currently available for loan is a sound/ slide kit entitled "G. Washington: A figure Upon the Stage Resource Kit." It includes 59 color slides of artifacts, photographs, and documents, and an audio cassette narrative with transcript. Other similar resource kits are being developed.

The Department of Public Programs now includes some of the offices that were formerly part of the Smithsonian Institution's Division of Performing Arts. Available resources are audio and video recordings, including the concerts and oral history project of the Black American Culture Program, aspects of American popular entertainment in the "American Musical Theater," "American Dance Experience," and "American Country Music" series, the "World Explorer" series of international artists, and chamber music on historic instruments. In addition, there are complete sets of photographic slides for past concerts and events.

Chamber Music Program
James Weaver, Director
(202) 357-4173

This office is responsible for the organizing of concerts presented at the museum. Many of these concerts make use of original instruments kept at the Division of Musical Instruments of the National Museum of American History and are comprised mostly

of eighteenth-century music and Americana. Other concerts organized by this office are presented in the museum or in other locations or for radio broadcast by the Smithsonian Chamber Players, the Smithsonian Chamber Orchestra, and the Smithsonian Quartet. Archival tapes are made for all performances. Some of these tapes are held at the Chamber Music Program office and some are at the Division of Musical Instruments. Many recordings are available through the Smithsonian Institution Press for general distribution (N11).

At this writing, permanent housing for other audiovisual archives produced by the former Division of Performing Arts is yet to be determined. Recordings of these materials represent various aspects of the American popular culture: dance, country music, musical comedy, and jazz. Some of this archival material also has been made available for distribution through the Smithsonian Institution Press (N11). For information regarding these materials, write to Harold Closter, Production Director, at the Department of Public Programs, Production Division, Room 310.

Program in Black American Culture
Bernice Johnson Reagon, Director
(202) 357–4176

This program is dedicated to the research and presentation of the rich black American cultural experience through concert series, conferences, workshops, and publications. The original African Diaspora Program was part of the Festival of American Folklife between 1972 and 1976 and concentrated on the relationship between black American culture and its African and Caribbean roots. Since 1976 more specific studies have been made on particular aspects of black American culture. For example, in 1980 a conference was held at the Smithsonian on the Civil Rights movement of the 1960s, which brought together over 100 singers, humanists, photographers, and other persons active in the movement. An ongoing study of pioneering composers of black gospel music has been conducted by scholars and performers, under the auspices of the Program in Black American Culture. To date the program has presented the work of Roberta Martin, Charles Albert Tindley, and William Herbert Brewster. Other related gospel music studies are a series on the quartet tradition and styles of individual performers.

Other presentations by the program include two studies on the blues tradition, a study of black hair styles (particularly braiding), and a conference on black American cultural scholarship. All programs presented by this office are documented on tape and are maintained as a permanent archive. Some recordings have been made from this archival material and are available for distribution either through this office or through the Smithsonian Institution Press (N11).

4 a. Listening facilities are available in some offices of the museum.

b. Appointments are necessary. There are restrictions on the use of some of the materials.

c. Fees are not charged to listen to recordings.

d. Some duplication of materials is permitted. Photoreproduction facilities are available through the departmental offices. Color transparencies and prints of some exhibits are available for purchase in the museum gift shop.

5. In addition to the above-mentioned *Guide,* the Archives Center maintains its own lists of manuscript collections. The Program in Black American Culture has logs and descriptions of most of its materials as does the Chamber Music Program. To keep abreast of recent gifts to the museum as well as information on museum programs, scholars should refer to the Smithsonian's *Annual Report.*

National Park Service (Interior Department)—Clara Barton National
Historic Site   See entry B31

C12 National Portrait Gallery (Smithsonian Institution)—Education Department

1 a. *8th and F Streets, N.W.*
      Washington, D.C. 20560
      (202) 357-2920

   b. 10:00 A.M.–5:00 P.M.   Monday–Friday

   c. Open to researchers for on-site use.

   d. Kenneth Yellis, Curator

2. The act of Congress creating the National Portrait Gallery stated that it would function as "a free public museum for the exhibition and study of portraiture and statuary depicting men and women who have made significant contributions to the history, development, and culture of the people of the United States, and the artists who created such portraiture and statuary." The special exhibitions of the gallery enlarge upon themes and subjects suggested by the permanent collection. Portraits, manuscripts, personal memorabilia, and other objects, many borrowed from public and private collections in the United States and abroad, are brought together to illuminate patterns in the national experience. The staff of the Education Department provides a number of services, including guided tours, lectures, films, and publications.

3. The Education Department arranges for the presentation of special performance events, including "Portraits in Motion," a dramatic and musical series illuminating the lives and times of notable Americans in the gallery's collections, and "Portraits in Motion Studio Theater," a series of informal and occasionally experimental dramatic, musical, storytelling and theater performances focusing on a wide range of themes in American cultural life, and "Portraits in American Song." Some of these presentations have been recorded by Radio Smithsonian (H22). Many of these programs are recorded on audio tape and are available for archival and scholarly use on-site.

4 a. Minimal viewing/listening facilities are available.

   b. Reservations are required.

   c. Fees are not charged.

   d. Reproduction of photographs or transparencies of portraits in the permanent collection is permitted only with the written permission of the gallery. Contact the Education Department regarding duplication of sound recordings.

5. The *Catalog of American Portraits,* a reference facility on American portraiture, is actively engaged in a nationwide survey and maintains photographs and data on more than 70,000 portraits in public and private collections. The gallery's *Permanent Collection Illustrated Checklist* is brought up-to-date in a new edition on a regular schedule. A brochure describing the gallery is available to individuals upon request.

C13 Navy Memorial Museum (Naval Historical Center)

1 a. *Washington Navy Yard, Building 76*
9th and M Streets, S.E.
Washington, D.C. 20374
(202) 433-2651 (Hours and Exhibit Information)
(202) 433-4882 (Additional Information)

  b. 9:00 A.M.–4:00 P.M.   Monday–Friday
     10:00 A.M.–5:00 P.M.   Weekends and holidays, except Thanksgiving, Christmas, and New Years's days.

  c. Open to the public.

  d. Commander T.A. Damon, Director

2. This organization is the Navy's central historical museum. It has over 30,000 square feet of indoor display area plus an outdoor park of almost equal size. The museum's displays depict the Navy's wartime operations, weapons, and leaders, as well as the service's peacetime contributions in such fields as aeronautics, diplomacy, electronics, exploration, humanitarian service, marine engineering, medicine, navigation, oceanography, and space flight.

3. In the museum is the special Naval Electronics Exhibit, depicting the development of the radio and consisting of three principal components: radio communications, componentry, and navigational aids. A number of the pieces on exhibit are on loan from the National Museum of American History of the Smithsonian Institution (C11).
    Radio Communications: 3-electrode amplifier tube, late 1930s, manufactured by Machllett Co., Stamford, Conn.; radio receiver, Neutrodyne Design, model NR-5 with headset (the first radio receiver installed in the White House, 1921, used by President Warren G. Harding; originally manufactured for the U.S.S. *Mayflower* by the Freed Eisemann Co.); Navy built receiver, 1915, model Ba, no. W83 (tuning range 10,000–1,000 meters, 30–300 kHz); radio receiver, very-low frequency, 1932, model RAC, type SE 4510, manufactured for the Bureau of Engineering by the Naval Research Laboratory (first naval receiver operated on alternating current, tuning range 25,000–3,750 meters, 12–80 kHz); portable wavemeter, 1918, type SE 965, manufactured by Wireless Improvement Co., New York, N.Y. (tuning range 100–800 meters, 375–3,000 kHz); portable spark-gap transmitter, 1917 (battery powered and used by the U.S. Army, on loan from the National Museum of American History of the Smithsonian Institution); radio receiver, 1920, model SE 1420C, manufactured by American Radio and Research Corp. (first naval receiver to incorporate the vacuum-tube detector internally; an alternate crystal detector was mounted externally; tuning range: 250–7,500 meters, 40–1,200 kHz); triple section crystal detector, 1909, type SE 183A, manufactured by Lowenstein Radio Co., Inc., Brooklyn, N.Y. (used by Navy prior to and during World War I); radio receiver, 1917, type CF 753, manufactured by DeForest Radio Telephone and Telegraph Co. (the detector is an externally mounted crystal or vacuum tube, tuning range 10,000–1,000 meters, 30–300 kHz); high-frequency transmitter-receiver, 1939, model TCS, type CMX-46195 (receiver), type COL-52245 (transmitter), manufactured by The Magnovox Co. for the Bureau of Ships of the Navy Department (tuning range 1,500–12,000 kHz, 20 watts (voice), 40 watts (continuous wave)); shipboard VHF transceiver, 1938, model TABS, type CRV 46068-A, Radio Corporation of America; transmitter, type CRV-52093 (tuning range 60–80 MHz); WW II superheterodyne receiver, 1940, model RBA, manufactured by

Federal Telegraph Co., Newark, N.J. (tuning range 14.5–600 kHz, 40 watts); WW II airborne VHF transceiver, 1943, model AN/ARC-1 (tuning range 11–156 MHz, 10 watts); high-frequency receiver, 1943, model RBS, type CCT-46217-A, manufactured by Stromberg-Carlson Co., Rochester, N.Y.; solid-state high-frequency transceiver, 1962, model AN/WRC-1, manufactured by General Dynamics (tuning range 2–30 MHz, 100 watts).

Componentry: Passive items include a Leyden jar, 1916 (on loan from the National Museum of American History, Smithsonian Institution), a mica capacitor, developed by William Dubilier, 1916; and various resistors, inductors, and other capacitors. Active items include a Coherer, 1899; a J receiving tube, 1915; an N receiving tube, 1922, Western Electric Company; an audion, 1907, developed by DeForest; an Acorn, 1935, RCA Corp.; a Lighthouse, 1940, General Electric Co.; and a Klystron, 1940 (invented by the Varian brothers). Solid state items include early devices such as integrated circuits, circuit cards, and modules. One interesting item is a BUSAC-7 laboratory model circuit card for one of the earliest transistorized digital computers built in the United States.

Navigational Aids: Shipboard radio detection finder receiver, 1940, model DP-12, manufactured by RCA Manufacturing Co. (frequency range 100–150 kHz, includes an operating pedestal, type CRV-69011); Loran receiver, 1942, Model DAS-3, manufactured by FADA Radio and Electric Company.

The museum also has additional items in storage. Contact Henry Vadnais, Curator (202/433–2318) for additional information.

4 c. Fees are not charged.

d. Visitors may take pictures with the permission of the museum office.

5. Copies of the *Navy Memorial Museum* brochure and *The Navy Memorial Museum's Guide to Willard Park* are available without charge on request.

C14 Phillips Collection

1 a. *1600 21st Street, N.W.*
Washington, D.C. 20009
(202) 387-2151

b. 10:00 A.M.–5:00 P.M.   Tuesday–Saturday
2:00 P.M.–7:00 P.M.   Sunday

c. Open to the public. Special permission is required to access sound recordings.

d. Laughlin Phillips, Director
Charles Crowder, Director of Music

2–3. Although the Phillips Collection was established as an art gallery, it is internationally known for its Sunday Afternoon Concert Series started in 1941. Not only do nationally and internationally known concert artists perform there, but also local artists perform each May. Some of the more notable performers include Glenn Gould, Gary Graffman, Charlie Byrd, and Jesseye Norman. All of the concerts have been recorded since September 1972. The performances take place on Sundays at 5:00 P.M., September through May, and are recorded on tape for broadcast on Washington's Education Radio Network, and for national distribution by Parkway Communications Corporation (Appendix II). The Phillips Collection maintains an archive of these tapes.

4 a. On-site listening equipment is not available.

5. Sound recordings are not cataloged.

Smithsonian Institution Libraries—Museum Reference Center Library
See entry A63

Smithsonian Institution Libraries—Museum Support Center
See entry A63

Smithsonian Institution—Office of Museum Programs   See entry K16

C15 Textile Museum—Arthur D. Jenkins Library

1 a. *2320 S Street, N.W.*
Washington, D.C. 20008
(202) 667–0441

b. 10:00 A.M.–5:00 P.M.   Wednesday–Friday
10:00 A.M.–1:00 P.M.   Saturday

c. Open to the public for on-site use only.

d. Katherine T. Freshley, Librarian

2. The research library contains 10,000 books and some 500 periodicals on the history and technology of handwoven textiles and rugs. The library also holds materials on contemporary fiber art as well as art, archeology, and anthropology. Geographic areas represented include Africa, China, Egypt, Japan, Near and Middle East, India, Indonesia, Spain, Pre-Columbian Peru, and the Indians of South, Central, and North America.

3. The library has some 35 lectures and talks, recorded on audio cassettes, presented at the International Conference on Oriental Carpets, October 17–19, 1980, at the Textile Museum. Session topics include "Carpets in America," "Turkish Carpets," "Chinese and East Turkeston Carpets," "Turkoman Carpets," "Classical Carpets," and "19th and 20th Century Carpets." Countries represented include United States, Turkey, China, Iran, and Morocco.

4 a. On-site listening equipment is not available. Researchers must provide their own equipment.

b. Reservations are required.

c. Fees are not charged.

d. Photocopy facilities are available.

5. There is a curator's card catalog, arranged by country. An annual journal and a quarterly newsletter are distributed to the museum's associate members.

C16 Woodrow Wilson House (National Trust for Historic Preservation)

1 a. *2340 S Street, N.W.*
Washington, D.C. 20008
(202) 673–4034

b. 10:00 A.M.–2:00 P.M.   Tuesday–Friday
12:00 Noon–4:00 P.M.   Saturday–Sunday

c. Open to the public. Admission fee for museum tour. Access to recordings is provided to serious researchers only and by prior appointment.

d. Earl James, Director
Nancy McCoy, Assistant Director

2. The Woodrow Wilson House, a memorial to President Woodrow Wilson, is the only presidential house museum in the nation's capital. Designed in 1915, and bought by Wilson in 1920, the house contains the President's furnishings, his library of books and record collection, and various mementos.

3. The sound recording collection reflects the President's varied interests and includes 151 commercial and private disc recordings spanning the early 1900s to 1940s. The two principal manufacturers are Columbia Graphophone Company and Victor Talking Machine Co. The selections consist of vocal performances and operatic excerpts, orchestral and other instrumental performances, minstrel music and ragtime, by various performers, including Bert Williams, University of Pennsylvania Quartette, John McCormack, Geraldine Farrar, Arthur Pryor's Band, George H. O'Connor, Josef Hofmann, Walter P. Phillips, Prince's Band, Van E.P.S. Banjo Orchestra, Enrico Caruso, J.P. Sousa Band, Harry Lauder, and Eugene Ysaye. One of the earliest recordings in the collection is *Telegraph Lessons* (8 disc set) produced by J.H. Bonnell and Co. in 1907. There are also 7 discs representing the American Red Cross.

Private recordings include the following: "Hatikva" performed by Efrem Zimbalist and Alona Gluck, September 11, 1918 (Victor Talking Machine Co.); political addresses by Wilson, including "Labor" and "The Tariff"; and recordings by Margaret Woodrow Wilson, including a performance of "The Low Back'd Car" and other songs.

Holdings also include a collection of oral history tapes consisting of interviews for the Kalorama History Project focusing on the immediate geographical area surrounding the house. The six interviews include Edwin Pilson interviewed on February 1, 1977, and March 8, 1977; Joel Barlow interviewed on January 28, 1977; George Reber Littlehales interviewed on February 4, 1977, and on March 10, 1977; and Eleanor Lunde interviewed on March 9, 1977. There are also interviews relating to Woodrow Wilson, including George B. Howard, chauffer to President Wilson and Mrs. Richard W. Hale, daughter of Henry Fairbanks (original owner of the house).

Yet another set of audio tapes consist of copies made from disc recordings of Woodrow Wilson and others. These include a recorded address to Indian tribes; League of Nations speech presented from the S Street Library, November 10, 1923; speeches on labor and the tariff; an address to farmers; a Democratic principles acceptance speech in 1912; a promotion of the League of Nations speech from E.R. Murrow's "I Can Hear It Now"; and various other recordings of speeches by Presidents Wilson, Roosevelt, Taft, and Harding.

The Woodrow Wilson House also has the President's personal playback victrola (style VV-SVI, 72016) manufactured by the Victor Talking Machine Co. probably during the 1920s.

4 a.   Playback facilities are not available.

   b.   Reservations are required.

   c.   No fees are charged except those for museum tours. However, a donation to be used in preserving the site and furnishings is graciously accepted.

   d.   A photocopy facility is not available.

5.   Currently there is a handwritten list of sound recordings. The recordings are filed in 11 binders (C-N).

D Embassies

Introductory Note

Generally, most embassies can be considered valuable initial sources for procuring information on organizations and, in some cases, manufacturers associated with the recording industries in their respective countries. Most of the embassies are willing to answer reference questions regarding their recordings, but they do prefer that researchers or other interested parties call or write in advance for permission to visit. The majority of the embassies queried have audio materials pertaining only to their respective countries.

Embassies are usually closed on their respective national holidays. Consult the United States Department of State's *Diplomatic List,* which cites those holidays, as well as other information, including names, addresses, and telephone numbers of the members of the diplomatic staffs of all missions. Additional useful information on embassies is included in the section, "Foreign Embassies, U.S. Ambassadors, and State Dept. Country Officers," in *Washington Information Directory, 1984–85* (Washington, D.C.: Congressional Quarterly, 1984), and in *Washington 84* (Washington, D.C.: Columbia Books, 1984). Another source that provides a list of foreign embassies and consulates in both the United States and abroad is *World-Wide Chamber of Commerce Directory* (Loveland, Colorado: Johnson, 1981).

In this section, embassies are given their official titles as indicated in the *Diplomatic List* and are arranged alphabetically according to their geographic name.

D1 Embassy of the Bahamas (The Commonwealth of the Bahamas)

1 a. *Tourist Office*
1730 Rhode Island Avenue, N.W., Suite 510
Washington, D.C. 20036
(202) 659–9135

b. 9:00 A.M.–5:00 P.M.   Monday–Friday

c. Researchers may borrow recordings by special arrangement, but the embassy prefers that users listen to the recordings on-site.

d. Mr. G. McNair Brown, Senior Regional Manager

2–3. An unspecified number of cassette recordings of calypso music produced in the Bahamas are held, primarily exemplifying music used in promotion of tourism.

4 a. The embassy has a cassette tape player, but prefers researchers to bring their own equipment.

D2 Embassy of Belgium

1 a. *Cultural Section*
3330 Garfield Street, N.W.
Washington, D.C. 20008
(202) 333–6900

b. 9:30 A.M.–1:00 P.M.; 2:30 P.M.–5:30 P.M.   Monday–Friday

c. Open to the public. Groups, educational institutions, and broadcasting stations may borrow recordings. Appointments are required.

d. Andrea Murphy, Cultural Officer

2–3. The embassy maintains a collection of some three hundred recordings of Belgian music, which have been produced in the United States and Belgium. Selections consist of sacred, early Flemish, folk, classical, and contemporary music. There are also a variety of recordings of the Belgian national anthem and recordings of performances at international music festivals held in Belgium. Included in the collection are recordings of the Queen Elizabeth International Music Competition for violin, piano, and composition.

4 a. The embassy has only one turntable.

b. Reservations are recommended to assure the availability of desired recordings.

c. Recordings are lent free of charge.

d. Recordings in the public domain may be copied with the permission of the embassy.

5. Borrowers may consult an inventory of recordings at the embassy.

D3 Embassy of Brazil

1 a. *3006 Massachusetts Avenue, N.W.*
Washington, D.C. 20008
(202) 797–0198

b. 9:00 A.M.–5:00 P.M.   Monday–Friday

c. An appointment must be made for arrangements to listen to the recordings.

d. Ms. Cybele S. Magro, Attaché

2–3. An unspecified number of discs and cassettes recorded in Brazil and consisting of that country's orchestras, bands, and vocalists are available

4 a. Users must supply their own listening equipment.

D4 Embassy of Cameroon (United Republic of Cameroon)

1 a. *2439 Massachusetts Avenue, N.W.*
Washington, D.C. 20008
(202) 265–8790

Office of the Cultural Counselor
(202) 332-6705

  b. 9:00 A.M.–1:00 P.M.; 2:00 P.M.–5:00 P.M.   Monday–Friday

  c. Research scholars may borrow recordings. Special permission, however, must be obtained in advance.

  d. Mr. Ejedepang-Koge, Cultural Counselor

2–3. One disc and 2 cassettes of sacred vocal music performed by Cameroon singers produced both in the United States and the United Republic of Cameroon are available. The embassy also has a small number of films, which may be projected at the embassy or outside the embassy by embassy staff.

4 a. On-site listening facilities are not available.

D5 Embassy of Chile

1 a. *Cultural Office*
1732 Massachusetts Avenue, N.W.
Washington, D.C. 20036
(202) 785–1746

  c. Open to the public, but researchers must telephone in advance for an appointment.

  d. Maria Pincus, Assistant to the Cultural Attaché

2–3. The embassy has 2 disc recordings of Chilean folk music produced in that country.

4 a. On-site listening equipment is not available.

D6 Coordination Council for North American Affairs (Republic of China on Taiwan)

1 a. *Cultural Division*
131 Van Ness Centre
4301 Connecticut Avenue, N.W.
Washington, D.C. 20008
(202) 686–1638

  b. 9:00 A.M.–5:00 P.M.   Monday–Friday

c. Films of Chinese movies may be borrowed by special arrangement. Researchers may view and listen to Chinese films and video cassettes of Chinese songs, etc., in the division, but must telephone in advance to make an appointment.

d. Ms. Evadne C. Yu, Secretary

2–3. The division has a collection of films and cassettes of Chinese movies and songs.

4 a. Taping may be done if special permission is secured, but organizations and individuals must supply their own tapes.

D7   Embassy of Costa Rica

1 a. *2112 S Street, N.W.*
Washington, D.C. 20008
(202) 234–2945

b. 9:00 A.M.–1:00 P.M.; 2:30 P.M.–4:00 P.M.   Monday–Friday

c. Recordings may be borrowed but researchers must telephone for an appointment.

d. Mirtha Virginia de Perea, Minister Counselor for Cultural Affairs

2–3. The embassy has an unspecified number of disc recordings of folk music, poetry, and the Costa Rican national anthem. Sound recordings and related materials were produced in Costa Rica.

4 a. On-site listening equipment is not available.

D8   Embassy of Cyprus

1 a. *2211 R Street, N.W.*
Washington, D.C. 20008
(202) 462–5772

b. 9:00 A.M.–5:00 P.M.   Monday–Friday

c. Research scholars must have special permission from the Press Counselor in order to examine the recordings. Please telephone ahead to make an appointment.

d. Dr. Marios Evriviaden, Press Counselor

2–3. The collection includes an unspecified number of native ethnic and traditional music recorded in Cyprus.

4 a. On-site listening equipment is not available.

D9   Embassy of Czechoslovakia

1 a. *3900 Linnean Avenue, N.W.*
Washington, D.C. 20008
(202) 363–6315

b. 9:00 A.M.–12:00 Noon; 2:00 P.M.–6:00 P.M.   Monday–Friday

c. Not open to the public. Recordings are loaned only to colleges. Please telephone in advance to make an appointment.

d. Vladimir Vedral, Third Secretary

2–3. The embassy has an unspecified number of disc recordings of Czech folksongs produced in Czechoslovakia.

4 a. On-site listening equipment is not available.

D10 Embassy of Finland

1 a. *Press Section*
3216 New Mexico Avenue, N.W.
Washington, D.C. 20016
(202) 363-2430

b. 9:00 A.M.–4:30 P.M.   Monday–Friday
9:00 A.M.–4:00 P.M.   Monday–Friday (summer hours)

c. Not open to the public. Disc recordings may be borrowed. Please telephone in advance for an appointment.

d. Benita Faggerström, Secretary

2–3. The embassy has some 30 disc recordings and 100 reel-to-reel tape recordings of Finnish classical, folk, military, and patriotic music. The audio tapes consist of music and speeches on the Finnish economic and political system. A number of the recordings were produced in Finland.

Some of the Finnish composers and performers represented in the collection include Jean Sibelius, Joonas Kokkonen, Martti Talvela, Leevi Madetoja, Erik Bergman, Uuno Klami, Selim Palmgren, Tauno Pylkkänen, Einojuhani Rautavaara, Bruno Dössekker, S. Einar Englund, Nils-Eric Fougstedt, Aarre Merikanto, Väinö Raitio, Taneli Kuusisto, and Ahti Sonninen.

4 a. Audio equipment is not available.

b. Reservations are recommended to assure the availability of desired recordings.

c. Recordings are lent free of charge.

d. Recordings in the public domain may be copied with the permission of the embassy.

5. A free listing of recordings is available upon request.

D11 Embassy of Ghana

1 a. *2460 16th Street, N.W.*
Washington, D.C. 20009
(202) 462-0761

b. 9:00 A.M.–5:00 P.M.   Monday–Friday

c. Tour groups and research scholars must make special arrangements to secure access to recordings.

d. Richard Horsley, Minister-Counselor

2–3. The embassy has an unspecified number of disc recordings of native folk music produced in Ghana.

4 a. On-site listening facilities are not available.

D12 Embassy of Grenada

1 a. *1701 R Street, N.W.*
Washington, D.C. 20009
(202) 265–2561

b. 9:00 A.M.–5:00 P.M.   Monday–Friday

c. Not open to the public. Users must telephone or write in advance requesting an appointment to examine recordings. Although recordings are not loaned, researchers may purchase copies of the recordings.

d. Samuel Orgias, Counselor

2–3. The embassy has 25 disc recordings on economic, political, and cultural topics related to Grenada. The recordings were produced in Grenada.

4 a. On-site listening facilities are not available.

D13 Embassy of Guyana

1 a. *2490 Tracy Place, N.W.*
Washington, D.C. 20008
(202) 265–6900

b. 9:00 A.M.–5:00 P.M.   Monday–Friday

c. Researchers must telephone or write for an appointment to examine recordings. Recordings may be borrowed, but with special permission only.

d. Gordon Daniels, Second Secretary

2–3. The embassy has a number of disc recordings of native folk and dance music.

4 a. On-site listening facilities are not available.

D14 Embassy of India

1 a. *Information Service*
2107 Massachusetts Avenue, N.W.
Washington, D.C. 20008
(202) 939–7000

b. 9:00 A.M.–5:00 P.M.   Monday–Friday

c. Not open to the public.

d. Mr. Murdhy, Librarian

2–3.   The embassy has some 20 audio cassettes of native Indian music produced in India.

4 a.   On-site listening facilities are not available.

D15 Embassy of Iraq

1 a. *Iraqi Interests Section*
1801 P Street, N.W.
Washington, D.C. 20036
(202) 232–6933 (Press Office)

b. 8:30 A.M.–4:00 P.M.   Monday–Friday

c. Researchers may borrow recordings, but must telephone or write for an appointment.

d. Mrs. Mahasin Yono, Secretary, Press Office

2–3.   The embassy has 4 cassette recordings in Arabic of the national anthem of Iraq, and songs about the country. The recordings were produced in Iraq. The embassy also has a number of films and video cassettes in Arabic and English.

4 a.   On-site listening facilities are not available.

D16 Embassy of Japan

1 a. *Japan Information and Culture Center*
Embassy of Japan
917 19th Street, N.W.
Washington, D.C. 20006
(202) 234–2266, ext. 416 cr 417

b. 9:00 A.M.–12:30 P.M.; 1:30 P.M.–5:00 P.M.   Monday–Friday

c. Open to the public. Researchers may borrow materials. Please telephone or write in advance.

d. Mr. Michio Shimizu, Deputy Director

2–3.   The embassy has some 10 disc recordings of traditional folk music produced in Japan. It may be of further interest that the embassy also maintains a collection of more than 100 films on Japan.

4 a.   On-site previewing and/or listening facilities are not available.

D17 Embassy of Jordan (Hashemite Kingdom of Jordan)

1 a. *Jordanian Information Bureau*
1701 K Street, N.W.
Washington, D.C. 20006
(202) 659–3322

b. 9:30 A.M.–5:30 P.M.   Monday–Friday

c. Researchers may borrow recordings, but must telephone or write for an appointment.

d. Dr. Akram Z. Barakat, Minister, Press and Information

2–3. The embassy has 3 disc recordings of Jordanian classical music produced in Jordan.

4 a. On-site listening facilities are not available.

D18 Embassy of Korea

1 a. *Information Office*
1717 Massachusetts Avenue, N.W., Suite 707
Washington, D.C. 20036
(202) 483–6892

b. 9:00 A.M.–12 Noon; 2:00 P.M.–5:00 P.M.   Monday–Friday

c. Open to the public, but researchers must telephone or write requesting an appointment.

d. Mr. Park Shinil, Information Director

2–3. The embassy has an unspecified number of disc and cassette recordings of classical and native music performed by Korean artists. The recordings were produced in Korea.

4 a. Listening facilities are available.

D19 Embassy of Norway

1 a. *Information Office*
2720 34th Street, N.W.
Washington, D.C. 20008
(202) 333–6000

b. 9:00 A.M.–4:00 P.M.   Monday–Friday

c. Recordings are loaned at the discretion of the embassy. Researchers must write or call for an appointment.

d. Per Aasen, Press and Cultural Counselor

2–3.   The embassy has an unspecified number of disc recordings which are lent to individuals, groups, or radio stations. The collection includes traditional folk music as well as classical and contemporary works by Norwegian composers. The recordings were produced in Norway.

4 a.   On-site listening facilities are not available.

D20   Embassy of Pakistan

1 a.   *2315 Massachusetts Avenue, N.W.*
Washington, D.C. 20008
(202) 939–6227/6228

b.   9:00 A.M.–5:00 P.M.   Monday–Friday

c.   Researchers must telephone or write for an appointment to examine the recordings.

d.   Mohammad Saleem, Second Secretary, Information

2–3.   The embassy has a small number of disc and cassette recordings of native folk and instrumental music produced in Pakistan. In addition, documentary films on Pakistan can be obtained on loan upon request.

4 a.   On-site listening facilities are not available.

D21   Embassy of the Philippines

1 a.   *Cultural Office*
1617 Massachusetts Avenue, N.W.
Washington, D.C. 20036
(202) 483–1414

b.   9:00 A.M.–12 Noon; 2:00 P.M.–4:30 P.M.   Monday–Friday

c.   Researchers may borrow recordings but with special permission only.

d.   Leoncio R. Cardenas, Jr., Third Secretary

2–3.   The embassy has an unspecified number of disc and cassette recordings of Philippine folksongs, as well as 5 films on various cultural topics.

4 a.   On-site listening facilities are not available.

D22   Embassy of Portugal

1 a.   *2125 Kalorama Road, N.W.*
Washington, D.C. 20008
(202) 265–1643

b.   9:00 A.M.–5:00 P.M.   Monday–Friday

c. Recordings are loaned to colleges but not individuals. It is also the embassy's policy to donate recordings to radio stations. Researchers must telephone or write in order to obtain specific information on the collection.

d. Luis Amorim de Sousa, Counselor, Press and Cultural Affairs

2–3. The embassy has some 20 to 30 disc recordings of folk, classical, and popular music of Portugal.

4 a. On-site listening facilities are not available.

D23 Embassy of South Africa

1 a. *Information Section*
3051 Massachusetts Avenue, N.W.
Washington, D.C. 20008
(202) 232–4400

b. 9:00 A.M.–5:00 P.M.   Monday–Friday

c. For current information on borrowing privileges, researchers must telephone or write.

d. Mr. P.K. Coetzee, Minister of Information

2–3. The embassy has some 194 disc recordings consisting primarily of South African classical, popular, folk, and traditional music. Some of the performing artists and composers include Mimi Coertse, Lourens Bogtman, Alan Naudé, and Sophie Mgcina. The collection also includes tourist films.

4 a. On-site listening facilities are not available.

5. A descriptive list of the collection is available by mail.

D24 Embassy of Spain

1 a. *Cultural Office*
4200 Wisconsin Avenue, N.W., Room 520
Washington, D.C. 20016
(202) 966–1077

b. 9:30 A.M.–4:00 P.M.   Monday–Friday

c. The embassy is not open to the public. Researchers must write or telephone for an appointment to examine recordings.

d. Demitrio Gonzalez, Audiovisual Librarian

2–3. The embassy has an unspecified number of disc and reel-to-reel tape recordings of Spanish regional music, writers, and poets.

4 a. On-site listening facilities are not available.

D25 Embassy of Switzerland

1 a. *2900 Cathedral Avenue, N.W.*
Washington, D.C. 20008
(202) 745–7900

b.· 9:00 A.M.–5:00 P.M.   Monday–Friday

c. Recordings may be borrowed, but users must write or telephone in advance.

d. Rita Blaser, Secretary

2–3.   The embassy has a *Musica Helvetica* record collection, which includes some 81 discs consisting of classical, folk and traditional, jazz, rock, Christmas music, patriotic songs, and marches. All of the composers and performing artists are Swiss, including Arthur Honegger, Frank Martin, Michael Studer, Edith Mathis, Emilie Haudenschild, Gottfried Stucki, Joseph Bovet, Luzi Bergamin, Kasimir Geisser, Max Lässer, Jürg Lüth, Kobelt Quartet, Swiss Jazz Quintet, and Roland Perrenoud.

4 a. On-site listening facilities are not available.

5.   A descriptive list of the collection is available by mail.

D26 Embassy of Thailand

1 a. *Office of the Public Relations Attaché*
2300 Kalorama Road, N.W.
Washington, D.C. 20008
(202) 667–3108

b. 9:30 A.M.–12:30 P.M.; 2:00 P.M.–5:00 P.M.   Monday–Friday

c. Recordings may be borrowed, but with special permission only.

d. Mr. Phong Pradit, Secretary

2–3.   The embassy's collection includes some 50 cassette recordings of native classical and popular music produced in Thailand.

4 a. Contact the embassy regarding listening facilities.

D27 Embassy of Togo (Republic of Togo)

1 a. *2208 Massachusetts Avenue, N.W.*
Washington, D.C. 20008
(202) 234–4214

b. 9:00 A.M.–5:00 P.M.   Monday–Friday

c. All public relations affairs are handled by David Apter and Associates, 1625 K Street, Suite 102, Washington, D.C. 20006. The firm manages the Togo Information

Service. Contact David Jewell at (202) 393–2200. Interested parties may visit the Apter firm in order to borrow recordings.

2–3. The Togo Information Service has 2 disc recordings consisting of Togo Music from West Africa, featuring various artists, and Dama Damawuzan, a Togo vocalist. The Togo Information Service is in the process of developing the collection.

4 a. On-site listening facilities are not available.

D28 Embassy of Turkey

1 a. *2010 Massachusetts Avenue, N.W., 6th Floor*
Washington, D.C. 20036
(202) 833–8411 (Office of the Press Counselor)

b. 9:30 A.M.–4:30 P.M.   Monday–Friday

c. Researchers wishing to meet with embassy personnel should write or telephone in advance to request an appointment.

d. His Excellency Sukru Elekdag, Ambassador

2–3. The Office of the Press Counselor maintains a small reference library with books and periodicals in English and Turkish on the history and culture of Turkey. The library also holds a number of recordings of Turkish music.

4 a. On-site listening facilities are not available.

E Religious Bodies

Introductory Note

Washington, D.C. has a number of substantial resources for both print and non-print materials that center on religious topics. The Washington Theological Consortium (E9) of colleges, universities, and divinity schools can provide additional information on these resources.

The researcher should be aware that several principal academic institutions described in section K of this *Guide* have theology schools or departments.

E1 Board of Jewish Education of Greater Washington (BJE)

1 a. *9325 Brookville Road*
Silver Spring, Maryland 20910
(301) 589–3180

  b. 9:00 A.M.–5:00 P.M.   Monday, Wednesday
    9:00 A.M.–12:00 Noon   Tuesday, Thursday, Friday

  c. Open to the public for on-site use. Some recordings circulate but with permission only.

2. The Board of Jewish Education of Greater Washington seeks to identify the Jewish educational requirements of the Washington metropolitan area and to support the individual and professional growth of the community. The BJE accomplishes this goal by supplying services to local schools as well as publishing a number of useful publications.

3. Notable holdings of the Board.

Teacher Center Library
(301) 589–3180

Judith Kupchan, Coordinator

The BJE maintains a Teacher Center Library, which contains a substantial collection of materials relating to Judaic studies. The collection contains some 5,000 books, 60 periodicals, several hundred films, some 1,200 filmstrips (100 of which are audio cassette/filmstrip kits), and individual cassette and disc recordings.

The library's audio collection includes specifically some 200 disc and 50 cassette recordings consisting primarily of Jewish music. A number of these materials were produced in Israel. Included among the cassette tapes are several lectures on Judaic themes presented by such notable persons as Abba Eban, Gershom Scholem, Emil Fackenheim, Harold Schulweis, and David Hartman.

4 a. On-site listening equipment is available.

b. No reservation requirements.

c. No fees are charged.

5. The BJE publishes *Teacher Center News,* a bulletin that describes and evaluates new publications, provides bibliographical listings for special occasions, and describes Teacher Center activities. Other publications include *Family Resource* and *Lamoreh— To the Teacher,* the latter being a newsletter about pedagogic issues. The library's sound recordings are not cataloged.

E2   DeSales School of Theology—Library

1 a. *721 Lawrence Street, N.E.*
Washington, D.C. 20017
(202) 269-9412

b. 9:00 A.M.-4:00 P.M.   Monday-Friday

c. Open to the public for on-site use only. Sound recordings do not circulate.

d. Ward Gongall, Head Librarian

2.   The library has some 18,800 books, which generally focus on theological subjects. Its periodical collection is maintained at the Periodical Center at the Dominican House of Studies (contact Father Raymond Vandegrift, 202/529-5300).

3.   The library has 380 single audio cassette tapes and filmstrip/ audio cassette programs. Most of the materials cover theological subjects, such as pastoral ministry, religious education, and spirituality and were produced commercially by the *National Catholic Reporter.* A few tapes are recordings of class and guest lectures.

4 a. On-site listening equipment is available.

b. No reservation requirements but prior permission is recommended.

c. Fees are not charged.

5.   The library maintains a shelf list in card catalog format for the sound recordings. Recordings are indexed and shelved according to title.

Dominican House of Studies—Archives   See entry B12

Georgetown University—Joseph Mark Lauinger Library—Woodstock Theological Center Library   See entry A31

E3 Interfaith Conference of Metropolitan Washington

1 a. *1419 V Street, N.W.*
Washington, D.C. 20009
(202) 234–6300

b. 9:00 A.M.–5:00 P.M.   Monday–Friday

c. Individuals should contact the conference for information regarding use of the collection.

d. Naomi U. Kaminsky, Administrative Assistant

2. The Interfaith Conference of Metropolitan Washington is the meeting ground for four major faith communities of the metropolitan area: Protestant, Roman Catholic, Jewish, and Islamic. Its purpose is to hold dialogues on shared concerns and to work together on critical issues facing the Washington area. Bishops, judicatory executives, ministers, rabbis, imams, and key lay leaders meet to find ways to express effectively the religious communities' concern for the quality of life in the community.

3. Although the conference does not have a formal library, it has the following recorded music performances on cassettes: Interfaith choral concerts (11/24/80, 11/23/81, 11/22/82); and interfaith service for the safe return of the hostages in Iran, held at the U.S. Capitol (1/29/81); an interfaith service for Dr. Martin Luther King, Jr. (1/16/83), and a ½-inch video cassette tape of "Interfaith Cooperation: A Christian View" from Bauman Bible Telecasts, featuring the Interfaith Conference. Its executive director, Rev. Clark Lobenstine; Roman Catholic Bishop Eugene A. Marino, and Muslim Imam Rajee Abdur Rashid are interviewed by Dr. Edward Bauman.

4 a. On-site listening equipment is not available.

5. The conference publishes a quarterly newsletter, *Interfaith Connector.*

Jewish Historical Society   See entry B18

E4 Oblate College Library

1 a. *391 Michigan Avenue, N.E.*
Washington, D.C. 20017
(202) 529–5244

b. 9:00 A.M.–9:00 P.M.   Monday–Saturday

c. Open to scholars and students of theology for on-site use.

d. George Croft, Librarian

2. The library holdings support the curriculum and areas of faculty specialization. The collection contains some 36,400 books, 200 periodical titles, and a number of non-print materials.

3. The audio collection includes 75 cassettes focusing on various moral, spiritual, and scriptural subjects.

4 a. On-site listening equipment is available.

b. No reservation requirements, although it is recommended that users telephone in advance of visiting the library.

c. Fees are not charged.

5. The library has a card catalog with author/title and subject access.

E5 Seventh-day Adventists—General Conference Ministerial/ Stewardship Association

1 a. *6840 Eastern Avenue, N.W.*
Washington, D.C. 20012
(202) 722–6000

b. 9:00 A.M.–5:00 P.M. Monday–Friday

c. Access to tape recordings is provided through subscription and purchase of individual items.

d. Rex D. Edwards, Director of *Aspire*

2. Ministerial outreach by the Seventh-day Adventists is provided through its program, *Aspire, Tape of the Month,* This is a monthly series of programs on evangelism, counseling, church affairs, preaching, and sermons, prepared for Seventh-day Adventist ministers and church leaders. Currently over 100 cassettes are available in the series. Other audio recordings include the North American Bible Conference (1974), talks presented at the Dallas Meetings for Ministers' Wives (1980), the Mission of the Church Meeting (1979), and the General Conference Session (1980).

3. A number of *Aspire, Tape of the Month* recordings for 1982–1983 are held in the Theofield G. Weis Library of Columbia Union College (A19).

4 a. On-site listening equipment is not available.

5. *Aspire, Tape of the Month: Subject Index* (1968–1983) is available by request.

E6 Shalem Institute for Spiritual Formation, Inc.

1 a. *Mount St. Alban*
Washington, D.C. 20016
(202) 966–7050

b. 9:00 A.M.–5:00 P.M. Monday–Friday

c. Open to scholars with prior permission. Audio materials may be borrowed with special permission.

d. Tilden Edwards, Jr., Director

2. The Shalem Institute for Spiritual Formation, founded in 1979, provides long-term group conferences, one-day conferences, retreats, and contractual work to assist individuals, parishes, and organizations with contemplative prayers and with spiritual development.

3. The institute maintains a small lending library, which holds 30 cassette tapes produced by various organizations. The recordings cover mostly contemplative prayer, spirituality, and healing and mystical life matters. Examples of sound recordings in the collection include *Life and Prayer: The Desert Source* (Thomas Merton) and *The Jesus Prayer* (George Maloney, 1976).

4 a. On-site listening equipment is not available.

 b. Prior appointment is recommended.

5. Sound recordings are accessible through a card catalog and are filed under individuals' names.

Trinity College—Sister Helen Sheehan Library   **See entry A66**

E7   Virginia Theological Seminary—Bishop Payne Library

1 a. *3737 Seminary Road*
   Alexandria, Virginia 22304
   (703) 370–6600

 b. Daytime Hours:
   9:00 A.M.–5:45 P.M.   Monday–Friday
   Evening Hours:
   7:30 P.M.–10:30 P.M.   Monday, Tuesday, Thursday
   9:30 P.M.–10:30 P.M.   Wednesday
   Weekend Hours:
   9:00 A.M.–5:00 P.M.   Saturday
   2:30 P.M.–5:45 P.M.; 7:30 P.M.–10:00 P.M.   Sunday
   Summer Hours:
   8:45 A.M.–4:45 P.M.   Monday–Friday

 c. Open to the public for on-site use.

 d. Jack H. Goodwin, Librarian

2. The library has 100,000 books and 325 periodical subscriptions.

3. The library has approximately 300–400 audio cassette tapes, which focus on religion and theology. All of the recordings are commercially produced.

4 a. Two tape recorders are available.

 c. Fees are not charged.

 d. A photocopy facility is available.

5. A dictionary catalog provides access to the main collection.

E8 Washington Bible College—Oyer Memorial Library

1 a. *6511 Princess Garden Parkway*
Lanham, Maryland 20706
(301) 552–1400, ext. 232

b. 7:30 A.M.–10:00 P.M.   Monday–Thursday
7:30 A.M.–8:00 P.M.   Friday
9:00 A.M.–8:00 P.M.   Saturday

c. Open to members of the college and pastors located in the area.

d. Carol A. Satta, Director of Library Services

2. The library has over 35,000 volumes with a major emphasis on religion.

3. Audiovisual materials include close to 500 filmstrips and over 1,200 audio cassettes focusing mostly on religion. Additional subjects represented in the collection include education, family life, history, language (German, Greek, Hebrew, Italian, Japanese, and Spanish), literature, management, music, and psychology. Included are sermons, lectures, teaching materials, speeches by Presidents Franklin D. Roosevelt, Truman, Eisenhower, and Nixon, and recordings of concerts presented at the college.

4 a. On-site listening equipment is available.

b. No reservation requirements.

c. Fees are not charged to listen to recordings.

d. A photocopy facility is available.

5. Audio cassettes can be located through a typewritten subject list current as of May 1983. A separate filmstrip subject catalog is current as of September 1983. Both lists are updated on an annual basis. The Washington Bible College Bookstore is described in Appendix I.

E9 Washington Theological Consortium

1 a. *487 Michigan Avenue, N.E.*
Washington, D.C. 20017
(202) 832–2675

b. 9:00 A.M.–5:00 P.M.   Monday–Friday

c. Open to scholars, teachers, and students for telephone reference.

d. Daniel F. Martensen, Director

2. The consortium, established in 1967, consists of a number of colleges, universities, and divinity schools, including Virginia Theological Seminary (E7), the School of Religious Studies at Catholic University, DeSales School of Theology (E2), Dominican House of Studies, Oblate College (E4), Lutheran Theological Seminary at Gettysburg, Wesley Theological Seminary (E10), Saint Paul's College, and the Washington Theological Union.

The consortium offers a variety of programs and activities, including borrowing privileges for constituents of the member institutions, open cross-registration in over 600 courses annually, and various consortium seminars.

3.   The newly established Washington Institute of Ecumenics, which is affiliated with the consortium, is establishing an Ecumenical Resources Collection. Included is documentation on the history of the ecumenical movement as well as on the international and regional work of the last twenty years. Materials otherwise unavailable in North America are now being secured.

4 a.   On-site listening equipment is not available.

5.   The consortium has published a number of brochures, such as *A Guide to the Libraries of the Washington Theological Consortium*. In addition, its *Union List of Periodicals of the Members of the Washington Theological Consortium and Contributing Institutions* (3rd ed., 1979) is useful for determining which journals focusing on audiovisual topics are held by member schools.

E10   Wesley Theological Seminary Library

1 a.   *4500 Massachusetts Avenue, N.W.*
Washington, D.C. 20016
(202) 885–8691

   b.   8:00 A.M.–10:00 P.M.   Monday–Thursday
8:00 A.M.–4:30 P.M.   Friday
9:00 A.M.–12:00 Noon   Saturday
6:00 P.M.–10:00 P.M.   Sunday
Hours vary during summer.

   c.   Open to researchers for on-site use only. Borrowing privileges extended to constituents of member institutions of the Washington Theological Consortium, and to the faculty and graduate students of the American University. Inter-library loan is available for printed materials only.

   d.   Roland E. Kircher, Director

2–3.   The library holds books, periodicals, microforms, and sound recordings with the major emphasis on theology. The sound recording collection includes 783 discs, 394 cassettes, and 394 reel-to-reel tapes. The disc collection consists mostly of commercially produced musical recordings, including in particular baroque, contemporary, jazz, and orchestral music. Among these discs are 15 sets produced by Time-Life Books (N14). Of particular significance are original cassette recordings of sermons and lectures by clerical and other visitors at the seminary, including, for example, Martin L. King, Sr. and Jr., Edward L. Elson, David E. Trueblood, George M. Docherty, John Wesley Lord, Francis Sayre, Helmut Thielicke, and Heinrich Ott. There are also 53 audio tapes of sermons by Reinhold Niebuhr. Among the special audio tape series at the library are the Martin Luther King Lecture Series, with James H. Cone, speaker, produced at the seminary; the Convocation Lectures; and a series of faculty and student sermons. The library also has a complete set of *Thesis Theological Cassettes* (Pittsburgh, Pennsylvania, Thesis), recording sermons and lectures on theological topics.

4 a.   The library has an audiovisual listening room on the second floor.

b. Reservations are not required.

c. No fees are charged.

d. Audio recordings may be duplicated but with special permission only. A photoduplication facility is available.

5. The library has a card catalog with author/title and subject entries. Currently there is no index to the disc collection. These recordings are shelved by composers' last names or by subject. The tape recordings are located through typewritten lists titled "Audio-Visual Holdings: Tape Recordings (Fall, 1971; supplement, 1974)."

F Services for the Handicapped

Introductory Note

In the Washington area, a number of services for the physically handicapped are available, including organizations (mentioned below) that loan materials and record printed materials upon request. A number of organizations only dispense information, but because of the nature of their services, they are included in this section.

There are a number of basic reference tools to aid in the identification of resources and services for the handicapped. *Library Resources for the Blind and Physically Handicapped* (Library of Congress, 1982) lists regional and subregional libraries affiliated with the Library of Congress program. Affiliated libraries located in the Washington area include Alexandria Library (F2), Arlington County Public Library (F5), Fairfax County Public Library (F8), Martin Luther King, Jr. Memorial Library (F10), Montgomery County Department of Public Libraries (F11) and Prince George's County Memorial Library (F17). Other published aids include *Directory of Radio Reading Services* (New York: American Foundation for the Blind, 1979) which lists special programming for the reading of newspapers, periodicals, and best sellers for blind and physically disabled persons, and *Volunteers Who Produce Books* (Library of Congress, 1981), which includes names and addresses for volunteers who record books on tape, or in braille and large type formats. The United States Department of Education's *Directory of National Information Sources on Handicapping Conditions and Related Services* (August 1982) cites resources, including annotations, concerning the resources' organizational structure, information services, publications, and collections of materials.

F1 Alexander Graham Bell Association for the Deaf (AGB)

1 a. *3417 Volta Place, N.W.*
Washington, D.C. 20007
(202) 337–5220

  b. 9:00 A.M.–4:30 P.M.   Monday–Friday

  c. Open to the public.

202 / Collections **F2–F3**

    d. William E. Castle, President
        Suzanne Neel, Director of Professional Programs and Services

2. The Alexander Graham Bell Association for the Deaf, founded in 1890, is dedicated to the development and use of speech by the hearing impaired (deaf and hard of hearing) and to the effective integration of the hearing-impaired child and adult in community life. AGB accomplishes this goal in a number of ways, including continuing education conferences, workshops, biennial international conventions, and a varied publications program.

5. The association has published *Speech and Voice Characteristics of the Deaf,* which provides training in diagnosing and planning therapy for deaf and hard-of-hearing clients with defective speech and voice by means of a series of five audio tapes. This audio tape training package is available for purchase and may be examined by appointment at the association's national offices by contacting Suzanne Neel (202/337–5220).

F2   Alexandria Library (City of Alexandria)—Special Services Division—Talking Books Department

1 a. *Talking Books Department*
     5651 Rayburn Avenue
     Alexandria, Virginia 22314
     (703) 838–4555

    b. 9:00 A.M.–5:00 P.M.   Monday–Friday

    c. Open to the public. Patrons must register at this office by application, with eligibility certified by a physician.

    d. Fred Boots, Chief of Special Services
        Patricia Bates, Supervisor, Talking Books Department

2. Registered blind and physically handicapped patrons may borrow books and magazines on records and flexible discs, which are produced by the National Library Service for the Blind and Physically Handicapped of the Library of Congress (F9). These materials may be ordered by both mail or telephone.

4 a. Special machines are needed for the use of these materials. These machines may be used on-site, but the library has them available on a loan basis.

5. Talking books are listed in a catalog, which is available in print and on tape.

F3   American Council of the Blind (ACB)

1 a. *1211 Connecticut Avenue, N.W., Suite 506*
     Washington, D.C. 20036
     (202) 833–1251
     (800) 424–8666 (toll-free)

    b. 9:00 A.M.–5:00 P.M.   Monday–Friday

c. Open to the public.

d. Oral O. Miller, National Representative

2. The American Council of the Blind is a national organization consisting of blind and visually impaired persons, who are dedicated to improving the living conditions of the blind and visually impaired. Their 51 state affiliates and 15 special interest organizations offer various services, such as information dissemination and referral, legal consultation, training, and monitoring existing service delivery systems.

5. Their monthly magazine, *Braille Forum,* is available in braille, disc, returnable cassette, and large print. Their type-written publication, *Periodicals and Newsletters: American Council of the Blind and ACB State and Special-Interest Affiliates* (February 1981) cites names, addresses, and publishing formats, including returnable cassettes.

F4   American Red Cross—Audio-Visual Production Center

1 a. *5816 Seminary Road*
Falls Church, Virginia 22041
(703) 379–8160

b. 9:00 A.M.–5:30 P.M.   Monday–Friday

c. Open to researchers with prior permission.

d. Al Rettig, Production Manager

2. The American Red Cross is the largest voluntary organization congressionally chartered to provide disaster relief and aid to both the military and the public. It is engaged in many worthwhile endeavors, including the collecting and distribution of blood.
The Audio-Visual Production Center is specifically involved in producing radio/TV, video, and film units centered on the nature and function of the American Red Cross. It also contains an archive of audio materials.

3. The collection contains hundreds of media spots and programs, which were recently discovered in the warehouse. The Production Center is in the process of transfering the material from disc format to reel-to-reel tape format. Topics include fund raising, entertainment personalities, original dramas, and speeches. Some of the recordings date from the 1930s on and were produced by various radio networks. A number of the programs dating from the 1940s were narrated by Arthur Godfrey. A recent disc, *Echos of a Century,* produced in 1981, features Jack Benny singing old Red Cross songs in celebration of its centennial.

4 a. On-site listening equipment is available.

b. An appointment is required.

c. Fees are not charged.

d. Contact the center for current duplication policy.

5. The Production Center is currently working on cataloging the sound recordings. They hope to have a list of audio materials available to researchers some time in the

future. Some of their holdings are, however, cited in the *National Library of Medicine Audiovisuals Catalog* (G2).

NOTE: At least 61 American Red Cross recordings are held in the Motion Picture, Broadcasting and Recorded Sound Division of the Library of Congress (A41) and Woodrow Wilson House (C16).

F5   Arlington County Central Public Library—Talking Book Service

1 a.   *1015 North Quincy Street*
      Arlington, Virginia 22201
      (703) 527–4777, ext. 56

  b.   9:00 A.M.–5:00 P.M.   Monday–Friday

  c.   Borrowing services available to the blind, physically handicapped, and reading disabled of Arlington County who have completed required application forms.

  d.   Mary M. Bergin, Talking Book Librarian

2.   This Talking Book Service is one of the subregional libraries in the Washington area with special materials available from the Library of Congress National Library Service for the Blind and Physically Handicapped (F9). The collection includes popular materials (books and magazines) on disc and cassette, as well as reference materials on blindness and other handicaps. Records and cassettes will be mailed to patrons upon request or they can be charged out in person.

4 a.   Special machines for these materials are available for loan. The Kurzweil Reading Machine, which translates printed material into synthetic speech, is also available for the visually impaired. Training is necessary and can be scheduled by calling the library. A variety of low vision aids can be lent to patrons.

  b.   No reservation requirements.

  c.   Fees are not charged.

  d.   Duplication of tapes is available. The library has a photocopy facility.

5.   Items for loan are listed in printed and recorded book catalogs and also on microfiche, produced by the Library of Congress. This is issued monthly with annual cumulations, and indexes by author, title, and subject. The library issues a patron newsletter.

F6   Better Hearing Institute (BHI)

1 a.   *1430 K Street, N.W., Suite 700*
      Washington, D.C. 20005
      (202) 638–7577 (local)
      (800) 424–8576 (toll-free)

  b.   9:00 A.M.–5:00 P.M.   Monday–Friday

c. Open to the public.

d. Karen Glooch, Helpline Coordinator

2. The Better Hearing Institute is a non-profit organization whose purpose is to inform hearing-impaired individuals and the general public about hearing loss and available medical, surgical, and hearing-aid rehabilitation. BHI conducts a number of public information, education, and publications programs.

4 a. On-site listening facilities are not available.

5. The institute publishes a number of audio cassette/slide presentations by well known personalities in the entertainment industry, which serve as informative tools to increase awareness of hearing disorders. One presentation *You and Your Hearing* is a concise introduction to hearing diseases and disorders.

BHI publishes a variety of booklets and reprints of a number of informative magazine and newspaper articles concerning hearing loss. Brochures and a publications list are available free upon request.

F7 Blinded Veterans Association (BVA)

1 a. *1735 DeSales Street, N.W.*
Washington, D.C. 20036
(202) 347–4010

b. 8:00 A.M.–5:00 P.M.   Monday–Friday

c. Open to the public.

d. Thomas H. Miller, National President

2. The Blinded Veterans Association, chartered by Congress, has three major programs: a field service program, which assists and counsels blinded veterans in obtaining their rightful benefits and in becoming rehabilitated, an outreach employment program, which assists blinded veterans in obtaining meaningful employment; and an information program (see category 5).

4 a. On-site listening facilities are not available.

5. Although the BVA does not have any audio recordings, they do publish a bi-monthly newsletter, *The BVA Bulletin,* which includes citations of recently published audio materials. *The BVA Bulletin* is also published in soundsheets compatible for use with talking book machines, which are available on loan from the Library of Congress.

F8 Fairfax County Public Library—Talking Book Service

1 a. *John Marshall Branch*
6209 Rose Hill Drive
Alexandria, Virginia 22310
(703) 971–0030

 b. 9:30 A.M.–9:00 P.M. Monday–Thursday
   9:30 A.M.–6:00 P.M. Friday
   9:00 A.M.–5:00 P.M. Saturday

 c. The Talking Book Service is available to blind, physically handicapped, and learning disabled residents of Fairfax County and surrounding communities. Patrons must complete a special application form. Most circulation is conducted by mail in response to patrons' telephone requests. However, walk-in service is available.

 d. Jean B. Gerhardt, Special Services Librarian

2. This service is part of the network provided by the National Library for the Blind and Physically Handicapped at the Library of Congress (F9). Materials consist of over 22,000 books and 50 magazine titles available on special cassettes and flexible discs. These are primarily recreational reading, including adventure, romance, other best sellers, and some current events.

3. Special materials and services include reference materials on blindness and other handicaps, family and child care in braille and on cassettes, volunteer-produced braille and cassettes, and print/braille books.

4 a. Special machines can be borrowed in person or through the mail or can be used in the library.

 b. No reservation requirements.

 c. Fees are not charged.

 d. Duplication of tapes is available.

5. Catalogs are available on microfiche, in book form, or on flexible disc. There are also braille and large-type versions. The library produces a patron newsletter.

F9 **Library of Congress—National Library Service for the Blind and Physically Handicapped (NLS/BPH)**

1 a. *1291 Taylor Street, N.W.*
  Washington, D.C. 20542
  (202) 287–5100 (General)
  (202) 287–9286 (Reference)

 b. 8:15 A.M.–4:15 P.M. Monday–Friday

 c. The Library of Congress program is available to those whose reading is impaired due to a physical handicap. The Library of Congress is open to the public. Most materials, however, can be obtained through its regional library system. In the Washington, D.C. metropolitan area there are 6 regional and subregional libraries. For a complete directory of member libraries, see *Library Resources for the Blind and Physically Handicapped* (1982) and *Address List* (1982) of regional and subregional libraries. Materials are sent to readers and returned by postage-free mail. The Library of Congress provides a reference service, as well as a small reference collection, which is available to professionals who work with blind and physically handicapped persons. Contact a member library for an application for free library service.

NOTE: See also F2, F5, F8, F10, F11, and F17.

d. Frank Kurt Cylke, Director
   Hylda Kamisar, Head, Reference Section
   Merrillyn Gibson, Reference Librarian

2. The National Library Service for the Blind and Physically Handicapped, established by an act of Congress in 1931, publishes books and magazines in braille and in recorded form on discs and cassettes for readers who cannot hold, handle, or see well enough to read conventional print because of a visual or physical impairment. Through a national network of state and local libraries, materials are loaned free to eligible readers in the United States and to its citizens living abroad.

The national book collection currently contains more than 38,000 titles. Each year 2,100 press-braille, disc, and cassette titles are mass-produced. A limited number of titles are also in Spanish and other languages. In addition 70 magazines on disc and in braille can be obtained through the program. Readers may request free subscriptions to such magazines as *U.S. News, National Geographic,* and *Consumer Reports.* Library of Congress' recorded books are on cassette (Philips cassettes, predominantly 4-track and $^{15}\!/_{16}$ inches per second) and on disc (predominantly 8⅓ revolutions per minute). Special playback equipment is needed to read these books and can be borrowed by the reader.

The Library of Congress publishes a variety of materials that list and describe specific services and recorded books and magazines currently available. The scholar can obtain in recorded format a number of research-related books and reference tools. See category 5 below for a description of these publications.

For more information on the program, consult *An Introduction to the National Library Service for the Blind and Physically Handicapped (1982).*

The Library of Congress Taylor Street headquarters maintains a small reference collection of books and some 506 periodical subscriptions, and an extensive vertical file collection for the use of the professional working with the blind and physically handicapped. Access to the vertical file materials is provided on-site through a book catalog containing subject headings, which include such audio topics as "Audiovisual Materials," "Talking Books," and "Tape Recordings."A combined author/title/subject card catalog is provided for the book collection.

3. Notable holdings of the library.

Music Section
Shirley P. Emanuel, Head
(800) 424–8567

The Music Section, established in 1962, provides instructional materials in special formats to the blind and physically handicapped music students, researchers, and other persons with an interest in music. Both books and periodicals are available only from the Music Section at the Taylor Street headquarters; not from the regional and subregional libraries. Musical recordings intended solely for listening pleasure are not covered by this service. The Music Section does provide, however, materials that are not readily available from other sources.

Currently the collection contains over 30,000 items, including scores in braille and large type, textbooks and books about music in braille and large type, and recorded forms, as well as elementary instruction books on various musical instruments. Handicapped scholars can obtain a number of basic works that will prove useful for conducting independent research. These include books on music theory and appreciation, history, biographical sketches of musicians and examples of their art, and interviews and master classes.

To assist the handicapped researcher, the Music Section provides an array of ref-

erence tools in recorded format. For example, the *Music Article Guide*, a quarterly annotated index to signed articles in some 175 American music periodicals, some of which are highly specialized, is available in both braille and cassette formats. The articles themselves will be reproduced by the Music Section upon request. There are also subscriptions in disc format to individual journals, such as *High Fidelity/Musical America* and *Music Journal*. In addition, a number of specialized dictionaries, encyclopedias, guides, and manuals for assisting the scholar in preparing research reports and theses are available in cassette, braille, and large-type formats. Refer to the publication, *Reference Books in Special Media* (September 1982) for a list of these research tools (see category 5 below).

The following publications, available on a free subscription, provide information on recent developments, as well as general and specialized articles on musical topics:

The Musical Mainstream (bimonthly), intended for the serious musician and educator, includes reprints of articles about classical music, criticism, and instruction. It lists new acquisitions in all formats, and is published in braille, cassette, and large-type formats. Recently published articles include those by distinguished authors like Ned Rorem and Nicolas Slonimsky.

Contemporary Sound Track: A Review of Pop, Jazz, Rock, and Country (bimonthly), intended for persons interested in popular music, contains articles reprinted from magazines about popular music, and is published on cassette (15/16 ips).

Two additional publications, *Music and Musicians: Instructional Cassette Recordings Catalog (1980)* and *Music and Musicians: Instructional Disc Recordings Catalog (1980)*, identify commercial recordings focusing on all aspects, styles, and periods of music. Recordings in these catalogs are grouped into several sections, and within sections alphabetically by title or composer. The catalogs provide annotations and contents, as well as record manufacturer numbers and sources of acquisition. Again, a number of these recordings are highly specialized and would prove useful to music researchers.

Both disc and cassette recordings concerning the lives of musicians, composers, and singers are listed with annotations in *Biography: The Arts* (1980). Anton Bruckner, Frederic Chopin, George Gershwin, Wolfgang Amadeus Mozart, and Igor Stravinsky are among the notable musicians represented in this work.

The Music Section is currently working on a union catalog of recorded books about music. Contact the Music Section for details on this project.

4 a. Although on-site listening equipment is not available at the NLS/BPH, equipment is available at the regional and subregional libraries.

b. No reservations are required.

c. Fees are not charged.

d. Photoduplication facility is available.

5. Principal guides to monographs recorded in disc and cassette formats include the following.

Talking Books Adult, a biannual (non-cumulative) catalog of books recorded from 1974 to the present in disc format and announced in *Talking Book Topics*. Includes fiction and nonfiction focusing on a variety of topics, such as biography, consumer affairs, government and the legal system, history, journalism and the media, medicine and health, music, poetry and literature, political science, psychology, religion, science, and sociology. Each entry includes a short description of the content.

Cassette Books, a catalog (non-cumulative) listing cassette books produced by NLS/BPH since 1968. Includes fiction and nonfiction focusing on a variety of topics, such as the arts, biography, business and economics, computers, diet and nutrition, education, government, law and politics, history, journalism, medicine and health, music,

philosophy, psychology, religion, science and technology, social science, and women. Each entry includes a short description of the content.

Talking Book Topics (bimonthly) covers news of developments and activities in library services, and lists recorded books and magazines available through a national network of cooperating libraries. Each entry is fully annotated.

Reference Books in Special Media (September 1982) is of particular use to handicapped researchers in that it cites reference tools, such as dictionaries, thesauri, encyclopedias, books on grammar, style and usage, guides to research and report writing, and other tools in specific subjects, such as languages, geography and maps, history, law and politics, mathematics, medicine, music and fine arts, psychology and psychiatry, radio and television, religion and philosophy, and the natural and social sciences, available in disc, cassette, braille, and large type formats. Each entry lists the source for obtaining the respective item.

NLS/BPH also has a variety of subject catalogs which list books in disc, cassette, large type, and braille formats, including: *Home Management* (1977); *Science* (1978); *Sports* (1977); *Bestsellers* (1979); *Science Fiction* (1979); *Religion* (1979); *Health* (1979); *Biography: Government and Politics* (1980); *Biography: The Arts* (1980); *Magazines* (1981); and *Mysteries* (1982). One additional subject catalog, *Libros Parlantes* (1980), covers Spanish titles recorded on disc or cassette that have been distributed to cooperating libraries between 1973 and 1980. Both fiction and nonfiction books are represented.

Refer to the following publications in order to stay abreast of current developments: *News* (quarterly); *Update* (quarterly); *Facts* (published occasionally); and *Library of Congress Information Bulletin*.

NLS/BPH is also described in *Guide to the Library of Congress* (1982).

F10 Martin Luther King, Jr., Memorial Library (District of Columbia Public Library)—Services for the Blind and Physically Handicapped

1 a. *901 G Street, N.W., Room 215*
Washington, D.C. 20001
(202) 727-2142

b. 9:00 A.M.–5:30 P.M.   Monday–Friday

c. Open to the public.

d. Grace Lyons, Chief

2. Anyone who is unable to read standard print materials due to visual or physical handicap can call or write for an application for free library service. Individuals may request books for magazines to be recorded in sound format or, if available in the collection, may borrow them. As a regional library for the blind and physically handicapped, the library provides assistance in borrowing recorded textbooks from such agencies as Recording for the Blind, Inc., and makes available a wide variety of audiovisual aids. Materials can also be obtained from the Library of Congress (F9).

3. Currently the collection consists of over 100,000 talking book phonograph discs, cassettes, and reel-to-reel tapes. Other materials are available in braille or large print.

4 a. On-site listening facilities are available.

b. Reservations are not required.

c. Fees are not charged.

d. Duplication facilities are available.

5. Materials are indexed in an author/title/subject card catalog, and on microfiche. Various brochures describing the service are available free upon request.

F11 Montgomery County Department of Public Libraries—Service for the Physically Handicapped

1 a. *99 Maryland Avenue*
Rockville, Maryland 20850
(301) 279–1679

b. 9:00 A.M.–5:00 P.M.   Monday–Saturday

c. Open to the public.

d. Martha Spencer, Supervisor of Library Services

2. The Service for the Physically Handicapped serves principally the residents of Montgomery County, Maryland. Recorded books on discs or cassettes may be borrowed from either the in-house collection or from the National Library Service for the Blind and Physically Handicapped at the Library of Congress (F9).

3. The collection currently includes some 8,000 items consisting of recordings as well as large print books and braille materials. In 1985, the service is planning to move to the Davis Library building at 6400 Democracy Boulevard, Bethesda, Maryland 20817.

4 a. On-site listening equipment is available.

b. Reservations are not required.

c. Fees are not charged.

d. Contact the library regarding the current duplication policy.

5. Principal catalogs include *Talking Book Catalog* (1980–1981), *Cassette Catalog* (1982), and *Talking Book Topics* (bimonthly). The latter catalog features the most recently recorded books, and is available in large print or recorded on disc. All of the catalogs are available free to patrons upon request.

F12 Narcotics Education, Inc. (NEI)

1 a. *6830 Laurel Street, N.W.*
Washington, D.C. 20012
(202) 722–6740

b. 8:30 A.M.–12:00 Noon   Monday–Thursday
1:00 A.M.–5:30 P.M.   Monday–Thursday
8:30 A.M.–12:00 Noon   Friday–Thursday

c. Open to the public by appointment.

d. Sherrie Thomas, Studio Services

2. Narcotics Education, Inc., is an organization devoted to the education of the public regarding the misuse of drugs, alcohol, and smoking.

4 a. On-site listening equipment is not available.

5. Included in its publication program are a number of audio cassette/slide/filmstrip presentations regarding drugs, narcotics, and alcohol. NEI also publishes a number of films, books, and pamphlets. The catalog *The Help They Need: A Narcotics Education Catalog* is available free upon request.

F13 National Epilepsy Library and Resource Center (NELRC) (Epilepsy Foundation of America)

1 a. *4351 Garden City Drive*
Landover, Maryland 20785
(301) 459–3700

  b. 9:00 A.M.–5:00 P.M.   Monday–Friday

  c. Open to the public.

  d. Cynthia W. Shockley, Assistant Director

2. The library and resource center maintains a collection of books, journals, reports, and non-print materials focusing on neurology and epilepsy.

3. Currently the collection includes some 25 audio cassettes and TEXTRACT, the NELRC new in-house database, provides comprehensive information on recently published print and audiovisual materials dealing with the psychosocial aspects of epilepsy. The database also indicates the ordering source for these materials.

4 a. On-site listening equipment is available.

  b. Contact the library for arranging an appointment.

  c. Fees are not charged.

  d. Photocopy facilities are available.

5. A guide to the library, as well as a number of special bibliographies, are available upon request.

F14 National Federation of the Blind (NFB)

1 a. *655 15th Street, N.W., Suite 300*
Washington, D.C. 20005
(202) 639–4028

Headquarters:
National Center for the Blind
1800 Johnson Street
Baltimore, Maryland 21230
(301) 659–9314
(800) 638–7518 (toll-free, only for information on employment of the blind)

b. Office hours vary. Contact the Maryland office for an appointment.

c. Open to the public by appointment.

d. James Gashel, Director of Governmental Affairs

2. The National Federation of the Blind, founded in 1940, is the largest organization of the blind in America. Their purpose is to achieve equal rights for the blind and to help insure a fair and complete integration of the blind into society. They fulfill their objective through a number of programs, services, and publications.

4 a. On-site listening equipment is not available.

5. Their monthly newsletter, *Braille Monitor,* is published in braille, print, and on record. Their catalog lists more than 65 reel-to-reel, cassette, and disc recordings, dealing with such topics as the blind and labor relations, discrimination, consumer education, careers, and legislation. There are recordings of NFB banquet speeches for the years 1968–1981, and NFB conventions for the years 1971–1981. Examples of types of materials individuals will find in the catalog include: *Local Organizations of the Blind: How to Build and Strengthen Them* (cassette); *Postsecondary Education and Career Development: A Resource Guide for the Blind, Visually Impaired, and Physically Handicapped* (cassette); *White House Conference Alternative Report* (disc/ cassette); *Education for the Handicapped Act (Public Law 94–142)* (disc); *Final Regulation to Implement Section 504 of the Rehabilitation Act of 1973 as Amended in 1974* (disc).

NOTE: Although the Washington, D.C., office dispenses information on the organization, it is best to contact the Baltimore headquarters for extensive reference consultation. Recordings should be ordered from that address as well. A brochure and catalog are available from either office to individuals upon request.

F15 Office of Information and Resources for the Handicapped (Education Department)—Clearinghouse on the Handicapped

1 a. *3132 Switzer Building*
400 Maryland Avenue, S.W.
Washington, D.C. 20202
(202) 245–0628

b. 9:00 A.M.–5:30 P.M.   Monday–Friday

c. Open to the public.

d. Helga Roth, Chief

5. At present the only audiovisual service the clearinghouse offers is through its various publications. For example, *Programs for the Handicapped,* a bimonthly publication, includes information on such audiovisual concerns as closed circuit radio for individuals, recent publications, and audio tapes.

The Clearinghouse on the Handicapped also publishes a *Directory of National Information Sources on Handicapping Conditions and Related Sources* (August 1982), which serves as a major reference tool for referrals and information on at least fourteen organizations that have audiovisual materials. The *Directory* may be purchased from the Government Printing Office (N5).

F16 President's Committee on Employment of the Handicapped

1 a. *Executive Office*
1111 20th Street, N.W., Suite 600
Washington, D.C. 20036
(202) 653–5044

b. 7:00 A.M.–6:00 P.M.   Monday–Friday

c. Open to the public by appointment.

d. Harold Russell, Chairman

2.   The President's Committee on Employment of the Handicapped was established by President Truman in 1947 to promote favorable attitudes regarding the employment of handicapped individuals. To achieve this objective the committee seeks to eliminate both physical and psychological barriers and to fully utilize educational training, rehabilitation and employment opportunities. The committee has at least twelve standing subcommittees, which work toward this goal. Their activities consist of annual meetings, various special events, the promotion of National Employ the Handicapped Week, held in October, and the dissemination of public information.

5.   The committee's major publication, *Disabled USA,* often features articles and news regarding handicapped activities. For example, a recent issue included articles on media and broadcasting for disabled people. Information on the committee is available by writing to the above address.

F17 Prince George's County Memorial Library System—Visually & Physically Handicapped Division

1 a. *Hyattsville Library*
6532 Adelphi Road
Hyattsville, Maryland 20782
(301) 779–9330

b. 10:00 A.M.–5:30 P.M.   Monday–Thursday
9:00 A.M.–5:00 P.M.   Saturday

c. Open to the public.

d. Shirley Bean, Head Librarian

2–3.   The Visually & Physically Handicapped Division serves principally the residents of Prince George's County, Maryland. The collection includes some 650 titles of recorded books on 1,570 individual discs and 2,424 titles of recorded books on 4,600 cassettes. Recorded books are available to registered handicapped readers for the current two year period only. The staff will attempt to locate recorded books not available in the collection. The collection also includes some 2,800 titles of large print books. Materials can also be obtained from the Library of Congress (F9).

4 a. On-site listening equipment is available.

b. Reservations are not required.

    c. Fees are not charged.

    d. A cassette duplication facility is available for the handicapped by special permission only.

5. The principal index for the holdings is on microfiche and can be searched by author/title, subject, narrator, and language. The library also subscribes to *Talking Book Topics* (Library of Congress).

F18 Recording for the Blind, Inc. (RFB)

1 a. *4000 Albemarle Street, N.W.*
Washington, D.C. 20016
(202) 244–8990

    Headquarters:
215 East 58th Street
New York, New York 10022
(800) 221–4792 (toll-free)

    b. 9:00 A.M.–5:00 P.M.   Monday–Friday

    c. Open to the public by appointment.

    d. Penny Williams, Director, Washington Office

2. The Washington RFB office is one of 28 recording studios located throughout the country, which records textbooks and educational materials in all subjects for students and other persons certified visually handicapped. The Washington, D.C., branch serves as a recording studio and clearinghouse for information on the program.

4 a. On-site listening equipment is not available.

5. RFB publishes a catalog *Recording for the Blind: Learning Through Listening* (1979/1980; supplements: 1980/1981, 1981/1982), which contains over 35,000 titles of recorded books, including materials in 17 languages. The catalog provides subject/author indexes. RFB will also record books not listed in the catalog.

F19 Recording Service for the Visually Handicapped

1 a. *P.O. Box 551*
Falls Church, Virginia 22046
(703) 553–7413

    b. 10:00 A.M.–2:00 P.M.   Monday–Friday

    c. Telephone reference service is provided.

    d. Susan Thomas, Coordinator of Services

3. Individuals may send copies of books and other printed materials to them. They will tape record the materials free of charge. Please allow several months for the recording process to be completed.

F20   Self Help for Hard of Hearing People, Inc.

1 a. *4848 Battery Lane, Suite 100*
       Bethesda, Maryland 20814
       (301) 657–2248

  b. 9:00 A.M.–5:00 P.M.   Monday–Friday

  c. Open to the public by appointment.

  d. Howard E. Stone

3. Self Help for Hard of Hearing People, founded in 1979, consists of individuals who are involved in the education, detection, management, and prevention of hearing loss. It works to generate research into all elements of hearing loss and to foster a climate in which the hearing impaired can seek alternative communication skills.

4 a. On-site listening equipment is not available.

5. The organization publishes a journal about hearing loss, *Shhh,* which is issued every other month. Articles relating to the subject of sound recordings are occasionally printed. For example, an article "Alternative Listening Devices," published in the January/February, 1981 issue discusses various types of listening devices that can be attached to radios, televisions, and sound recording amplifiers. Also, eight situational brochures are in production to show people what devices they can use to help them with the telephone, at mealtime, on the street, etc.

F21   Volunteers for the Visually Handicapped (VVH)

1 a. *4405 East-West Highway, Suite 109B*
       Bethesda, Maryland 20814
       (301) 652–4347

  b. 9:00 A.M.–4:00 P.M.   Monday–Friday

  c. Open to the public.

  d. Catherine Couch, Executive Director

3. This non-profit United Way Agency provides a variety of services to blind and visually impaired persons in the Washington area. Volunteers are provided for reading, home visiting, and tape recording of printed materials. VVH also serves as an information and referral organization for information on audio materials.

4 a. On-site listening equipment is not available.

5. VVH catalogs of aids and appliances are available in large-print, braille, and voice-indexed cassette editions.

F22 Washington Ear, Inc.

1 a. *35 University Boulevard East*
Silver Spring, Maryland 20901
(301) 681–6636

b. 9:00 A.M.–5:00 P.M.   Monday–Friday

c. Open to the public for telephone reference.

d. Margaret Rockwell-Pfanstiehl, Chief Executive Officer

3.   Washington Ear is a non-profit closed-circuit radio-reading and information service for the blind and physically handicapped who cannot effectively read print. The service operates through the efforts of approximately 120 weekly volunteers and 6 professional staff members, and is funded by federal, county, and municipal governments, and private sources.

The organization uses the subcarrier channel of WETA-FM to transmit its programs to listeners within a 35-mile radius of the station's tower in Arlington, Virginia. Listeners must have a pretuned crystal control receiver in order to pick up the closed-circuit programming. These receivers are free of charge for persons who qualify (through applications). Washington Ear can also be heard through special communications systems established at several area hospitals and nursing homes and through special arrangements made with Arena Stage and the John F. Kennedy Center for the Performing Arts.

Programming provided by the service includes *The Washington Post* (N16), as well as other national and local papers, popular magazines and best-selling books, consumer and grocery shopping information, home management for the handicapped, legislation affecting the handicapped, general rehabilitation materials, sports, music, and foreign affairs. A new service is "Audio Description," heard in conjunction with certain public TV dramatic programs and plays presented at the Arena Stage and the Kennedy Center. Hours of broadcasting are 6:20 A.M. to 11:00 P.M., Monday through Friday, and 8:30 A.M. to 11:00 P.M., Saturday and Sunday.

4 a. On-site listening equipment is not available.

F23 Washington Volunteer Readers for the Blind (WVRB)

1 a. *901 G Street, N.W., Room 215*
Washington, D.C. 20001
(202) 727–2142

b. 9:00 A.M.–5:30 P.M.   Monday–Friday

c. Open to the public by appointment.

d. Dr. Heidi Franklin

3.   The Washington Volunteer Readers for the Blind is a non-profit organization, incorporated under the laws of the District of Columbia, which assists the blind and physically handicapped residents of the District of Columbia and the Washington metropolitan area by providing them with tape recordings and in-person reading of books, periodicals, and other printed materials.

Specifically, WVRB will record materials for individuals, any organization or agency, public or private, which needs taping of materials to serve the blind and physically handicapped. All services are free of charge. Individuals and organizations must, however, provide the original materials to be taped. There are a number of other very reasonable requirements, which can be ascertained by contacting the WVRB.

4 a. On-site listening equipment is not available.

   d. Duplication services are provided (see category 3 above).

5. A flyer that describes the service in detail will be sent to individuals and organizations upon request.

G Data Banks

Introductory Note

The transfer of information and utilization of information through computerized means in the Washington area is enormous. Many Washington area libraries, government agencies, academic institutions, and research organizations maintain their own series of subscriptions to a wide variety of data banks and data bank vendors. Other Washington organizations maintain their own in-house databases. For audiovisual materials, a number of databases in both the humanities and sciences provide access to either printed audiovisual materials or audiovisual software. This section includes those data banks.

For more comprehensive information, check *Computer-Readable Databases: A Directory and Data Sourcebook* (Washington, D.C.: American Society for Information Science, 1982); the Subject Index of that publication contains an entry on audiovisual materials. Note also the forthcoming *Data Base Directory* (White Plains, New York: Knowledge Industry Publications), scheduled for publication in 1984.

G1 Agricultural Online Access (AGRICOLA) (Agriculture Department — National Agricultural Library)

1 a. *Reference Section*
10301 Baltimore Boulevard, Room 111
Beltsville, Maryland 20705
(301) 344–3755/3756 (Information and Reference)

b. 8:00 A.M.–4:30 P.M.   Monday–Friday

c. Reference questions may be submitted by letter or telephone. On-line access is offered through Bibliographical Retrieval Services and DIALOG Information Retrieval Systems.

d. Mary Lassanyi, Head of Reference

2. AGRICOLA includes a number of databases consisting of indexes to international journals and monographic literature and United States government reports on various agriculture-related topics. The coverage amounts to more than 1.2 million records from 1970 to the present. Subjects covered include all aspects of agriculture and related topics, such as animal industry, botany, chemistry, ecology and environmental science,

energy engineering, entomology, fertilizers, foods, forestry, human nutrition, hydroponics, pesticides, plant sciences, rural sociology, soils, and water management.

In addition, a number of oral history transcripts, which are held in the National Agricultural Library may be identified using this file (see B25 for a description of NAL's oral history program).

3. The Food and Nutrition Information Center has the only subfile of AGRICOLA that contains citations concerning audiovisual materials, such as audio recordings. The primary emphasis is on human nutrition research and education. For a full description of these materials, see the Food and Nutrition Information Center of the Agriculture Department (L4).

4 c. Fees are not charged for limited searches.

5. Manual searches may be performed through publications that are derived from the databases and include *The Bibliography of Agriculture Library Catalog*, and the *Catalog* of the Food and Nutrition Information Research Center. Brochures describing AGRICOLA are available free to researchers.

Arthritis Information Clearinghouse (Health and Human Services Department—National Institutes of Health—National Institute of Arthritis, Diabetes, and Digestive and Kidney Diseases)   See entry L1

G2   Audiovisuals Online (AVLINE) (National Library of Medicine)

1 a. *Technical Services*
8600 Rockville Pike
Bethesda, Maryland 20209
(301) 496–5497 (Technical Services)
(301) 496–6097 (Audiovisual Librarian)

b. 8:00 A.M.–5:00 P.M.   Monday–Friday
Hours vary during the summer.

c. On-line searches for the public are conducted with the assistance of an NLM search analyst. Immediate retrieval or hardcopy prints may be requested. AVLINE can be used for search and retrieval at some 1,000 institutions in the United States that belong to the National Library of Medicine's on-line network.

d. Alice Jacobs, Coordinator
Alvin J. Barnes, Audio-Visual Coordinator

2. This computerized on-line data file, in operation since 1975, was created in response to the increasing production of audiovisual materials, widely ranging in their quality. Between 1976 and February 1982, much of the material produced for educational purposes was included in the file only after it had passed a critical review for accuracy and quality by specialists recommended by the Association of American Medical Colleges. The review process has been discontinued as of 1982. Other materials categorized as educational events have always been included without review. These items include lectures, grand rounds, continuing education courses, society meetings, seminars.

3. AVLINE, a component of MEDLARS, is truly unique in its comprehensiveness of audiovisual coverage. Currently, the file contains approximately 11,000 items encompassing video cassettes, slides, motion pictures, filmstrips, kits, and audio cassettes. Some 100 items are added monthly. All of the material indexed in AVLINE is available in the National Library of Medicine (A55).

A typical entry in the file for an audio cassette covers title, organization or person responsible for the work, sale or loan source, series, audience, review data, physical description, NLM call number, credits, prices, procurement source, and unique citation identification number.

4 c. Fees are charged for a conducted search.

   d. Photocopy facilities are available.

5. Most, but not all, of the items indexed in the file can be searched manually in the *NLM Audiovisual Catalog* (three quarterly issues and an annual cumulation). In addition, selected audiovisual serial titles are indexed in the *Index to Audiovisual Serials in the Health Sciences.* Users may also request the AVLINE *Online Services Reference Manual* for information on the system. A number of articles have been written about AVLINE and should prove useful to those interested in the history and application of the file. See, for example, "AVLINE: A Data Base and Critical Review System of Audiovisual Materials for the Education of Health Professionals," in *Journal of Medical Education,* vol. 57, no. 2, February 1982, pp. 140–155, and Emanuel Suter and Wendy H. Waddell, "Attributes of Quality in Audiovisual Materials for Health Professionals," in *The Journal of Biocommunication,* vol. 8, no. 2, July 1981, pp. 5–12.

Corporation for Public Broadcasting (CPB)   **See entry H9**

G3   Educational Resources Information Center (ERIC) (Education Department—National Institute of Education)

1 a.   *Central ERIC*
1200 19th Street, N.W.
Washington, D.C. 20208
(202) 254–7934 (Information)
(202) 254–5500 (Central ERIC)

   b.   8:00 A.M.–4:30 P.M.   Monday–Friday

   c.   The database is open to the public. Researchers should refer to the *Directory of ERIC Search Services,* which provides information on where ERIC can be accessed as well as fee schedules. Contact ERIC Processing and Reference Facility, 4833 Rugby Avenue, Suite 303, Bethesda, Maryland 20014 (301/656–9723).

   d.   Charles Hoover, Chief

2.   The Educational Resources Information Center (ERIC) was established in 1964 by the United States Office of Education. ERIC, now administered by the National Institute of Education, acquires, selects, indexes, stores, retrieves, and disseminates current education-related materials, and contains over 3 million items. There are 16 ERIC clearinghouses in the network, and each one is responsible for a major area of

education. Reports are selected by these clearinghouses for inclusion in the ERIC abstract journal, *Resources in Education* (RIE). The database can be searched manually or by computer using a variety of descriptors.

3. The type of materials in the database include books, current research findings, project and technical reports, speeches, unpublished manuscripts, and journal articles. Audiovisual materials can be located under such descriptors as "Audiotape Cassettes," "Audiotape Recordings," "Audiovisual Aids," "Audiovisual Centers," "Audiovisual Communications," "Audiovisual Coordinators," "Audiovisual Instruction," and "Oral History."

4 c. Fee schedules are printed in *Director of ERIC Search Services.*

   d. The full text of the documents identified may be purchased in hardcopy or microfiche from ERIC Document Reproduction Service, P.O. Box 190, Arlington, Virginia 22210.

5. ERIC publishes a number of indexes, handbooks, and pamphlets. *Resources in Education* (RIE), a monthly abstract journal, cites research reports, programs, and other educational documents. The section, "How to Order ERIC Documents," lists current information on prices for documents, microfiche, and subscriptions to microfiche collections.

   Current Index to Journals in Education (CIJE), a monthly publication, indexes 700 educational journals by subject, author, and journal title. Other publications include *Thesaurus of ERIC Descriptors* (10th ed., 1984), and *Directory of ERIC Microfiche Collections* (1983). A useful tool that introduces the user to the ERIC system is *ERIC: What It Is, How to Use It,* available from the National Audiovisual Center (L7). The kit contains three audio tapes and accompanying printed materials and slides.

   In addition, contact the various clearinghouses for information regarding topical bulletins and flyers. For example, the ERIC Clearinghouse on Teacher Education (One Dupont Circle, N.W., Suite 610, Washington, D.C. 20036; telephone: 202/293–2450) publishes a semiannual *Bulletin,* which reports the clearinghouse's latest news and developments.

Food and Nutrition Information Center (FNIC) (Agriculture Department)
See entry L4

Government Printing Office (GPO)   See entry N5

National Clearinghouse for Alcohol Information (NCALI) (Health and Human Services Department—Public Health Service—Alcohol, Drug Abuse, and Mental Health Administration—National Institute on Alcohol Abuse and Alcoholism)—Library   See entry L9

National Health Information Clearinghouse (NHIC) (Health and Human Services Department—Public Health Service—Office of Disease Prevention and Health Promotion)   See entry L12

National Institute of Justice/NCJRS (Justice Department)   **See entry L13**

G4   **National Referral Center (Library of Congress)**

1 a.   *John Adams Building, 5th Floor, Room 5225*
Washington, D.C. 20540
(202) 287–5670 (Referral service or to schedule visits)
(202) 287–5680 (Registration of information resources)
(202) 287–5683 (Information about publications or database developments)

b.   8:30 A.M.–5:00 P.M.   Monday–Friday

c.   Request for referral services may be made by letter, telephone, or in person. Telephone requests are encouraged because they allow for discussion and refinement of complex questions. The center will accept requests on any topic. When a subject is not covered in the data file, the center will attempt to locate new information resources from its extensive contacts.

d.   Edward MacConomy, Chief

2.   The National Referral Center is a free service that directs individuals with questions to the appropriate organizations. The referral service uses a subject-indexed, computerized file of 13,000 organizations. A description of each resource includes its special field of interest and the type of information service it is willing to provide. The center is accessible to readers at the Library of Congress through the RECON computer network operated by the Department of Energy. The center maintains systematic coverage of resources throughout the United States; its file also includes some international and foreign resources.

The concept of information resource is broadly defined to include any organization, institution, group, or individual with specialized information in a particular field and a willingness to share it with others. This includes not only traditional sources of information, such as technical libraries, information and documentation centers, and abstracting and indexing services, but also such sources as professional societies, university research bureaus and institutes, United States government and state agencies, industrial laboratories, museums, testing stations, hobby groups, and grassroots citizens organizations.

3.   Currently, the database includes a number of organizations that have audiovisual holdings, as well as information services. Some of these organizations include APM Library of Recorded Sound, Association for Recorded Sound Collections, Inc. (ARSC) (M29), Broadcasting Foundation of America, Educational Media Center at the University of Colorado at Boulder, Library of Congress (A41), National Archives and Records Service (B27), and Recording Industry Association of America.

4 c.   Fees are not charged.

d.   Photocopy facilities are available.

5.   The center occasionally compiles directories of information resources covering a broad area, for instance, the *Social Sciences* directory (revised edition), which appeared in 1973. These are published by the Library of Congress under the general title, *A Directory of Information Resources in the United States* with varying subtitles, and are sold through the Superintendent of Documents, United States Government

Printing Office, Washington, D.C. 20402. A brochure describing the center is available upon request.

G5   National Rehabilitation Information Center (NARIC) (Education Department—National Institute of Handicapped Research)

1 a. *Catholic University of America*
  4407 8th Street, N.E.
  Washington, D.C. 20017
  (202) 635–5822

  b. 9:00 A.M.–5:00 P.M.   Monday–Friday

  c. Research room and the library are open to the public. Consultation is provided for users and information specialists.

  d. Susan Flowers, Director

2. NARIC, the National Rehabilitation Information Center, is a unique research and information resource. Its mission is to foster utilization of research; hence it collects, catalogs, houses, and disseminates disability knowledge, including information on rehabilitation products.

NARIC has two separate computer databases. The first, called REHABDATA contains information about documents in the library's collection on disability. The second database, ABLEDATA, provides information on commercially available rehabilitation equipment and technical aids. All information and documents listed in these databases are in the library and readily accessible for reference.

On-line searching of NARIC's bibliographic database by users can be arranged for those having compatible terminals and a subscription to BRS (Bibliographic Retrieval Service). Some kinds of requests can be handled immediately while comprehensive, in-depth requests can take up to several weeks.

3. NARIC's collection includes research and proceeding reports, books, journals, and audiovisual materials on all aspects of disability and rehabilitation.

4 c. Fees are charged for photocopy service.

  d. Photocopies of NARIC documents are provided.

5. NARIC publishes a variety of materials, including a periodicals list, thesaurus, and special bibliographies. A number of information services brochures are available upon request.

National Technical Information Service (NTIS) (Commerce Department)   See entry N7

ORGANIZATIONS

Organizations Entry Format

1. Address and Telephone Numbers
2. Chief Official/Key Resource Person
3. Objectives and/or Programs
4. Collections/Research Facilities
5. Publications

NOTE: The organizations format outlines the categories and sequence of information contained within each organization entry. The numbers of the entry format correspond to the numerical arrangement of each entry. If a particular number does not appear in an entry, that category of information was either not applicable or not available.

H Broadcasting Organizations

Introductory Note

The broadcasting industry is one closely allied to the concept of sound and sound recording collections. Aside from the radio stations located in the Washington area, there are many associations that play a variety of roles in the industry and that could be regarded as resource centers to scholars researching the field. Many of these are national organizations with headquarters in the nation's capital, while others are located in the area to better represent their members in legislative and regulatory matters. There are also a number of special interest groups representing the concerns of women, blacks, Catholics, and Spanish-speaking citizens in the broadcasting industry. Other organizations listed in this section function as liaisons between the industry and the educational institutions with broadcast curricula. Although most of these associations do not have a sound recording library per se, they do share an interest in public service and information distribution. Washington metropolitan area radio stations with significant collections of sound recordings are described in Appendix III.

Radio bureaus not included here are cited in *Washington 84* (Washington, D.C.: Columbia Books, 1984). In addition, major media contacts and agencies not cited in this study are listed in *Washington Information Directory: 1984-85* (Washington, D.C.: Congressional Quarterly, 1984).

As noted in the introductory note to section C (Museums and Galleries), Washington, D.C., has a number of museums and other repositories that hold artifacts representing the development of radio communications. The National Museum of American History of the Smithsonian Institution (C11) owns a varied collection of early receivers and componentry. An excellent collection of special-contract receivers, transceivers, navigational aids, and componentry is found in the Navy Memorial Museum (C13). Many of its items were acquired from the Naval Research Laboratory (NRL), which undertook the development of radio communications technology during the 1920s and 1930s. A number of historic pieces have been presented also to the National Museum of American History by the Naval Research Laboratory. Occasionally the NRL (4555 Overlook Avenue, S.W., Washington, D.C. 20375) arranges for exhibiting noteworthy artifacts from the Smithsonian collections. For information on these exhibits, contact Linda Greenway, Exhibit Manager, in the Information Services Office of the Naval Research Laboratory; telephone (202) 767-2541. The National Bureau of Standards Museum (C7) holds various artifacts, including receivers, among which is the first AC radio developed for use in the home. The Motion

Picture, Broadcasting and Recorded Sound Division of the Library of Congress (A41) and the National Archives and Records Service (B27) also have significant holdings in this field.

African Bibliographic Center, Inc. (ABC)   See entry J2

H1   Agriculture Department—Radio and Television Division (Office of Governmental and Public Affairs)

1. *Room 410-A*
    12th Street and Independence Avenue
    Washington, D.C. 20250
    (202) 447–4330

2. James L. Johnson, Acting Chief

3. The Radio and Television Division produces a variety of materials, which are adaptable to several types of programming on radio and television. These range from farm shows to programs for consumers, women's interest groups, and general news and commentary. Department officials, scientists, economists, and specialists are participants in these productions. The division also records and maintains audio tapes of various speeches, interviews, and remarks by the current Secretary of Agriculture and other high level USDA officials. Older, non-current recordings (RG 16) have been transferred to the National Archives and Records Service (B27).

4. "Consumer Time."A weekly series of six programs featuring food, marketing, clothing, pest control, gardening, and many other topics of interest to consumers; produced since 1966.
    "Agri-Tape/Farm Program Report." A weekly reel of five programs including a USDA news summary, interviews, etc.; produced since 1957.
    "Agriculture USA." A weekly documentary program. Wide range of subjects directed at the general public; produced since 1954.
    "Hispanic Information Service." A weekly reel of at least 4 programs; content aimed at concerns of Hispanic audience; produced since 1979.
    "USDA Radio News Service." A continuous 24-hour report on telephone of one to six spot news items (telephone: 202/488–8358 or 8359).

5. The service also provides the series, "Radio Home Features," which is a monthly script service featuring a variety of short items on consumer subjects.

H2   American Broadcasting Company (ABC)—Washington Bureau

1. *1717 DeSales Street, N.W.*
    Washington, D.C. 20036
    (202) 887–7777

2. Edward Fouhy, Vice President and Bureau Chief

4. The ABC News and Public Affairs Collection for the years 1943–1967 (RG 200) is maintained in the National Archives and Records Service (B27). The collection contains some 27,000 items. Original video tapes of television daily news programing from 1976 to the present are also held by NARS.

5. ABC evening newscasts can be accessed in *Television News Index and Abstracts* (Vanderbilt University Library, Nashville, Tennessee 37203; telephone: 615/322–2927).

American Chemical Society (ACS)—Education Division—Radio-TV Service   See entry M8

H3   American Women in Radio and Television, Inc. (AWRT)

1. *1321 Connecticut Avenue, N.W.*
    Washington, D.C. 20036
    (202) 296–0009

2. Phyllis G. Tritsch, Executive Vice President

3. American Women in Radio and Television, Inc., founded in 1951, describes itself as the nation's oldest continuing broadcast organization. It seeks to provide its members with a network for sharing information about the industry and to promote the role of qualified women in it. Members are professionals in administrative, creative, and executive positions in the electronic media and other agencies and service organizations involved with radio and television. The AWRT Foundation, chartered in 1960, conducts professional and student seminars and symposia, and provides grants and scholarships.

4. The Soaring Spirit Program, which consists of audio tapes produced for children in hospitals, is available only through local chapters.

5. AWRT publications include a newsletter, *News and Views* (6 issues per year), an annual membership directory, and various manuals and treatises focusing on the broadcasting industry. For example, *Women on the Job: Careers in the Electronic Media,* published in cooperation with the Women's Bureau, U.S. Department of Labor, describes various careers in the media.

H4   Broadcast Education Association (BEA)

1. *1771 N Street, N.W.*
    Washington, D.C. 20036
    (202) 293–3510

2. Harold Niven, Executive Secretary

3. The Broadcast Education Association is the academic organization for colleges and universities offering courses in broadcasting. Closely affiliated with the National Association of Broadcasters (H14), it acts as a liaison between the industry and the schools, promoting the improvement of curricula and teaching methods. BEA has

several committees including History of Broadcasting, Internships, and Industry Liaison.

The Washington office can provide information about the organization and can put scholars in touch with the appropriate personnel in other parts of the country.

5.   BEA publications include the following journals: *Feedback* (quarterly), *Journal of Broadcasting* (quarterly), and *Broadcast Monographs* (annual).

Broadcast Pioneers Library (BPL)   See entry B8

H5   Citizens Communication Center of the Institute for Public Representation (CCC/IPR)

1.   *Georgetown University Law Center*
600 New Jersey Avenue, N.W.
Washington, D.C. 20001
(202) 624–8047

2.   Wilhelmina Reuben Cooke, Director

3.   The Citizens Communication Center, operating since 1969, functions as a public interest and communications law firm, whose purpose has been to increase diversity in the media and to make the broadcast industry and the Federal Communications Commission more responsive to and aware of citizen and public input. In 1981, the center merged with the Institute for Public Representation at Georgetown University, funded by the Ford Foundation, also as a public interest law firm.

The organization aids citizens and groups without resources or technical skills in participating in the regulatory and decision-making process and obtaining media access. They also act as a referral center for education advocates to assert these rights. In addition, CCC/IPR serves, to a large extent, as a resource for persons interested in matters of broadcast law.

4.   The organization has no sound recordings, but maintains files of test cases and studies. For example, they have the papers from the World Administration Radio Conference held in Geneva in 1980.

H6   Clear Channel Broadcasting Service (CCBS)

1.   *1776 K Street, N.W., Suite 1100*
Washington, D.C. 20006
(202) 429–7020

2.   R. Russell Eagan, Counsel

3.   The Clear Channel Broadcasting Service is a non-profit informal trade association representing the interests of the nation's clear channel stations to the Federal Communications Commission and to Congress. Current membership includes Class I-A and I-B stations. These stations are set aside to provide AM coverage to wide areas,

both day and night. CCBS seeks to preserve that service and to improve its reliability by maintaining higher power.

Aside from legal support, CCBS also provides engineering counsel, and undertakes special projects, such as monitoring of clear channels to check interference and examining the feasibility of AM stereophonic broadcasting.

4. Audio tapes of monitoring and other projects can be made available to researchers. Some member stations have their own historical audio materials. For example, WSM in Nashville, Tennessee, one of the oldest clear channel stations, has a collection of materials focusing on the Grand Ole Op'ry.

5. CCBS publishes a leaflet that explains what clear channels are and why their service is important to maintain.

H7 Columbia Broadcasting System (CBS)—Washington Bureau

1. *2020 M Street, N.W.*
   Washington, D.C. 20036
   (202) 457–4321

2. Jack Smith, Vice President and Director, News

4. Researchers may access CBS radio network broadcasts, for the years 1957 and 1960–1967 in the Motion Picture, Broadcasting and Recorded Sound Division of the Library of Congress (A41). In addition, a collection of CBS materials (226 items), dating from about 1937–1943, is held in the Broadcast Pioneers Library (B8). CBS radio broadcasts (Milo Ryan Phono Archive Collection) for the years 1939–1945 and original video tapes of television daily news programing from 1974 to the present and the CBS bicentennial radio programs (RG 200) are located in the National Archives and Records Service (B27).

5. Pertinent research tools for CBS broadcasts include the annual *CBS News Index: Key to the Television News Broadcasting* (Microfilm Corp. of America, 21 Harristown Road, Green Rock, New Jersey, 07482; telephone: 201/447–3000) and *Television News Index and Abstracts* (Vanderbilt University Library, Nashville, Tennessee, 37203). Frances Stone, the CBS Information Services Manager (202/457–4484) can offer assistance in identifying news transcripts and newscast tapes.

H8 Commerce Department—Broadcast Branch (News Relations Division)

1. *14th Street and Constitution Avenue, N.W., Room 5058*
   Washington, D.C. 20230
   (202) 377–5610

2. E.R. Nassikas, Supervisory Public Affairs Specialist

3–4. The Commerce Department's Broadcast Branch has two programs available for use by the private sector. Radio stations may subscribe to these services and individuals may listen to the reports on the telephone. The first program, "A Growing Nation," is accessed by telephone (202/393–4102) consists of 3.5 minute segments on

a variety of topics. Such segments often take the form of interviews with various officials as participants. The second program, "Daily Economic Report," takes the form of a news report (telephone 202/393–4100).

Programs are stored for three years then destroyed. Transcripts are available. With special permission, researchers may visit the division to listen to past programs.

H9   Corporation for Public Broadcasting (CPB)

1.   *Office of Corporate Communications*
     1111 16th Street, N.W.
     Washington, D.C. 20036
     (202) 293–6160

2.   Edward J. Pfister, President

3.   The Corporation for Public Broadcasting is a non-profit non-governmental agency, authorized under the Public Broadcasting Act of 1967 and funded by the United States government and private sources. Its primary function is to promote the growth and development of non-commercial radio and televison, dividing its budget between corporate administration, project administration, and grants, contracts, and services.

CPB projects and services provide grants to local public radio and television stations, program production centers, and regional networks; conduct audience research and studies concerning emerging telecommunications technologies; and provide support for the Public Broadcasting Service and National Public Radio (B33).

4.   CPB maintains a data bank on American public broadcasting, including statistics on listening ranges and audience, as well as budgetary information.

5.   Publications include a weekly newsletter, an annual report, and monographs, such as *Public Radio Programming: Content by Category* (1979), and *Teletext and Public Broadcasting* (1980).

H10   Economics News Broadcasters Association (ENBA)

1.   *18 H Ridge Road*
     Greenbelt, Maryland 20770
     (301) 474–8300

2.   Jim Newman, President
     Robert L. Gray, Executive Vice President

3.   The Economics News Broadcasters Association, founded in 1977, consists of broadcasters who are devoted to expanding the forum for financial news and to increasing public awareness of the significance of financial events in relation to the individual and community.

4.   ENBA has a small collection of both audio and video tapes consisting of broadcasts of financial and economic news.

5.   Publications include the *Newsletter* (monthly) and reports of annual conventions.

H11 FOCUS

1. *1755 Massachusetts Avenue, N.W.*
   Washington, D.C. 20036
   (202) 328–5026

2. Kent A. Price, Coordinator

3. FOCUS is a Washington consortium for public affairs programming. Members include the American Association for the Advancement of Science (J3), the Brookings Institution (J5), the Conservation Foundation (J9), the Consultative Group on International Agricultural Research (J10), the Overseas Development Council (J13), the Johns Hopkins University School of Advanced International Studies (K15), and Resources for the Future (J14), which also serves as the consortium's administrative headquarters.

   FOCUS completed eight years of radio broadcasting in 1983. Weekly programs are produced throughout the year and distributed via two networks; some 240 mostly public stations throughout the country subscribe to the series through the Longhorn Radio Network of the University of Texas (P.O. Box 7158, Austin, Texas 78712) and each program is also broadcasted via satellite to the 281 member stations of the National Public Radio (B33) network.

   FOCUS shows run for 29 minutes and feature staff members and guests of the sponsoring organizations in an interview/discussion format. The series is produced and directed by Mike Waters, public radio producer, and is hosted by media professionals such as Harry Ellis of the *Christian Science Monitor,* Cokie Roberts of National Public Radio, and Robert San George of United Press International. Topics span the spectrum of interests represented by members of the consortium.

4. FOCUS maintains an archive of some 20 programs on-site. Listening facilities are not available. Researchers must provide their own equipment. Duplication of programs is possible. Researchers should contact the above-mentioned networks for access to other programs in the series.

5. Plans are being made for sale and distribution of program cassettes.

H12 Foreign Broadcast Information Service (FBIS)

1. *P.O. Box 2604*
   Washington, D.C. 20013
   (202) 351–2927
   (202) 351–7676 (Public Affairs)

2. John D. Chandlee, Director

3–4. The Foreign Broadcast Information Service, an agency of the United States government, publishes a series, *Daily Reports,* consisting of translations of selective foreign language material collected from foreign radio and television broadcasts, news-agency transmissions, magazines, newspapers, and periodicals. *Daily Reports* is issued for a number of geographic areas, and include translations of speeches of foreign dignitaries, government reports, special news reports concerning political, cultural, and scientific developments, and various other articles and editorials. Individuals may

obtain edited versions of *Daily Reports,* in both printed and microfiche formats, on a subscription basis from the National Technical Infomation Service (N7). Another useful FBIS publication, *Broadcasting Stations of the World* (4 volumes, 1974) is available from the Government Printing Office (N5).

5. *Index to the Daily Reports,* from 1975 to the present, is published by Newsbank (P.O. Box 645, 135 East Putnam Avenue, Greenwich, Connecticut 06830; telephone: 203/966–1100). Included are subject, geographic, and name accesses.

H13 Joint Council on Educational Telecommunications (JECT)

1. *1111 16th Street, N.W.*
    Washington, D.C. 20036
    (202) 293–6160

2. Edwin Cohen, President

3. The Joint Council on Educational Telecommunications, founded in 1950, was instrumental in persuading the Federal Communications Commission to reserve channels for educational television and radio. Currently, the organization consists of a consortium of non-governmental associations and non-commercial broadcasting organizations including National Public Radio (B33), the Corporation for Public Broadcasting (H9), and the American Library Association (M14). The council continues to address vital concerns pertaining to the communications field.
    JECT conducts seminars and provides a forum for its members for discussion of new telecommunications technology and other matters, and it serves as education's advocate to the Federal Communications Commission. It also serves as a clearinghouse for information on communications and public policy. In 1971, JECT helped to organize the World Administrative Radio Conference on Space Telecommunications.

National Aeronautics and Space Administration (NASA)—Broadcast and Audiovisual Branch   See entry L6

H14 National Association of Broadcasters (NAB)

1. *1771 N Street, N.W.*
    Washington, D.C. 20036
    (202) 293–3500

2. Edward O. Fritts, President

3. The National Association of Broadcasters, founded in 1922, is the trade association of the commercial broadcasting industry. The association represents the industry before Congress, at the White House, and before federal regulatory agencies. NAB's mandate is to defend and to promote the American system of broadcasting as a powerful means of free communication. The association offers its member stations services in radio and television management workshops, publications, training sessions,

seminars, engineering, and research. It conducts the world's largest annual broadcasting industry convention. The National Association of Broadcasters is supported by over 5,000 radio and television stations and all the commercial networks.

4. Since 1946, NAB has maintained a library designed to serve members and staff. Holdings include 6,600 volumes (5,200 titles) relating to broadcasting; 225 periodicals; and NAB publications, including member newsletters, reports, news releases, conference papers, and a collection of audio tapes of convention sessions. The collection emphasizes industry economics, station management and operation, and legislative and regulatory activities. The library is open to the public by appointment. Although telephone reference is limited, the staff is knowledgeable about other private and public collections in the Washington area, as well as other parts of the country.

The library hours are 10:00 A.M. to 5:00 P.M., Tuesday through Friday by appointment. The library director is Susan Hill (202/293–3578).

NOTE: The Broadcast Pioneers Library (B8) holds a NAB collection of archival materials (some 1,556 items) consisting of research studies, surveys, promotional items, station publications, and documents relating to early educational broadcasting. In addition, the Motion Picture, Broadcasting and Recorded Sound Division of the Library of Congress (A41) has NAB disc recordings, including a 1952–1953 Voice of Democracy Contest.

5. NAB publications include the following: *Highlights* (weekly), *Radioactive* (monthly), and *Telemedia* (bimonthly).

H15 National Association of Spanish Broadcasters (NASB)

1. *1140 Connecticut Avenue, N.W., Suite 809*
Washington, D.C. 20036
(202) 293–3873

2. Carmen Junco, President

3. The National Association of Spanish Broadcasters, established in 1979, is the trade association representing Spanish language format radio and television stations in the United States and Puerto Rico. Its most important function is to promote and protect the interests of Spanish broadcasters. NASB performs various services for its members, such as providing legislative and regulatory representation for its members at congressional hearings and with the Federal Communications Commission, providing economic advice and support by informing Spanish broadcasters of funding sources, conducting research, preparing papers, and disseminating information on topics of interest to Spanish broadcasters. NASB conducted the first national marketing survey of the Hispanic population.

4. NASB maintains a small library and information service focusing on Hispanic population characteristics, media, and buying habits. The library has newspaper clippings and other archival material.

5. Publications include *News/Noticias* (bimonthly) and *U.S. Hispanics—A Market Profile*.

NOTE: Operations suspended as of October 31, 1983.

H16 National Black Media Coalition (NBMC)

1. *516 U Street, N.W.*
    Washington, D.C. 20001
    (202) 387–8155

2. Carmen Marshall, Executive Director

3. The National Black Media Coalition, consisting of some 40 black associatons, seeks to encourage the elimination of racism from the media and to promote the broadcasting of black issues. This organization acts as a representative of the black broadcasting community in Federal Communications Commission and legislative arenas. NBMC also contributes to the development of black-owned broadcasting stations and of black-oriented programming, as well as participating in FCC legislation.

4. NBMC maintains a current news article file of information relevant to its membership. It also disseminates information about employment opportunities.

5. Publications include *Media Line* (monthly newsletter), *For the Record* (a compilation of employment statistics on blacks in the media), and various brochures describing goals and services of the organization.

H17 National Broadcasting Company (NBC)—Washington Bureau

1. *4001 Nebraska Avenue, N.W.*
    Washington, D.C. 20016
    (202) 686–4000

2. Robert McFarlane, Chief

3. NBC has transferred its entire radio archive of 175,000 recordings of radio programs and events broadcast from 1933 to 1970 to the Motion Picture, Broadcasting and Recorded Sound Division of the Library of Congress (A41). Included in the collection are 7,500 to 8,000 hours of broadcasts from the World War II period; a number of recordings from the Salzburg Music Festival; over 300 Metropolitan Opera Broadcasts; concerts and rehearsals of the NBC Symphony Orchestra; speeches broadcast by presidents and national political figures; comedy and variety programs, including Fred Allen, Amos and Andy, Jack Benny, Eddie Cantor, Bob Hope, and Will Rogers; news coverage of national political conventions (1936–1948); olympic games; founding of the United Nations; and the 1939 World's Fair. In addition, original video tapes of daily news programming for 1976 to the present are located in the National Archives and Records Service (B27).

5. Scholars may obtain transcripts of newscasts from the NBC office in New York (30 Rockefeller Plaza, New York, New York 10020; telephone 212/664–4444). Video tapes of the evening newscasts are listed in *Television News Index and Abstracts* (Vanderbilt University Library, Nashville, Tennesse 37203; telephone: 615/322–2927).

H18 National Federation of Community Broadcasters (NFCB)

1. *1314 14th Street, N.W.*
Washington, D.C. 20005
(202) 797–8911

2. Thomas J. Thomas, Vice President

3–4. The National Federation of Community Broadcasters is a national organization devoted to the support and growth of community non-commercial broadcasting stations. The organization provides services to its members and represents them in the development of legislative and regulatory policies through Congress and the Federal Communications Commission.

A wide variety of services are provided to its 175 stations (national and international), including program distribution and consultation, training, operational assistance, financial and funding advice, and a publications program. NFCB also places some emphasis on minority participation.

The organization provides reference material, sample documents, and practical information to stations and producers. Its extensive program distribution service includes radio dramas, such as "Moment of Madness: The Civil War" and "Jack of London," a series of classical music, and political documentaries. There are also special programs to coincide with special events, such as Black History Month and International Women's Day.

5. Publications include the *NFCB Newsletter, NFCB Legal Handbook* (1980), *Audiocraft: An Introduction to the Tools and Techniques of Audio Production* (1982), as well as occasional special reports.

H19 National Oceanic and Atmospheric Administration (NOAA) (Commerce Department)—Office of Public Affairs

1. *Commerce Department Building, Room 6013*
14th Street and Constitution Avenue, N.W.
Washington, D.C. 20230
(202) 377–8090

2. Robert Buchanan, Public Affairs Officer

3–4. National Oceanic and Atmospheric Administration produces radio spot programs under the series name, "Sea and Air." Currently some 15 radio stations in Washington, D.C., air the program which consists of 3-minute segments. A number of past programs (RG 370) were 10 to 12 minutes in length and are available at the National Archives and Records Service (B27). Programs are produced on the average of once a month and consist of a variety of topics related to NOAA programs. The Office of Public Affairs stores past programs, consisting of some 50 titles. Although there is no listening facility, researchers may telephone for information on accessing the collection. NOAA officials occasionally are participants in the Department of Commerce's production, "A Growing Nation." (See entry H8 for additional information.)

5. A typewritten list of programs is available for use on-site.

National Public Radio (NPR)—Library   **See entry B33**

H20 National Radio Broadcasters Association (NRBA)

1. *1705 DeSales Street, N.W., Room 500*
    Washington, D.C. 20036
    (202) 466–2030

2. Sally Johnson, Director of Operations

3. The National Radio Broadcasters Association consists of both commercial and non-commercial radio stations, and it is the only association representing radio exclusively. Its primary functions are to promote time sales and listenership of radio, to provide legislative representation, and to promote technical advancement for the industry.

  In representing the radio industry in Congress and the Federal Communications Commission, the greatest focus of NRBA has recently been on the deregulation of radio. The association also provides regular membership services, such as assisting member stations in such areas as sales, management, and engineering.

4. NRBA has conducted various research projects and has maintained files of studies made. The organization can serve as a resource center for persons with specific questions about the radio industry.

5. NRBA publishes a variety of materials, including *Resources Service* (newsletter), *Sales and Promotion News, Station Profile, Washington Memo, Monday Morning Memo, NRBA Radio New Tech,* and *Radio Pro-Gram.*

National Republican Congressional Committee (NRCC)—Communications Division   See entry B34

H21 Radio Free Europe/Radio Liberty, Inc. (RFE/RL)

1. *1201 Connecticut Avenue, N.W.*
    Washington, D.C. 20036
    (202) 457–6900

2. James L. Buckley, President

3. RFE/RL, is a private, non-profit broadcasting corporation, under the oversight of the Board for International Broadcasting. In Munich it maintains the largest private research center in the West concentrating on East European and Soviet affairs. The Radio Free Europe division broadcasts to Bulgaria, Czechoslovakia, Hungary, Poland, and Romania; the Radio Liberty division to the Soviet Union.

4. The office has available some recordings and transcripts of broadcasts, although comprehensive materials can be found only in Munich. Inquiries to Munich can be

directed to RFE/RL, Oettingenstrasse 67, am Englischen Garten, D-8000 Munich 22, West Germany.

5. The Radio Free Europe division issues three kinds of publications: *Situation Reports, Background Reports,* and *Media Surveys.* The latter consists of English translations of important East European Press articles. The Radio Liberty division publishes *Research Bulletin, Press Surveys,* and *Samizdat Archive.*

The major bibliographic tool for locating RFE reports is the annual *Subject Index,* which lists items by both country and subject.

The annual report of the Board for International Broadcasting provides graphic details on the success and shortcoming of RFE/RL, Inc., operations. It is available on request. A six-page analysis entitled *Radio Free Europe Research* is available free on request from RFE/RL, Inc., as are a handy fact sheet and a brochure on research publications.

H22 Radio Smithsonian (Smithsonian Institution—Office of Telecommunication)

1. *National Museum of American History, Room CMB06*
   10th Street and Constitution Avenue, N.W.
   Washington, D.C. 20560
   (202) 357-1935

2. Jesse Boggs, Producer

3. Radio Smithsonian is a weekly half-hour program covering the wide variety of exhibition and educational activities of the Smithsonian Institution. Nationally distributed, it is currently being broadcast by more than 50 stations across the country. The Radio Smithsonian office also produces "Smithsonian Galaxy," a 2½ minute radio feature, as well as films, television productions, and special programs.

4. Audio holdings include tapes of all programs produced by Radio Smithsonian since it began broadcasting in 1969. The subjects represented by these productions are as varied as the activities of the Smithsonian Institution itself, including art, science, music, history, and space exploration. A sample of program titles is as follows: "On the Trail of the Dinosaur," "Saving the African Lion," "An Oral History of Aviation," "Presidents on Wheels," "Rodin True or False, " "The Museum as an Iceberg," "The Shaker Way," "Mayans and the Supernatural," "String Bands—Two Traditions," "Blacks in the Westward Movement," "The Supreme Court–Has It Really Changed?," "Loch Ness–Search for a Monster," "Old and New—Are the Beatles as Good as George Gershwin?," "Dressing the Muppets," "Champions of American Sport," "The Golden Age of Animation," "FDR Remembered," "Voices of the Civil Rights Movement," and "The Cold War Today."

The tapes are held at Radio Smithsonian for approximately two years after which they are sent to the Smithsonian Institution Archives (B42) for permanent housing. Researchers should contact the Radio Smithsonian office for information on using and/or duplicating materials at either location. Office hours are 9:00 A.M. to 5:00 P.M., Monday through Friday.

5. There is a chronological list of tapes with a brief description of each program. There is no index to the collection.

H23 Radio-Television News Directors Association (RTNDA)

1.   *1735 DeSales Street, N.W., Room 501*
     Washington, D.C. 20036
     (202) 737–8657

2.   Ernie Schultz, Executive Vice President

3.   The Radio-Television News Directors Association, founded in 1946, is the principal national advocate for broadcast journalism. The organization's primary function is to "safeguard the constitutional rights of news broadcasters against judicial, legislative, and bureaucratic encroachment, and to join with others in a common defense of the First Amendment."

RTNDA holds an annual international conference with special events, speakers, and exhibits of products and services available to the broadcast news industry. The organization conducts research and a continuing education program. It also presents annual awards to both stations and individuals, and offers scholarships and career information to students in broadcast journalism.

4.   Aside from its information-sharing activities, RTNDA maintains files of texts of convention speeches and resolutions, and a chronicle of the organization's development and achievements. Tape recordings of major addresses are collected by the Washington office. Later they are sent to the University of Iowa where they are permanently maintained. Examples of tape recordings in the collection include: "Three Mile Island: Did We Make It Worse than It Was?"; "Future of Radio Network News"; "Libel and Slander Insurance (with Steve Nevas, attorney with National Association of Broadcasters)"; and Charles Osgood reading poetry.

5.   Publications include the monthly newsletter, *Communicator,* an annual directory, a career pamphlet for students, a small market radio guide, and other publications representing special projects and events.

H24 Telecommunications Research and Action Center (TRAC)

1.   *P. O. Box 12038*
     Washington, D.C. 20005
     (202) 462–2520

2.   Samuel A. Simon, Executive Director

3.   The Telecommunications Research and Action Center is a non-profit organization that seeks to improve the quality of broadcasting. The committee's activities are varied, such as conducting projects to determine public interest in public broadcasting. TRAC also evaluates programming performance of radio and television stations and networks, and conducts telecommunications research, taking legislative action where necessary. TRAC is the only media group advocating consumer interest on the Citizens Utility Board to monitor rate making from American Telephone and Telegraph. TRAC also acts as a forum for other media groups and events and is the cooperative representative for issues regarding cable broadcasting.

4. A small library of some 30 periodicals and around 200 books on the subject of telecommunications and broadcasting is maintained. It is open to the public by appointment.

5. TRAC publications include *Reverse the Charges,* a consumer's guide to telephone usage; *Telecommunications and the Future;* and a journal, *Access* (monthly), which focuses on public interest issues and communications. A video tape of *Reverse the Charges* is available for purchase or rental.

H25 Unda-USA

1. *3035 Fourth Street, N.E.*
   Washington, D.C. 20017
   (202) 526–0780

2. Rev. John Geaney, CSP

3–4. This organization serves as the American branch of Unda, the International Catholic Association for Radio and Television ("unda" is the Latin word for wave, in this case, air wave.)Unda is the trade association for Catholic broadcasters and allied communicators.

Unda presents the Gabriel awards to honor commercial and religious broadcasters who have produced programs that "exemplify the broadcast art and contribute to a deeper understanding of the human values that will enhance the lives of viewers and listeners."

Although the organization does not maintain a tape collection, Unda does serve as a clearinghouse for those individuals interested in its projects and in Catholic broadcasting.

5. Unda produces "Real-to-Reel," a 15-minute TV program sent weekly to subscribers. Printed materials include the bimonthly newsletter, *White Paper* (an educational resource on telecommunication), a membership directory, and *Media Inventory,* which is a catalog of programs, and various pamphlets and brochures describing services.

Voice of America (VOA) (U.S. Information Agency)—Music and Tape Libraries   See entry A72

Washington Ear, Inc.   See entry F22

The White House—Office of the Press Secretary—News Summary and Audio Services   See entry B54

J Research Centers

Introductory Note

Research centers in the Washington area are substantial resources for sound recordings. It should be noted that due to current interest and availability of funds, programs and personnel often undergo changes. The audio resources held by research institutions frequently reflect these changes. Several of the centers produce regular radio programs reflecting the nature of their research concerns (see entries J2, J3, J5, J9, J10, J13, J14, and J15).

Organizations that engage in research activities but are not cited in this section include history divisions of federal government agencies, described in section B, and radio broadcasting organizations, described in section H.

The principal sources for accessing research organizations in Washington, D.C., are *Research Centers Directory* (9th ed., 1984), *Government Research Centers Directory* (2nd ed., 1982), both published by Gale Research Company, and *Research Institutions and Learned Societies* (Westport, Conn.: Greenwood Press, 1982). The first two guides provide addresses, telephone numbers, and concise descriptions of programs and services. The third guide centers on only the more significant research institutions, but offers lengthy descriptions, and bibliographies of additional readings.

J1 Academy for Educational Development (AED)—International Operations Division

1. *1414 22nd Street, N.W.*
   Washington, D.C. 20037
   (202) 862–1900 (Academy)
   (202) 862–1938 (Division)

2. Stephen F. Mosley, Director, International Operations Division

3. The Academy for Educational Development, founded in 1961, is an international planning and research organization, which works in all aspects of education, including elementary, secondary, and higher. AED is also involved in projects in communications, world affairs, and in studies for improving the facilities of institutions that serve the public. AED is currently conducting 139 projects in the United States and 53 projects in the developing countries.

AED is involved in media production, including films and video tapes for use by international agency and country officials in seminars and workshops. The International Division Programs assist individuals in learning how to manage an information resource library, as well as individuals who would like to learn about audiovisual products or the uses of satellite communications for development. AED also produces and assists others in broadcasting instructional radio programs, as well as evaluating instructional radio series. For instance, since the early 1980s AED has written and produced some 500 English-language radio lessons in Nairobi, Kenya.

4. AED maintains a small library consisting of 1,200 documents that center on the application of communication systems to the delivery of social services in isolated rural areas of the developing world.

Library materials are listed under various subjects in a manual card file. Some subjects worth examining include "Broadcast-Radio" and "Teleconferencing-Audio."

5. AED publishes a number of monographs, reports, occasional papers as well as the newsletter, *Academy News* (3 times a year.) The last source is a good starting point for learning of the various non-print activities and projects of the academy. Catalogs and brochures are available upon request at the Washington, D.C., office or by writing to the New York office at 680 Fifth Avenue, New York, New York 10019.

J2   African Bibliographic Center, Inc. (ABC)

1.   *1346 Connecticut Avenue, N.W., Suite 909*
Washington, D.C. 20036
(202) 223–1392

Mail:
P.O. Box 13096
Washington, D.C. 20009

2.   Daniel G. Matthews, President and Executive Director

3–4.   The African Bibliographic Center was founded in 1963 as an information center for researchers and the general public. The ABC research program has several components; part of it is ongoing, and another part depends on contracts from governments and foundations. The results of the ongoing research are a series of bibliographies and information programs on the radio.

ABC produces "Habari," which is a free information and 24-hour news service about Africa, available via telephone (202/659–2529). The recordings last several minutes and are purchased by various radio stations for broadcast. ABC transcribes each report. There are transcripts available for purchase on a weekly, monthly, or quarterly plan. Transcripts are held from 1976 to the present.

5.   One of the more significant publications of ABC is *A Current Bibliography on African Affairs* (quarterly).

Alexandria Archaeological Research Center (City of Alexandria— Department of Historic Resources)   See entry B1

J3   American Association for the Advancement of Science (AAAS)

1.   *1101 Vermont Avenue, N. W. (10th Floor)*
Washington, D.C. 20005
(202) 842-9590
(202) 467-4360 (Library)

2.   William D. Carey, Executive Director
Kathryn Wolff, Publications

3.   The American Association for the Advancement of Science, founded in 1848, is dedicated to supporting the research of scientists and to facilitate cooperation among them, and to help promote public understanding of science. This goal is accomplished through an extensive program of publications, meetings, seminars, educational activities, and public sector activities. The Washington office handles the association's activities and programs, which are implemented at regional, national, and international levels.
    The association's audiovisual programs are varied. At least 94 cassette recordings of the annual meeting of January 1982 have been made available for purchase from Mobiltape Company, Inc., 1741 Gardena Avenue, Glendale, California 91204; telephone 800/423-2050 (toll-free). The following tapes serve as examples of the wide array of scientific subjects represented in the collection: *Academia, Industry, and Government: The Organizational Frontier of Science Today* (James B. Hunt, Jr.; cassette 82AAAS/3); *Theories of Choice in the Making of Decisions* (James G. March; cassette 82AAAS/4); *A Symposium to Honor Mina Rees: Contributions to the Study of Artificial Intelligence* (cassettes 82 AAAS/106-107); *Biocommunication: New Discoveries and Ideas* (cassettes 82 AAAS/116-119); *The Brain Sciences and Education* (cassettes 82AAAS/28-29; *A Challenge for American Education: Scientific Literacy in Japan, the Germanies, and the Soviet Union* (cassettes 82AAAS/168-169); *Reflections on the Recombinant DNA Controversy* (cassettes 82AAAS/162-165); *Bioactive Marine Products* (cassettes 82AAAS/188-189). Similarly available for purchase from Mobiltape Company are 104 cassette recordings of the May 1983 annual meeting. A brochure *AAAS 1983 Annual Meeting Detroit Tapes* is sent free on request.
    The AAAS Office of Communications is involved in a number of media programs. In 1981, for example, it began a daily radio science program, "Report on Science," co-sponsored by CBS Radio Stations News Service. Since 1977 the office has also produced radio programs for non-commercial radio stations including National Public Radio stations. AAAS is a member of FOCUS (H11), a Washington consortium for public affairs radio programming. AAAS's contributions to FOCUS have typically involved programs consisting of two 15-minute discussions of distinct topics. Illustrative examples of these programs, relying on scientists from the Washington, D.C., community, were "Management Techniques in National Parks" and "Women in Science," in 1983; and "Trident Submarines" and "Using Pets to Alleviate Stress" in 1984. Joan Wrather, Senior Communications Associate (202/467-5441), is responsible for AAAS's programming for FOCUS.

5.   The official journal of the AAAS since 1900 is *Science*. This magazine, in addition to featuring scientific articles and reports of note, cites audiovisual information. For example, the audio cassette tapes of the 1982 AAAS meeting were listed in the 28 May and 9 July 1983 issues of the journal. Another journal, *Science Books and Films*, published five times a year, includes annotated entries for recently published cassettes with filmstrips for such subjects as data processing, library and information sciences,

psychology, sociology, anthropology, natural resources/environmental issues, social problems and services, mathematics, astronomy, physics, life sciences, zoological sciences, and medical sciences. These and numerous other publications are cited in an array of brochures and catalogs available from the association.

American Educational Research Association (AERA)   **See entry M9**

J4   American Enterprise Institute for Public Policy Research (AEI)

1. *1150 17th Street, N.W.*
    Washington, D.C. 20036
    (202) 862–5800

2. William J. Baroody, Jr., President
    Robert C. Doyle, Television Programs

3. The AEI, established in 1943, is an independent, non-profit, nonpartisan, research and educational organization that studies public policy issues, both national and foreign. Through its continuing series of Public Policy Forums, the institute features scholarly discussions on major public policy problems of current interest. Between 1970 and 1981 proceedings of 123 of these forums were made available in reel-to-reel audio tapes, as well as in video tapes and video cassettes. AEI is resuming this program in 1984.

4. The institute's small reference library (Evelyn Caldwell, 202/862–5831) of some 15,000 volumes is open to the public by appointment only.

5. Publications of AEI include *Public Opinion* (bimonthly), *Regulation* (bimonthly), and two newsletters, *AEI Economist* (monthly) and *Memorandum*. An annual catalog of *New Publications* is available on request.

Anacostia Neighborhood Museum (Smithsonian Institution)—Research Department   See entry C1

J5   Brookings Institution

1. *1775 Massachusetts Avenue, N. W.*
    Washington, D.C. 20036
    (202) 797–6000

2. Bruce K. MacLaury, President
    Roger D. Semerad, Executive Vice President
    Margaret M. Rhoades, Public Affairs Director

3.   The Brookings Institution is a private, non-profit organization devoted to research, education, and publication in economics, foreign policy, government, and the social sciences. Its principal purpose is to shed light on current and emerging public policy problems facing the United States and to publish its findings to inform the public. Its research activities are carried out by its programs in Economic Studies, Governmental Studies, and Foreign Policy Studies. Other activities are carried out by the Advanced Study Program, the Social Science Computation Center, and the Publications Program. In addition to Senior Fellows, Research Associates, and Research Assistants, Brookings offers temporary appointments and fellowship opportunities including dissertation-stage Research Fellowships, postdoctoral Economic Policy Fellowships, Federal Executive Fellowships (for senior U.S. government officials), and a pre- and/or postdoctoral Guest Scholar Program, which allows scholars whose research is related to Brookings' purposes access to the institution's facilities. The Advanced Study Program sponsors conferences, seminars, round table luncheons, and other activities, which are by invitation or subscription only.

Brookings is a member of FOCUS (H11), a Washington consortium for public affairs programming. Institution members have been interviewed, as well as participated in discussions, to be broadcast via public radio stations. Recently, Brookings has contributed the following programs: "Industrial Policy" with Charles Schultze, Senior Fellow, in the fall of 1983; and "Ballistic Missile Defense" with Ashton Carter, Affiliated Scholar, and "Our Changing Financial Institutions" with Andrew S. Carron, Senior Fellow, both in the spring of 1984.

4.   Brookings maintains a specialized library of books and periodicals designed to meet the needs of its research programs. Current holdings include 60,000 volumes, 625 periodical titles, vertical files of pamphlets and government documents, and a selective collection of United Nations documents. Although the library is restricted to resident staff members, outside researchers with a demonstrated need may request permission to use the facility by contacting the librarian, Laura P. Walker (202/797– 6234).

The Social Science Computation Center (202/797–6180) provides computer services for Brookings and some 60 other organizations engaged in social science research and public administration. On-line data are mostly numerical and statistical. A fee schedule for outside users is available.

5.   The Brookings Institution Publications Program supports a large number of publications on a variety of topics each year. Also available are *The Brookings Bulletin,* the annual report, program descriptions, and a complete list of publications that are in print and for sale.

J6   Center for Applied Linguistics (CAL)

1.   *3520 Prospect Street, N.W.*
     Washington, D.C. 20007
     (202) 298–9292

2.   G. Richard Tucker, Director

3.   The Center for Applied Linguistics, established in 1959, is dedicated to the study of language and the application of linguistics to educational, cultural, and social concerns. Their three principal objectives are to improve the teaching of English as a second or foreign language, to improve the teaching of seldom taught languages, and

to incorporate the findings of the language sciences into the American education process.

CAL is organized into five operating departments: the Native and English Language Education Division, the Foreign Language Education Division, the Research Division, the Office of Communication and Publications, and the Office of Language and Public Policy.

5.   One of the center's principal publications is *Your New Life in the United States,* which consists of refugee orientation handbooks with accompanying audio cassettes for Vietnamese, Lao, Hmong, Khmer (Cambodia), and Cantonese Chinese languages.

The Office of Communication and Publications has produced a number of bilingual phrasebooks with accompanying audio cassettes for the languages named above. Since September 1983, these have been available for purchase from Nancy McCloughan, Operations Manager, HBJ International, 757 Third Avenue, New York, New York 10017 (telephone 212/888–3980).

A useful publication to consult is the *Dictionary Catalog of the Library of the Center for Applied Linguistics,* 4 vols. (Boston: G.K. Hall, 1974).

J7   Chamber of Commerce of the United States

1.   *1625 H Street, N.W.*
     Washington, D.C. 20062
     (202) 659–6000 (General)
     (202) 463–5690 (Broadcast Division)

2.   Richard Lesher, President
     Robert Adams, Vice President for Broadcasting

3.   The Chamber of Commerce, created in 1912, has a membership of some 213,000 corporations and individuals, trade and professional organizations, and local and state chambers of commerce. The nation's largest business federation represents the views of American business on national issues through the work of several divisions and regional offices. The Chamber of Commerce organizes seminars and conferences that focus on diverse business interests.

In addition, BizNet, The American Business Network of the United States Chamber of Commerce, offers a satellite television subscription service as well as syndicated programs for on-air and cable, covering the wide range of government and regulatory matters affecting small business, regional, state and local chambers of commerce, industries, corporations, and trade and professional associations. The two-way interactive television system offers coverage of daily business and political events, as well as in-depth education and management seminars.

5.   The Chamber of Commerce also publishes a number of non-print materials. For example, the Nation's Business Executive Seminars in the Sound Division produces, for purchase, 2 audio cassette programs: *Manage Your Ways to Personal Success* (6 cassettes) and *Executive Seminars in Sound* (8 cassettes), the latter focusing on the handling of business problems and situations.

Also available from the United States Chamber of Commerce are a variety of video tapes, films, and slide programs, plus reports, surveys and other materials on business, trade, and the economy.

J8 Clearinghouse on Development Communication (Academy for Educational Development)

1. *1414 22nd Street, N.W.*
   Washington, D.C. 20037
   (202) 862–1900 (Academy)
   (202) 862–1914 (Clearinghouse)

2. Judy Brace, Director

3. The Clearinghouse on Development Communication is an international center for information and services to promote the appropriate use of communications in Third World development programs. The clearinghouse supports a network of development practitioners in more than 150 countries by regularly providing them with information on communication strategies that can give access to information and services for improving the daily lives of the rural and urban poor in the developing world. There is a strong emphasis on the use of radio for disseminating educational information in order to complement, facilitate, and extend development activities.

4. The clearinghouse provides technical information to development professionals and maintains a reference collection of both print and non-print materials. Individuals may obtain permission to use these materials on-site. Audiovisual materials such as video tapes and films on communication may be viewed on-site or rented.

5. The clearinghouse publishes *Development Communication Report,* a quarterly newsletter on Third World uses of communications for social services.

J9 Conservation Foundation (CF)

1. *1717 Massachusetts Avenue, N.W.*
   Washington, D.C. 20036
   (202) 797–4300

2. William K. Reilly, President

3. Through research, citizen training, and communication with opinion leaders in the United States and abroad, the Conservation Foundation encourages wise management of the earth's resources—its land, water, air, and energy. It conducts programs in land use (rural resources, urban conservation, public lands, international comparative land use), coastal and water resources, economics and the environment, pollution and toxic-substances control, and energy. CF conducts interdisciplinary research, education, and information programs to develop knowledge, improve techniques, and stimulate public and private awareness and action to improve the quality of the environment. It carries out demonstration planning programs; and offers a variety of conservation services at home and abroad.

   The Conservation Foundation is a member of FOCUS (H11), a Washington consortium for public affairs radio programming, and regularly produces programs broadcast via public radio stations. Gordon Binder, Assistant to the President, directs the preparation of the CF programs, which have included "Environmental Mediation," and "Hazardous Wastes" in 1983, and an interview with William D. Ruckelshaus, administrator of the Environmental Protection Agency, in 1984.

4. CF maintains a library of over 5,000 books, 76 vertical file drawers, and over 200 periodicals. The focus is on environmental issues. The library (Barbara Rodes, librarian, 797–4300) is open to the public from 9:00 A.M. to 5:00 P.M., Monday through Friday.

5. The foundation's publications include *Conservation Foundation Letter* (monthly), books, and reports. It also produces films.

J10 Consultative Group on International Agricultural Research (CGIAR)

1. *1818 H Street, N.W.*
   Washington, D.C. 20433
   (202) 477–5347

2. Curtis Farrar, Executive Secretary
   Olivia Vent, Information Officer

3. The Consultative Group on International Agricultural Research was organized in May 1971 to bring together countries, public and private institutions, international and regional organizations, and representatives from developing countries in support of a network of international agricultural research centers and programs. The World Bank provides the Executive Secretariat of the Consultative Group, which is advised by the Technical Advisory Committee, whose secretariat is provided by the Food and Agriculture Organization of the United Nations.

Since 1983 the CGIAR has been a member of FOCUS (H11), a Washington consortium for public affairs radio programming. Programs contributed in 1984 by CGIAR have included "International Agricultural Research" and "Genetic Diversity."

5. The Consultative Group issues a quarterly newsletter, *News From CGIAR*.

Education Department—Office of Educational Research and Improvement
See entry B13

J11 Government Institutes, Inc.

1. *966 Hungerford Drive, No. 24*
   Rockville, Maryland 20850
   (301) 251–9250

2. Charlene Ikonomou, Publications Coordinator

3. Government Institutes was founded as a publishing and educational organization whose programs include courses, conferences, and seminars on matters relating to energy and environmental topics of governmentally related interest.

5. The organization publishes numerous handbooks and conference proceedings focusing on legal, regulatory, technical, and economic topics related to the energy and environmental fields. Some of these proceedings are available in audio cassette format.

Examples include the first *European Environmental Laws and Regulations Conference* held in December 1981, which consists of 7 tapes; the second *Cogeneration: Current Prospects and Future Opportunities Seminar,* held in October 1982, which consists of 7 tapes; and the *Environmental Compliance Audit* course, held in November 1982, which consists of a notebook and 5 tapes. Each March, for the past 10 years, Government Institutes has sponsored the Energy Technology Conference, their largest, in Washington. Several materials from their most recent conference, Energy Technology X, include: *Cogeneration: Current Prospects and Future Opportunities III* (a notebook and 5 tapes); *Fluidized Bed Combustion* (a notebook and 3 tapes); *Natural Gas Pricing* course (3 tapes); *Photovoltaic Energy Conversion* course (a notebook and 4 tapes); *Electricity Regulation: Supply and Price* (a notebook and 4 tapes); *Wind Energy* course (4 tapes); and *Market for Energy Efficient Products and Services* course (4 tapes). Sixty-three individual cassettes from the 1983 Energy Technology Conference are also available from Government Institutes. Examples of these individual courses include: *State of Energy, Financing Energy Management Projects,* and *Efficient Industrial Boilers.* Cogeneration III materials are very popular and they focus on legislation, regulations, court decision, tax incentives, and other economic factors affecting cogeneration and alternate energy sources. A thumbnail catalog (a catalog that lists all publications for sale at Government Institutes along with their prices) and flyers describing the above-mentioned publications and other energy and environmental books are available free upon request.

Howard University Libraries—Manuscript Division—Moorland-Spingarn Research Center   See entry A36

J12   National Council on Aging (NCOA)—Senior Center Humanities Program

1.   *600 Maryland Avenue, S.W., West Wing, Room 100*
       Washington, D.C. 20024
       (202) 479–1200

2.   Edmund H. Worthy, Jr., Director

3–4.   The Senior Center Humanities Program is available to any organization that serves older people. It consists of study units on a variety of topics, which serve as texts to generate discussion. The units are comprised of anthologies and accompanying tapes and posters; sample titles are *The Search for Meaning, The Heritage of the Future,* and *A Family Album: the American Family in Literature and History.* Program materials also include a *Manual for Leading Humanities Discussion Groups.* As a result of this program, sites making use of these materials have developed collections of taped discussions and oral histories of participants. The National Council on Aging holds transcriptions of many of these collections and is available as a clearinghouse for further information on aging and related topics.

5.   In addition to the above-mentioned publications, the Senior Center Humanities Program also publishes a quarterly, *Collage: Cultural Enrichment and Older Adults.*

J13   Overseas Development Council (ODC)

1.   *1717 Massachusetts Avenue, N.W.*
Washington, D.C. 20036
(202) 234–8701

2.   John W. Sewell, President

3.   ODC is an independent, nonprofit research center concerned with increasing American understanding of the economic and social problems confronting developing countries. The council stresses the importance of these countries to the United States in an increasingly interdependent world, and pursues its objectives through research, conferences, publications, and liaison with mass-membership organizations interested in U.S. relations with the developing world.

Prominent emphasis in the council's current work programs includes analysis of the implications of the increasing interdependence of economic growth or stagnation in the industrialized and developing countries; assessment of the costs and benefits for all countries of the major proposals for a new international economic order (North-South dialogue); identification of improved ways to achieve Third World health and population goals, including analysis of how development can affect health and fertility; continued study of alternative development strategies; and refinement of a new tool for measuring development achievement.

ODC is a member of FOCUS (H11), a Washington consortium for public affairs programming. Staff members and associates of the council are interviewed or serve as participants in discussions broadcast via public radio stations. Contributions by ODC have included interviews with Shridath Ramphal on "Brandt Commission Report" and with John P. Lewis on "Developing Countries" in 1982, as well as with Richard Feinberg on "Central America" in the spring of 1984.

4.   ODC has a small research library primarily for the use of the staff.

5.   ODC has an extensive publications program of monographic studies, occasional papers, and communiques. The ODC annual report and a catalog of publications is available free.

J14   Resources for the Future (RFF)

1.   *1755 Massachusetts Avenue, N.W.*
Washington, D.C. 20036
(202) 328–5000

2.   Emery N. Castle, President

3.   Resources for the Future is a non-profit research organization, which studies domestic and international issues relating to energy, environmental quality, and natural resources. The resident staff of researchers, most of whom are economists, is augmented by a varying number of visiting scholars.

RFF is a member of FOCUS (H11), a Washington consortium for public affairs programming. Staff members and others are interviewed, or serve as participants in discussions to be broadcast via public radio stations. RFF recently prepared the fol-

lowing programs: "World after Nuclear War," and "Air Pollution and Health" in the fall of 1983, and "American Agriculture" in the spring of 1984.

5. The organization publishes a newsletter, *Resources,* and a series of monographs and research papers. The annual report and a publication list are available upon request.

Society for History in the Federal Government   See entry B44

Supreme Court Historical Society   See entry B48

Takoma Park Historical Society   See entry B49

Telecommunications Research and Action Center (TRAC)   See entry H24

J15   Woodrow Wilson International Center for Scholars (WWICS)

1.   *Smithsonian Institution Building*
     1000 Jefferson Drive, S.W.
     Washington, D.C. 20560
     (202) 357-2429

2.   James H. Billington, Director

3.   The Woodrow Wilson International Center for Scholars was created by the United States Congress in 1968 as the nation's official living memorial to its twenty-eighth president. As a national institution with international interests, the center seeks to encourage the creative use of the unique human, archival, and institutional resources in the nation's capital for studies illuminating our understanding of the past and present.
     Through its residential fellowship program of advanced research the center seeks to commemorate both the scholarly depth and the public concerns of Woodrow Wilson. The center welcomes outstanding project proposals representing a wide diversity of scholarly interests and approaches from individuals throughout the world. It has no permanent or tenured fellows. Its fellowships are awarded for periods ranging from four months to one year or more, in one broadly defined program and five more focused programs of research. Projected as a sixth is the European Program, covering both Western and Eastern Europe (outside the USSR), for which the first fellowship competition will be held in the fall of 1984. The others are the Kennan Institute for Advanced Russian Studies, the Latin American Program, the International Security Studies Program, the East Asia Program, and the Program in American Society and Politics. The broadly defined program—History, Culture, and Society—enables the center to support superior projects from the entire range of scholarship in the humanities and social sciences, particularly those that promise to make major contributions to our understanding of the human condition or that attempt broad synthesis involving different fields or different cultures. The center also operates a Guest Scholar

Program for the short-term use of the center's facilities by a small number of visiting scholars and specialists.

The center has a long standing interest in the history and theory of motion picture, television, and broadcasting. From 1975 to 1984 the following scholars held fellowships in the audiovisual fields at the center: Peter Braestrup, Marc Ferro, Eric Barnouw, Thomas Cripps, Lawrence Lichty, David Culbert, Frank McConnell, Gladys and Kurt Lang, Herbert Marshall, Julianne Burton, and Chidananda Dasgupta.

The center's activities include frequent colloquia, evening seminars, and other discussions designed to foster intellectual community among the participants. In 1982–1983, for instance, discussions were held on the following topics: "Prospects for Radio Free Europe/Radio Liberty," and "Radio Broadcasting to the Soviet Union." The scheduled events are announced in the monthly *Calendar of Events*.

From 1978 to 1983, the center participated in a Washington education and research consortium as a sponsor of the public-affairs radio show FOCUS (H11). It has become increasingly committed to bringing the richness of its discussions and its scholars' insights to radio listeners across the nation. Distributed by National Public Radio via satellite to its member stations, and by the University of Texas Longhorn Network to some 230 United States educational stations, the FOCUS programs were tightly edited presentations of major international issues. Most were moderated by members of the center's senior staff. During 1982–1983, the Wilson Center broadcast 14 programs through the FOCUS series, including "Science and Technology in China," "Germany Between East and West," "Education in Language and Culture," "Field Anthropology," "Latin American Debt," "Revolutionary Violence," and "Oral Culture."

In January 1984, the Wilson Center expanded its FM radio offerings by producing its own once-per-week 30-minute program entitled DIALOGUE, which is also distributed by National Public Radio (B33) and Longhorn Radio Network. This 52-week program is built around the center's fellows and guest scholars, as well as drawing upon meeting and conference participants. Programs on "Churches in Eastern Europe and the Soviet Union," "Japanese Industrial Policy," "Israel: Likud, Labor, and Future of Arab-Israeli Relations," "Walt Whitman: Poetry and Politics," and "Minorities in America" were included among those broadcast in 1984. The weekly broadcast is also available on cassettes and is marketed to schools, colleges, and public affairs groups. For station information and a catalogue of cassettes, contact Radio Coordinator for DIALOGUE, Genie Beth Skarstrom (202/357-2185).

In addition, the center occasionally contributes to "Radio Smithsonian" (H22), a weekly half-hour radio program offering a variety of people and events throughout the Smithsonian Institution. In 1983 these programs included "Comparison of Ideologies of the United States and the Soviet Union" and "American Growth Policy since World War II." A special Films at the Archives series, "The Vietnam War on TV (April 5, 12, and 18, 1978)" was sponsored by the Wilson Center and the National Archives and Records Service. This featured presentation of ABC, CBS, and NBC network evening news coverage of the Vietnam War, 1965–1973, as compiled by Lawrence W. Lichty, Wilson Center Fellow, includes discussions by reporters who covered the war. A set of 5 audio reel tapes of remarks for the series (RG 64) was deposited in the Motion Picture, Sound & Video Branch of the National Archives and Records Service (B27).

4. The Wilson Center has a working library containing 16,000 volumes of basic reference works, bibliographies, and essential monographs in the social sciences and humanities with an emphasis on the areas covered by the center's programs. The library subscribes to and maintains the backfiles of about 300 scholarly journals and periodicals. As part of a National Presidential Memorial, the library has special access

to the collections of the Library of Congress and other government libraries. The librarian is Zdenek V. David (202/357–2567).

5. The Wilson Center's publications are varied and reflect the interest and research activities shared by its members. Of particular significance to those interested in audiovisuals and Washington, D.C., is the center's series of *Scholars' Guides to Washington, D.C.* Each *Guide* surveys the collections, institutions, and organizations, and other resources pertinent to the study of particular geographic areas, including Russia/ Soviet Union (2d edition), Latin America and the Caribbean, East Asia, Africa, Central and Eastern Europe, the Middle East, South Asia, Southeast Asia, and Northwest Europe. A forthcoming *Guide* focuses on Southwest European Studies. Each *Guide* contains sections on non-print media, including "Collections of Music and Other Sound Recordings." A separate *Guide* will cover film and video collections in the Washington, D.C., area and will serve as a companion volume to this survey. All of the *Guides,* available from the Smithsonian Institution Press (P.O. Box 1579, Washington, D.C. 20013), have useful information on audio resources not necessarily duplicated in this study. Therefore, researchers may wish to refer to them as well.

The *Wilson Quarterly* (105,000 circulation) carries occasional articles within the audiovisual field. Clusters of three or four articles with bibliographic essays have appeared on the following topics: "TV News and Politics" (spring 1977), "Television in America" (winter 1981), and "The News Media" (special issue 1982). The center's programs issue several series of *Occasional/Working Papers,* which are distributed free of charge to interested parties, upon request. The *Annual Report* and an occasional bulletin, the *Wilson Center News,* are sent to former fellows and other friends of the Wilson Center.

J16   World Future Society (WFS)

1.   *4916 St. Elmo Avenue*
     Bethesda, Maryland 20814
     (301) 656–8274

2.   Julia Larson, Book Service Director

3.   The World Future Society is a clearinghouse for information on present and projected societal and global trends. The society works to encourage public awareness of the future and especially social and economic trends. In this way, society can "avert potential disasters and capitalize on future opportunities."Futurists are concerned with trends in science, computer techniques and application, food consumption, education, space, employment, industry, business, communications, environment, ecology; in sum, all aspects of society.

5.   The WFS achieves its goal of dissemination of information by distributing for purchase books, papers, monthly abstracts, bulletins, films, games, and tape cassettes.

The WFS *Tape Catalog: 1982* includes more than 175 sessions recorded during the Society's Third General Assembly, "Through the '80s: Thinking Globally, Acting Locally," held in July 1980. In addition, there are 175 tapes sessions, luncheon speeches, and special events of the Fourth General Assembly, "Communications and the Future," held in July 1982. Topics covered include arts, business, communications, computers, defense, economics, education, employment, government, health, information industry, international relations, law, management, mass media, and space. All of the speakers are distinguished in their respective fields. Tapes are also available

of the "Work and Career Conference," held in Washington in August 1983. See WFS *Book Catalog,* fall 1983.

J17 World Peace Through Law Center (WPTLC)

1. *1000 Connecticut Avenue, N.W., Suite 800*
    Washington, D.C. 20036
    (202) 466–5428

2. Charles S. Rhyne, President

3. The World Peace Through Law Center is a world-wide organization of judges, lawyers, law professors, and law students representing 151 nations, including the ASEAN (Association of Southeast Asian Nations) states and Burma, dedicated to the replacement of force by law in international affairs. A non-profit and non-political organization, the center draws its members from its constituent professional associations: World Association of Judges, World Association of Lawyers, World Association of Law Professors, and World Association of Law Students. WPTLC maintains separate specialized sections for dealing with issues, such as human rights and international legal education.

   The center sponsors World Law Day, and biennial World Law Conferences, featuring demonstration trials on such themes as human rights and law of the sea, at different locations throughout the world.

4. Audio tape recordings have been made of just a limited number of past conferences. The recordings, as a rule, are available for use only by members of the organization.

5. WPTLC's extensive publications include: *The Law and Woman* (1975); *Model Code of Conduct for Transnational Corporations* (1977); *Peace with Justice under World Rules of Law* (1977); and *Law and Judicial Systems of Nations* (1978). The center also publishes a bimonthly newsletter, *The World Jurist,* as well as the *World Law Review,* which contains the proceedings of the biennial conferences. A list of the center's publications and *A Report on the Activities of the World Peace Through Law Center* is available on request.

K Academic Programs and Departments

Introductory Note

Several academic institutions in the Washington metropolitan area offer undergraduate and graduate students courses in a variety of audio topics, including production, editing, operations, maintenance, and materials in both practical and theoretical approaches. Through the Consortium of Universities (K7), students can enroll in courses at several institutions and receive credit from their home university. For further information on academic programs, individuals should contact the director or departmental chairperson of the institution.

Organizations not described in this section, but which offer self-instructional recordings for creating slide-tape programs include the Association for Educational Communications and Technology (M28) and the National Audiovisual Center (L7).

K1 Aerospace Education Foundation (Affiliate of the Air Force Association)

1. *1750 Pennsylvania Avenue, N.W.*
   Washington, D.C. 20006
   (202) 637–3370

2. Don C. Garrison, President
   Michael J. Nisos, Managing Director

3–4. The Aerospace Education Foundation reproduces and distributes Air Force technical courses for civilian use. These courses were developed on-site at Air Force training centers and are accredited through the auspices of the Community College of the Air Force (CCAF), Maxwell, Alabama. Currently 58 instructional classroom programs and 11 home study packages are offered. These courses, many of which include audiovisuals cover a broad spectrum of vocational studies.

Currently three audio-related courses are offered. The "Audio Specialist" course provides a student with a basic understanding of all audio operations including use and maintenance concepts of audio equipment. The "Audiovisual Equipment Repairman" course provides basic theory and practical experience in the maintenance of audio equipment. The "Audiovisual Methods" course affords a student both training

and practical experience in the selection, design, pre-production, application and validation of audiovisual software. The "Audio Specialist" course consists of print materials only, the "Audiovisual Equipment Repairman" course contains 6 videotapes, and the "Audiovisual Methods" course contains 11 sound/slide programs (also on videotape) and 2 audio/only cassettes.

5. A catalog of courses is available free from the foundation upon request.

American Sociological Association (ASA)—Teaching Services Program
See entry M25

K2   American University—Department of Physics

1. *McKinley Building, Room 106*
   Massachusetts and Nebraska Avenues, N.W.
   Washington, D.C. 20016
   (202) 885–2741
   (202) 885–2743

2. Romeo Segnan, Program Director

3. The Department of Physics offers a B.S. degree in audio techniques. The program concentrates on the technology of electronic recording and reproduction of sound. The program is multidisciplinary, combining the resources of the School of Communication, the Department of Performing Arts, Audio Visual Services, and the Department of Physics. Course subjects are varied and include such topics as "Audio Technology," "Electronics," "Studio Techniques," "Mass Media," and "Electronic Music Synthesis." The Department has an extensive recording studio/laboratory, which includes a Moog Synthesizer.

4. The libraries of the American University are described in entries A5 and A6.

5. A brochure describing the program is available.

K3   American University—School of Communication

1. *Mary Graydon Center, Room 300*
   Massachusetts and Nebraska Avenues, N.W.
   Washington, D.C. 20016
   (202) 885–2060
   (202) 885–2058

2. Glen Harnden, Acting Dean
   John Doolittle, Director of Broadcast Journalism

3–4. The School of Communication offers B.A. and M.A. degrees in broadcast journalism. The program focuses on radio and television news reporting, writing and broadcasting, and radio and television production. Students prepare and broadcast

daily news programs on WAMU-AM. Only one course focuses on the production of audio recordings and is entitled "Editing: Film, Video and Audio." Also offered is a minor in mass media studies for students who want to become informed consumers of the mass media.

4. The libraries of the American University are described in entries A5 and A6.

K4 Bowie State College—Department of Communications

1. *Bowie, Maryland 20715*
    (301) 464–3000 (General)
    (301) 464–03283 (Department of Communications)

2. Elaine Bourne-Heath, Chairperson

3. The Department of Communications offers a Communications Media Program leading to either a B.A. or B.S., whereby students are prepared for employment in the administration of educational and professional media programs and the educational use of media in the teaching professions. Courses include "AV Materials Production and Utilization," which focuses on the methods of facilitating learning through the use of pictures, films, radio and television recordings, and "Individualized Multimedia Instructions."

4. The Bowie State College Library is described in entry A12.

5. A catalog of courses is available free upon request.

K5 Catholic University of America—School of Education

1. *Michigan Avenue and Fourth Street, N.E.*
    Washington, D.C. 20064
    (202) 635–5800

2. Raymond J. Steimel, Dean

3. The School of Education offers an undergraduate course, "Audiovisual Methods and Materials for Instruction," which serves as an introduction to theoretical and practical implications relating to the use of media in all areas of instruction.

4. Library facilities are described in entries A15 and A16.

K6 Catholic University of America—School of Library and Information Science

1. *Michigan Avenue and 4th Street, N.E.*
    Washington, D.C. 20064
    (202) 635–5085

2. Raymond F. Vondran, Acting Dean

3. The School of Library and Information Science offers two graduate courses, "Design and Production of Audiovisual Materials" and "Media Services in Libraries," which explore the role of non-print media, including sound recordings and equipment, in all types of libraries and information/media centers.

4. Library facilities are described in entries A15 and A16.

K7 Consortium of Universities of the Washington Metropolitan Area

1. *1346 Connecticut Avenue, N.W., Suite 531*
    Washington, D.C. 20036
    (202) 466-2628

2. Darrell Lemke, Coordinator of Library Programs

3. The major colleges and universities of Washington, D.C., have joined in a co-operative effort for coordinating the use of their facilities and disseminating information on library holdings of each institution. In 1984, an Audiovisual Advisory Committee was formed to discuss ways in which the schools can share in developing non-print media. The member institutions include the American University, the Catholic University of America, Gallaudet College, George Mason University, George Washington University, Georgetown University, Howard University, Mount Vernon College, Trinity College, and the University of the District of Columbia. Under certain conditions, students who are registered at any member institution may take courses for credit at other member institutions. Faculty and graduate degree candidates in the consortium may borrow library materials from the main libraries of the member schools.

4. Combined holdings of the member libraries total 5,500,000 volumes, 3,500,00 items of microform, and 62,000 serial subscriptions.

5. The publications issued by the Consortium of Universities include a *Guide to Libraries* (January 1984), which lists pertinent information for each member school, and a useful reference aid, *Consortium Union List* (4th ed., 1981), which lists alphabetically some 33,289 serial titles totaling approximately 62,330 items held by eight colleges and universities. This list is particularly useful for identifying and comparing periodicals whose subject matter focuses on audiovisuals.

Another recommended reference tool is the *Guide to Library Audio-Visual Facilities in the Libraries of the Consortium of Universities of Washington, D.C.* (August 1981), edited by Diana Vogelsong of the American University Library. Information includes addresses, hours of operation, descriptions of the audiovisual collections, listings of equipment owned, identification of playback facilities, services offered, and statements of use policy.

Another publication, *Consortium Calendar* (bi-monthly), lists all of the significant events, such as lectures and concerts, taking place at the member schools.

Individuals should inquire at any member library's reference desk for these publications.

Foreign Service Institute (State Department)   **See entry L5**

K8   George Mason University—Department of Communication

1.   *4400 University Drive*
     Fairfax, Virginia 22030
     (703) 323–3575

2.   Anita Taylor, Chairperson

3.   The Department of Communication offers a B.A. degree with a major in speech communication. The program prepares the undergraduate student for graduate study and/or a career in four areas of communication, including journalism and mass communication. Courses in this department include "Radio Workshop," "Broadcast Journalism," "Radio Broadcast Operations," and "Broadcast Announcing," as well as a full slate of courses in public and interpersonal communication.

4.   The George Mason University Library collections are described in entry A26.

5.   The university catalog is available from the Admissions Office, Finley Building.

K9   George Mason University—Department of History

1.   *Library Building, Fifth Floor*
     4400 University Drive
     Fairfax, Virginia 22030
     (703) 323–2242

2.   Joseph Lee Harsh, Chairman
     Roy Rosenzweig, Assistant Professor of History and Director of Oral History

3.   Both credit and noncredit courses on the techniques and uses of oral history are taught through the Department of History. Recent examples are "Using Oral History in Your Community," and "An Introduction to Oral History," free courses open to the public.

4.   The relevant collections and research materials of the George Mason University Library are described in entry A26.

5.   The University catalog is available from the Admissions Office, Finley Building.

K10 George Washington University—Department of Education

1.   *2201 G Street, N.W.*
     Washington, D.C. 20052
     (202) 676–6940

2.   John G. Boswell, Chairman

3.   The Department of Education offers a graduate course, "Instructional Materials, Media, and Resources," which serves as an introduction to the selection, evaluation,

and use of audiovisual materials, including the administrative problems in care, operation, maintenance, and use of such materials and equipment.

4. Library facilities are described in entries A27, A28, and A29.

K11 George Washington University—Department of History

1. *Lisner Hall*
    2023 G Street, N.W.
    Washington, D.C. 20052
    (202) 676–6230

2. Charles Herber, Chairman

3. The Department of History in association with the American Studies Program offers an undergraduate course "Oral History and Interview Techniques," which serves as an introduction to theory and practice of obtaining and using historical data through recorded interviews. Included is an examination of major published works on oral history and ongoing oral history projects in the Washington area.

4. George Washington University libraries are described in entries A27, A28, and A29.

K12 Howard University—School of Communications

1. *2400 6th Street, N.W.*
    Washington, D.C. 20059
    (202) 636–7690

2. Lionel C. Barrows, Jr., Dean

3. The School of Communications is composed of the following departments: Communication Arts and Sciences; Journalism; and Radio, Television and Film. Both the Department of Radio, Television and Film and the Department of Journalism offer a B.A. in broadcast production. An M.A. in communication arts, an M.S. in communication sciences, and a Ph.D. in communication arts and sciences are offered through the Graduate School of Arts.

4. Howard University libraries are described in entries A33, A34, A35, and A36.

K13 International Conservatory of Music

1. *1346 Connecticut Avenue, N.W., Office 230-A*
    Washington, D.C. 20036
    (301) 835–9669

2. Tim Healy, Executive Director

3. The conservatory sponsors master classes, symposia, and performances in music. Serving as an educational source for musicians and teachers, these programs frequently feature internationally known artists. For example, Sergiu Natra, foremost composer from Tel Aviv, Israel, was featured in a workshop at the Jewish Community Center's Kreeger auditorium with members of the D.C. Chapter of the American Harp Society; they performed all of Natra's written works for solo concert harp on April 12, 1982.

4. The organization maintains a small collection of reel-to-reel and cassette tapes of various events sponsored by the Conservatory. Included, for example, among the tapes are concerts devoted to "Classical Arabic Music" and "Traditional Music of China," the latter performance was presented by Louis Chen, cheng player from Hong Kong, on February 28, 1982. The conservatory has been the recipient of gifts from various embassies, including, for example, 10 disc recordings of Romanian classical and folk music. Plans are underway for adding a considerable number of tapes to the collection. With special permission, individuals may listen to these recordings. An on-site listening facility is not available.

5. The conservatory publishes *Music Calendar,* which lists scheduled events.

International Masonry Institute Apprenticeship and Training (IMIAT) See entry M35

National Center for Devices and Radiological Health (Health and Human Services Department—Public Health Service—Food and Drug Administration)—Training Resources Center   See entry L8

K14   NAVA, the International Communications Industries Association (NAVA/ICIA)

1. *3150 Spring Street*
   Fairfax, Virginia 22031
   (703) 273–7200

2. Terri Campbell, Program Coordinator

3. NAVA/ICIA's projects in various areas of the audiovisual field are sponsored jointly with the Audiovisual Center of Indiana University, Bloomington, Indiana. Currently, NAVA/ICIA's Audio-Visual Institute for Effective Communications conference is held in March and in October on the campus of Indiana University. It offers a wide variety of courses, including "Production of Sound Use with Visuals," "Audiovisual Facilities Design," and "Managing Media Collections." NAVA/ICIA's Institute for Professional Development conference is held in July also in Bloomington, Indiana. Directed mainly at audiovisual business professionals, it offers courses, such as "Selling and Design of Audio-Visual Facilities." NAVA/ICIA is involved in other programs and activities as well; see entry M48.

5. Flyers describing the above programs are available to interested persons.

K15 School of Advanced International Studies (SAIS) (The Johns Hopkins University)

1. *1740 Massachusetts Avenue, N.W.*
   Washington, D.C. 20036
   (202) 785–6804

2. George R. Packard, Dean
   Susan Crowley, Director of Public Affairs

3. The School of Advanced International Studies is a graduate division of the Johns Hopkins University. SAIS offers a 2-year course of study leading to a master of arts degree. It also offers a degree of Master in International Public Policy and has a small Ph.D. program. The school sponsors numerous public and private lectures and symposia in which visiting scholars, SAIS faculty members, and members of the local diplomatic and foreign policy community participate.

Since 1983 SAIS has been a member of FOCUS (H11), a Washington consortium for public affairs radio programming. Faculty members and others have been interviewed and served as participants in discussions to be broadcast via public radio stations. Among the programs contributed by SAIS have been "U.S.-Japanese Mutual Perceptions," and "NATO," in 1983, and "Central America" in 1984.

K16 Smithsonian Institution—Office of Museum Programs

1. *Arts and Industries Building, Room 2235*
   900 Jefferson Drive, S.W.
   Washington, D.C. 20560
   (202) 357–3101

2. Jane Glaser, Director

3. The goal of the Office of Museum Programs is to share the resources of the Smithsonian with other museum professionals throughout the United States and abroad, and at the same time work to preserve our culture as represented by the Smithsonian collections and research activities. The office conducts workshops and provides internships and a visiting professionals program for training in all areas of museum practices, techniques, and skills. Of particular interest is the Native American Museums Program, which offers workshops, internships, written materials on funding resources, and technical assistance to those individuals involved with American Indian, Eskimo, and Aleut museums. The office also provides career counseling, publishes materials and sponsors national and international conferences on subjects related to the museum profession. The Museum Reference Center (A63), a library of museological information, also serves the Office of Museum Programs.

4. The Office of Museum Programs produces and distributes a number of video tapes and slide cassette programs in conjunction with its various training programs. The primary subject emphasis is on conservation awareness, or preventive care of collections for nonconservators who handle museum materials. Other topics include educational programs in museums, security of museum materials, handling of tribal archives, and museum careers. These 116 programs are available for sale or loan. The office is open to the public from 9:00 A.M. to 5:00 P.M., Monday through Friday.

5. The office has prepared the *Survey of Audiovisual Programs Produced by the Smithsonian Institution* (1982). This is a comprehensive list of films, video tapes, slides, filmstrips, and sound recordings produced by the various offices and museums within the Smithsonian Institution, including what is available for distribution and what is for in-house use. It contains detailed information about each item plus title, subject, medium, and bureau indexes. It will be updated periodically. The booklet is primarily for staff use, but it is available for reading in the Museum Reference Center library in the Office of Museum Programs.

K17 University of Maryland—College of Library and Information Services (CLIS)

1. *Hornbake Library, Room 4105*
   College Park, Maryland 20742
   (301) 454–5441

2. Claude Walston, Dean

3. The College of Library and Information Services offers a course, "Problems of Non-Book Materials," which is an examination of non-book materials, such as audio records, motion pictures, maps, video records, machine-readable data files, and realia. The course also focuses on technical services applicable to non-book material. In addition, the college occasionally offers a minicourse focusing on oral history, such as "Oral History and Folklore Sound Collections," taught in summer 1984.

4. University of Maryland libraries are described in entries A68 and A70.

K18 University of Maryland—Communication Arts and Theatre Program

1. *Tawes Fine Arts Building, Room 1147B*
   College Park Campus
   College Park, Maryland 20742
   (301) 454–3311

2. Patti Gillespie, Chairperson

3. The department offers an M.A., B.A., and a Ph.D. in each of the three following divisions: speech communication; theater; and radio, television and film (RTVF). Both the undergraduate program and the graduate program offer an extensive array of courses in RTVF including "Advanced Sound Production," "Introduction to RTVF," and "RTV Station Management."

4. University of Maryland libraries are described in entries A68 and A70.

K19 University of Maryland—Department of History

1. *Francis Scott Key Hall, Room 2115*
   College Park Campus
   College Park, Maryland 20742
   (301) 454-2843

2. Emory G. Evans, Chairman

3. The Department of History offers an undergraduate course, "Oral History (309E)," and a graduate independent reading course, "Oral History (619G)." Currently, the courses are conducted by Martha Ross (301/454–4203), who is a specialist in the field.

4. The University of Maryland libraries are described in entries A68 and A70.

L United States Government Agencies

Introductory Note

Federal agencies and departments hold some of the more significant collections of sound recordings in Washington, D.C. Most agencies have specialists who are available to provide information about their collections and to discuss individual research projects with scholars.

The manner in which the acquisition, production, and distribution of audio recordings by the federal government is handled is somewhat complex. Historically, the Federal Audiovisual Committee of the Office of Federal Management Policy was established in 1974 to serve as a public advisory committee; it would advise and assist the General Services Administration in the establishment of policies for audiovisual programs and activities within the federal government. Member agencies included the Departments of Agriculture, Commerce, Defense, Education, Health and Human Services, Housing and Urban Development, Interior, Justice, Labor, State, Transportation, and Treasury; Civil Service Commission; Environmental Protection Agency; Federal Communications Commission; General Services Administration; National Aeronautics and Space Administration; U.S. Information Agency; and Veterans Administration.

In 1978 the Office of Management and Budget (OMB), under Executive order, was directed to assume the primary responsibility of prescribing policies and procedures for improving the management of federal audiovisual activitives. OMB issued Circular no. A-114 which established the National Audiovisual Center (NAC) (L7) as the "central information source to the public and federal agencies concerning the availability of audiovisual products produced by or for the government." Circular A-114 also contains guidelines for the production and management of audiovisual products, facilities, and equipment.

Each year all federal agencies involved in administering media programs are also required to submit a report of their activities to NAC, which in turn compiles that information for release in its publication, *Federal Audiovisual Activity*. Researchers can use this report for identifying agencies that are involved in sound recording activities. Information in the report includes a summary of federal audiovisual activity, including dollars expended, acquisitions, production and duplication, and addresses and telephone numbers of the agencies.

For further information on the role of OMB and the implementation of this policy, contact Charles Clark in the Office of Federal Procurement Policy of OMB (202/395–3254). Contact John A. Constance, Chief of the NAC Agency Liaison Staff for further

information on Circular A-114. The Agency Liaison Staff also provides assistance to individual agencies in program management, production, and distribution planning.

Although currently out of print, a key source for identifying the individuals responsible for federal audiovisual programs is *Directory of U.S. Government Audiovisual Personnel* (7th ed., 1980). The directory is organized by agency within each branch of the government, and includes titles, names, and telephone numbers. Yet another useful directory is *Federal Staff Directory* (1984), which lists key personnel associated with various audiovisual programs.

Sound recordings are acquired or produced by the government for various purposes. First, recordings are produced to support programs in various government training facilities, which are usually open only to federal employees. Although most of these recordings are useful only to the individuals associated with these programs, a number of recordings that are considered to have wider application are distributed, for purchase, to the public through the National Audiovisual Center. NAC serves as the central and distribution source for all federal audiovisual productions.

Audio recordings are produced or acquired by federal agencies as part of their day-to-day operations. Some of these recordings are held on-site by various agencies or are added to the holdings of certain government libraries. After a certain amount of time has passed, and, if the recordings have archival value, many of them are retired to the National Archives and Records Service (B27). Copies of some of these recordings are also available, for purchase, to the public from either the National Audiovisual Center or directly from various agencies, including the Library of Congress and the Smithsonian Institution. In certain cases, researchers can arrange to make copies of recordings held in the National Archives.

Audio-related print materials are produced and handled in much the same way, except that they are available to the public through the Government Printing Office (N5) and the National Technical Information Service (N7).

Information regarding recently enacted and pending legislation related to audiovisual matters is cited in *Congressional Quarterly Weekly Report, Congressional Quarterly Almanac,* and the *Federal Register.* For example, in the February 16, 1983 issue, the latter publication cited information regarding recent U.S. import duties legislation for educational non-print materials.

In pursuing their studies, researchers should be aware of the Freedom-of-Information Act (Public Law 89–487 of 1966, as amended by Public Law 93–502 of 1974), which provides that any citizen has the right of access to, and can obtain copies of, any document, file, or other record in the possession of any federal agency or department, with specific exceptions (including certain personnel records and classified documents whose classification can be justified as essential to national security).

In this section, entries are arranged alphabetically by the name of the individual collection or organization. However, functional descriptors precede the generic name; e.g., *Agriculture Department* rather than the *Department of Agriculture.*

Agriculture Department—Radio and Television Division (Office of Governmental and Public Affairs)   See entry H1

**Army Center of Military History (CMH) (Army Department)
See entry B5**

Army Corps of Engineers (Army Department)—Historical Division
See entry B6

L1 Arthritis Information Clearinghouse (Health and Human Services Department—National Institutes of Health—National Institute of Arthritis, Diabetes, and Digestive and Kidney Diseases)

1. *P.O. Box 9782*
Arlington, Virginia 22209
(703) 558-8250

2. Lois Lunin, Project Director

3. The Arthritis Information Clearinghouse collects and disseminates information about print and audiovisual educational materials that focus on arthritis and related musculoskeletal diseases. Specifically, such information deals frequently with patient, public, and professional education, community demonstration programs, and federal programs in the rheumatic diseases.

4-5. The clearinghouse maintains its own database whereby it can create hard copy products consisting of bibliographies, catalogs, and reference sheets. The database contains information on films, microfiche, slides, video tapes, filmstrips, and audio tapes, in single or kit formats. Most of the materials have been released since 1975. The clearinghouse has prepared the *Audiovisual Materials Catalog* (1981), the entries of which have been selected from the database. The catalog lists audio cassette tapes consisting of clinical seminars, courses, and self-learning series on practically every aspect of the field. Listed are 45 separate titles of audio cassettes, 1 audio cassette title with microfiche, 14 audio tapes with filmstrips, and 4 titles of audio tapes with slides. A typical entry includes author, title, source/producer, year of release, physical description, name and address of distributor, rental and purchase costs, and annotation.
A number of bibliographies, guides, federal publications, reference sheets, and catalogs are available from the clearinghouse on request.

Census Bureau (Commerce Department)—Census History Staff
See entry B9

Commerce Department—Broadcast Branch (News Relations Division) See entry H8

Education Department—Office of Educational Research and Improvement
See entry B13

Energy Department (DOE)—History Division See entry B14

L2   Federal Judicial Center

1.   *Dolly Madison House*
      1520 H Street, N.W.
      Washington, D.C. 20005
      (202) 633–6415

2.   A. Leo Levin, Director
      Kenneth C. Crawford, Director, Division of Education and Training

3.   The Federal Judicial Center, established in 1967, conducts research, development, and training within the federal judicial system. Its four divisions include the Research Division, the Division of Innovations and Systems Development, the Division of Inter-Judicial Affairs and Information Services, and the Continuing Education and Training Division.

4.   The Federal Judicial Center maintains a Media Library within the Media Services Unit. The library lends materials to federal court employees only. Included in the library are some 1,800 titles, which consist of seminars and workshops dealing primarily with legal issues recorded on audio cassette tapes. Subjects represented in the collection include constitutional law, civil rights law, anti-trust law, bankruptcy law, appellate matters, and case and court management. These topics are discussed by well-known professors, judges, and practicing attorneys. There are also a few cassette tapes dealing with non-legal topics, including office management and personnel issues. Library hours are from 9:00 A.M. to 5:30 P.M., Monday through Friday. On-site listening equipment is available to qualified researchers who have obtained permission from the center's director to use the library.

L3   Federal Reserve System—Board of Governors

1.   *20th Street and Constitution Avenue, N.W.*
      Washington, D.C. 20551
      (202) 452–3000

2.   Paul A. Volcker, Chairman

3.   The Federal Reserve System is the United States' central bank. It is comprised of a seven-member Board of Governors located in Washington, D.C., and 12 Federal Reserve Banks and their 25 branches. The Federal Reserve's purpose is to conduct monetary policy and to assist in maintaining a commercial banking system and a payments mechanism that are stable and flexible to meet the nation's domestic and international financial needs and objectives.

4–5.   As part of its public awareness program, the Federal Reserve System has produced a number of films and filmstrips/with accompanying audio cassettes, designed for educators, bankers, economists, and the general public. These materials focus on the history of banking, inflation, economy, the Federal Reserve in action, and other topics. All of the audiovisual materials currently available are listed in the catalog *Public Information Materials* (October 1983); they are generally loaned free of charge, except for a few titles, which are available for purchase. Individuals must refer to this

catalog in order to determine which Federal Reserve Banks distribute materials listed in the catalog.

The Federal Reserve publishes and distributes a variety of publications, including periodicals, reports, and newsletters, many of which are available free of charge. Useful publications include *The Federal Reserve System: Purposes and Functions* (1984); *Historical Beginnings . . . The Federal Reserve* (1977); and *Monetary Policy Objectives* (published semi-annually). Contact the Publications Services Office at the above address for copies of publications and catalogs. Researchers may also want to visit the Research Library of the Board of Governors (Ann Roane Clary, Chief Librarian; 202/452–3332). The library does not hold any audiovisual materials.

Food and Drug Administration (FDA)—Medical Library   See entry A24

L4   Food and Nutrition Information Center (FNIC) (Agriculture Department—National Agricultural Library)

1.   *10301 Baltimore Boulevard, Room 304*
     Beltsville, Maryland 20705
     (301) 344–3719 (24-hour answering service)

2.   Robyn Frank, Director
     Pam Kosh, Audio Visual Coordinator

3.   The Food and Nutrition Information Center's holdings include print and nonprint materials focusing on human nutrition research and education, food service management, foods, and food technology. The audiovisual collection includes motion picture films, filmstrips, slides, film loops, posters, charts, games, transparencies, and audio recordings. Materials contained in the collection represent diversified opinions regarding nutrition.

4–5.   The audiovisual materials held by FNIC are listed in various publications: Audiovisual materials acquired by FNIC from 1973 to 1978 are cited in *Audiovisual Resources in Food and Nutrition* (Phoenix, Arizona: Oryx Press, 1979). The entries cited in this compilation were taken from cataloging records prepared by FNIC for the National Agricultural Library's AGRICOLA (G1) database covering 1973–1978 acquisitions. The compilation is fully annotated including title, author, publisher, place, date, descriptors used in indexing the item, and an abstract of the intellectual contents of the item. The guide has author, title, media, and subject indexes. The Media Index is particularly useful in that it lists all of the items that are available on audio tape format. There are 96 audio tapes listed in this section. Other sections in the Media Index include disc recordings of which 5 titles are cited, filmstrips, and slides, many of which are accompanied by either cassette or disc recordings. Some of the topics treated on the sound recordings include nutrition (all aspects), herbal medicine, communications and nutrition, management, vegetarianism, metric measurement and dietetics, obesity, food, population and environment, quackery, behavior therapy, and allergies and food. When using this guide be sure to check entries under the term "Audiovisual" in the Subject Index. An update to this guide is scheduled for publication in 1984 by the Oryx Press.

Meanwhile, FNIC has prepared "Audiovisual Resources Update," a printout that

lists acquisitions received through December 22, 1981. Most, if not all of FNIC audiovisual items are available on a loan basis. The center accepts lending requests by mail, telephone, and on-site visit. Researchers are encouraged to contact the center for additional information on its loan procedures.

Another source, *Food and Nutrition Bibliography*, 10th ed. (Phoenix, Arizona: Oryx Press, 1982), covers materials collected by FNIC in 1979. Included are filmstrips, slides, kits, and motion pictures. The 11th edition, which covers acquisitions during 1980, was published in 1984. Before visiting the center, researchers may obtain a free copy of *FINC: A User's Guide to the Food and Nutrition Information Center.*

L5 **Foreign Service Institute (FSI) (State Department)**

1. *1400 Key Boulevard*
   Arlington, Virginia 22209
   (703) 235–8750
   (703) 235–08759

2. Stephen Low, Director
   John T. Sprott, Deputy Director
   Eloise Shouse, Staff Aide

3. The Foreign Service Institute was created by Congress in 1946 to provide training to employees of the Department of State and other U.S. government agencies involved in foreign affairs. Each year over 20,000 students enroll full or part-time in about 145 FSI courses offered through the Schools of Professional Studies, Area Studies, and Language Studies.

4–5. The School of Language Studies offers intensive language training in Washington in some 40 languages. Part-time programs also are conducted in Washington and at some 200 overseas posts in about 60 languages. In order to maintain this comprehensive program, the institute has an Audio-Visual Division, including a language laboratory, where audio materials for every language are prepared for use within the institute. This facility is not open to the public.

Many of the audio materials prepared by FSI are available for purchase through the National Audiovisual Center (L7). Individuals can request the NAC catalog, *A List of Audiovisual Materials Produced by the United States Government for Foreign Language Instruction* (1983) where no less than 1,550 "Basic," "Introductory," and "Programmatic" cassette tapes and accompanying texts are available in 39 languages. FSI audio tapes are also cited in *A Reference List of Audiovisual Materials Produced by the United States Government* (National Audiovisual Center, 1978; supplement, 1980).

FSI has its own library (William Bennett, Librarian, 703/235–8717) but it holds no audiovisual materials.

Forest Service (Agriculture Department)—History Section
See entry B16

Government Printing Office (GPO)   **See entry N5**

L6   National Aeronautics and Space Administration (NASA)

1.   *400 Maryland Avenue, S.W.*
     Washington, D.C. 20546
     (202) 453–1000

2.   James M. Beggs, Administrator

3.   National Aeronautics and Space Administration activities include the arranging of scientific resources of the U.S. with other nations engaged in aeronautical projects for peaceful purposes. It disseminates information concerning its activities and results. NASA also maintains a comprehensive historical archives of its activities, and contracts with outside researchers and consultants.

4.   Collections and research facilities of the administration.

Broadcast and Audiovisual Branch
400 Maryland Avenue, S.W.
Washington, D.C. 20546
(202) 453–8375

8:00 A.M.–4:30 P.M.   Monday–Friday

Joseph L. Headlee, Chief

Open to the public. This is the principal unit of NASA that records and produces audio tapes of all-NASA related programs. The public is not allowed to borrow or listen to these tapes on-site. However, many of the tapes are available through the National Audiovisual Center (L7). The following NASA radio programs are released on broadcast quality audio cassettes to thousands of radio stations, nationwide.
   The Space Story. A weekly 4½-minute series of topical programs featuring people, projects, and sounds of the space age; mailed every four weeks, released in sets of four.
   NASA Special Report. A monthly 14½-minute series of actuality documentaries featuring detailed treatment of a particular story of current interest. All upcoming Space Shuttle missions are covered by these programs.
   NASA Audio News Feature. Periodic sets of interview features released prior to major events.
   NASA Space Notes. 60-second informational announcements issued in sets of ten, and updated every three months.
   Some of these tapes also include Space Age Sound Effects highlights of 11 Apollo missions, the Apollo-Soyuz mission, Gemini and Mercury missions, 4 Skylab missions, and Space Shuttle missions.
   The U.S. news media are provided with ready access to the collection. Each service can be provided with one free copy of a program in the collection. Currently NASA supplies 3,000 radio stations with cassettes each month. This department also maintains a photo library of over one million items and produces a monthly video tape for Media (TV) distribution only.

History Office Archives
7th & D Streets, S.W., Room 706
Washington, D.C. 20546
(202) 453–8303

8:00 A.M.–4:30 P.M.   Monday–Friday

Sylvia D. Fries, Director
Lee D. Saegesser, Archivist

The NASA History Office maintains an archives, publishes histories and reference books by its staff and contractors, assists outside researchers, and advises NASA field installations on their historical activities. The holdings of the archives include periodical clippings, press releases, reports, correspondence, and oral history tapes and transcripts.

The oral history reel-to-reel and cassette tapes with transcripts were produced for the most part under contracts for books being written on the history of NASA and include interviews with several hundred individuals, all of whom are associated with aeronautics either directly or indirectly. Included are NASA administrators, astronauts, scientists, government personnel, etc. Examples of persons interviewed include James H. Doolittle, Benjamin Foulois, John Glenn, Dr. George E. Mueller, Gen. Samuel Phillips, Alan Shepard, Dr. Ed C. Welsh, James E. Webb, Thomas O. Paine, Robert C. Seamons, Dr. Hugh R. Dryden, George M. Low, Dr. Homer Newell, Willis Shapley, Dr. Wernher von Braun, Dr. John Naugle, Jerome C. Hunsaker, Glover Loening, and Richard Whitcomb.

The earliest interviews focus on the activities of the National Advisory Committee for Aeronautics in 1915. Most interviews, however, date from the 1960s to the present. The transcripts are available to qualified researchers and are arranged in the biography file alphabetically by name of person and thereunder chronologically. Additional oral history materials related to NASA are included in the Oral History Program of the Office of Air Force History (B37).

5.   The most useful introduction to the History Office holdings is *A Guide to Research in NASA History* (6th ed., 1982), available to individuals upon request. The examples of cassettes of mission flights in the Broadcast and Audiovisual Branch described above are listed in the branch's catalog, *NASA Films* (1982), which is also available to individuals. Also useful is *NASA/1980 Photography Index*. Persons interested in the most current technical information on magnetic tape recording should refer to *Magnetic Tape Recording for the Eighties* (NASA Reference Publication 1075; April 1982) prepared by the Tape Head Interface Committee and produced by NASA's Scientific and Technical Information Branch.

Labor Department Library   See entry A40

National Aeronautics and Space Administration (NASA)—Headquarters Library   See entry A50

L7   National Audiovisual Center (NAC) (National Archives and Records Service—General Services Administration)

1.   *8700 Edgeworth Drive*
     Capital Heights, Maryland 20743
     (301) 763–1896 (301) 763–1891 (Order Section)

Mail:
National Audiovisual Center
Information Services Center
Washington, D.C. 20409

2. John McLean, Director

3. The National Audiovisual Center is the central information and distribution source for more than 13,000 films, videocassettes, filmstrips, audio/slide sets, sound recordings, and other media produced by and for federal agencies for public use. For researchers who wish to identify federal agencies that produce audiovisual materials, NAC serves as an ideal source of referral. Although printed materials issued by the center are the primary means of keeping individuals informed about federal media programs, the Information Services staff will respond to telephone or written inquiries. Other public services include research and special presentations, and, if requested, on-site previews of available programs for persons seriously interested in purchasing.

Individuals will find that the Center's subject concentrations are varied, including medicine, library science, aerospace science, education, language, mental health, women's studies, health and safety, science and technology, environment and energy issues, administration, and labor. A partial list of agencies which produce or sponsor audiovisual programs include:

Coast Guard
Department of Energy
Disaster Preparedness Staff (National Weather Service)
Division of Dental Health (National Institutes of Health)
Environmental Protection Agency
Food and Drug Administration
Foreign Service Institute
National Air and Space Museum
National Cancer Institute
National Center on Child Abuse and Neglect (Department of Health, Education, and
 Welfare)
National Highway Traffic Safety Administration
National Institute of Allergy and Infectious Diseases
National Institute of Education
National Institute of Mental Health
National Library of Medicine
National Medical Audiovisual Center
Occupational Safety and Health Administration
Office of Federal Equal Employment Opportunity (Civil Service Commission)
Public Health Service
Right to Read Program (Office of Education)
Women's Bureau (Department of Labor)

Audiovisual programs produced or sponsored by the above agencies are cited in the publications described in category 5.

4. It is not possible to list every audiovisual program distributed by NAC, but descriptions of some of the significant series are noted: *The Makings of a Modern Library* consists of a three-part selection of instructional kits, which assist individuals in obtaining a foundation in library science. Included are 10 audio cassettes, which provide an introduction to basic reference tools, and 6 audio cassettes/ with slides, which focus on the maintenance and preservation of non-book materials; both are sponsored by

the Office of Education. Useful also is *Development of a Slide-Tape Instructional Presentation* (1979) produced by the National Medical Audiovisual Center (NMAC). Other programs distributed by NAC include some 1,550 audio cassettes, produced by the Foreign Service Institute (FSI) (L5), for instruction in 39 languages, and the series *Flight,* produced by the National Air and Space Museum (NASM) (C6), consisting of 21 audio cassettes with filmstrips, which focus on the history of aviation and space exploration. Individuals should also be alerted to the extensive number of slide/tape presentations on medicine produced by the National Medical Audiovisual Center (NMAC).

5.   The National Audiovisual Center's flyer *The Central Source* serves as a useful introduction to the programs and services provided by the center. NAC issues a variety of publications that assist individuals in identifying federal agencies involved in producing audiovisual materials. Each year all federal agencies involved in administering media programs are required by law to submit a report of their activities to NAC, which in turn compiles that information for release in its publication *Federal Audiovisual Activity.* Information in the report includes a summary of federal audiovisual activity, including dollars expended, acquisitions, production, and duplication of audiovisual materials, and an appendix that lists agencies, including addresses and telephone numbers, which were involved in media programs for the respective fiscal year.

The principal publication for identifying individual audiovisual materials, including sound recordings, is *A Reference List of Audiovisual Materials Produced by the United States Government* (1978; supplement, 1980). Each entry includes the name of producer/sponsor of item, with both a physical and content description of the item. The publication, *Directory of U.S. Government Audiovisual Personnel* (7th ed., 1980), which is out of print, lists most of each federal agency's key audiovisual personnel, including addresses and telephone numbers, who are involved in television, motion pictures, still photography, sound recordings, and exhibits.

Other publications, such as booklets and flyers that list and describe audiovisual programs on specific topics, include *A List of Audiovisual Materials Produced by the United States Government for Foreign Language Instruction* (1980), *A List of Audiovisual Materials Produced by the United States Government for Library and Information Science* (1980), *Kits for Education* (1982), *Medical Catalog of Selected Audiovisual Materials Produced by the United States Government, 1980,* and *A List of Audiovisual Materials Produced by the United States Government: Spanish Language Soundtracks* (1980).

NAC maintains a Master Data File, which is the central resource for all federal audiovisual activity, and includes information on withdrawn titles and other programs for which no duplicating materials exist, as well as those which are available. Inquiries concerning this file should be directed to the Information Services Center.

National Bureau of Standards (NBS) (Commerce Department)—Library and Information Division   See entry A51

L8 **National Center for Devices and Radiological Health (Health and Human Services Department—Public Health Service—Food and Drug Administration)**

1. *12720 Twinbrook Parkway*
    Rockville, Maryland 20857
    (301) 443–1038

2. John C. Villforth, Director

3. The National Center for Devices and Radiological Health is involved in a national program to control unnecessary human exposure to potentially hazardous ionizing and nonionizing radiation and to ensure safe use of radiation. The center disseminates its information and research in scientific journals and in its own technical reports.

    The bureau maintains a library (Room 408-T), which has a number of books, journals, and non-print materials. Although the library contains no audio recordings, it does maintain a very small collection of reference books on audiovisuals. The books are easily accessed by scanning the subject catalog under such terms as" Audiovisual" and "Sound Recordings."

4. Collections and research facilities of the center.

Training Resources Center, HFX-73
5600 Fishers Lane
Rockville, Maryland 20857
(301) 443–4647

William S. Properzio, Acting Director

Through its Training Resources Center, the National Center is able to effectively assist radiation control personnel and user groups in greater numbers. The center produces movies, video cassettes, and audio cassettes.

5. A number of publications that will assist researchers in identifying audiovisual materials are available from the center. One such source, *Radiological Health Training Resources Catalog 1983* (HHS pub. FDA 83-8023), lists video materials and self-learning packages having audio cassettes. Examples of these kits include: *Radiation Protection during Medical X-ray Examinations, Dental Radiology,* and *Radiation Protection for Nuclear Medicine Procedures,* and are available from the National Audiovisual Center (L7). Another publication, *Sourcebook: Medical Radiation Material for Patients* (HHS pub. FDA 80-8113), lists a few audio cassettes on radiation that are available from sources outside the D.C. area. Information on recent audiovisual materials produced by the center is included regularly in its *Bulletin.*

L9 **National Clearinghouse for Alcohol Information (NCALI) (Health and Human Services Department—Public Health Service—Alcohol, Drug Abuse, and Mental Health Administration—National Institute on Alcohol Abuse and Alcoholism)**

1. *1776 East Jefferson Street, Fourth Floor*
    Rockville, Maryland 20852
    (301) 468–2600

Mail:
P.O. Box 2345
Rockville, Maryland 20852

2.   Molly Wolfe, Program Director

3.   The National Clearinghouse for Alcohol Information collects information on studies and programs related to prevention, training, and treatment of alcohol abuse and alcoholism. Its goal is to make available current information to professional audiences, as well as the general public. Clearinghouse activities include an active publications program, providing literature searches of computerized files containing citations and abstracts for documents in the sciences and humanities related to alcoholism.

4.   The clearinghouse maintains a library and reading room having reference and referral services. The head of reference services is Leonor Burts (301/468–2253). Hours are from 9:00 A.M. to 5:30 P.M., Monday through Friday. The library has a small collection of audio tapes, films, filmstrips, and slides dealing with alcoholism. Typical examples include *The Big Fight 1974–75),* produced by Human Resources Association, and consisting of 12 tapes dealing with alcoholism prevention and treatment, and *No Power* (1981–1982), the alcohol control kit.

5.   Clearinghouse publications include two subscription services, which provide the reader with current information on research reports and reviews of new books, *Alcohol Health and Research World* (quarterly), and *Alcohol Awareness Service* (bi-monthly). A number of flyers and brochures are available free to interested individuals from the clearinghouse.

National Defense University (NDU) (Defense Department)—Library
See entry A53

L10   National Endowment for the Arts (NEA)—Media Arts: Film/Radio/ Television Program

1.   *1100 Pennsylvania Avenue, N.W.*
Washington, D.C. 20506
(202) 682–5452

2.   Maria R. Goodwin, Program Specialist

3.   The National Endowment for the Arts is an independent federal agency established by Congress in 1965 to encourage and assist the nation's cultural resources. The endowment is advised by the National Council of the Arts, a presidentially appointed body consisting of a chairman and 26 distinguished private citizens who are each well known in the arts.
    The Media Arts: Film/Radio/Television Program assists in supporting those organizations and individuals who seek to bring all the arts to a wide public through broadcast. In so doing, new work by artists of exceptional talent is encouraged while giving millions of citizens the opportunity to watch and hear our greatest performers and artists.

4. Some of the Washington area broadcasting organizations that have been funded by NEA include National Public Radio (B33), Borrowed Time Productions, Corporation for Public Broadcasting (H9), Feminist Radio Network, The New Classroom, Washington Ear, Inc. (F22) Watershed Foundation, and Radio Station WETA (Appendix III).

Copies of films, video tapes and audio tapes (mostly cassettes) produced under grants from NEA are held in the NEA archives. To date there are in the archives some 300 audio cassettes, many of which consist of radio programs, and 100–200 additional tapes are added each year. A number of video productions that focus on dance, music, drama, and crafts are also available at the Motion Picture, Broadcasting and Recorded Sound Division of the Library of Congress (A41).

5. Publications available to individuals from NEA include *Application Guidelines* for grants, and a list of *Grants in Radio* for the years 1971–1981.

L11 National Endowment for the Humanities (NEH)

1. *1100 Pennsylvania Avenue, N.W.*
    Washington, D.C. 20506
    (202) 786–0438

2. William J. Bennett, Chairman

3. The National Endowment for the Humanities is an independent federal agency established by Congress in 1965 to promote and support research and other activities in the humanities. NEH provides grants to individuals, groups, and institutions through its five divisions: Education Programs; Fellowships and Seminars; General Programs; Research Programs; and State Programs. The Office of Planning and Policy Studies is also involved in grant provision.

4. Collections and Research facilities of the endowment.

DIVISION OF GENERAL PROGRAMS
Media Program
Room 426
(202) 786–0278

Richard M. Huber, Assistant Director of Division

Since 1972, the Media Program has supported over 480 hours of television and 360 hours of radio programs for national and regional (radio) broadcast. Of these at least 13 documentaries and series produced in cassette format have been produced in part from grants supplied by NEH. A number of these cassette radio series have been produced and/or distributed by National Public Radio (B33), including *A Question of Place* (1980), a documentary radio series that examines twelve key thinkers in modern history, and *The World of F. Scott Fitzgerald* (1979), consisting of eight cassette programs co-produced by National Radio Theater of Chicago. NEH retains one copy of projects such as the above which are funded through the Media Program.

DIVISION OF RESEARCH PROGRAMS
Research Resources Program
Room 319
(202) 786–0200

Harold Canon, Director of Division

The Research Resource Program supports oral history documentation projects. Copies of projects that have been funded in the past are maintained as an archival collection. A finding list is not currently available.

NEH maintains a small library of books and periodicals, and publications that have resulted from NEH grants. The library is open to the public for reference use only from 9:00 A.M. to 5:30 P.M., Monday through Friday.

5. The Public Affairs Office has recently published its *Media Log: A Guide to Television, Film & Radio Programs Supported by the National Endowment for the Humanities.* This catalog describes in detail over 315 productions supported by NEH, and provides names and addresses for media distributors. In addition, the Public Affairs Office publishes an *NEH Annual Report* containing detailed information on programs and grants, and a number of tree brochures and pamphlets having information on programs and deadlines for grant applications. Individuals may also be interested in the NEH bimonthly journal *Humanities,* available by subscription.

L12 National Health Information Clearinghouse (NHIC) (Health and Human Services Department—Public Health Service—Office of Disease Prevention and Health Promotion)

1. *1555 Wilson Boulevard, Suite 600*
   Arlington, Virginia 22209
   (703) 522–2590
   (800) 336–4797 (toll-free)

   Mail:
   P.O. Box 1133
   Washington, D.C. 20013

2. Joanne Angle, Director

3–4. The National Health Information Clearinghouse identifies groups and organizations that provide health information to the public. NHIC provides information on health resources, but does not give medical advice. An in-house database contains descriptions of about 2,000 health-related organizations and programs throughout the country, including some 250 organizations that have audiovisual materials. An individual may request a particular search that, if successful, produces a printout containing several labeled paragraphs of information, including that concerning audio materials. An example of a Washington organization included in the database is the American Council of the Blind (F3). Its printout includes such information as location, telephone number, abstract of the organization's function, list of the council's publications, and keywords used in indexing the entry. Inquiries regarding the clearinghouse services can be made during the hours 8:30 A.M. to 5:00 P.M., Monday through Friday.

5. The clearinghouse has available to individuals resource guides on a variety of health topics, such as a list of toll-free telephone numbers for health information resources throughout the country.

National Institute of Education (NIE) (Education Department)—Educational Research Library   See entry A54

L13 National Institute of Justice (Justice Department)—National Criminal Justice Reference Service (NCJRS)

1. *1600 Research Boulevard, Second Floor*
    Rockville, Maryland 20850
    (301) 251–5500

    Mail:
    P.O. Box 6000
    Rockville, Maryland 20850

2. James K. Stewart, Director, National Institute of Justice

3. The National Criminal Justice Reference Service is a centralized information resource on all aspects of criminal justice, juvenile justice, law enforcement and court administration service practitioners, researchers, students, and the general public. NCJRS also offers assistance to libraries that want to improve service to the criminal justice community, as well as maintaining extensive document loan and conference support programs.

4. The NCJRS collection of materials include some 73,000 documents in both printed and microform formats. In addition, holdings include films, video tapes, slide/cassette kits, and audio reel-to-reel and cassette tapes.

    The audio recordings total over 60 titles and focus on a variety of criminal justice topics, produced by both public and private organizations, including the American Association for the Advancement of Science (J3), Center for the Study of Democratic Institutions, and National Council of Juvenile and Family Court Judges. Notable series in the collection include the second and third *National Conference on Juvenile Justice, Crime and American Society (proceedings of the 1977 convocation of the Center for the Study of Democratic Institutions),* and the *National Symposium on Child Placement, 1978.* These and other audio tapes may be borrowed through inter-library loan. Individuals should contact local, academic, or agency libraries to borrow documents. To verify holdings, telephone Customer Service, (301) 251–5500. NCJRS maintains a reading room which is open to the public, 8:30 A.M. to 5:15 P.M., Monday through Friday.

5. There are a number of NCJRS catalogs and other publications that researchers will find useful. The *Directory of Criminal Justice Information Sources* (September 1981) lists repositories that hold audiovisual materials. Available, for purchase, is *Audiovisual Materials: A Listing of Criminal Justice Films and Videotapes from the NCJRS Collection,* whose 2d edition (1983) lists some 400 titles available for loan and *Document Retrieval Index* (microfiche) and its four supplements, together covering 1972 to the present. Announcements for selective recent documents and audiovisual

materials added to the NCJRS database are listed in *NIJ Reports* which is issued bimonthly.

A number of flyers describing NCJRS programs and services are available free upon request.

National Oceanic and Atmospheric Administration (NOAA) (Commerce Department)—Office of Public Affairs   See entry H9

National Technical Information Service (NTIS) (Commerce Department) See entry N7

L14   National Trust for Historic Preservation (NTHP)

1.   *1785 Massachusetts Avenue, N.W.*
      Washington, D.C. 20036
      (202) 673–4000

2.   Michael L. Ainslie, President

3.   The National Trust for Historic Preservation, established in 1949, is the only national, private non-profit organization chartered by Congress with the responsibility for encouraging public participation in the preservation of sites, buildings and objects significant in American history and culture. The National Trust sponsors a number of conferences and workshops and disseminates information on local, state, and national preservation programs.

4.   The organization maintains an audiovisual library as part of its Information Services Division. Audio tapes are primarily from National Trust sponsored conferences. The library is open to National Trust members, by appointment, 9:00 A.M. to 5:00 P.M., Monday through Friday. Call Cary Schneider, Librarian, at (202) 673–4038.

5.   Some of the significant publications of the National Trust include *Preservation News* (monthly), *Historic Preservation* (bimonthly), *Conserve Neighborhoods* (six issues per year), *Preservation Law Reporter* (bimonthly).

Naval Air Systems Command—Technical Library (Navy Department)   See entry A57

Office of Information and Resources for the Handicapped (Education Department)—Clearinghouse on the Handicapped   See entry F15

Office of Personnel Management Library   See entry A59

Soil Conservation Service (SCS) (Agriculture Department)   See entry B46

State Department—Bureau of Public Affairs—Office of the Historian   See entry B47

Voice of America (VOA) (U.S. Information Agency)—Music and Tape Libraries   See entry A72

M Associations (Academic, Professional, Cultural)

Introductory Note

Associations that have Washington offices number in the hundreds. Moreover, each year numerous organizations open new offices in the Washington area. A considerable number of associations record their convention meetings, presentations by guest speakers, and other events related to their operational activities and programs. Many of these recordings are available for purchase. Other associations have prepared audiovisual instructional materials as part of their educational programs, ranging from management to sociology and medical sciences. The best source for identifying associations is *Encyclopedia of Associations, 1985* edited by Denise S. Akey (19th ed. Detroit: Gale Research Company, 1984), 2 volumes in 3.

For a list of associations that produce audiovisual materials, see *Associations' Publications in Print 1984* (New York: R. R. Bowker, 1983). Relevant materials are cited in the subject index under the headings "Audio-Visual" and "Oral History."

M1 Air Force Association (AFA)

1. *1501 Lee Highway*
    Arlington, Virginia 22209
    (703) 247–5800 (Information)
    (202) 637–3333 (Communications)

2. Russell E. Dougherty, Executive Director

3. The Air Force Association (founded in 1946) is a national, non-profit, non-political organization, which supports "a strong national defense posture for the security and peace of the nation and the free world and is dedicated to the application of aerospace technology for the betterment of all mankind." It has more than 200,000 members, many of whom are organized in chapters in all 50 states and abroad.

4.   The Communications Department has tape recordings of national AFA symposia on national security issues (AFA conducts seven a year throughout the nation), speeches, addresses and keynotes of senior government and military leaders. The materials are currently in storage, under the supervision of Robin Whittle, Director, Communications Department. With special permission, it may be possible for qualified researchers to gain access to the collection. AFA also maintains a research library, which is open to researchers. Holdings include some 2,000 books, with an emphasis on military aviation and history and Congressional hearings on the military budget. Library hours are from 9:00 A.M. to 5:30 P.M., Monday through Friday. Contact Pearlie Draughn, librarian (703/247–5800), for additional information.

5.   AFA publishes a monthly magazine, *Air Force*. A brochure describing the AFA is available upon request.

Alexander Graham Bell Association for the Deaf (AGB)   See entry F1

M2   American Association for Counseling and Development (AACD)

1.   *5999 Stevenson Avenue*
       Alexandria, Virginia 22304
       (703) 823–9800

2.   Patrick McDonough, Executive Vice-President

3.   The American Association for Counseling and Development represents more than 40,000 professional counselors and related human development specialists who work in the nation's schools, colleges, mental health agencies, rehabilitation programs, community agencies, business, industry, and private practice settings. Services of the AACD are varied including annual conventions, professional development workshops, and an extensive publications program, including books and periodicals, films, and audio recordings.

4.   The AACD has a library containing current publications, periodicals, and reports.

5.   Currently, the AACD has available, for purchase, the following audio cassette series: *Counseling for Personal Mastery* (8 cassettes by John Vriend and Wayne W. Dyer, 1974). The *Counseling Resource Catalog* (1984) is available upon request.

American Association for the Advancement of Science (AAAS)
See entry J3

M3   American Association of Blood Banks (AABB)

1.   *1117 North 19th Street, Suite 600*
       Arlington, Virginia 22209
       (703) 528–8200

2.   Joyce Duncan, Publications Manager

3.   The American Association of Blood Banks, founded in 1947, is a non-profit scientific and administrative organization devoted to blood banking and blood transfusion services. The association consists of institutions and individuals, and offers a variety of services. For example, it fosters scientific investigation, clinical application, education, and the exchange of information relating to the field of blood banking.

4.   The association achieves its goal, in part, by having available for distribution a variety of publications, including books, manuals, journals, and audiovisual materials. Available for purchase from the association are a number of *Radio Spots* discussing the need for blood.

5.   AABB publishes a scientific journal, *Transfusion,* and a monthly bulletin, *News Briefs.* Various brochures and catalogs are available free upon request.

M4   American Association of Community and Junior Colleges (AACJC)

1.   *One Dupont Circle, N.W., Suite 410*
Washington, D.C. 20036
(202) 293-7050

2.   Mark Winter, Public Sales Manager
Rosemarie Wallers, Librarian

3.   The American Association of Community and Junior Colleges plays a vital role in promoting two-year community-based colleges, while serving as a forum for administrators, faculty, and trustees to express concerns and interests. A research and data office collects and disseminates information on national trends and developments.

4.   AACJC maintains a library, which contains some 200–300 audio cassettes, among other materials. The tapes are not cataloged and do not circulate. Researchers must telephone or write in advance for an appointment to listen to the tapes. Included among these recordings are public service announcements, tapes of annual conventions, and interviews from radio stations. The emphasis is on education.
The association also distributes, for purchase, a number of sound recordings. For example, it made available 91 cassettes of forums and special sessions of the AACJC 1981 annual convention whose theme was the "Shaping of Society: The Community College Role." Among these tapes are the following representative examples: *Telecommunications and the Adult Learner: Projects and Prospects for the Future* (no. 81185–090); *Summer College for Gifted Kids: A Response to Community Needs* (no. 81185–160); *Community Colleges and the Law: The Shape of Things to Come* (no. 81185–190); *Cable TV: The Future is Now* (no. 81185–480); *Faculty Renewal and the Art of Teaching* (no. 81185–500); *Dynamics of a Successful Fund-Raising Program for a Fine Arts Center* (no. 81185–550); *Thinking About Women Today* (no. 81185–610); *1980 International World Futurist Conference Report: Implications for Community College Planning* (no. 81185–770); *Report of the Commission on the Humanities: Issues and Implementation* (no. 81185–810); *Industrial Program Development and Management* (no. 81185–850); *Two Models for Linking Community Colleges and Community Agencies Serving the Disabled* (no. 81185–860); *How to Work Effectively with State Legislatures* (no. 81185–870); *Women's Programs: New Clients, New Delivery, New Applications* (no. 81185–890); *The National Human Services Consortium* (no. 81185–900). Similarly, 56 cassettes were taped at the 1982 annual Convention

("Opportunity with Excellence: A College and Community Partnership"), and 82 cassettes at the 1983 annual convention ("High Technology: Policies, Programs, and People"). The audio cassettes from the 1982 and 1983 conventions are available for purchase from ACTS, 1025 East Clayton Road, Ballwin, Missouri 63011 (telephone 314/394–0611).

5. AACJC publishes *Community and Junior College Journal* (eight times per year), a newsletter, *AACJC Letter,* and the annual *Community, Technical, and Junior College Directory.* Flyers describing services and programs are available on request.

M5 American Association of Sex Educators, Counselors and Therapists (AASECT)

1. *11 Dupont Circle, N.W., Suite 220*
    Washington, D.C. 20036
    (202) 462–1171

2. Virginia Castle, Administrative Director

3. The American Association of Sex Educators, Counselors and Therapists is devoted to developing professional competency and ethical and training standards for sex educators, counselors, and therapists. The organization's central mission is the dissemination of knowledge in sexology, as well as research into aspects of the specialty to benefit the public and the profession.

4–5. Although AASECT does not have a library available to the public, it does offer for purchase a variety of audio cassettes on various aspects of the discipline. The following citations are examples of tapes produced by AASECT, and are abstracted from presentations at national sex institutes by authorities in the fields of sex education, counseling, and therapy: *The Evolution of Leadership Organization in the Developing World: International Family Planning and Sex Education* (Marilyn E. Schima; no. G14); *Family Planning Attitudes among Blacks in a Rural Population* (Walter Farrell, Jr. and Marvin P. Dawkins; G17); *Biofeedback Principles and Technology in Sex Research, Diagnosis and Therapy* (Richard A. Pigott; D10); *Instruments to Measure Attitudes towards Abortion and Knowledge of Abortion* (Stanley Snegroff; E14); *Sex and the Law* (Frank Susman; E16); *Audio/Visual Sex Education* (Milton Diamond; F7); *Teaching Sexual Communication in the Classroom* (Marilyn Mason and Bruce Fisher; F49); *Shere Hite Keynote Address* (F51); *Cognitive Methods of Sex Therapy* (Albert Ellis; F59).

AASECT publishes the *Journal of Sex Education and Therapy* (semiannual), as well as the *AASECT Letter,* and an annual *National Register* of AASECT certified sex educators, counselors, and therapists. Catalogs listing some 130 tape recordings are available on request from the above address.

M6 American Association of University Women (AAUW)

1. *2401 Virginia Avenue, N.W.*
    Washington, D.C. 20037
    (202) 785–7700
    (202) 785–7763 (Library)

2.   Mary Purcell, President
Nancy Floyd, Library Information Assistant

3.   The American Association of University Women is the largest and oldest national organization in America working for the advancement of women. It emphasizes advocacy, action, research, and life-long learning.

4.   AAUW maintains an Educational Foundation Library, which is open to its professional staff and association members, and to scholars and graduate students by special permission. The collection includes some 4,000 books and 145 periodicals. The library also maintains the archives of the AAUW.

Audio holdings include approximately 400 reel-to-reel tapes of AAUW conventions and speeches from other public gatherings. The content of the tapes reflects the wide range of AAUW interests, such as environmental issues, education, and women's issues. A few tapes of activities of AAUW are held in the Marguerite Rawalt Resource Center of the Business and Professional Women's Foundation (A14).

5.   Flyers are available from the association. An index to the audio collection is in the process of compilation.

M7   American Bankers Association (ABA)—Audio Visual Department

1.   *1120 Connecticut Avenue, N.W.*
Washington, D.C. 20036
(202) 467–4196

2.   Raphael J. Milio, Manager, Audio Visual Department

3.   The American Bankers Association, established in 1875, seeks to help banks and bankers realize their full potential for serving the needs of the public. ABA councils and committees help determine commercial banking's position of proposed federal legislation and assist in determining what educational activities are implemented.

4.   ABA educational activities are comprehensive. Available to ABA members and the public are numerous publications, such as speeches, conferences, courses, seminars, workshops, symposia, conventions, research studies, and extensive audiovisual materials, including films, video cassettes, filmstrips, slides, and audio cassettes.

Currently, ABA has available, for purchase, no less than 456 audio cassettes representing the activities mentioned above for such topics as agricultural banking, branch banking, competition, correspondent banking, deposits, education, international banking, marketing, operations, protection, and trust. Audio cassettes are available through ABA's Order Processing Department, 44 Industrial Park Circle, Waldorf, Maryland 20601 (telephone: 301/843–8800).

5.   ABA publishes numerous books and pamphlets, including a useful *Bank Fact Book* available through the ABA editorial department. *American Bankers Association Catalog* lists all of ABA publications, including audiovisual materials, and is available upon request from the Communications Department (202/467–4196).

M8   American Chemical Society (ACS)—Education Division

1.   *1155 16th Street, N.W.*
     Washington, D.C. 20036
     (202) 872–4588 (Education Division)
     (202) 872–4446 (Radio-TV Service)

2.   Herldleen Russell, Program Assistant, Radio-TV Service
     Harold G. Walsh, Head, Education Division

3.   The American Chemical Society, founded in 1876, consists of some 130,000 professional chemists and chemical engineers seeking to advance chemical science and education. ACS activities are numerous, including the publication of books and periodicals, the administration of grants and awards, the sponsoring of local, regional, and national meetings, and the dissemination of current information in the field. The latter activity is carried out in part by a series of cassette tapes that are broadcast on many radio stations.

4.   The society's continuing education program is one of its significant activities. Over 50 continuing education courses are available in the ACS audio courses series. The courses consist of lectures on audio tape cassettes with integrated study manuals containing reference and illustration materials. Subjects include analytical chemistry, polymer chemistry, organic chemistry, chemical engineering, history of chemistry, radiochemistry, and business topics and professional skills, such as management, oral communication, introduction to patents, and new product development.

   Examples of titles in the collection include the following: *Polymer Chemistry and Technology* (Raymond B. Seymour, Ph.D.; 5 audio cassettes with manual, no. 61); *Carbon-13 NMR Spectroscopy* (George C. Levy, Ph.D. and Gordon L. Nelson, Ph.D.; 6 audio cassettes with manual, no. 31); *Free Radical Chemistry* (Glen A. Russell, Ph.D.; 8 audio cassettes with manual, no. 63); and *Electroorganic Synthesis* (Norman L. Weinberg, Ph.D.; 6 audio cassettes with manual, no. 48). One interesting title in particular deserves mention: *Scientific German* (Eric S. Belz and Carol Kempf, 6 audio cassettes with manual, no. 50) is a course designed to assist individuals in translating German technical articles into English.

   The Radio-TV Service distributes for purchase (subscription or selection) a scientific series *Dimensions in Science* (formerly *Man & Molecules*), which consists of some 200 cassette tapes. These science documentaries are designed to help individuals keep up with current research and future trends in science and society, health and medicine, the natural world, energy, space, and environment, among many others. All of the scientists featured are notable, including Glenn T. Seaborg, Linus Pauling, Norman Borlaug, Herbert C. Brown, and James Cronin, to name only a few.

5.   The society publishes over 20 journals and magazines, and more than 500 books embracing every major area of chemistry. Its two best known periodicals are *Chemical & Engineering News* and *Chemical Abstracts,* the latter being a compendium of current research in chemistry (also available as a computer data service). ACS has published an audio aid for researchers and library science professionals *Chemical Abstracts: An Introduction to its Effective Use* (John T. Dickman, Ph.D., Michael O'Hara, and O. Bertrand Ramsay, Ph.D.; 2 cassettes with manual, no. 52). An audio tape series also produced by ACS and which is a comprehensive survey of the professional literature is *Use of the Chemical Literature* (Samuel H. Wilen, Ph.D.;8 cassettes and manual, no. 39). ACS has a number of brochures which describe the above materials in detail available free.

American Council of the Blind (ACB)   **See entry F3**

M9   **American Educational Research Association (AERA)**

1.   *1230 17th Street, N.W.*
Washington, D.C. 20036
(202) 223-9485

2.   Amy E. Shaughnessy, Director of Publications

3.   The American Educational Research Association is concerned with the improvement of the educational process through the encouragement of scholarly inquiry related to education, the dissemination of research results, and their practical application. The association has ten divisions including: Administration; Counseling and Human Development; Curriculum Studies; Education in the Professions; History and Historiography; Learning and Instruction; Measurement and Research Methodology; Postsecondary Education; Social Context of Education; and Social Evaluation and Program Development.

4–5.   AERA has had available, for purchase, over 400 audio cassette tapes consisting of highlights of its annual meetings for the years 1971–1983. Included among the tapes are presentations by well-known educators, state-of-the art lectures, research-in-progress reports, panel discussions, and symposia. The recordings represent virtually all aspects of education and its relation to a wide variety of other disciplines. Some of the representative titles include: *International Perspectives on Education Research* (Erwin Miklos, 1978 annual meeting; K21); *Alternative Research Approaches to Learning and Teaching* (Vito Perrone, 1978 annual meeting; K16); *Educational Administration: A Forty-Year Perspective* (H. Thomas James, 1981 annual meeting; LA-1420); *Education in China* (Peter Seybolt, C.K. Yang, William Hinton, Robert Chin, and Francis Hso, 1974 annual meeting; F6); *Instructional Psychology: Past, Present, Future* (Robert Glaser, 1976 annual meeting; H3); *Speculations on the Future of Early Childhood Education* (Sheldon H. White, 1975 annual meeting; G11); *Priorities in Educational Research* (Roger Heyns, 1973 annual meeting; E4).

   AERA also has available, for purchase, its *AERA Research Training Tape Series.* Included in the series is *Alternative Methodologies in Educational Research* (Richard M. Jaeger, editor; 8 cassettes).

   AERA publishes a host of journals and books, including *Educational Researcher* (ten times per year), *American Educational Research Journal* (quarterly), *Review of Educational Research* (quarterly), and others. Flyers listing audio materials available, for purchase, are sent upon request.

American Federation of Labor and Congress of Industrial Organizations (AFL-CIO)—George Meany Center for Labor Studies   **See entry B2**

M10 American Federation of Teachers (AFT)

1. *11 Dupont Circle, N.W., Suite 500*
    Washington, D.C. 20036
    (202) 797–4458

2. Albert Shanker, President
    Scott Widmeyer, Public Relations

3. The American Federation of Teachers, organized in 1916, provides support for the professional concerns of its members through research, legislative and educational activities, and public relations. Some of AFT research and educational interests include teacher certification, competency testing, education for the handicapped, and in-service education for teachers.

4. AFT maintains a small collection of no more than 50 audio cassettes and reel-to-reel tapes, dating from 1979 to the present, consisting of speeches, convention proceedings, and workshops on such topics as tuition tax credits, competency tests, teacher lay-offs, vocational and general education. Telephone or write in advance to obtain permission to examine the collection. The tapes are not cataloged. On-site listening equipment is not available. Hours are 9:00 A.M. to 5:00 P.M., Monday through Friday.

5. AFT publishes a wide variety of materials, including educational studies, periodicals, and a number of films and video tapes. Of the five periodicals published, *American Teacher* (monthly, with exceptions) and *American Educator* (quarterly) are perhaps of most significance. *The AFT Press Kit,* containing an assortment of brochures, is available upon request.

M11 American Financial Services Association (AFSA)

1. *1101 14th Street, N.W.*
    Washington, D.C. 20005
    (202) 289–0400

2. Robert B. Evans, President

3–4. The American Financial Services Association (AFSA) established in 1916, is a trade association that represents more than 800 finance and industrial banking companies throughout the United States. It engages in a number of programs and activities including, for example, conventions, conferences, and committee meetings, all of which provide specialized training and beneficial interaction between members. In addition, the association provides information and guidance in research, training, communication, and legislation.

5. The association publishes a host of monographs and periodicals, including, *Credit Magazine* (a bi-monthly journal), *Thrift Reporter* (a monthly newsletter), and *Finance Facts* (a monthly report).
    The association distributes, for purchase, a number of self-instructional audio materials in the fields of personnel training and management. These cassette programs are printed in the *AFSA Services Catalog,* which is available upon request.

M12 American Forest Institute (AFI)

1.   *1619 Massachusetts Avenue, N.W.*
     Washington, D.C. 20036
     (202) 797–4500
     (800) 424–2485 (toll-free)

2.   Robert Lehrman, President
     Wende A. Taylor, Communications Assistant

3.   The American Forest Institute is an association of individuals, industries, educators, and others who are dedicated to provide both nationwide and local programs of information, education, and research to achieve a better understanding and use of America's forests.

5.   The AFI has available, for purchase, films and audio cassette materials, the latter focusing on the potential of America's forests. AFI also has a Tree Farm Broadcast Kit, which includes six 60-second announcements on reel-to-reel tape concerning the management of private forest land. An *AFI Guide to Audio/Visual Materials* is available upon request.

M13 American Home Economics Association (AHEA)

1.   *2010 Massachusetts Avenue, N.W.*
     Washington, D.C. 20036
     (202) 862–8300

2.   Kinsey B. Green, Executive Director

3.   Founded in 1909, the American Home Economics Association is an educational and scientific association serving the home economics profession. It works to improve the quality of life for all, and especially the family unit.
     The American Home Economics Association offers a number of services to its membership including support for family research, state and national workshops and conferences, and the development of an accreditation program for institutions offering home economics programs.

5.   AHEA publishes a number of periodicals and monographs as well as audiovisual productions and booklets relating to the field. Audio output consists mainly of cassette tapes of speakers and sessions at annual meetings. These can be ordered through the annual publications list.

M14 American Library Association (ALA)—Washington Office

1.   *110 Maryland Avenue, N.E., Box 54*
     Washington, D.C. 20002
     (202) 547–4440

2.   Carol C. Henderson, Deputy Director, ALA Washington Office

3.   The Washington Office has represented ALA constituency regarding video and audio copyright legislation currently under consideration by Congress. An article "Washington Hotline" in *College and Research Libraries News,* vol. 43, no. 9, October 1982, p. 313, discusses ALA testimony on the subject. Subsequent developments are reported by Carol Henderson in later issues.

5.   The ALA has published a useful manual, *Oral History: From Tape to Type* (1977), which focuses on the collecting, processing, and dissemination of oral history. Available for purchase from Eastern Audio Associates (Appendix II) are educational cassettes recorded live at the 1983 ALA National Convention. Researchers may request a copy of *ALA Publications Checklist 1984.*

M15 American Management Associations (AMA)

1.   *440 1st Street, N.W.*
     Washington, D.C. 20001
     (202) 347–3092

2.   Thomas R. Horton, President

3.   The American Management Associations consist of some 100,000 managers who rely upon the AMA for providing a forum for personal development and for sharing ideas and commitment to common goals. The AMA is divided into 12 divisions and offers educational programs, courses, and seminars.

4–5.   AMACOM, the AMA in-house publishing division, located at 135 West 50th Street, New York, New York 10020, publishes a variety of business management books, periodicals, newsletters, survey reports and audiovisual materials.
     A number of audio cassette programs feature in-depth conversations with leaders and management pioneers, including Chris Argyris, Peter F. Drucker, James L. Hayes, George Odiorne, Robert Montgomery, and Rensis and Jane Likert, can be purchased from AMACOM. A number of multimedia program kits for management training are also available to the purchaser's representative who is trained by an AMA specialist.
     AMA journals include *Supervisory Management Magazine* (monthly) and *Organizational Dynamics* (quarterly), among others. Brochures and a publications catalog are available upon request.

M16 American Occupational Therapy Association, Inc. (AOTA)

1.   *1383 Piccard Drive*
     Rockville, Maryland 20850
     (301) 948–9626

2.   James Garibaldi, Executive Director

3.   The American Occupational Therapy Association consists of professional occupational therapists, occupational therapy assistants, occupational therapy students and organizations supportive of occupational therapy. Occupational therapists assist individuals with physical, developmental, and emotional disabilities in gaining the skills

necessary to live independent, productive lives. The association disseminates information through various programs and publications, including books, manuals, reports, brochures, films, video tapes, slides, and audio cassettes.

4. The American Occupational Therapy Foundation, at the same address maintains a collection of occupational therapy and related literature available through interlibrary loan. The librarian is Sheila Richards (301/948-9626).

5. Currently there are 4 audio cassette/slide programs available for purchase or on a rental basis from the association: *Patient Care Evaluation (1978)* (cassette and slides, D-41); *OT on Target (1976)* (cassette and slides, J-2); *AOTPAC [American Occupational Therapy Political Action Committee]: A Capital Idea (1978)* (cassette and slides, J-4); *The Total Child (1978)* (cassette and slides, J-5), a description of sensorimotor processing and illustration of its affect on a child's general development and classroom behavior.

A detailed description of these and other materials is found in the association's *Multi-Media Catalog*, which is available on request.

M17 American Physiological Society (APS)

1. *9650 Rockville Pike*
   Bethesda, Maryland 20814
   (301) 530-7164

2. Orr E. Reynolds, Executive Secretary-Treasurer

3. The American Physiological Society, founded in 1887, is an organization of professionals devoted to the research of physiology and the education and training of those working in the field.

4-5. APS achieves its objectives in large part due to an extensive publications program. It publishes 10 professional journals, books, various clinical physiology series, and special publications, such as the *World Directory of Physiologists, 1980.* It also publishes a number of educational materials, including the series *Instructional Slide/Tape Programs in Physiology,* which is designed for the medical school level. Included in this series are at least 38 cassettes with accompanying slides of programs representing the following subjects: peripheral circulation; electrophysiology of the heart; cardiac physiology; renal physiology; renal pathophysiology; and acid/base physiology. All of the program instructors are recognized experts who are actively involved in the teaching of physiology. Examples of topics in the series include: *Hemodynamics* (Shu Chien, M.D., Ph.D.; cassette/slide 1201); *The Electrical Anatomy of the Heart* (Rory W. Childers, M.D.; cassette/slide 1104-05); *Mechanics of the Intact Heart* (W.W. Parmley, M.D.; cassette/slide 604); *Understanding Renal Hemodynamics 1* (L.G. Navar, Ph.D.; cassette/slide 805); and *Edema* (Cecil H. Coggins, M.D.; cassette/slide 903).

The society's audiovisual materials are ordered from: Audio/Visual Medical Marketing, 404 Park Avenue South, New York, New York 10016; telephone (800) 221-3995 (toll-free). Annotated catalogs describing the audiovisual materials are available.

M18 American Podiatry Association

1. 20 Chevy Chase Circle, N.W.
    Washington, D.C. 20015
    (202) 537–4992

2. Norman Klombers, Executive Director

3. The American Podiatry Association is a professional society of podiatrists.

4. The association's publications include audio cassette and disc recordings. Currently available are 8 subjects on a disc recording on radio spot announcements on foot health, 13 cassette recordings of the Podogeriatric Training Program held at St. Vincent Hospital and Medical Center in Toledo, Ohio, in 1967, 10 cassette tapes of lectures on chemotherapy in podiatric medicine presented at The University of Connecticut in 1970, and 15 cassette tapes of the symposium on "The Neglected Foot" held at Medical College of Virginia in Richmond in 1973. Other materials available, for purchase or on a rental basis, include films, slides, and filmstrips.

    The association has an audiovisual department, headed by George Dame (202/537–4992).

5. The association distributes a current Catalog of Audiovisual Information and Educational Materials (1984) upon request. A number of items are also listed in the National Library of Medicine's Audiovisuals Catalog (A55).

M19 American Psychiatric Association (APA)

1. 1400 K Street, N.W.
    Washington, D.C. 20005
    (202) 682–6080

2. Zing Jung, Director, Library and Archives

3. The American Psychiatric Association disseminates information and material on current developments in psychiatry, psychology, clinical psychology, psychoanalysis, psychosomatic medicine, nursing, and mental hospitals.

4. The association maintains a library and reference collection of educational materials, including a number of audio cassettes of lectures delivered at annual meetings of the APA. There are also 24 audio cassette tapes of personal interviews with prominent psychiatrists. Some of these oral histories are transcribed. Although the library has a card catalog, the tapes are not cataloged.

5. The association's publications include American Journal of Psychiatry (monthly), Hospital and Community Psychiatry (monthly), and Psychiatric News (twice monthly). Some of APA's publications are listed in the National Library of Medicine's Audiovisuals Catalog (A55).

M20 American Public Health Association (APHA)

1. *1015 15th Street, N.W.*
    Washington, D.C. 20005
    (202) 789–5670

2. Sue Mekkelson, Audiovisual Resources

3. The American Public Health Association, founded in 1892, works to eradicate communicable diseases, encourages public and private involvement in international health issues, helps to set standards for the improvement of health and the environment, and serves as an advocate of national health policies that promote preventive care and basic health services. To meet these goals, APHA offers technical advisory services, conducts research, holds conferences, workshops, and seminars.

4. Audio materials produced by APHA include cassette tapes, available for purchase, for the APHA annual meetings. Topics at the meetings typically cover epidemiology, sports medicine, diseases, dentistry, pharmacology, health care, public hospitals, hostages and victims of terrorism, radiology, population, energy, environment, health education, drugs and tobacco, food and nutrition, law, mental health, community studies, and women's studies. Tapes covering the 1983 APHA annual meeting (some 170 cassettes) can be ordered from AVW Audio Visual, 2418 Converse Street, Dallas, Texas 75207; telephone (214) 638–0024.

5. APHA publishes monographs and newsletters on health topics. Brochures describing the association and audio cassettes are available free.

M21 American Society for Industrial Security (ASIS)

1. *1655 North Fort Myer Drive, Suite 1200*
    Arlington, Virginia 22209
    (703) 522–5800

2. E.J. Criscuoli, Executive Vice President

3. The American Society for Industrial Security, founded in 1955, seeks to raise the level of professionalism in security and to encourage the development of education in the security field. The activities of the society include diversified publications and various educational programs, seminars, and conferences.

4. The society publishes for purchase a number of audio cassette tapes recording key speakers and panel sessions at its annual seminars. Currently available is a set of tapes of the 29th Annual Seminar and Exhibits, held in Washington, D.C., September 12–15, 1983. No less than 65 cassettes represent a wide array of topics, including banking and finance, security, management, fire prevention and safety, health care services, investigations, oil, gas, petrochemical and mining, public utilities, standards and codes, and crime. Tapes are ordered from the society's distributor, Audio-Video Transcripts, 250 West 49th Street, New York, New York 10019 (telephone: 212/586–1972).

5. ASIS publishes a number of studies, including its *ASIS Reprint Series* in security management.

M22 American Society for Microbiology (ASM)

1. *1913 Eye Street, N.W.*
    Washington, D.C. 20006
    (301) 833–9680

2. Riley D. Housewright, Executive Director

3. The American Society for Microbiology, founded in 1899 as the Society of American Bacteriologists, is a scientific and educational society that promotes the advancement of knowledge in the field of microbiology. The society consists of five divisions: Publications, Meetings, Education and Training, Public Affairs, and the American Academy of Microbiology. Its objectives include promoting the scientific knowledge of microbiology through its meetings and publications, stimulating research and encouraging its practical application, improving education in microbiology, and increasing recognition of the discipline.

4. The society produces audiovisual comprehensive programs covering the essentials and recent developments in general microbiology, clinical microbiology, genetics, mycology, virology, and immunology. Included are at least 15 cassette/slide programs totaling over 30 individual cassettes, as well as a number of additional video-taped presentations. The following are representative types of programs available for purchase: *The Bacterial Cell: Structure and Function* (Linda L. Klimowski; 2 cassettes with slides, no. 6401–02); *Interaction of Soil Microorganisms and Herbicides* (D. Roy Cullimore; 1 cassette with slides, no. 6601); *Bacterial Sporulation* (Roy H. Doi; 1 cassette with slides, no. 6801); *Malaria Parasite Detection and Identification* (Dean "Ike" Armstrong; 1 cassette with slides, no. 6710); *Mycoplasma* (Michael G. Gabridge; 1 cassette with slides, no. 6701).

5. The *Audiovisual Resource Catalog* (1980), describing 750 programs and over 90 distribution sources, is compiled by, and available from, the society. The society's audiovisual materials are ordered from, Audio/Visual Medical Marketing, Dept. MIC, 404 Park Avenue South, New York, New York 10016 (telephone: 800/221–3995 (toll-free)).
    The society publishes books, manuals, and 8 journals, including the *Journal of Bacteriology, Journal of Virology, Journal of Clinical Microbiology,* and *Bacteriological Reviews*, as well as a monthly magazine, *ASM News*.

M23 American Society of Association Executives (ASAE)

1. *1575 Eye Street, N.W.*
    Washington, D.C. 20005
    (202) 626–2742

2. Richard Farkas, Publications Manager

3. The American Society of Association Executives provides a forum for information exchange on the principles, activities, and functions of associations. The emphasis is on management and standards of association executives. The society's membership includes executives of professional, technical, and business associations.

4–5. Although the society conducts reference service for individuals and maintains a library, access to audio materials is available only through purchase.

The more than 300 cassette tapes that have been produced cover ASAE educational seminars, meetings, and conventions spanning the years 1971–1983. Typical subjects include career advancement, communications, computers, electronic data processing, financial management, investing, accounting, economics, law, politics, government relations, research, and marketing. The following are representative titles in the collection: *Association Marketing Techniques* (Frank Martineau; no. 80013–280); *Information Sources in Washington* (Matthew Lesko; no. 80013–310); *Understanding Association Tax Laws* (John C. Vickerman; no. 79013–160); *Associations—An Information Systems Direction Using Computers* (no. 79013–430); *Marvin Kalb Speaking on Kissinger* (no. 74013–080); *The Role of Associations in Europe* (Bernard de Rouvray; no. 75013–060); and *Computer Uses for Association Activities* (Douglas Fisher; no. 80013–290).

ASAE publishes a *Cassette Catalog: Resources in Sound,* which is available upon request.

M24 American Society of International Law (ASIL)

1. *2223 Massachusetts Avenue*
    Washington, D.C. 20008
    (202) 265–4313

2. Seymour J. Rubin, Executive Director

3. The American Society of International Law, founded in 1906, is devoted to encouraging and promoting the study of international law and international relations based on law and justice. The society achieves its mission by providing a forum for exchange of current legal topics relating to international activities, by serving as a research center for traditional and new issues of international law, and by maintaining a varied publications program.

4. The society's library (open to the public from 9:00 A.M. to 5:00 P.M., Monday through Friday; Helen S. Philos, librarian, 202/265–4313) contains over 20,000 items consisting of treatises, books, documents, briefs, pamphlets, periodicals, and basic reference aids. Some specialized material in the collection is not easily obtainable elsewhere. The library's holdings include 28 audio cassette tapes of the society's 76th annual meeting held in Washington, D.C., April 22–24, 1982. A few of the significant titles in the audio collection include: *U.S.–Iranian Claims Tribunal; Islamic Law; The United Nations Conference on the Law of the Sea; ICJ Decision in the Libya-Tunisia Continental Shelf Case; Choosing a Forum for International Commercial Arbitration; International Protection of the Independence of the Judicial Process; Workshop on the Falkland Island Crisis.* These tapes are available for purchase from American Audio Association, P.O. Box 511, Floral Park, New York 11002 (telephone 212/740–0186). The society intends to produce similar audio cassettes covering its subsequent annual meetings. Audio transcripts of the 1983 annual meeting are available from Audio Video Transcripts, 250 West 49th Street, New York, New York 10019 (telephone 212/586–1972).

5. The society publishes *American Journal of International Law* (quarterly) and *International Legal Materials* (bi-monthly). A descriptive brochure, *The American Society of International Law,* and a list of audio cassettes that may be purchased are available free.

M25 American Sociological Association (ASA)—Teaching Services Program

1. *1722 N Street, N.W.*
   Washington, D.C. 20036
   (202) 833–3410

2. Carla B. Howery, Professional Associate

3. The American Sociological Association, founded in 1905, is an organization of persons interested in the research, teaching, and application of sociology. It seeks to stimulate and improve research, instruction, and discussion, and to encourage co-operative relations among persons engaged in the scientific study of society.

4. The Teaching Services Program is specifically dedicated to improving effective teaching within the discipline of sociology. Although the ASA does not have a collection of audio recordings, the Teaching Services Program will refer individuals to sources for obtaining audio recordings appropriate for classroom use.

5. The association's varied publications include three specialized quarterly journals: *Social Psychology Quarterly, Sociology of Education: A Journal of Research in Socialization and Social Structure,* and *Journal of Health and Social Behavior. Teaching Newsletter* can be obtained from the Teaching Services Program. Flyers describing the ASA are available upon request.

M26 American Women Composers, Inc. (AWC)

1. *7315 Hooking Road*
   McLean Station
   McLean, Virginia 22101
   (703) 893–6524

2. Tommie Ewert Carl, President/Founder

3. American Women Composers, Inc., was founded in 1976 for the purpose of promoting and supporting the works of women composers and performers in the United States. The organization, which consists of composers, performers, musicologists, and librettists, regularly produces live concerts of music of women composers, as well as other supporting activities.

4. AWC maintains a music library of over 2,500 scores, a small collection of books, and some 200 disc, cassette and reel-to-reel recordings of music of women composers. Many of the discs are commercially produced by such manufacturers as Orion, CRI, Leonarda, and Opus One. Other recordings cover live performances. In all, some 300 women are represented in the collection. The disc collection does not circulate. Tape recordings circulate depending upon age and condition. For further information, researchers should contact AWC during the hours of 10:00 A.M. to 4:00 P.M., Monday through Friday.

5. AWC has recently began issuing sound recordings under its own label: Capriccio Records. In addition, its *AWC News/Forum* (quarterly) regularly includes information on recent recordings and collections acquired by the library and other news regarding sound recordings.

M27 Armenian General Benevolent Union of the U.S.—Washington Chapter

1. *7504 Newburg Drive*
    Lanham, Maryland 20801
    (301) 552–1347

2. Rita Balian, President
    Annie Simonian Totah, Executive Committee Member

3. The Armenian General Benevolent Union, founded in Cairo, Egypt, in 1905, has a Washington, D.C., chapter, which was organized in 1917. The local chapter has about 110 members. The nationwide membership is approximately 5,000. The purpose of the union is to provide educational and welfare assistance to Armenians in the United States and to help preserve the ethnic heritage, religion, and culture of Armenian-Americans. In achieving this objective, the Washington Chapter sponsors activities related to Armenian culture. Many of the events may be attended by the public.

4. The Washington Chapter plans to sponsor a weekly radio program devoted to Armenian culture. The program, not yet in production, would be based on "The Heritage of Armenian Culture" currently aired on SDET FM in Detroit, Michigan. The Washington Chapter has a number of the tapes in the series, as well as a typewritten list of programs. Subjects include music, musical performers, and poetry.

M28 Association for Educational Communications and Technology (AECT)

1. *1126 16th Street, N.W., Suite 310*
    Washington, D.C. 20036
    (202) 466–4780

2. Lyn Gubser, Executive Director

3. The Association for Educational Communications and Technology is dedicated to the improvement of instruction through media and technology. It accomplishes its goal through a variety of programs offered through its several divisions, special publications, and an annual conference. In a special project, AECT collaborates with several state departments of education that assist their local schools in the application of information technology.

4–5. AECT publishes a number of reference tools and checklists on non-print media. A few illustrative titles include: *Media in Instruction: 60 Years of Research* (1980); *Standards for College and University Learning Resource Programs* (1983); and *Learning with Microcomputers* (1983).
    AECT also publishes filmstrip/audio cassette kits. Currently 6 kits are available, including *Understanding Educational Technology* (1977); *Creating Slide/Tape Programs* (1980); and *Freedom to Learn* (1979). The latter discusses court cases related to intellectual freedom and intellectual freedom in public schools.
    AECT journals include *Instructional Innovator* (10 times per year), *Educational Communications & Technology Journal* (quarterly), and *Journal of Instructional Development* (quarterly). All of the publications described above are cited in the asso-

ciation's catalog, *Media and Technology for Educational Training* (1984), which is available free upon request.

M29 Association for Recorded Sound Collections, Inc. (ARSC)

1. *118 Monroe Street, Apartment 610*
    Rockville, Maryland 20850

    Mail:
    Box 1643
    Manassas, Virginia 22110

2. Timothy Brooks, President
    Les Waffen, Executive Director
    Gerald Gibson, Chairman, ARSC/AAA

3. The Association for Recorded Sound Collections is a non-profit organization serving the interests and concerns of the private collector, discographer, librarian, archivist, and specialty dealer in all fields of collecting historical-discographic information. ARSC works to encourage the preservation of historic recordings, to promote the exchange and dissemination of research and information about sound recordings, and to foster an increased awareness of the importance of recorded sound in our cultural heritage. A Washington metropolitan area chapter was formed in 1984. The chapter president is Phillip Rochlin (301/283–3177).

4. ARSC has been involved in a number of projects related to sound recordings, and has published *Rules for Archival Cataloging of Sound Recordings*. The most significant ARSC project yet undertaken is the recently completed *The Rigler and Deutsch Record Index—A National Union Catalog of Sound Recordings, Part I: An Index to the 78-rpm Sound Recordings in the Association for Recorded Sound Collections/ Associated Audio Archives [ARSC/AAA] Member Libraries, Made Possible by a Grant from Lloyd E. Rigler and Lawrence E. Deutsch and a Grant from the National Endowment for the Humanities*. The index includes microfilm photographs of some 615,000 "pre-lp," commercial disc, sound recordings held by the ARSC/AAA members, the Library of Congress (A41), the Rodgers and Hammerstein Archives of Recorded Sound of the New York Public Library, the Belfer Audio Laboratory and Archive of Syracuse University, the Archive of Recorded Sound of Stanford University, and the Yale Collection of Historical Sound Recordings of Yale University. Key data transcribed into a computer database from the photographs permits bibliographic access to the discs by author/composer, title, performer, label name, issue number, matrix number, and holding institution. The complete index is held by each of the AAA member institutions and ARSC. The index on microfilm is available to other archives, libraries, and individuals, on a non-profit basis. ARSC is negotiating placement of the machine record in one or more national on-line data storage and exchange networks. ARSC has applied for grant funding to index some 650,000 "lp/45" recordings held by ARSC/AAA members and prepare a bibliographic enhancement of the operatic material contained in *The Rigler and Deutsch Record Index*. The proposals are under review by potential funding sources. Information on these projects is available from ARSC/AAA Project Coordinator Elwood McKee.

5. ARSC publishes a journal (issued three times a year), which is devoted to the results of major research, technical developments, unusual discoveries, discographies, record reviews, and articles of general interest in the field; an annual bulletin contains

reports of meetings and conventions, and a newsletter is issued quarterly. Flyers describing ARSC and its various projects are available by mail.

M30 Association for Supervision and Curriculum Development (ASCD)

1   *225 North Washington Street*
Alexandria, Virginia 22314
(703) 549–9110

2.   Gordon Cawelti, Executive Director

3.   The purpose of the Association for Supervision and Curriculum Development is to seek balanced instructional programs for assuring equal and quality educational opportunities for all students. The association provides opportunities for individuals to develop supervisory and leadership skills through annual conferences and national curriculum study institutes. ASCD publishes a variety of materials and provides a research information service, as well as audio and video cassette tapes for staff development purposes. ASCD also reviews and disseminates information about educational practice, research media, and materials.

4–5.   The association has approximately 80 audio cassettes available for purchase. Subjects represented include: curriculum, assessment, evaluation and testing, humanistic education, leadership, middle school/high school, school and society, supervision, and teaching/learning. Some representative titles include: *Future Directions for Gifted and Talented Programs* (Marvin Gold; no. 109); *Research on Women in Leadership Roles* (Jacqueline Clement; no. 86); *Recent Research on Learning Styles and Practical Implications for Supervisors and Teachers* (Rita and Kenneth Dunn; no. 94); *Reading Skills—What We Know and Don't Know* (Marshall Smith; no. 147); and *Definition and Identification of the Gifted/Talented* (Donald Treffinger; no. 150).

ASCD publishes a journal *Education Leadership* (8 issues per year), as well as a number of books, a newsletter, and a yearbook. Its publications catalog is available upon request.

M31 Association for the Study of Afro-American Life and History, Inc.

1.   *1401 14th Street, N.W.*
Washington, D.C. 20005
(202) 667–2822

2.   M. Sammye Miller, Executive Director

3.   The Association for the Study of Afro-American Life and History is dedicated to the study of black history and civilization. The organization collects documentary material on the contributions of blacks to society, and since 1926, has sponsored the National Afro-American (Black) History Month.

4.   The association maintains a library, which is available to the public by special permission only. Preliminary reference questions may be posed by either telephone or letter. The collection consists of books, journals, photographs, maps and charts, correspondence, and sound recordings. The audio holdings consist of cassette tape recordings of the association's conventions, which have been based on various themes for National Afro-American History Month.

5. Publications of the association include two quarterlies: *Journal of Negro History* and *Negro History Bulletin*.

Association of Former Members of Congress (FMC)   **See entry B7**

M32 Association of Trial Lawyers of America (ATLA)—Education Fund

1. *1050 31st Street, N.W.*
    Washington, D.C. 20007
    (202) 965-3500
    (800) 424-2727 (toll-free)

    Mail:
    P.O. Box 3717
    Washington, D.C. 20007

2. C. Thomas Bendorf, Executive Director

3. The Association of Trial Lawyers of America consists of lawyers, judges, law professors, and students whose objectives are to advance the science of jurisprudence, to train in all fields and phases of advocacy, to promote the administration of justice for the public good, and to uphold and improve the adversary system and trial by jury.

4–5. ATLA has over 75 audio cassette tape programs available for purchase. These include lectures, arguments, and panel discussions on such topics as wrongful death, class action litigation, trends in worker's compensation, railroad law, admiralty law, commercial litigation, family law, aviation law, special problems in military law, tort litigation, strategies in products liability cases, trial and settlements techniques, and medical and professional liability. The catalog, *ATLA: New Horizons in Legal Education* (1983), describes these programs in detail, and is available to individuals upon request. Major publications of ATLA include *ATLA Law Reporter* (10 issues per year), *ATLA Advocate* (monthly), and *Trial Magazine* (monthly).

Atomic Industrial Forum (AIF)—Audiovisual Library   **See entry A11**

Better Hearing Institute (BHI)   **See entry F6**

Blinded Veterans Association (BVA)   **See entry F7**

Broadcast Education Association (BEA)   **See entry H4**

M33 Council for Exceptional Children (CEC)

1. *1920 Association Drive*
    Reston, Virginia 22091
    (703) 620–3660

2. Lynn Smarte, Information Specialist

3. The Council for Exceptional Children consists of individuals committed to supporting each other through professional development and whose goal it is to ultimately enhance the education of all exceptional children. The emphasis is on the designing of technical assistance and training for the development of existing or new programs for exceptional children.

4–5. The council carries on a limited program of audio publication. Examples of audio recordings include *They Shall Create: Gifted Minority Children* (Paul Torrance; no. 78) and *Everybody Counts!A Workshop Manual to Increase Awareness of Handicapped People* (M. J. Ward, R. N. Arkell, and J. H. Wise; no. 189). Multi-media kits cover, for example: *PL 94–142, Implementing Procedural Safeguards: A Guide for Schools and Parents* (includes 3 audio cassettes), and *We Can Help; A Specialized Curriculum for Educators on the Prevention and Treatment of Child Abuse and Neglect* (includes 2 audio cassettes).

In the past the council made available audio cassette tapes of a number of CEC conferences: *The CEC Invisible College Conference on Learning and Behavioral Problems of Handicapped Students in Secondary School Programs* (M. Angele Thomas, editor; 6 cassettes, no. 161) and *The CEC Invisible College Conference on Education's Responsibility for Disruptive, Alienated, and Incarcerated Youth* (M. Angele Thomas, editor; 6 cassettes, no. 201). This particular program has been discontinued.

The council publishes several periodicals, in particular, *Exceptional Children* (8 times per year) and *Teaching Exceptional Children* (quarterly). For a fee, the council will conduct computer searches of the Exceptional Child Education Resources (ECER) database and the Educational Resources Information Center (ERIC) database (G3). The *CEC Catalog* is available on request. A number of the council's publications are listed in the National Library of Medicine's Audiovisuals Catalog (A55).

Economics News Broadcasters Association (ENBA)   **See entry H10**

M34 Electronic Industries Association (EIA)

1. *2001 Eye Street, N.W.*
    Washington, D.C. 20006
    (202) 457–4900
    (202) 457–4919 (Director of Educational Services)

2. Peter F. McCloskey, President

3. The Electronic Industries Association, established in 1924, is a national trade organization that represents companies involved in the manufacture of electronic components, equipment, and systems for government, industry, and consumer ap-

plications. EIA sponsors trade shows, disseminates current information, and often acts as a lobby organization to Congress, the Executive branch, and the regulatory agencies.

4.   Individuals interested in audiovisual publications should contact the Service Technical Development Program, which maintains current information on the newest audio servicing techniques and products.

5.   EIA publishes and sponsors a number of audiovisual publications. *Audio Servicing* series includes, for example, text, lab manual, and *Instructor's Guide* (published by Gregg/McGraw-Hill). A catalog and flyer, as well as consumer education pamphlets, are available from the association upon request.

Inter-American Development Bank—Felipe Herrera Library
See entry A37

M35 International Masonry Institute Apprenticeship and Training (IMIAT)

1.   *815 15th Street, N.W., Suite 711*
Washington, D.C. 20005
(202) 347–2333

2.   Bruce N. Voss, Executive Director

3.   The International Masonry Institute Apprenticeship and Training is the educational division of the masonry industry. As part of its on-going program of assisting in the education of the professional mason, the institute develops textbooks and audiovisual training aids, and provides consultation to masonry training organizations. The institute also conducts biennial seminars for apprentices and journeymen.

4–5.   Currently available for purchase are 13 programs on audio cassettes (with accompanying slides) for instruction in pointing, ceramic tile, cutting, rigging, use and applications of the mason's level, setting pavers, panel assembly and installation, basic bricklaying, basic blocklaying, arch construction methods, laying headers, rowlocks and soldiers, lifting and hoisting hand signals, as well as information on the trowel trades as a career.

M36 International Newspaper Promotion Association (INPA)

1.   *The Newspaper Center*
Dulles International Airport
(703) 620–9560

Mail:
P.O. Box 17422
Washington, D.C. 20041

2.   Paula Markiewicz, Executive Director
Micheael G. Kane, Special Projects Manager

3. The International Newspaper Promotion Association is a network of more than 1,400 experts in every area of newspaper promotion, including marketing, advertising, circulation, research, and public relations. INPA serves as an information resource, providing ideas for practical solutions to complex marketing and promotion problems.

4. Each year INPA compiles all of the winning television and radio spots in the E & P Promotion Contest in both video and audio cassette formats. Copies of these spots, considered to be the best media productions of their type produced throughout the country, are available for purchase directly from INPA.

INPA maintains a library containing several hundred items, including cassettes of radio and television spots, promotion textbooks, camera-ready promotion advertisements, speeches of industry leaders, and audiovisual marketing and sales presentations.

5. Major INPA publications include *The Idea Newspaper,* an annual publication that features some of the best ads created by INPA members, *Films About Newspapers, INPA Yearbook,* and various monographs on promotional topics and trends.

M37 Namysto (The Necklace) Singing Ensemble

1. *1003 La Grande Road*
    Silver Spring, Maryland 20903
    (301) 434–6075

2. Peter Krul, Musical Director

3. The group has six vocalists and three instrumentalists (bass guitar, lead guitar, and electric organ). The ensemble performs five to six concerts a year in the Washington, D.C., area and other major cities, including New York. Namysto sings mostly festive, modern Ukrainian songs.

4. Peter Krul has a collection of musical arrangements, about 20 books and 30 to 40 records of Ukrainian songs and music.

5. The group has recorded two albums on Namysto's own label; they are available at the address given above. In the future Mr. Krul hopes to publish some of the songs and music he has arranged.

National Association of Broadcasters (NAB)   See entry H14

M38 National Association of Housing and Redevelopment Officials (NAHRO)

1. *2600 Virginia Avenue, N.W., Suite 404*
    Washington, D.C. 20037
    (202) 333–2020

2. Robert W. Maffin, Executive Director
    Mary L. Pike, Deputy Director of Member Services

3. The purpose of National Association of Housing and Redevelopment Officials is to work toward the provision of adequate housing for all persons, as well as the goal of having ecologically and economically sound communities. This objective is pursued through working at the administrative level, through engaging in research, conducting meetings and conferences, and through maintaining a publications program.

4. NAHRO has a collection of approximately 500 cassette and reel-to-reel tape recordings covering conferences, conventions, and lectures. A number of individuals featured include housing and urban development officials and members of NAHRO. Topics cover federally assisted housing, community development and redevelopment, communications, management, energy conservation, finance, legal issues, and finance, among others.

5. NAHRO has available for purchase at least 60 audio cassettes from conventions and conferences since 1978. Examples of individual recordings available for purchase include *Housing Policy Options from the President's Commission on Housing* (Samuel Pierce; no. 2–141–81); *Special User Housing: Concepts, Problems and Solutions* (Judy L. Morris; no. 13–90–78); *Community and Economic Development* (David Alberts; no. 16–90–78); *Rehabilitation and Neighborhood Conservation* (Paul Brophy; no. 17–90–78); and *Assessing and Analyzing Financial Documents, Annual Reports and Other Data* (no. 8–110–81). Cassettes may be ordered from Audio Transcripts, P.O. Box 487, Times Square Station, New York, New York 10108 (telephone: 212/245–7897).

NAHRO publishes a variety of printed materials including *Journal of Housing* (monthly), *NAHRO Monitor* (semi-monthly newsletter), the bulletin *Action Alert,* and a number of technical books and pamphlets. Brochures and catalogs listing sound recordings and citing other information are available upon request.

M39 National Association of Secondary School Principals (NASSP)

1. *1904 Association Drive*
    Reston, Virginia 22091
    (703) 860–0200

2. Scott D. Thomson, Executive Director
    Linda Durham, Assistant

3. The purpose of the National Association of Secondary School Principals is to keep abreast of current developments and trends in education. The organization informs its members of current information covering a wide variety of subjects, ranging from management techniques to curriculum programs. This goal is achieved, in part through the association's extensive publications program.

4. The association maintains an audio tape library of materials, which can be used on-site with permission. Contact the association during the hours of 8:15 A.M. to 4:30 P.M., Monday through Friday, for additional information. Most of the audio tapes maintained in the library are available for purchase.

5. Currently, the association's catalogs list over 200 audio cassette tapes consisting of NASSP annual convention programs for 1981–1983, dialogues, lectures, and reports. The tapes focus on a wide variety of subjects including administrative leadership, community involvement, public relations, education in the future, computers and instructional television, learning styles and evaluation, school improvement, schools and the law, skill development, special problems and programs, and career planning.

Examples of individual sound recordings include *Improving Achievement through Computer Managed Instruction* (Olcott Gardner; no. 4308004); *Using ITV to Strengthen Science and Language Arts* (Helen Callison and Robert Reese; no. 4308015); *Education, Youth, and Crime* (Walter G. Whitlach and Milton Rector; no. 4307606); *Mainstreaming Handicapped Students: One School's Success Story* (Cecil Mosenson and Kevin O'Shea; no. 4307813); *Competency-Based Education: The Instructional Side* (Robert French and William Habermehl; no. 4307912); *Starting a High School Gifted and Talented Program* (no. 4308250); *Washington Merry-Go-Round* (Jack Anderson; no. 43082109).

NASSP publishes a number of monographs, special papers, bulletins, reports, and newsletters. Its catalog, *Publications 1983–1984,* is available to individuals upon request.

National Association of Spanish Broadcasters (NASB)   **See entry H15**

National Black Media Coalition (NBMC)   **See entry H16**

M40 National Education Association (NEA)

1.   *1201 16th Street, N.W.*
       Washington, D.C. 20036
       (202) 833–4000
       (202) 822–7266 (Publications Department)

2.   Don Cameron, Executive Director
       Neal Hall, Assistant Manager, Telecommunications Studio

3.   The National Education Association, founded in 1857, consists primarily of college and university professors, elementary and secondary school educators, administrators, principals, and other educators interested in all aspects of education.

4–5.   NEA maintains a library, which contains over 1,000 reel-to-reel and cassette recordings of conventions, meetings, conferences, and speeches. One notable set of recordings consists of NEA conventions held during the 1930s. Copies of the recordings held in the library are available for purchase through NEA catalogs, and the staff prefers that individuals purchase recordings rather than listening to them in the library.

Some recordings listed in the association's *Publications and Audiovisual Materials: Catalog* include a number of in-service training multimedia programs for such educational topics as discipline, gifted and talented, motivation, parent involvement, copyright, education of the handicapped, multi-ethnic education, and law related education. Another useful series is *Critical Issues in Education* (4-part cassette series with printed overviews, discussion questions, and biographical information), which includes comments by Karl A. Menniger, Arthur M. Schlesinger, Jr., Andrew Young, Margaret Heckler, Barbara Jordan, and Walter Mondale.

Other cassette tapes focus on topics such as parent/community involvement, social studies, music, poetry, and women's rights. Examples of individual titles representing the collection include: *Hubert Humphrey: Friend of Education* (Humphrey speaking to the NEA assembly in Minneapolis in 1977; no. 1969–5–06); *Future Issues in Rights Enforcement* (Attorney General Ramsey Clark, 1973; no. 0540–6–06); and *ERA:*

The Equal Rights Amendment and You (Margaret M. Heckler, 1975; no. 0589–9–06). These and other recordings may be ordered from NEA Distribution Center, The Academic Building, Saw Mill Road, West Haven, Connecticut, 06516 (telephone: 203/934–2669).

NEA publishes *Today's Education* (quarterly), *Reporter* (8 times a year), *Handbook* (annual), *Oral History as a Teaching Approach* (1976), and various bulletins.

NOTE: The Motion Picture, Broadcasting and Recorded Sound Division of the Library of Congress (A41) has at least 4 disc recordings of 8 NEA-sponsored radio programs broadcasted in 1953. In addition, the National Archives and Records Service (B27) has a number of NEA recordings (RG 48).

National Federation of Community Broadcasters (NFCB)   **See entry H18**

National Federation of the Blind (NFB)   **See entry F14**

M41 National League of Cities (NLC)

1.   *1301 Pennsylvania Avenue, N.W.*
      Washington, D.C. 20004
      (202) 626–3000 (General)
      (202) 626–3200 (Conference Management & Planning)
      (202) 626–3210 (Library)

2.   Alan Beals, Executive Director
      Olivia Kredel, Manager, Municipal Reference Service

3.   The National League of Cities, established in 1924, represents 49 leagues and more than 1,000 cities directly and, through the membership of the state municipal leagues, almost 15,000 additional cities. The league represents its members in Washington in the legislative, administrative, and judicial processes that affect them, as well as providing training, and technical information to municipal officials for improving the quality of local government.

4.   The league holds conferences and conventions annually, which consist of seminars, workshops, panel discussions, and lectures on virtually every topic related to cities. Most of the sessions have been recorded on audio cassettes and are available for purchase. For example, the "1981 Congress of Cities: New Directions for Cities" has been recorded on 83 cassettes, which focus on such topics as energy, transportation, crime, handicapped needs, taxes, employment, recreation, environment, education, housing rehabilitation, state resources, solar power, foreign investment, and social services. The "1982 Congressional Cities Conference" has been recorded on 51 cassettes, which focus on women in municipal government, energy, environment and natural resources, finance, human development, transportation, and housing. Audio cassettes for two conferences held in 1983 are also available. Orders are filled by Eastern Audio Associates, Inc., 8980-B Route 108, Columbia, Maryland, 21045.

5.   Flyers describing the audio cassettes and various other publications are distributed free of charge upon request.

M42 National Mental Health Association (NMHA)

1. *1021 Prince Street*
    Alexandria, Virginia 22314
    (703) 684–7722

2. Douglas Waterstreet, Acting Executive Director

3. The National Mental Health Association is a voluntary organization whose mission is to promote mental health, prevent mental illness, and improve the care and treatment of the mentally ill. It has 650 chapters throughout the United States whose activities include education, advocacy, and the dissemination of information.

4. NMHA publishes a host of materials including books, pamphlets, campaign kits, and a significant number of audiovisual materials including films, slides, and audio cassettes. Films make up the greater part of these materials. Currently, the audio cassettes available for purchase consist mostly of public service announcements narrated by the actor Cliff Robertson. Other materials include a disc on membership recruitment and a cassette on the subject of tension.

5. The association has a catalog of publications available to interested individuals.

M43 National Office Products Association (NOPA)

1. *301 North Fairfax Street*
    Alexandria, Virginia 22314
    (703) 549–9040

2. Donald P. Haspell, Executive Vice-President

3. The National Office Products Association, founded in 1904, consists of retailers, wholesalers, and manufacturers' representatives dedicated to a number of objectives, including conducting economic research, seminars, and management and sales training programs.

4–5. NOPA has a variety of audio and video tape training aids available for purchase that focus primarily on management. NOPA publications include *Office Products Industry Report* (biweekly) and *Special Report to the Office Products Industry* (bimonthly). A catalog of publications is available upon request.

National Radio Broadcasters Association (NRBA)   **See entry H20**

M44 National Science Teachers Association (NSTA)

1. *1742 Connecticut Avenue, N.W.*
    Washington, D.C. 20009
    (202) 328–5800

2. Bill G. Aldridge, Executive Director

3. The National Science Teachers Association, established in 1944, seeks to improve the quality of teaching and of educational systems, particularly those relating to science education. It achieves this through its various convention programs, special projects, and publications.

4–5. The use of audiovisual materials is important to science educators. Therefore, at its national annual convention, NSTA arranges for a major exhibit of recent and noteworthy audiovisuals in the field.

NSTA publishes a set of audiotaped interviews with six women scientists titled "Women in Science" (interviews are conducted by Donah Moche). Other publications include monographs, bulletins, and journals, including *The Science Teacher, Science and Children,* and the *Journal of College Science Teaching.* A flyer describing the association and a catalog of publications is available on request.

M45 National Society for Children and Adults with Autism (NSAC)

1.   *1234 Massachusetts Avenue, N.W., Suite 1017*
Washington, D.C. 20005
(202) 7830–0125

2.   Bradford A. Tatum, Interim, Executive Director

3.   The purpose of the National Society for Children and Adults with Autism is to further the education and welfare of people with autism. The society achieves this goal by promoting additional legislation and research and by providing various information and referral services.

4–5. NSAC maintains an active and varied publications program. Available for purchase are approximately 70 cassette recordings of the NSAC International Symposium on Autism held during July 14–18, 1981. Included are lectures, panel presentations, and conference workshops for parents and professionals. Topics include communication, language, ecological studies, neurochemistry, neuropsychology, neurobiology, social studies, music, education, legislation, ethnic groups, and international studies. Examples of recorded sessions at the symposium include *Issues in Language and Communication Research* (session no. 1; Paula Menyuk and Loes Schuler); *The Identification of Research Needs in Natural Settings* (session no. 4; Anne M. Donnellan and Martin Kozloff); *Language and Communication* (session no. 6; Dorothy W. Davis, Margaret P. Creedon, and others); *U.C.L.A. Clinical Research Center* (session no. 15; Marion Sigman, Judy Ungerer, Illene Tonick, and Fred Frankel); *Biological Studies in Childhood Autism* (session no. 19; Donald J. Cohen); *Neuropsychological Study of Autism and Treatment of Autism, Including the Asperger Syndrome in East Europe* (session no. 24; Andor J. Tari); *Dermatoglyphic Analysis of Autistic Children* (session no. 25; Angel Riviere); *The Language of Music: Right Hemisphere Power* (session no. 35; piano recital by Eileen Coughlin who has autism). Recordings are ordered from American Audio Association, P.O. Box 511, Floral Park, New York, 11002 (telephone: 212/740–9186).

NSAC also publishes a variety of printed materials including their newsletter, *The Advocate* (bi-monthly) and an annual proceedings of national NSAC conferences. An audio catalog, as well as various book and film catalogs, are available on request.

M46 National Society for Performance and Instruction (NSPI)

1. *1126 16th Street, N.W., Suite 315*
   Washington, D.C. 20036
   (202) 861–0777

2. Kay Schaeffer, Executive Director

3–4. The National Society for Performance and Instruction, founded in 1962, is an international organization of over 2,000 individuals interested in the application and advancement of various technologies. The society's work consists of analysis, research, and application for developing solutions to human performance problems. The society conducts a variety of programs including annual conferences and workshops. Some of the programs center on innovations in instructional technology. For example, one of the post-conference workshops held in April 1982 was devoted to media production. A number of guest speakers discussed the topic, "How to Develop Audio Visual Training Modules."

5. The society publishes the journal *Performance & Instruction* (monthly, except January and August) in which articles are printed frequently on media evaluation and production. Flyers describing NSPI objectives and programs are available upon request.

M47 National Symphony Orchestra (NSO)

1. *John F. Kennedy Center for the Performing Arts*
   Washington, D.C. 20566
   (202) 785–8100 (Public Relations Office)

2. Mstislav Rostropovich, Music Director
   Henry Fogel, Executive Director
   Patricia J. O'Kelly, Public Relations

3–4. The National Symphony Orchestra has produced numerous recordings under its various music directors, including Hans Kindler, Howard Mitchell, Antal Dorati, and Mstislav Rostropovich. Recording companies have included Columbia, Deutsche Grammophon, London, RCA, Richardson, Turnabout, and Westminster. Although a complete set of recordings made by the NSO are not available in any one repository, the Motion Picture, Broadcasting and Recorded Sound Division of the Library of Congress (A41) has a representative selection.

5. A complete typewritten discography prepared by Richard Freed is available for reference in the Public Relations Office. In addition, a printed discography of currently available recordings is provided to individuals upon request.

National Wildlife Federation—Frazier Memorial Library   See entry A56

M48 NAVA, International Communications Industries Association (NAVA/ICIA)

1.   *3150 Spring Street*
     Fairfax, Virginia 22031
     (703) 273–7200

2.   Ronald D. Henry, President

3.   NAVA, International Communications Industries Association, established in 1939, is the international trade organization of the audiovisual communications industry and consists of media and business professionals who seek to promote more advanced and effective methods to educate, communicate, and train its constituency. NAVA/ICIA serves as a clearinghouse for information about every sector of the audiovisual industry, as well as representing the industry in various lobbying activities.

The association's services and programs are extensive. Each year NAVA/ICIA holds a convention and exposition for recent hardware and software developments. There are also various council activities representing various segments of the industry. NAVA/ICIA also offers a comprehensive training program for persons who distribute audiovisual products (K14) and for those who use audiovisual communications products.

5.   NAVA/ICIA publishes a variety of materials including a slide/tape program *To Communicate with Imagination* (also available in video audiovisuals); a multi-image show, *Today's World, Tommorrow's Future;* a bi-weekly newsletter, *Communications Industries Report,* which contains current information on the audiovisual industry; *The Membership Directory,* and *The Audio-Visual Equipment Directory* (1983–1984).

M49 OPERA America

1.   *633 E Street, N.W.*
     Washington, D.C. 20004
     (202) 347–9262

2.   Martin I. Kagan, Executive Director

3.   OPERA America, founded in 1970, consists of 91 opera companies, who collectively promote the production and enjoyment of opera through education, information dissemination, and intercompany communications.

4.   OPERA America has an Education Division, which maintains a collection of multiple copies of tape recordings of selected operas produced by member opera companies including the Metropolitan Opera Company, Greater Miami Opera Association, Michigan Opera Theatre, and the New York City Opera. The tapes were produced with the assistance of grants from OPERA America.

The recordings are designed to be used by handicapped persons, particularly blind individuals. Almost all of the tapes include critical commentaries and synopses of the operas by well-known critics, such as Andrew Porter. To date, the collection consists of 41 operas, recorded on some 390 audio cassettes. Examples include *Norma* (Vincenzo Bellini); *Lulu* (Alban Berg); *Elixir of Love* (Gaetano Donizetti); *Hansel and Gretel* (Engelbert Humperdinck); *Pagliacci* (Ruggiero Leoncavallo); *Cavalleria Rusticana* (Pietro Mascagni); *Cosi fan Tutte* (Wolfgang Amadeus Mozart); *The Magic*

Flute (Wolfgang Amadeus Mozart); *Dialogues of the Carmelites* (Francis Poulenc); *Manon Lescaut* (Giacomo Puccini); *Tosca* (Giacomo Puccini); *Turandot* (Giacomo Puccini); *L'Italiana in Algeri* (Gioacchino Rossini); *The Masked Ball* (Giuseppe Verdi); and *La Traviata* (Giuseppe Verdi). Currently, the tapes can be borrowed by the constituents of the member opera companies.

M50 Oral History in the Mid-Atlantic Region (OHMAR)

1. *P.O. Box 266*
    College Park, Maryland 20740

2. Patricia Cooper, President

3. Oral History in the Mid-Atlantic Region (Delaware, District of Columbia, Maryland, New Jersey, Pennsylvania, Virginia, and West Virginia) is an organization whose purpose is to share information about the techniques and applications of oral history, to promote standards among those engaged in producing oral histories, and to assist individuals interested in learning about the subject. Its members include historians, librarians, archivists, teachers, folklorists, independent researchers, and others interested in oral history. Society meetings take place twice yearly. Members of OHMAR serve as excellent resource persons for information on oral history programs and collections in the District of Columbia. Write Patricia Cooper, President, for additional information.

5. OHMAR publishes a newsletter (3 times a year), which reports on the organization's activities and projects, and D.C. area oral history collections and programs. A brochure describing OHMAR is available to individuals upon request.

Radio-Television News Directors Association (RTNDA) See entry H23

Society for History in the Federal Government See entry B44

M51 Society for Neuroscience

1. *11 Dupont Circle, N.W., Suite 130*
    Washington, D.C. 20036
    (202) 462–6688

2. Nancy Beany, Executive Director

3. The Society for Neuroscience is a scientific organization dedicated to the exchange of information among scientists working on the nervous system. The membership is interdisciplinary including biochemistry, neurochemistry, neurology, physiology, anatomy, and psychiatry. The society seeks to advance the understanding of nervous systems and the part they play in determining behavior. The society's programs include annual meetings, workshops, public lectures, exhibits, and publications.

4. Currently the only non-print media publications offered by the society for purchase include a 4-part set of 8 audio cassettes and slides titled *The Structure of Nervous*

Tissue by Edward G. Hones, M.D., Ph.D. The set is designed for use at medical schools, and can be ordered from Medical Marketing, Inc., 404 Park Avenue South, New York, New York 10016 (telephone: 800/221–3995 (toll-free)).

5. Included among the society's publications are *Neuroscience Training Programs Handbook, Neuroscience Commentaries, The Journal of Neuroscience,* and *Neuroscience Newsletter* (quarterly). Brochures describing the society and its publications are available free upon request.

M52 Society of Colonial Wars—Washington Chapter

1. *6654 Barnaby Street, N.W.*
   Washington, D.C. 20005
   (202) 347–2882

2. Nicholas Donnell Ward, Governor, Washington Chapter

3. The Society of Colonial Wars consists of some 4,000 individuals, including 110 members locally, who are related to persons who provided civil and military service to the colonies before the American Revolution.

4. The Washington Chapter has issued a sound recording, "The Roast Beef of Old England," which is a re-creation of music, including 45 different tunes, associated with a traditional British regimental dinner.

5. An article, "Old Musick," about the society and the recording, was published in *The Washington Post* (September 7, 1983).

Society of the Cincinnati   See entry B45

M53 Society of Woman Geographers

1. *1619 New Hampshire Avenue, N.W.*
   Washington, D.C. 20009
   (202) 265–2669

2. Elizabeth Fagg Olds, President
   Eleanor Mitchell, Librarian/Archivist/National Membership Chairman

3. The Society of Woman Geographers is an international organization consisting of a highly selective group of widely travelled women who have sought out and studied the little-known or unique places, people, and cultures of the world. The society, founded in 1925, has a central purpose of serving as a forum for the exchange of experiences and ideas while supporting and encouraging young women in the advanced study of geography.

4. The society maintains a library consisting of an extensive array of materials by and about its members. Included in the holdings are a number of unique and fascinating oral history tapes. Currently there are some 281 cassettes and 4 reel-to-reel tapes

consisting of experiences on travel, exploration, and study as recounted by members of the society. There are interviews with 56 women, as well as recordings of a number of society meetings held in Chicago, New York, San Francisco, and Washington, in addition to Society Executive Council meetings.

The collection is unique in that many of this country's notable women have been captured on tape. Some of the tapes were produced in various parts of the world on behalf of the society. Examples of recordings include Gertrude Emerson Sen, explorer in India (recorded on 3 cassettes), Eugenie Clark, ichthyologist, speaking at the 50th anniversary banquet of the society, and the Amelia Earhart: Flight into Yesterday symposium held at the National Air and Space Museum (C6) on June 18, 1982, as well as various tapes by and about Margaret Mead. Individual scholars may have access to the collection but with special permission granted on an appointment basis only. Hours during which researchers may contact the staff are 10:00 A.M. to 3:00 P.M., Wednesday and Friday.

5.   The society publishes a newsletter and an annual bulletin, which are available to its members. Information on the oral history collection is cited in the latter.

Treasury Historical Association (THA)   See entry B51

Unda-USA   See entry H25

M54 United Nations Association of the USA—Capital Area Division

1.   *3141 N Street, N.W.*
Washington, D.C. 20007
(202) 337–5551

2.   Sophie Degan, Executive Director

3.   The Capital Area Division of the United Nations Association of the USA serves as a source of information concerning United Nations meetings and events. The division had received a set of oral history and radio interviews with international political figures at the United Nations, 1974–1979. This set of tapes was donated to the American University Library (A5). The Motion Picture, Broadcasting and Recorded Sound Division of the Library of Congress (A41) has custody of a special "United Nations Recordings Collection" consisting of U.N. proceedings for the years 1946–1963.

The association also maintains a book and gift store next door (Appendix I).

M55 United States Capitol Historical Society (USCHS)

1.   *200 Maryland Avenue, N.E.*
Washington, D.C. 20515
(202) 543–8919

2.   Fred Schwengel, President

3.   The United States Capitol Historical Society's mission is to preserve the rich heritage of the Capitol and to interpret to the American people the functions and role of the Congress. The society, founded in 1962, operates the Capitol Visitor Center in the Capitol, where information on Congress, assistance to visitors, and publications relative to the Capitol are provided throughout the year. General hours are from 8:30 A.M. to 4:30 P.M., every day except Christmas, Thanksgiving, and New Year's. The society is open until 10:00 P.M. during the summer. An oral history program was conducted from 1978–1982. Transcripts of the interviews were deposited in the Manuscript Division of the Library of Congress (B20).

4–5.   Currently the society has one sound recording available for purchase: *The Voice of the People,* narrated by Helen Hayes and E.G. Marshall, provides an introduction to the history of the Capitol and the Capitol building. The recording is available from the society in both disc and cassette formats. The society also publishes a quarterly newsletter, *The Capitol Dome.*

M56 Washington Saengerbund, Inc.

1.   *2434 Wisconsin Avenue, N.W.*
      Washington, D.C. 20007

2.   Nancy Pierce, Assistant Archivist

3.   The Washington Saengerbund, founded in 1851, has carried on its tradition of combining serious choral singing and conviviality within the framework of a single club. Although the society is not formally open to the public, individuals may visit the club on Friday evenings when rehearsals are conducted.

4.   The club has 18 reel-to-reel tape recordings of various concerts presented by the Saengerbund. Some of the tapes include fall, spring, and Christmas concerts from 1973–1974, and 1976 to the present. The music presented on the tapes includes folk songs, lieder, various other art songs, and selections from both opera and operettas. The club maintains a file of programs of concerts that have been taped. It is possible to purchase copies of the tapes, but with special permission only.

5.   The Saengerbund has recently published *The Washington Saengerbund, a History of German Song and German Culture in the Nation's Capital* (1982).

M57 Women's Institute for Freedom of the Press

1.   *3306 Ross Place, N.W.*
      Washington, D.C. 20008
      (202) 966-7783

2.   Donna Allen, Director

3.   The Women's Institute for Freedom of the Press is an association of women whose purpose it is to improve women's role in communications media, to aid networking

and to increase communication among women both nationally and internationally, and to generate more information on women.

4.   The institute has a small collection of sound recordings consisting of 25 cassette tapes of its annual conventions for the years 1979–1982, which took place at the National Press Club, Washington, D.C. (B32). The primary topic for the conventions centered on plans for an international communication network for women. Individuals must request special permission to listen to these recordings. Once obtained, researchers must supply their own listening equipment.

5.   The institute has available for purchase 7 cassette tapes entitled *Dateline Copenhagen: Woman's View* produced at the World Conference of Women, July 14–30, 1980, in Copenhagen, Denmark. The series includes Third World women in teleconference dialogues by satellite with women in six U.S. cities and dialogues among Third World women about projects to meet the needs of women in employment, education, health, and a special focus on rural women. The institute publishes an annual *Index: Directory of Women's Media* (1984), which lists women's media groups, including those for radio and television, multi-media, and music. This compilation also lists recording companies and stores that distribute recordings. Researchers will also want to refer to *Media Report to Women,* which lists and describes news items and documents issued since 1972 in over 100 subject areas, including broadcasting, music, public broadcasting, radio, and records. It also monitors the release of new media products, such as records and tapes.

World Peace Through Law Center (WPTLC)   **See entry J17**

N Publications and Print Media

Introductory Note

This section lists audio-related publications, issued in the Washington area, which include reviews of recordings and articles of special interest. Also cited here are companies that produce and distribute audio recordings and printed materials. Commercial firms that distribute recordings but do not produce them are listed in Appendix I.

N1 BNA Communications, Inc. (Bureau of National Affairs, Inc.)

1. *9439 Key West Avenue*
   Rockville, Maryland 20850
   (301) 948–0540

2. Hunter Williams, Sales Representative

3. BNA Communications advertises itself as the world's largest producer and distributor of training materials in the fields of management development, supervisory training, sales, safety, labor relations, motivation, communications, and employee health. Many of the training programs are conducted by leading behaviorial scientists or expert management consultants. The company produces many of its programs in an audiovisual format.

5. BNA's *Catalog of Training Programs* lists numerous audio cassettes and is available upon request. Training programs listed in the catalog may be previewed free of charge at the above address. Write or telephone for details. A number of BNA audio materials are cited in *Management Media Directory* (Detroit: Gale Research, 1982).

N2 Congressional Quarterly, Inc.

1. *1414 22nd Street, N.W.*
   Washington, D.C. 20037
   (202) 887–8578

2.   Peter Harkness, Executive Editor
Kathryn Gest, Managing Editor

5.   Congressional Quarterly, Inc., publishes a *Weekly Report* on legislation and committee hearings in Congress. Issues regarding the piracy, counterfeiting, and off-the-air home recording of sound recordings have recently been discussed in Congress, and cited in *Weekly Report*. For example, issue 20 of volume 40 (May 15, 1982), p. 1106, reports that one bill which would increase "penalties for record, tape, and film piracy and counterfeiting" was cleared in Congress. Individual reports on audio recordings and copyright may be found in the *Weekly Report* index under the term "recordings."

N3   Development Publications

1.   *5605 Lamar Road*
Bethesda, Maryland 20816
(301) 320–4409
(301) 229–2680

2.   Kim Mullen, Director

3.   Since 1965, Development Publications has been publishing and distributing resources used for training, consulting, and development. In 1980 the firm became the exclusive distributor for three consulting and training organizations including Organization Renewal, Inc., Project Associates, Inc., and International Consultants Foundation.

5.   Development Publications publishes books, pamphlets, reprints, films, and audio cassette learning modules. Currently available for purchase are 5 learning programs having a total of 21 audio cassette tapes with accompanying pamphlets and manuals. The program titles are *Coping with Change and Conflict, People in Planning, The Consulting Process in Action, Reality Practice: Theory and Skills of Role Playing Methods,* and *The Life/Work Goals Exploration Workbook Kit.* The *Multi Media Resources Catalog* is available upon request.

N4   Forecast

3.   This discontinued monthly magazine was published in Silver Spring, Maryland , from 1963 to 1982. It listed FM radio and television programs, and concerts in and around the Washington area. A regular department of the magazine, "Classics in Review," by Robert E. Benson, featured critiques of classical music recordings. The magazine listed the programs of radio stations WAMU–FM, WETA–FM, and WGTS–FM (Appendix III).

Government Institutes, Inc.   **See entry J11**

N5 Government Printing Office (GPO)

1. *Main Bookstore*
   710 North Capitol Street, N.W.
   Washington, D.C. 20402
   (202) 275-2091 (Main Bookstore)
   (202) 783-3238 (General Orders and Inquiries)

   Mail:
   Superintendent of Documents
   U.S. Government Printing Office
   Washington, D.C. 20402

   Commerce Department Bookstore
   First Floor, Room 1604
   14th and E Streets, N.W.
   Washington, D.C. 20230
   (202) 377-3527

   Health and Human Services Bookstore
   North Building, Room 1528
   330 Independence Avenue, S.W.
   Washington, D.C. 20201
   (202) 472-7478

   State Department Bookstore
   North Lobby, Room 2817
   21st and C Streets, N.W.
   Washington, D.C. 20520
   (202) 632-6575

   Laurel Bookstore
   8660 Cherry Lane
   Laurel, Maryland 20810
   (301) 953-7974

   Pentagon Bookstore
   Main Concourse, South End, Room 2E171
   Washington, D.C. 20301
   (703) 557-1821

2. Danford L. Sawyer, Jr., Public Printer
   Raymond M. Taylor, Superintendent of Documents

3-5. The Government Printing Office publishes and sells the reports and publications of United States government agencies and Congress. Close to 25,000 titles are currently available. New items are added and backlist titles are dropped at the rate of 2,000 to 3,000 per year. The GPO also publishes and maintains catalogs of these publications. See the *Monthly Catalog of United States Government Publications* (with semiannual indexes and annual cumulations also available through a computer database) for individual listings. A handy means for locating audiovisual printed materials in this catalog is the *Cumulative Index* (2 vols.) for 1970–1976, where relevant items are listed in the index under such topics as Audio-Visual Education, Audio-Visual Equipment, Sound Recordings, and Tape Recorders. A complete sales catalog, *The GPO*

Sales Publications Reference File is available bimonthly on microfiche and accessible through a computer database, *Publications Reference File* (PRF) through BRS and DIALOG. Inclusive dates for computer coverage are July 1976 to the present. In addition, subject bibliographies are available for more than 270 topics, including agriculture, annual reports, area handbooks, armed forces, directories and lists of persons and organizations, foreign affairs, foreign languages, International Trade Commission publications, maps, military history, motion picture films, audiovisual materials, national and world economy, national defense and security, naval history, statistics, and treaties.

Two free catalogs include *U.S. Government Books* and *New Books*. The latter is issued every two months and lists all publications that have been added to the sales inventory since the previous issue.

Researchers should note that specific types of government publications are also available from several other federal agencies, including the National Audiovisual Center (L7), National Technical Information Service (N7), Library of Congress (A41), General Services Administration, Smithsonian Institution Press (N11), Bureau of Mines, Defense Mapping Agency, General Accounting Office, National Ocean Survey, and the United States Geological Survey. The Printed Archives Branch of the National Archives and Records Service (B27) is the official repositiory archive for all GPO publications.

N6   National Geographic Society—Educational Services

1.   *17th and M Streets, N.W.*
Washington, D.C. 20036
(202) 857–7305

2.   George Peterson, Editor, Educational Services

3–4.   The National Geographic Society is well-known for its many publications and international adventures. The society itself has a print library and a film library but has no audio tape holdings. The Educational Services department does produce audiovisual materials mostly for use in schools. Over 125 filmstrips with accompanying cassettes in all areas of science, social studies, and language arts are available for purchase, in addition to other media.

The National Geographic also offers its periodicals and some book titles in braille and/or flexible disc or cassette for the blind and physically handicapped. Likewise available are captioned filmstrips for those with impaired hearing. These materials may be ordered directly through the National Library Service for the Blind and Physically Handicapped, Library of Congress, 1291 Taylor Street, N.W., Washington, D.C. 20542.

5.   All audiovisual material along with complete ordering information are described in the annual *National Geographic Society Educational Services Catalog*.

N7 National Technical Information Service (NTIS) (Commerce Department)

1. *5285 Port Royal Road*
   Springfield, Virginia 22161
   (703) 487–4600 (General Information)
   (703) 487–4650 (Sales)

2. Joseph F. Caponio, Director

3–5. The National Technical Information Service is the primary source of the public sale of U.S. government-sponsored research, development, and engineering reports. It also publishes foreign technical reports and other studies prepared by national and local government agencies. The NTIS information collection contains over 1.4 million titles. These titles are listed in *Government Reports, Announcements & Index* (bi-weekly). One may search for various titles using a number of indexes, including personal author, corporate author, and keyword. Studies related to sound recordings are readily located through the keyword index under the term "Audiovisual". NTIS also offers a standing order service called *SRIM (Selected Research in Microfiche),* issued bi-weekly, and 28 weekly abstract newsletters.

Another convenient method of locating, recent technical reports or for compiling subject groups of abstracts is to conduct an NTIS bibliographic database on-line search. One need only identify an organization that maintains the database for public use through its contractual relationship with NTIS.

Various federal government agencies use NTIS for publishing their audiovisual reports. For example, the National Medical Audiovisual Center although no longer in operation has a number of its reports published by NTIS.

Telephone inquiries may be directed to NTIS during the hours 7:45 A.M. to 4:15 P.M., Monday through Friday. Individuals may request a free NTIS *General Catalog of Information Services No. 8a* (1983).

N8 Organization of American States (OAS)—Inter-American Musical Editions

1. *1889 F Street, N.W.*
   Washington, D.C. 20006
   (202) 789–3157

2. Efrain Paesky, Director
   Karen Cardullo, Program Manager

3–4. The OAS publishes a series of 19 disc recordings representing the variety of musical traditions, both serious and popular, as performed by leading soloists, or-chestras, and ensembles of member states. Included are songs of Argentina, Bolivia, Brazil, Caribbean, Chile, Columbia, Cuba, Mexico, Peru, and Venezuela, as well as traditional guitar music and a representative collection of classical music.

5. A leaflet describing the recordings is available free upon request.

N9   Recorded Books

1.   *6306 Aaron Lane*
     Clinton, Maryland 20735
     (800) 638–1304 (toll-free)
     (301) 868–7856 (Maryland residents only)

2.   Sandy Spencer, Manager

4.   Recorded Books produces abridged and unabridged books on cassettes. Subjects include drama, poetry, presidential speeches, current affairs, and language instruction courses. Tapes may be either rented or purchased. Only mail order service is provided.

5.   A catalog of titles is available free to individuals upon request.

N10   Robert J. Brady Co. (Prentice-Hall Publishing and Communications Co.)

1.   *Routes 450 and 197*
     Bowie, Maryland 20715
     (301) 262–6300
     (800) 638–0220 (toll-free)

2.   Eileen Cassidy, Sales Manager

5.   The Brady Co. publishes a number of audio cassette tapes whose subjects focus on nursing and emergency medical services. Catalogs are available upon request. A number of Brady materials are cited in the National Library of Medicine's, *Audiovisuals Catalog.*

N11   Smithsonian Institution Press (Smithsonian Institution)

1.   *955 L'Enfant Plaza, Suite 2100*
     Washington, D.C. 20560
     (202) 287–3788
     (202) 357–1793 (Distribution Section)

     Mail:
     P.O. Box 1579
     Washington, D.C. 20013

2.   Felix C. Lowe, Director

3.   The Smithsonian Institution Press is an integral division of the Smithsonian Institution, which issued its first publication in 1848. The press was given its present name in 1966 and is a member of the Association of American University Presses. The Press publishes in numerous fields, principally air and space, anthropology, fine arts, biology, natural and life sciences, and regional interests.

5. Of particular significance to individuals interested in audiovisual materials in Washington, D.C., is the series *Scholars' Guides to Washington, D.C.* (sponsored by the Woodrow Wilson International Center for Scholars (J15)). Each *Guide* surveys the collections, institutions, organizations, and other resources in the metropolitan area pertinent to the study of particular geographic areas, including Russia/Soviet Union, Latin America and the Caribbean, East Asia, the Middle East, Africa, Central and East Europe, South Asia, Southeast Asia, and Northwest Europe. Each *Guide* contains sections on non-print media, such as "Collections of Music and Other Sound Recordings."A separate *Guide* covers film and video collections in the Washington, D.C., area and serves as a companion volume to the present study. All of the *Guides* have useful information on audio resources not necessarily duplicated in this volume.

Another Smithsonian publication, *Prelude to the Space Age: The Rocket Societies, 1924–1940*, includes a list of interviews, some of which are taped, and housed in the National Air and Space Museum Library (C6).

The recordings collection department was transferred from the former Division of Performing Arts to the Press in October 1982. Sound recordings produced by the Smithsonian Institution are available by mail order from Smithsonian Recordings, P.O. Box 10230, Des Moines, Iowa 50336, or on-site in the various museum shops (Appendix I). The majority of the items are either performances of the Smithsonian Chamber Players using original eighteenth-century instruments from the collections of the National Museum of American History (C11), or existing historical recordings of American music, like jazz, musical theater, and country music.

An annual catalog of the Smithsonian publications is available upon request.

N12 Tape Worm, Inc.

1. *P.O. Box 5524*
   Rockville, Maryland 20855
   (301) 258–7618

2. Ann Somerset, President

4. Tape Worm produces unabridged fiction and non-fiction books on cassettes. Included are contemporary and classic fiction, poetry, 23 language courses, success motivation and management, and sports tapes. Cassettes may be either rented or purchased.

5. A catalog is available free upon request. Orders are accepted by mail or phone. Only retail pickup is available at Sportzone, Wintergreen Plaza, Rockville Pike, Rockville, Maryland.

N13 Tapes for Readers

1. *5078 Fulton Street, N.W.*
   Washington, D.C. 20016
   (202) 362–4585

2. Stephen Banker, Director

5.   Tapes for Readers publishes a series of cassette tapes consisting of interviews with individuals associated with the arts, black studies, consumer affairs, entertainment, human behavior, psychology, native American studies, literature, living history, politics, sports, and women's studies. All interviews are conducted by Stephen Banker. Titles representing the collection include *Joseph H. Hirshhorn* (discusses his life, collections and role as a patron of the arts); *Julian Bond* (interview conducted in 1969); *The Cashless Society* (growth of the credit card with Tom Dowling, Richard Bittner, Senator Sam Ervin, Senator William Proxmire, and John Diebold); *Zubin Mehta* (conductor of the New York Philharmonic Orchestra); *Psychiatry and Creativity* (Myron Marshall and Charles Newman); *John Kenneth Galbraith* (an interview); and *Panama Treaty Signing* (September 1977, with Omar Torryos, Sol Linowitz, John McLean, Nancy Collings, and Strom Thurmond), as well as additional interviews with James Michener, Isaac Bashevis Singer, John Updike, Saul Bellow, Woody Allen, Hubert Humphrey, Maya Angelou, and Gloria Steinem.

A number of recordings in the collection have been reviewed in *Booklist* (The American Library Association). A catalog and various flyers will be sent upon request.

N14   Time-Life Books

1.   *777 Duke Street*
     Alexandria, Virginia 22314
     (703) 838-7000

2.   Reginald K. Brack, Jr., President

3.   Time-Life Books is a subsidiary of Time Incorporated of New York, specializing in illustrative documentation publications.

5.   The 1983 catalog *Time-Life Books and Records* lists recordings of big bands and classical, country, and western music. A number of sets of recordings are based on thematic ideas, including "Great Performers," "American Musicals," and "Great Men of Music." The catalog is available upon request.

N15   University Press of America

1.   *4720 Boston Way, Suite K*
     Lanham, Maryland 20706
     (301) 459-3366

2.   James Lyons, Managing Editor

3.   University Press of America publishes books intended for the academic community, covering a wide range of topics, including economics, history, literature, philosophy, political science, religion, and sociology. The press uses a cost-efficient approach, employing a photoreproduction process to print typewritten and typeset manuscripts prepared by the authors.

5.   A catalog, which is available upon request, lists many monographs on music, broadcasting, and various topics in communications. One or more of the books on music contain individual discographies pertaining to the musical areas discussed.

N16 Washington Post

1. *1150 15th Street, N.W.*
    Washington, D.C. 20071
    (202) 334-6000

2. Benjamin C. Bradlee, Executive Editor

3. This daily newspaper regularly features record reviews. Some of the critics include Joseph McLellan (classical), Lon Tuck (classical), Boo Browning (popular music), and Richard Harrington (jazz and popular music).

5. Reviews of recordings are indexed since 1979 in *The Official Washington Post Index* (monthly; Woodbridge, Conn: Research Publications) and in the *Newspaper Index to the Washington Post* (Wooster, Ohio: Bell and Howell; Micro Photo Division) until 1981.

N17 Washington Star

3. The *Washington Star* daily newspaper, which ceased publication August 7, 1981, regularly published reviews of recordings. During the last year of publication, reviewers included Boris Weintraub (country music), Crispin Sartwell (rock), and Theodore W. Libbey, Jr. (classical music). The complete files of the *Washington Star,* including 1 million photographs, 13 million clippings, numerous articles, scrapbooks, and awards, are held as a permanent collection in the Washingtoniana Division of the Martin Luther King, Jr., Memorial Library (A42).

5. The Microfilming Corporation of America has indexed the *Washington Star* for the period 1852–1973.

N18 Washington Times

1. *3600 New York Avenue, N.E.*
    Washington, D.C. 20002
    (202) 636-3000 (Information)

2. James R. Whelan, Editor and Publisher

3–4. Financially underwritten by the Unification Church, the daily *Washington Times* began publication in 1982, in part to fill the void created by the *Washington Star*'s failure in 1981.
    The *Times* regularly features record reviews. Critics include David Charvonia, Mike Dolan, Glenn Garvin, and Lawrence D. Ink.

APPENDIXES

I Record Stores and Other Distributors of Sound Recordings

This appendix includes a selection of stores that stock sound recordings of potential interest to scholars and other researchers. A number of these establishments deal exclusively in out-of-print recordings. Stores that stock only popular music are not included here but may be identified through the Washington, D.C. area telephone books.

Entry Format

1. Address and Telephone Number

2. Hours

3. Stock

Audubon Book Shop

1. *1621 Wisconsin Avenue*
   Washington, D.C. 20007
   (202) 337–6062

2. 10:00 A.M.–5:00 P.M.   Tuesday, Wednesday, Friday, Saturday
   10:00 A.M.–9:00 P.M.   Thursday

3. The Audubon Book Shop has available, for purchase, some 20 tape recordings of bird songs, as well as an extensive array of printed materials.

Audubon Naturalist Society Gift Shop

1. *8940 Jones Mill Road*
   Chevy Chase, D.C. 20815
   (202) 652–9188

2. 10:00 A.M.–5:00 P.M.   Monday–Friday
   10:00 A.M.–3:00 P.M.   Saturday–Sunday

3.   The Audubon Naturalist Society gift shop has available, for purchase, 15 to 20 different recordings of bird songs. Organizational papers and sound recordings of the Audubon Naturalist Society are held in the Smithsonian Institution Archives (B42) The society publishes a monthly magazine, *Audubon.*

Common Concerns

1.   *1347 Connecticut Avenue, N.W.*
Washington, D.C. 20036
(202) 463-6500

2.   10:00 A.M.–9:00 P.M.   Monday–Thursday
10:00 A.M.–10:00 P.M.   Friday, Saturday
12:00 Noon–6:00 P.M.   Sunday

3.   Common Concerns has a selective collection consisting of jazz, political protest, and international recordings of such areas as Latin America, Africa, Palestine, and the Caribbean.

Disc Shop

1.   *5300 Wisconsin Avenue*
Washington, D.C. 20015
(202) 966-3466

2.   10:00 A.M.–9:00 P.M.   Monday–Friday
10:00 A.M.–6:00 P.M.   Saturday
12:00 Noon–5:00 P.M.   Sunday (holiday season only)

3.   The Disc Shop stocks a broad selection of recordings, including a larger number of imported international music from such areas as the Middle East and Asia. It also carries an assortment of documentary materials, classical stories, and language courses.

Folger Shakespeare Library—Bookstore

1.   *201 East Capitol Street, S.E.*
Washington, D.C. 20003
(202) 546-2626

2.   10:00 A.M.–4:00 P.M.   Monday–Saturday

3.   The bookstore has available for purchase 5 disc and 44 cassette recordings consisting of music composed at the time of Shakespeare, plays of Shakespeare, and such other individual recordings as *A History of the English Language, The Decameron,* and a 2 disc/cassette recording of *Shakespeare in Hollywood* performed during the 1930s. The bookstore will accept mail orders. A catalog is available by request.
    The Folger Shakespeare Library is described in entry A23.

Globe Book Shop

1. *1700 Pennsylvania Avenue, N.W.*
    Washington, D.C. 20006
    (202) 393–1490

2. 9:00 A.M.–6:00 P.M.   Monday–Friday
    10:00 A.M.–6:00 P.M.   Saturday

3. The Globe Book Shop has a selection of literature and music on recordings. Also sold are two types of language courses; one teaches foreign languages, the other teaches English from foreign languages. Both are sold on records and tapes.

House of Musical Traditions

1. *7040 Carroll Avenue*
    Takoma Park, Maryland 20912
    (301) 270–0222
    (301) 270–09800

2. 12:00 Noon–7:00 P.M.   Tuesday–Saturday
    12:00 Noon–5:00 P.M.   Sunday

3. This commercial enterprise primarily sells folk music. It offers recordings of American folk, ethnic folk, and most D.C. artists. Also sold are blues, jazz, calypso, and Louisiana Cajun.

I Hear Your Hand

1. *P.O. Box 26*
    Greenbelt, Maryland 20770

3. This firm sells disc and cassette recordings of deaf awareness songs. A catalog is available to individuals by writing to the above address.

Indian Spice and Gift Store

1. *4110 Wilson Boulevard*
    Arlington, Virginia 22203
    (703) 522–0149

2. 11:00 A.M.–8:00 P.M.   Monday–Saturday
    11:00 A.M.–7:00 P.M.   Sunday

3. The Indian Spice and Gift Store caters to the South Asian ethnic community and provides a good assortment of South Asian music on discs, and reel and cassette

tapes. The store's stock of music contains both regional folk and contemporary popular music.

Institute of Applied Natural Science (IANS)—Hypnotism Book Store

1. *3000 Connecticut Avenue, N.W., Suite 308*
    Washington, D.C. 20008
    (202) 387–7749

2. 11:00 A.M.–6:00 P.M.   Monday–Friday
    12:00 Noon–4:00 P.M.   Sunday

3.   The Hypnotism Book Store has available for purchase a wide variety of audio cassettes for such topics as induction management, autohypnosis, hypnotherapy, sexuality, stress reduction, biofeedback, and sound effects. A catalog, which includes some 50 titles, can be obtained upon request. A mail order service is available.

International Learning Center

1. *1715 Connecticut Avenue, N.W.*
    Washington, D.C. 20009
    (202) 232–4111

2. 10:00 A.M.–7:00 P.M.   Monday–Saturday

3.   International Learning Center stocks 30 to 40 cassettes and records of music and instruction from all over the world. Instructional tapes to learn English from foreign languages are also available.

Lammas

1. *321 7th Street, S.E.*
    Washington, D.C. 20003
    (202) 546–7292

2. 11:00 A.M.–6:00 P.M.   Tuesday–Friday
    10:00 A.M.–6:00 P.M.   Saturday
    1:00 P.M.–5:00 P.M.   Sunday

3.   Lammas functions as a place of information exchange for Washington's feminist community. The store stocks books, journals, disc and cassette recordings whose topics center on women's issues.

Library of Congress—Sales Shop

1. *Thomas Jefferson Building*
    1st Street, S.E.
    (between Independence Avenue and East Capitol Street)
    Washington, D.C. 20540

2. 9:00 A.M.–9:00 P.M.   Monday, Tuesday, Thursday, Friday
    9:00 A.M.–5:00 P.M.   Wednesday, Saturday, and holidays
    1:00 P.M.–5:00 P.M.   Sunday

3. The Sales Shop sells Library of Congress publications, postcards, slides, facsimiles, posters, folklife articles, and sound recordings. The recordings are produced through the auspices of the divisions of Music, Hispanic, and Archive of Folk Culture. Subjects include poetry and literature, religion, and the series "Folk Music of the U.S." A number of brochures listing recordings available for purchase are available free upon request.

Melody Record Shop

1. *1529 Connecticut Avenue, N.W.*
    Washington, D.C. 20036
    (202) 232–4002

2. 10:00 A.M.–9:00 P.M.   Monday–Saturday
    12:00 Noon–5:00 P.M.   Sunday

3. Melody Record Shop stocks a selection of American music, international music, and instructions in foreign languages of such countries as Turkey, Indonesia, and of South America.

Modern Language Book & Record Store

1. *3160 O Street, N.W.*
    Washington, D.C. 20007
    (202) 338–8963

2. 10:00 A.M.–6:00 P.M.   Monday–Friday
    10:00 A.M.–5:00 P.M.   Saturday

3. A modest collection of disc recordings of folk, contemporary, and popular, and spoken arts of mostly European and Latin American countries. Also available for purchase are disc and cassette language instructional recordings representing some fifteen languages. Mail order service is not provided.

Old Record Shop

1. *2405 Linden Lane*
    Silver Spring, Maryland 20910
    (301) 585–7070

2. 4:00 P.M.–8:00 P.M.   Thursday
    11:30 A.M.–6:00 P.M.   Saturday

3.   The Old Record Shop carries a complete line of used records (78s and lps only), including jazz, country, classical, and international music. The stock always varies according to the material the public brings in. They also sell machines adapted to play the 78s and lps.

Pyramid Bookstore

1. *2849 Georgia Avenue, N.W.*
    Washington, D.C. 20001
    (202) 328–0190

2. 10:00 A.M.–7:00 P.M.   Monday–Friday
    11:00 A.M.–5:00 P.M.   Saturday
    12:00 Noon–5:00 P.M.   Sunday

3.   Pyramid Bookstore sells books and records by and about people of African descent. They sell reggae, African music, jazz, used records, and speeches by well-known persons, such as, Malcolm X, Martin Luther King, Jr., Karenga, and Dr. Francis Welding.

Record & Tape, Ltd.

1. *1239 Wisconsin Avenue, N.W.*
    Washington, D.C. 20007
    (202) 338–6712

    Other locations:
    1900 L Street, N.W.
    Washington, D.C. 20036
    (202) 785–5037

    1340 Connecticut Avenue, N.W.
    Washington, D.C. 20036
    (202) 785–2662

    106 South Union Street
    Alexandria, Virginia 22314
    (703) 684–0030

2.   Wisconsin Avenue store
10:00 A.M.–10:00 P.M.   Monday–Thursday
10:00 A.M.–12:00 Midnight   Friday, Saturday
12:00 Noon–6:00 P.M.   Sunday

3.   This commercial enterprise carries one of the largest selections of international recordings in the metropolitan area. They offer full-length language courses plus a special 2-cassette travel package for the foreign visitor. Also sold are recordings to teach the English language from other foreign languages. Music from most areas of the world is available. The stores also sell compact discs, used records, and budget cassettes.

Record Collections

1.   *8231 Woodmont Avenue*
Bethesda, Maryland 20814
(301) 652–5500

2.   10:00 A.M.–6:00 P.M.   Monday–Friday
11:00 A.M.–5:00 P.M.   Saturday
1:00 P.M.–5:00 P.M.   Sunday (winter hours)

3.   Along with a line of American music, poetry, and international music, this establishment carries a wide variety of out-of-print material, including soundtracks for films, political campaigns, and political campaign songs. A tape duplication service is available.

Serenade Record Shop

1.   *1713 G Street, N.W.*
Washington, D.C. 20006
(202) 638–6648

Other locations:
1800 M Street, N.W.
Washington, D.C. 20036
(202) 452–0075

1710 Pennsylvania Avenue, N.W.
Washington, D.C. 20006
(202) 638–5580

2.   9:30 A.M.–7:00 P.M.   Monday–Friday
9:30 A.M.–6:00 P.M.   Saturday

3.   Serenade Record Shop has an excellent stock of classical music, especially import labels on both discs and tapes. In addition, there are over 200 titles to choose from on compact discs. One may subscribe to the shop's newsletter, *Serenade News*. A mail order service is provided.

Smithsonian Institution—Museum Shops

1.   *Mail:*
     Capitol Gallery Building, Suite 295B
     600 Maryland Avenue, S.W.
     Washington, D.C. 20560
     (202) 287–3563 (Information)

2.   10:00 A.M.–5:30 P.M.   Daily

3.   Each museums operates a separate giftshop, selling material pertaining to its museum. The specialty audio material is available in three shops: American History (202/357–1528), which sells spoken classics; Air and Space (202/357–1387), offering science fiction and also spoken tapes of astronauts; and Arts and Industries (202/357–1369), which carries recordings of Victorian novels and poetry. Also available is *The Guide to the Smithsonian,* tapes for the handicapped and blind. These can be purchased in the National Museum of American History shop. Mail order service for recordings produced by the Smithsonian are available through the Smithsonian Institution Press (N11).

United Nations Association of the U.S.A.—Capital Area Division—Gift Shop

1.   *3143 N Street, N.W.*
     Washington, D.C. 20007
     (202) 337–5553

2.   11:00 A.M.–5:00 P.M.   Monday–Saturday

3.   The Gift Shop of the United Nations Association has available for purchase a selection of disc recordings produced by the United Nations Children Fund (UNICEF). Included is the series *Sing Children Sing* representing the songs of such countries as Austria, France, Israel, Mexico, and the United States. Mail order service is not available.

Victor Kamkin, Inc.

1.   *12224 Parklawn Drive*
     Rockville, Maryland 20852
     (301) 881–5973

2.   9:00 A.M.–5:00 P.M.   Monday–Saturday

3.   This commercial enterprise provides a wide selection of Russian classical, folk, and spoken arts disc and cassette recordings, most of which are produced in the Soviet Union.

Vietnam Imports

1.   *922 West Broad Street*
     Falls Church, Virginia 22046
     (703) 534–9441

2.   10:00 A.M.–8:00 P.M.   Monday–Saturday

3.   A commercial establishment, Vietnam Imports offers a selection of Vietnamese instrumental and vocal music on audio tapes.

Washington Bible College—Bookstore

1.   *6511 Princess Garden Parkway*
     Lanham, Maryland 20706
     (301) 552–1400

2.   9:00 A.M.–9:00 P.M.   Monday, Tuesday
     9:00 A.M.–6:00 P.M.   Wednesday–Friday
     12:00 Noon–5:00 P.M.   Saturday

3.   Washington Bible College Bookstore sells both music and spoken word recordings. In the music category they carry gospel, classical, and inspirational music. These are sold on both records and tapes. Their spoken tapes vary from the spoken Bible in three languages, English, Korean, and Spanish, to lectures and seminars. These lectures are presented by visiting scholars and professors. The main emphasis of these lectures is Genesis and other Biblical teachings. Also available are counseling tapes by Tim Lahye and Dr. James Dobson. A children's section is also available, which contains both books and songs on either record or tape. Also for purchase are book abridgements with such titles as *The Home* (Howard Hendricks), *Act of Marriage* (Tim Lahye), and *Strong Willed Children* (Dr. James Dobson). The Bookstore will also ship the recordings anywhere in the world.
     The Washington Bible College—Oyer Memorial Library is described in entry E8.

Watershed Foundation—Poet's Audio Center

1.   *930 F Street, N.W., Suite 612*
     Washington, D.C. 20004
     (202) 347–4823

     Mail:
     P.O. Box 50145
     Washington, D.C. 20004

2.   9:30 A.M.–5:30 P.M.   Monday–Friday

3.   The foundation sells primarily spoken arts recordings, including novels and poetry by such persons as Daisy Aldan, Marvin Bell, Lucille Clifton, Owen Dodson,

Jessica Hagedorn, Shirley Kaufman, Julius Lester, Heather McHugh, George Oppen, and Sonia Sanchez. One special 10-cassette series, *A Kind of Hearth,* consists of contemporary literature as produced for public radio by the North American Poetry Network.

West Indian Record Mart

1. *700 Columbia Road, N.W.*
    Washington, D.C. 20001
    (202) 232–8226

2. 11:00 A.M.–9:30 P.M.   Monday–Saturday

3. A major source for reggae, calypso, and other music of the Caribbean area. Also sells recordings of African and other ethnic music. An article discussing the West Indians residing in Washington, D.C., in which the West Indian Record Mart is described, is "Washington's Growing Calypso Crowd," *The Washington Post* (January 3, 1982).

Zodiac Record Shop

1. *1754 Columbia Road, N.W.*
    Washington, D.C. 20009
    (202) 328–6533

2. 7:00 A.M.–9:00 P.M.   Seven days a week.

3. The Zodiac Record Shop is a commercial enterprise specializing in popular music and poetry from Latin America and the Caribbean.

II Recording Studios and Transcription Services

Listed here are organizations that provide, for a fee, cassette duplication, recording, and transcription services. Recording studios that focus on popular music are not included.

Entry Format

1. Address and Telephone Number

2. Chief Offical/Key Resource Person

3. Objectives and/or Programs

4. Collections/Research Facilities

5. Publications and Bibliographic Aids

Byron Motion Pictures

1. *Studios and Laboratory*
   65 K Street, N.E.
   Washington, D.C. 20002
   (202) 789–1100

2. Pat Patton, Director of Sound

3–4. Byron Motion Pictures has a complete video services and production laboratory and studio. Of particular interest is the availability of approximately 300 disc, cassette, and reel-to-reel sound recordings, which can be used in conjunction with the production of film. Included among these recordings is a comprehensive set of sound effects. Byron offers a number of recording services for a fee.

5. The firm's catalog will be sent for free upon request.

Center for Oral History

1.   *7507 Wyndale Road*
     Chevy Chase, Maryland 20815
     (301) 986-0418

2.   Ellen Robinson Epstein, Director

3.   The Center for Oral History contracts for oral history projects for individuals, institutions, and businesses. Clients receive the cassette tape(s) and full abstracts. Transcripts are also made upon request. Interested parties may telephone for quotes on current fees.

4.   The center holds some 100 audio tapes. Call or write for additional information.

Charles J. Linden, Inc.

1.   *1402 King Street*
     Alexandria, Virginia 22314
     (703) 549-4424

2.   Katherine Monteith, President

3.   Provided is cassette and cartridge duplicating of mostly studio work, but not recordings of bands. The firm does extensive narration work and will supply a narrator. Audio material can be reproduced, sold, or rented.

Christine Jennings

1.   *1218 National Press Building*
     Washington, D.C. 20045
     (202) 737-7957

2.   Christine Jennings, Director

3.   Christine Jennings administers a tape recording transcription service; news interviews, conferences, oral history, speeches, and seminars are transcribed from recording to hard copy. Prices depend on deadline and quality of audio on tape. Individuals may telephone for quotes on specific projects.

Cutting Studios, Inc.

1.   *4200 Wisconsin Avenue, N.W.*
     Washington, D.C. 20016
     (202) 363-3566

2.   Katie Barnard, Schedule Director

3.   Cutting Studios has recording services for all 8-track and 4-track tapes. Tape duplication, however, is offered for cassettes only. Though most services are done in the studio, some on-location convention contracting is available.

Eastern Audio Associates

1.   *8980/B Route 108*
Columbia, Maryland 21045
(301) 596–3900

2.   Herb Swisher, Director

3.   Eastern Audio has a branch office in Atlanta and they will travel all over the country to cover conventions. The firm has held contracts with such groups as American Bankers Association (M7); American College of Emergency Physicians; and American Health Consultants. Also offered is cassette and reel-to-reel duplication.

House of Representatives—House Recording Studio   See entry B17

Lion and Fox Recording

1.   *1905 Fairview Avenue, N.E.*
Washington, D.C. 20002
(202) 832–7884

2.   Rick Starkwether, Director

3.   Lion and Fox Recording has a full line recording studio starting with 24-track recordings. Recordings are also made of radio spots, industrial films, seminars, and conventions.

Memory Makers

1.   *11961 Tech Road*
Silver Spring, Maryland 20904
(301) 622–5900 (24 hours a day)

2.   Jim Corrado, Director

3.   Memory Makers carries a full line of audio tapes and can do duplications of up to 3,000 copies a day. Echo sound and special effects are also sold. The majority of convention recordings are health-oriented. The firm has had contracts with such organizations as National Parents Federation Against Drug Abuse, Preventive Medicine, and the American Dentist Association. It also makes audio recordings of ad hoc meetings. For instance, in November 1983, Memory Makers recorded the proceedings

of the Martin Luther Jubilee Conference and the Nutritional Conference for Medical Professionals.

4.   One collection rentable from Memory Makers includes a number of Kennedy assasination news tapes. For more information contact Jim Corrado.

Parkway Communications Corporation

1.   *7979 Old Georgetown Road*
       Bethesda, Maryland 20814
       (301) 657–9808

2.   Richard N. Currie, President

3.   Parkway Communications Corporation describes itself as America's fine arts broadcasting service. It syndicates and distributes concerts and productions, such as "First Hearing," "BBC Promenade Concerts," "In Recital," "The Vocal Scene," "Talking About Music," "Matinee," "Paul Temple, Detective," "America in Concert," and others. It also records concerts by The Philadelphia Orchestra and by other symphonies in the United States. Locally, Parkway records the recitals presented at the Phillips Collection (C14). In addition, Parkway produces a weekly news program, "European Perspectives."

4.   The series, "America in Concert," consisting of some 160 audio tapes, was presented to the Motion Picture, Broadcasting and Recorded Sound Division of the Library of Congress (A41) on February 23, 1982. This collection includes performances by orchestras, chamber orchestras, and choral groups. The series represents an excellent cross-section of lesser known performing ensembles throughout the United States.
       Parkway has a library, which contains several thousand disc, cassette, and reel-to-reel recordings. Copies of audio recordings are available for purchase by radio stations only.

5.   An in-depth description, entitled "'America in Concert' Collection Established at the Library," of the Parkway gift to the Library of Congress was published in the *Library of Congress Information Bulletin,* vol. 41, no. 9, February 26, 1982.

Recording for the Blind, Inc. (RFB)   See entry F18

Recording Service for the Visually Handicapped   See entry F19

Senate Recording Studio (U.S. Senate)   See entry B41

Soundwave, Inc.

1. *2000 P Street, N.W.*
    Washington, D.C. 20036
    (202) 861–0560

2. Jim Harmon, President

3. Soundwave, Inc. offers a variety of services. Creative audio production is the firm's specialty, which includes gathering on-location sound effects of your choice, casting narrators for scripts, cassette and reel-to-reel duplication, and conference contracting.

Washington Volunteer Readers for the Blind (WVRB)   **See entry F23**

III Radio Broadcasting Stations

Listed here are radio stations that have significant collections of sound recordings. Radio stations devoted solely to popular music are not listed here but can be located through D.C. area telephone books. Most radio stations provide printed program guides. Highlights of radio programs are printed in the *Washington Post* (N16), and the *Washington Times* (N18).

Entry Format

1. Address and Telephone Number
2. Chief Official/Key Resource Person
3. Programs
4. Collections
5. Program Guides

WAMU–FM

1. *The Broadcast Center*
    The American University
    Massachusetts and Nebraska Avenues, N.W.
    Washington, D.C. 20016
    (202) 885–1030

2. Nina Kern, General Manager
    Craig Oliver, Program Director

3. WAMU is a listener-supported public radio station broadcasting classical, jazz and popular music, a variety of public affairs programs, as well as a wide selection of vintage radio programs from the 1930s and 1940s. In certain cases, for a fee, the station will provide copies of certain broadcasts. Contact the station for further information.

4. The station's collection consists of some 3,500 disc recordings of classical music and jazz.

5. All of the station's programs are listed in its monthly publication, *The Guide*.

Washington Community Broadcasting Company (WCBC)

1. *1340 G Street, N.W.*
Washington, D.C. 20006
(202) 737–6400

2. Donn Miller, Program Director

3. WCBC primarily broadcasts popular music on weekdays. On weekends, however, community oriented programs are aired. Two shows on Saturday are "Confidential Hot Line" and "Sound Off" with Dr. Calvin Rolark. "New Horizons" and "People Want to Know" are aired on Sundays.

WDCU–FM

1. *4200 Connecticut Avenue, N.W.*
Washington, D.C. 20008
(202) 364–6092

2. G. Godwin Oyewole, General Manager

3. WDCU–FM is a noncommercial radio station licensed to the University of the District of Columbia (UDC). WDCU–FM consists of various types of information, cultural, and educational programs. Daily from midnight to 6:00 A.M. "Jazz Unlimited"; from 6:00 A.M. to noon, Monday through Friday, weekday morning jazz "Rise and Shine" is aired; from 12:00 noon to 12:15 P.M. weekdays are a variety of programs, including "Arab Press Review" on Mondays, "Israeli Press Review" on Tuesdays, and "Week at the U.N." on Wednesdays; 12:15 P.M. to 2:00 P.M. weekdays is "Cross Talk," a show concerning business, education, and home; from 2:00 P.M. to 3:30 P.M. is "The Art of" featuring either one particular artist or geographical area; "Public Affairs" is aired from 3:30 P.M. to 4:00 P.M.; an afternoon jazz, "Caravan," is aired weekdays from 4:00 P.M. to 6:30 P.M.; 6:30 P.M. to 7:00 P.M. is another public affairs program; finishing off the day from 7:00 P.M. to 10:00 P.M. is "Sounds of Jazz." Weekends follow a different schedule; 6:00 A.M. to 12:00 noon is "Blessed Assurance," which is recorded gospel music; on Saturday from 12:00 noon to 4:30 P.M. is "Mbari Mbayo," which is African and West Indian music and information; on Sundays from 3:30 P.M. to 4:00 P.M. is "Quarto Mundo," a bicultural Hispanic program; "Caravan" is aired from 4:00 P.M. to 5:30 P.M.; "UDC Spotlight," interviews with UDC students, is aired from 6:30 P.M. to 7:00 P.M.; and jazz is presented from 7:00 P.M. to 10:00 P.M.

5. A monthly program guide is available free upon request.

WEAM–AM

1. *2131 Crimmins Lane*
Falls Church, Virginia 22043
(703) 534–1390

2.   Stan Karas, Program Director

3.   On Sundays, WEAM has 8 continuous ethnic programs; 9:00 A.M. to 12:00 noon, Jewish programs; 12:00 noon to 1:00 P.M., music and news for the Italian-American community; 1:00 P.M. to 2:00 P.M. is an hour of French culture; 2:00 P.M. to 4:00 P.M. is an Indian show; 4:00 P.M. to 5:00 P.M. is an Irish program; 5:00 P.M. to 6:00 P.M. is a Turkish show.

WETA-FM

1.   *5217 19th Road, North*
      Arlington, Virginia 22207
      (703) 998-2790

2.   Allan Meckler, Record Librarian

3.   WETA-FM broadcasts primarily classical music. Three different shows are aired: Saturdays and Sundays from 6:00 A.M. to 12:00 noon; Monday through Friday, 10:00 A.M. to 12:00 noon; and from 8:00 P.M. to 12:00 midnight. Public affairs and news programs include, "All Things Considered," broadcast at 5:00 P.M. daily, and "Wall Street Week," broadcast at 6:30 P.M. Sunday.

4.   The radio station has some 11,000 disc and 200 reel-to-reel recordings, consisting mostly of classical music, 800 jazz albums, and 100 recordings of broadway shows and movie soundtracks.

5.   The station's program guide is published in *The Dial,* a monthly magazine, which also includes articles on popular topics. For information regarding the magazine contact the Washington, D.C. office: P.O. Box 2626, Washington, D.C. 20013 (telephone: 703/998-2626).

WGMS-AM and FM

1.   *11300 Rockville Pike*
      Rockville, Maryland 20852
      (301) 468-1800

2.   Paule W. Teare, Program Director

3.   WGMS, "Washington's Good Music Station," broadcasts primarily classical music. One notable feature of its programming includes interviews with notable musicians and radio talks that focus on the fine arts produced in the National Gallery of Art's recording studio. They are broadcast during the intermission of the Sunday concerts presented at the gallery. In 1982, 39 such talks were presented. A number of these radio talks are held in the Education Department Film Office of the National Gallery of Art (C8).

4.   The station's collection consists of some 50,000 disc recordings of mostly classical music, but also some jazz. Unique items include a number of unpublished pieces of music recorded on disc, as well as a variety of imported recordings received from

various embassies. The collection also includes a number of taped interviews with classical artists and composers.

5.   The WGMS monthly program guide is published in *Ovation,* whose address is Ovation Magazine Associates, 320 West 57th Street, New York, New York 10019.

WGTS–FM

1.   *7600 Flower Avenue*
      Takoma Park, Maryland 20912
      (301) 891–4200

2.   Don Wheeler, General Manager

3.   WGTS is a listener-supported radio station broadcasting primarily classical music and a number of religious and public affairs programs, focusing on health, politics, and consumer awareness.

4.   The station's collection also includes a number of taped public affairs shows, including interviews with local public officials and health professionals.

5.   All of the station's programs are printed in its monthly *Program Notes.*

WHUR–FM

1.   *529 Bryant Street, N.W.*
      Washington, D.C. 20059
      (202) 232–6000

2.   Oscar Fields, Music Director

3.   WHUR–FM is a commercial station. From 6:00 A.M. to 10:00 A.M., Monday through Friday, "The Morning Show" is aired, and on Sundays a health show replaces it. Other than these two news shows, WHUR–FM broadcasts primarily jazz, blues, and a small amount of popular music.

4.   The collection includes some 6,000 disc recordings, mostly from the 1960s and 1970s; however, some recordings date back to the 1930s.

WRC–AM

1.   *National Broadcasting Company*
      4001 Nebraska Avenue, N.W.
      Washington, D.C. 20016
      (202) 686–4422

2.   Gordon Peil, Program Director

3.   WRC–AM is a news and talk show station exclusively. Airing daily is "Morning

Drive," 5:00 A.M. to 9:00 A.M.; a public talk show, 9:00 A.M. to 5:00 P.M.; political topics are discussed from 5:00 P.M. to 7:00 P.M.; health-oriented programs, 7:00 P.M. to 8:00 P.M. Weekend shows vary and include the following Sunday programs: "Federal Employees," 10:00 A.M. to 12:00 noon; "Agronsky & Company," 12:00 noon to 12:30 P.M.; and "Meet the Press," 12:30 P.M. to 1:00 P.M.

4.   The station's sound recordings are in storage but may be examined by serious researchers. Included in the collection are some 20,000 disc and 2,000 reel-to-reel recordings. A number of disc recordings date from the 1920s. WRC to AM also has news recordings dating from 1975. For additional information, contact Gordon Peil. A WRC radio collection of broadcasts during 1955 is held in the Motion Picture, Broadcasting and Recorded Sound Division of the Library of Congress (A41).

5.   A program guide is available for free upon request.

WTOP-AM,

1.   *4646 40th Street, N.W.*
Washington, D.C. 20016
(202) 364-5800

2.   John Watkins, News Director

3.   The WTOP-AM collections are included in the University of Maryland Collection in RG 200 (entry B27) of the National Archives and Records Service, 8th Street and Pennsylvania Avenue, N.W. (202/523-3218).

WWDC-AM

1.   *1150 Connecticut Avenue, N.W.*
Washington, D.C. 20036
(202) 828-9932

2.   Don Davis, Program Director

3.   WWDC is primarily a music station. It does, however, broadcast a news program from 7:00 A.M. to 9:00 A.M., Sunday. This program is a weekly analysis of headline news and interviews with newsmakers. A number of WWDC radio documentaries from 1973-1975 (RG 200) are in the National Archives and Records Service (B27).

IV Audio Collections by Size

Some Washington, D.C. organizations do not maintain precise statistics on current audio holdings. Therefore, the following list provides estimates only.

More than 1 million sound recordings
Library of Congress (A41, B19)

100,000–150,000 sound recordings
National Archives and Records Service (NARS) (General Services Administration) (B27)
Prince George's County Memorial Library System (A61)
Voice of America (VOA) (U.S. Information Agency)–Music and Tape Libraries (A72)

50,000–100,000 sound recordings
Montgomery County Department of Public Libraries (A48)

25,000–50,000 sound recordings
Fairfax County Public Library (A21)
Library of Congress—National Library Service for the Blind and Physically Handicapped (NLS/BPH) (F9)
University of Maryland —Libraries (A68, A70)

15,000–25,000 sound recordings
Martin Luther King, Jr., Memorial Library (A42)

10,000–15,000 sound recordings
American University Library (A5)
Catholic University of America—John K. Mullen Memorial Library (A15)
Montgomery College Libraries (A47)

5,000–10,000 sound recordings
Arlington County Central Public Library (A9)
Georgetown University—Joseph Mark Lauinger Library (A31)
Mary Riley Styles Public Library (City of Falls Church, Virginia) (A43)
National Public Radio (NPR)—Library (B33)
Prince George's Community College—Learning Resource Center (A60)
Smithsonian Institution—Office of Folklife Programs—Folklife Program Archive (B43)

V Housing, Transportation, and Other Services

This section is prepared to help outside scholars who come to Washington, D.C., for short-term research, to find suitable housing. It also contains data on local transportation facilities and information services. Prices quoted are current as of March 1984 and are subject to change.

HOUSING INFORMATION AND REFERRAL SERVICE

For persons interested in leasing an apartment or house, *Apartment Shoppers' Guide and Housing Directory* (ASGHD) (updated every 3 months) is a valuable source of information. The directory, which quotes current rental prices, terms of leases, and directions to each of the facilities listed, is available at People's Drug Stores in the Washington area. It is published by ASGHD (202/363–8016), located at 3301 New Mexico Avenue, N.W., Suite 310, Washington, D.C. 20016. The staff provides a housing-referral service, for a fee, from 9:00 A.M.–5:30 P.M., Monday–Friday.

Faculty at local colleges and universities who are planning sabbaticals are sometimes willing to rent their homes to other scholars for periods of 6 months to a year. Using The American University as one example, contact the College of Arts and Sciences, Gray Building, Room 107, Washington, D.C. 20016, and ask for a copy of the "Monday-Times Picayune," a typed newsletter that lists names, addresses, and conditions of houses available for rent.

Scholars can also obtain assistance from the following local university housing offices:

George Washington University Off-Campus Housing Resources Center
2121 I Street, N.W. (Rice Hall), 4th Floor
Washington, D.C. 20052
(202) 676–6688
Summer: 8:30 A.M.–6:00 P.M.   Monday–Friday
Winter: 8:30 A.M.–5:00 P.M.   Monday–Friday
This office has listings of apartments and other housing in the Washington area. Open to the public, the office also distributes the *Apartment Shoppers' Guide and Housing Directory* (see above), maps of Washington, D.C., and a *Guide to Off-Campus Housing* (annual), prepared for students by the office.

Georgetown University Off-Campus Housing Office
Healy Building Basement, Room G08
37th and O Streets, N.W.
Washington, D.C. 20057
(202) 625–3026

1:00 P.M.–4:00 P.M.   Monday–Friday
Open to the public, this office offers services similar to those at the George Washington University Off-Campus Housing Resources Center.

Catholic University of America Off-Campus Housing Office
St. Bonaventure Hall, Room 106
Washington, D.C. 20064
(202) 635–5618
9:00 A.M.–5:00 P.M.   Monday–Friday
Open to the public, this office provides services similar to those of the other schools listed above.

Northern Virginia Community College
Annandale Campus Housing Board
Student Activities Center
Science Building, Room 225-A
8333 Little River Turnpike
Annandale, Virginia 22003
(703) 323–3147
8:30 A.M.–5:00 P.M.   Monday–Friday
The board maintains a listing of rooms available in private homes.

NOTE: The off-campus housing offices of The American University, Howard University, and the University of Maryland handle inquiries and requests from their own students and faculty members only.

Short-term Housing

For those scholars who intend to stay for a short period of time—a few days to a few weeks or months—the following facilities may be useful:

International Guest House
1441 Kennedy Street, N.W.
Washington, D.C. 20011
(202) 726–5808
Rates: $12.38 per bed per day, or $74.78 per week (breakfast and evening tea with shared rooms); half-price for children 6 to 16 years of age.

International Student House
1825 R Street, N.W.
Washington, D.C. 20009
(202) 232–4007
Rates: $385.00 to $485.00 per month (minimum, one-semester stay) for room and board (2 meals, 7 days). Single rooms and shared double or triple rooms are available. The house maintains a nationality quota policy that permits no more than 10 Americans or 3 citizens from any one foreign country at any time.

The Woodner Hotel Apartment Buildings
3636 16th Street, N.W.
Washington, D.C. 20010
(202) 328–2800
The hotel has furnished efficiency and one-bedroom apartments. Rates per month: $355–400 for an efficiency; $455–600 for 1-bedroom.

The Capitol Park
800 4th Street, S.W.
Washington, D.C. 20024
(202) 479–6800
(Near the Library of Congress)
Rates: Furnished 1-bedroom apartments, $60 single, $70 double, Monday through
Thursday, and $55 single or double, Friday through Sunday; and monthly, $700 single
and $800–900 double.

Long-term Housing

Individuals wishing to rent an apartment or house for one year or more should consult
not only the *Apartment Shoppers' Guide and Housing Directory* and the local university
housing offices, but also the following rental agencies:

Millicent Chatel	(202) 338–0500
Lynch Realty	(202) 232–4100
Nyman Realty Co.	(301) 474–5700
Edmund Flynn Co.	(202) 554–4800 (or 537–1800)
H.A. Gill	(202) 338–5000
Shannon & Luchs	(202) 659–7000
Norman Bernstein	(202) 331–7500
Snider Bros. P.M.I.	(301) 986–9500

Home and apartment rents vary greatly from area to area around Washington. Normally, rents are lower in suburban Virginia and Maryland than in Washington, D.C.
One should also remember that it is difficult to find furnished apartments in the
Washington area through regular real estate agents. People who need furnished quar-
ters may have to take unfurnished apartments and rent furniture through furniture
rental agencies listed in the D.C. area phone books.

TRANSPORTATION

In preparing for a visit to Washington, D.C., scholars should consider purchasing a
copy of the *Washington, D.C. and Vicinity Street Map* from the Alexandria Drafting
Company, 417 Clifford Avenue, Alexandria, Virginia, 22305. Free maps of the Washington metropolitan area, depicting streets and metro subway routes, are available
from the District of Columbia Department of Transportation Map Office at Room
519, 415 12th Street, N.W., Washington, D.C. 20004. The office is open from 8:15
A.M.–4:45 P.M., Monday through Friday (telephone: (202/727–6562). For mail requests, include a stamped (88 cents for U.S.A. delivery), self-addressed, 7″ x 10″
envelope. Other area street maps are available for purchase at any number of People's
Drug Stores.
   In general, the Metro subway and buses are the most preferable and inexpensive
means of traveling in and around the city. For persons using automobiles, parking
space in-town is not only limited but also relatively expensive. Commercial lots are,
however, available. Metered parking is sometimes available for periods up to two
hours. Many streets have restrictions for parking during rush hour (7:00–9:30 A.M.
and 4:00–6:30 P.M.). Regulations are strictly enforced and violaters can expect to be
ticketed or towed.

To National Airport

Public transportation to and from National Airport includes Metrobus No. 11, which
leaves from 10th Street and Pennsylvania Avenue, N.W., and a Metro subway train
that can be accessed from various downtown stations. A bus and train leaves every

10 minutes or less. A limousine service runs between the airport and the Capital Hilton Hotel, 16th and K Streets, N.W., daily until 11:15 P.M. For further information, call the hotel (202/393–1000).

To Dulles International Airport

Buses to Dulles International Airport leave from the Capital Hilton Hotel, 16th and K Streets, N.W., once every hour in the morning starting at 5:15 A.M., every 30 minutes in the afternoon from 2:15 until 8:15 P.M., and sporadically thereon until 11:45 P.M. There is a single Metrobus to Dulles that departs each day at 8:25 A.M. from 11th and E Streets, N.W., and arrives at Dulles Airport at 9:45 A.M.

To Baltimore-Washington (Friendship) International Airport

Buses to Baltimore-Washington (Friendship) International Airport leave from 16th and K Streets, N.W., making one stop at Greenbelt Station, Maryland . For further information, call (301) 441–2345. The Trailways and Greyhound bus terminals are located near Metro subway stops.

Train

The terminal for all passenger trains serving Washington, D.C., is located in-town at 50 Massachusetts Avenue, N.E. An on-site subway station is there as well. The Library of Congress is within walking distance from the station.

Taxi

Taxi fares in Washington, D.C., are based on a zone system and are reasonable. Taxi fares that cross into and out of Maryland and Virginia are fairly expensive. The major cab company phone numbers are:

Capital Cab	(202) 546–2400
Checker Cab	(202) 484–7888
Diamond Cab	(202) 387–6200
Yellow Cab	(202) 544–1212

Metro Subway System

The Metro subway is a regional transportation system, which links Maryland and Virginia with the District of Columbia, and, although still under construction, is for the most part completed. All Metro station entrances are identified by pylons with a clearly marked "M" on all sides. In the station below, large maps of the entire Metrorail System and maps showing the surrounding neighborhood are illuminated. Information booths are also available. Trains operate every ten minutes during non-rush hours and every five minutes during rush hours (6:00–9:30 A.M. and 3:00–6:30 P.M.). Metrorail is in operation Monday through Friday from 6:00 A.M. to midnight, Saturday from 8:00 A.M. to midnight, and Sunday from 10:00 A.M. to 6:00 P.M. Many of the organizations listed in the present study are accessible using the system. Individuals may wish to obtain a free copy of *All About Metro* by writing to Washington Metropolitan Area Transit Authority, Consumer Department, 600 Fifth Street, N.W., Washington, D.C., 20001, or by telephoning (202) 637–2437 from 6:00 A.M. to 11:30 P.M., seven days a week. Copies are also available at various Metro stops.

Bus Systems

Almost every area of Washington, D.C. and vicinity is linked by the Metrobus system. Brochures on individual routes, including express bus service, current information on fares, and hours of normal and holiday service are available at Metro headquarters,

as well as at local public libraries. Individuals may want to pick up a copy of *Metrobus Guide to Washington, D.C. and Suburban Maryland* from the Washington Metropolitan Area Transit Authority (address and telephone cited above).An important point to remember: Exact fare is required on Metrobus; operators do not give change.

Montgomery County, Maryland, maintains its own ride-on bus system, and is inexpensive. For route and fare information, call (301) 251–2225 from 7:30 A.M. to 5:00 P.M., Monday through Friday.

The city of Fairfax, Virginia, maintains a commuter express bus service between the city of Fairfax and Washington, D.C., with an intermediate stop at the Pentagon. Passengers must obtain a faircard to use the city's bus system. For information and a brochure citing route and fare information, call (703) 385–7859 or write to Public Information, Room 308, City of Fairfax, Fairfax, Virginia, 22030.

OTHER SERVICES

Foreign Student Service Council of Greater Washington (FSSC)
1623 Belmont Street, N.W.
Washington, D.C. 20009
(202) 232–4979
The Foreign Student Service Council provides services to foreign students living in or visiting Washington, D.C. Arrangements for board, seminars, program assistance, information on travel and lodging, and various productions are some of the services provided by FSSC.

NOTE: Because there are a large number of foreign students attending area colleges and universities, some of the schools have established offices for disseminating information of all types to foreign students.

International Visitors Information Service (IVIS)
801 19th Street, N.W.
Washington, D.C. 20006
(202) 872–8747 (24-hour service)
The International Visitors Information Service consists of some 78 independent groups that assist international visitors in the Washington area. Services and programs are varied, including a 24-hour telephone answering service available to international visitors for emergency problems after business hours and a multilingual referral service which includes information, maps, and brochures. All services are provided free by volunteers. A reception center is available at the above address and also at Dulles International Airport.

Washington International Center (WIC)
Meridian House
1630 Crescent Place, N.W.
Washington, D.C. 20009
(202) 332–1025
The Washington International Center, established in 1950, by the American Council on Education, provides services to international visitors in Washington, D.C.

OTHER SOURCES OF INFORMATION

There are a number of excellent publications, which cite additional organizations that provide assistance to foreign visitors in the nation's capital: The *Directory of Resources for Cultural and Educational Exchanges and International Communication* (1979), published by the United States International Communications Agency; the directory

lists both government and private organizations. Various indexes help facilitate the use of this *Guide*. See also *Directory of Community Organizations Serving Short-Term International Visitors* (1983–1984), published by the National Council for International Visitors. Additional guides for dining out in Washington, as well as for places to see, are available at most area bookstores.

VI   Federal Government Holidays

Federal government offices are closed on the following holidays:

New Year's Day	January 1
Washington's Birthday	Third Monday in February
Memorial Day	Last Monday in May
Independence Day	July 4*
Labor Day	First Monday in September
Columbus Day	Second Monday in October
Veterans Day	November 11*
Thanksgiving	Fourth Thursday in November
Christmas	December 25*

*If this date falls on a Saturday, the holiday is on Friday; if the date falls on a Sunday, the holiday is on Monday.

The public area of the Smithsonian Institution and the General Reading Room of the Library of Congress are open on most holidays.

VII   Standard Entry Formats

A-G. Collections Entry Format

1. General Information
   a. address; telephone numbers
   b. hours and days of service
   c. conditions of access
   d. name/title of director and key staff members

2. Size and Subjects of Collection
   a. general holdings
   b. sound recordings and related materials (transcripts, scores, manuscripts)

3. Notable Holdings

4. Facilities for Study and Use
   a. availability of audiovisual equipment
   b. reservation requirements
   c. fees charged
   d. reproduction services

5. Bibliographic Aids Facilitating Use of Collection

H-N. Organizations Entry Format

1. Address and Telephone Numbers

2. Chief Official/Key Resource Person

3. Objectives and/or Programs

4. Collections/Research Facilities

5. Publications

Appendix I.   Record Stores and Other Distributors of Sound Recordings Entry Format

1.   Address and Telephone Number
2.   Hours
3.   Stock

Appendix II.   Recording Studios and Transcription Services Entry Format

1.   Address and Telephone Number
2.   Chief Official/Key Resource Person
3.   Objectives and/or Programs
4.   Collections/Research Facilities
5.   Publications and Bibliographic Aids

Appendix III.   Radio Broadcasting Stations Entry Format

1.   Address and Telephone Number
2.   Chief Official/Key Resource Person
3.   Programs
4.   Collections
5.   Program Guides

BIBLIOGRAPHY

Bibliography

Reference sources consulted for identification of collections and organizations included in this *Scholars' Guide*.

Alternatives in Print: An International Catalog of Books, Pamphlets, Periodicals and Audiovisual Materials. New York: Neal Schuman, 1980.

American Association of Museums. *The Official Museum Directory*. Washington, D.C.: American Association of Museums, 1983.

American Library Directory. 37th ed., 2 vols. New York: Bowker, 1984.

Audiovisual Market Place: A Multimedia Guide. New York: Bowker, 1983.

Bhatt, Purnima M. *Scholars' Guide to Washington, D.C. for African Studies*. Washington, D.C.: Smithsonian Institution Press, 1980.

Brown, Allison, ed. *Organizations Serving International Visitors in the National Capitol Area*. 4th ed. Washington, D.C.: International Visitors Information Service, 1973.

Brown, James W., ed. *Educational Media Yearbook: 1983*. Littleton, Colo.: Libraries Unlimited, 1983.

Brownson, Charles B., comp. *1984 Congressional Staff Directory*. Mount Vernon, Va.: Congressional Staff Directory, 1984.

————. *1984 Federal Staff Directory*. Mount Vernon, Va.: Congressional Staff Directory, 1984.

Charles, Sharon A. *Drugs: A Multimedia Source Book for Children and Young Adults*. New York: Neal Schuman, 1980.

Cook, Patsy A. *Directory of Oral History Programs in the United States*. Sanford, N.C.: Microfilming Corporation of America, 1982.

Dillon, Kenneth J. *Scholars' Guide to Washington, D.C. for Central and East European Studies*. Washington, D.C.: Smithsonian Institution Press, 1980.

Diplomatic List. Washington, D.C.: U.S. Department of State, August 1984.

Directory of Archives and Manuscript Repositories in the United States. Washington, D.C.: National Archives and Records Service, 1978.

Directory of Historical Societies and Agencies in the United States and Canada. Tracy Linton Craig, ed., 12th ed. Nashville: American Association for State and Local History, 1982.

Directory of U.S. Government Audiovisual Personnel. Washington, D.C.: National Audiovisual Center, 1980.

Dorr, Steven R. *Scholars' Guide to Washington, D.C. for Middle Eastern Studies*. Washington, D.C.: Smithsonian Institution Press, 1981.

Encyclopedia of Associations, 1985. Denise S. Akey, ed., 19th ed., 2 vols. in 3 parts. Detroit: Gale, 1984.

Fisher, Perry O., and Linda J. Lear. *A Selected Bibliography for Washington Studies and Descriptions of Major Local Collections*. Washington, D.C.: George Washington University, 1981.

Grant, Steven A. *Scholars' Guide to Washington, D.C. for Russian/Soviet Studies*. 2d ed., rev. by Bradford P. Johnson and Mark H. Teeter. Washington, D.C.: Smithsonian Institution Press, 1983.

Grow, Michael. *Scholars' Guide to Washington, D.C. for Latin American and Carribean Studies*. Washington, D.C.: Smithsonian Institution Press, 1979.

Hamer, Phillip M., ed. *A Guide to Archives and Manuscripts in the United States*. New Haven: Yale University Press, 1965.

Jennings, Margaret S., ed. *Library and Reference Facilities in the Area of the District of Columbia*. 11th ed. Washington, D.C.: American Society for Information Science, 1983.

Kim, Hong N. *Scholars' Guide to Washington, D.C. for East Asian Studies*. Washington, D.C.: Smithsonian Institution Press, 1979.

Kruzas, Anthony T., and John Schmittroth, Jr., eds. *Encyclopedia of Information Systems and Services*. 5th ed. Detroit: Gale, 1982.

————. *Medical and Health Information Directory*. Detroit: Gale, 1980.

Mayerchak, Patrick M. *Scholars' Guide to Washington, D.C. for Southeast Asian Studies*. Washington, D.C.: Smithsonian Institution Press, 1983.

McKee, Gerald. *Directory of Spoken-Word Audio Cassettes*. New York: Jeffrey Norton, 1983.

Meckler, Alan M., and Ruth McMullin, comp. *Oral History Collections*. New York: Bowker, 1975.

Parsons, Richard. *Guide to Specialized Subject Collections in Maryland Libraries.* Baltimore: Maryland State Department of Education, 1974.

Pitschmann, Louis A. *Scholars' Guide to Washington, D.C. for Northwest European Studies.* Washington, D.C.: Smithsonian Institution Press, 1984.

Provan, Jill, and Maryruth Phelps Glogowski. *Management Media Directory.* Detroit: Gale, 1982.

Rahim, Enayetur. *Scholars' Guide to Washington, D.C. for South Asian Studies.* Washington, D.C.: Smithsonian Institution Press, 1981.

Research Centers Directory. Mary M. Watkins and James A. Ruffner, eds.,9th ed. Detroit: Gale, 1984.

Rowan, Bonnie G. *Scholars' Guide to Washington, D.C.,Film and Video Collections.* Washington, D.C.: Smithsonian Institution Press, 1980.

U.S. National Archives and Records Service. Office of the Federal Register. *The United States Government Manual, 1983–84.* Washington, D.C.: Government Printing Office, 1983.

Washington 84. Washington, D.C.: Columbia Books, 1984.

Washington Information Directory, 1984–85. Washington, D.C.: Congressional Quarterly, 1984.

Wasserman, Paul, ed. *Consumer Sourcebook.* 4th ed., 2 vols. Detroit: Gale, 1983.

Weber, Jack, ed. *The Selective Guide to Audiovisuals for Mental Health and Family Life Education.* 4th ed. Chicago: Marquis, 1979.

Young, Margaret. *Directory of Special Libraries and Information Centers.* Detroit: Gale, 1979.

INDEXES

I Personal Names Index

This index contains the names of oral history interviewees, lecturers, radio broadcast personalities, and others appearing on recordings cited in this *Guide*. Included also are the names of persons whose personal papers contain recordings. This list is intended only as a representative sampling of recordings researchers can expect to find in the organizations and institutions described herein. (It does *not* include the names of the administrative personnel of the collections and organizations covered in this volume.)

II Subject Index

This index covers broad categories and includes geographic headings. It points out collections and organizations in which a given topic is prominently featured. Entry symbols correspond to the following sections of the *Guide:*

A—Libraries (Government, Academic, Public, Special)
B—Archives and Manuscript Repositories
C—Museums and Galleries
D—Embassies
E—Religious Bodies
F—Services for the Handicapped
G—Data Banks
H—Broadcasting Organizations
J—Research Centers
K—Academic Programs and Departments
L—United States Government Agencies
M—Associations (Academic, Professional, Cultural)
N—Publications and Print Media

III   Organizations and Institutions Index

Entry symbols correspond to the following sections of the *Guide:*

> A—Libraries (Government, Academic, Public, Special)
> B—Archives and Manuscript Repositories
> C—Museums and Galleries
> D—Embassies
> E—Religious Bodies
> F—Services for the Handicapped
> G—Data Banks
> H—Broadcasting Organizations
> J—Research Centers
> K—Academic Programs and Departments
> L—United States Government Agencies
> M—Associations (Academic, Professional, Cultural)
> N—Publications and Print Media

Anacostia Neighborhood Museum (Smithsonian Institution) C1
  Research Department C1
Andrews Air Force Base (AAFB) Library A7
Antioch School of Law Library A8
Archives of American Art (Smithsonian Institution) B3
Arlington County Central Public Library A9, F5
  Special Services A9
    Virginiana Collection A9
  Talking Book Service F5
Armenian Assembly of America B4
Armenian General Benevolent Union of the U.S.—Washington Chapter M27
Army Center of Military History (CHM) (Army Department) B5
Army Corps of Engineers (Army Department)—Historical Division, B6
Army Department A25, B5, B6
  Army Center of Military History B5
  Army Corps of Engineers B6
    Historical Division B6
  Fort Myer Post Library A25
Arnold and Porter Law Library A10
Arthritis Information Clearinghouse (Health and Human Services Department—National Institutes of Health—National Institute of Arthritis, Diabetes, and Digestive and Kidney Diseases) L1
Association for Educational Communications and Technology (AECT) M28
Association for Recorded Sound Collections, Inc. (ARSC) M29
Association for Supervision and Curriculum Development (ASCD) M30
Association for the Study of Afro-American Life and History, Inc. M31
Association of Former Members of Congress (FMC) B7
Association of Trial Lawyers of America (ATLA)—Education Fund M32
Atomic Industrial Forum (AIF)—Audiovisual Library A11
Audiovisuals Online (AVLINE) (National Library of Medicine) G2

Bahamas, Embassy of the Commonwealth of the D1
Belgium, Embassy of D2
Better Hearing Institute (BHI) F6
Blinded Veterans Association (BVA) F7
BNA Communications, Inc. (Bureau of National Affairs, Inc.) N1
Board of Jewish Education of Greater Washington (BJE) E1
  Teacher Center Library E1
Bowie State College A12, K4
  Department of Communications K4
  Thurgood Marshall Library A12
  Music Listening Laboratory A12
Brazil, Embassy of D3
Brazilian-American Cultural Institute (BACI) Music Library A13
Broadcast Education Association (BEA) H4
Broadcast Pioneers Library (BPL) B8
Brookings Institution J5
Business and Professional Women's Foundation—Marguerite Rawalt Resource Center A14

Council for Exceptional Children (CEC) M33
Cyprus, Embassy of D8
Czechoslovakia, Embassy of D9

Defense Department A53
    National Defense University (NDU) Library A53
Democratic National Committee (DNC)—Press Office B11
DeSales School of Theology—Library E2
Development Publications N3
District of Columbia General Hospital—Medical Library A20
Dominican House of Studies—Archives B12

Economics News Broadcasters Association (ENBA) H10
Education Department A54, B13, F15, G3, G5
    National Institute of Education A54, G3
        Educational Research Library A54
        Educational Resources Information Center (ERIC) G3
    National Institute of Handicapped Research G5
        National Rehabilitation Information Center G5
    Office of Educational Research and Improvement B13
    Office of Information and Resources for the Handicapped F15
        Clearinghouse on the Handicapped F15
Educational Resources Information Center (ERIC) (Education Department) G3
Electronic Industries Association (EIA) M34
Embassies. *See* under the name of the country
Energy Department (DOE)—History Division, B14

Fairfax County Public Library A21, F8
    Talking Book Service F8
Fairfax Hospital—Jacob D. Zylman Memorial Library A22
Federal Judicial Center L2
Federal Reserve System—Board of Governors L3
Finland, Embassy of D10
FOCUS H11
Folger Shakespeare Library A23
Folklore Society of Greater Washington (FSGW)—Archive B15
Food and Drug Administration (FDA)—Medical Library A24
Food and Nutrition Information Center (FNIC) (Agriculture Department) L4
Forecast N4
Ford's Theatre (Interior Department—National Park Service)—Petersen House Library C2
Foreign Broadcast Information Service (FBIS) H12
Foreign Service Institute (M/FSI) (State Department) L5
Forest Service (Agriculture Department)—History Section B16
Fort Myer Post Library (Army Department) A25
Freer Gallery of Art Library (Smithsonian Institution) C3

Gadsby's Tavern Museum (City of Alexandria—Department of Historic Resources) C4
General Services Administration B27, L7
    National Archives and Records Service B27
        Civil Archives Division B27
            Judicial, Fiscal and Social Branch B27

The author, James R. Heintze, was born in Washington, D.C., in 1942. He attended Peabody Conservatory of Music and Loyola College (B.S. in Music, 1967) and received his M.A. in Musicology from American University in 1969 and his M.L.S. in Library Science from the University of Maryland in 1972. The author has published articles, reviews, and discographies in journals, such as *The Musical Quarterly, Library Quarterly, Maryland Historical Magazine,* and *Notes,* as well as having compiled *American Music Studies: A Classified Bibliography of Master's Theses* (1984). Currently, the author is Associate Librarian at the American University as well as editor of *Bibliographies in American Music,* published by The College Music Society.

Trudi W. Olivetti attended Boston University (B.A. in Fine Arts in 1968), Simmons College (M.L.S. in 1971), and The American University, where she is completing an M.A. in Musicology. She has taught library science at the University of Vermont and George Mason University in Fairfax, Virginia, and has worked as a librarian at Northern Virginia Community College, Mount Vernon College, and the American University Library Record-Score Collection. She is currently a cataloger at the National Gallery of Art Library.

Consultant Michael H. Gray is the Chief of the Tape and Music Libraries at the Voice of America in Washington, D.C. He worked in the Cataloging Department of the Library of Congress from 1972 to 1976.

Consultant Leslie C. Waffen is the Reference and Acquisitions Archivist in the Special Archives Division of the National Archives and Records Service in Washington, D.C.

Series editor, Zdeněk V. David has been Librarian of the Woodrow Wilson International Center for Scholars since 1974. He attended Wesleyan University (B.A. 1952), Harvard (Ph.D. 1960), and Rutgers (M.L.S. 1970), and taught history at Harvard, the University of Michigan in Ann Arbor, and Princeton, as well as library science at Rutgers University. He served as Slavic Bibliographer of the Princeton University Library from 1966 to 1974. He is coauthor of *Peoples of the Eastern Habsburg Lands, 1526–1918* (1984).